W9-BTE-303

THE WORKS OF JOHN MILTON

THE WORKS OF JOHN MILTON

VOLUME XI

NEW YORK
Columbia University Press
1935

PRINTED IN THE UNITED STATES OF AMERICA
BY THE PRINTING HOUSE OF WILLIAM EDWIN RUDGE, INC.
MOUNT VERNON, NEW YORK

JOANNIS MILTONI Angli,

Artis Logicæ Plenior Institutio, AD PETRI RAMI Methodum concinnata,

Adjecta est Praxis Annalytica & *Petri Rami* vita. Libris duobus.

LONDINI,

Impensis *Spencer Hickman*, Societatis Regalis Typographi, ad insigne *Rosæ* in *Cœmeterio*, *D. Pauli*. 1672.

A fuller institution

of the

ART OF LOGIC,

arranged after the method of

PETER RAMUS,

BY

JOHN MILTON,

an Englishman.

An analytic praxis and a life of *Peter Ramus* are appended.

In two Books.

London,
Printed for *Spencer Hickman*, Printer to the Royal Society, at the sign of the *Rose* in *St. Paul's Churchyard.*
1672.

ARTIS LOGICÆ PLENIOR INSTITUTIO

LIBER PRIMUS

De Argumentorum inventione

A FULLER INSTITUTION OF THE ART OF LOGIC

EDITED AND TRANSLATED BY ALLAN H. GILBERT

THE FIRST BOOK

Of the invention of arguments

LIBER SECUNDUS

De Argumentorum dispositione

THE SECOND BOOK

Of the disposition of arguments

ARTIS LOGICÆ
PLENIOR INSTITUTIO

PRÆFATIO.

QUANQUAM Philosophorum multi, suopte ingenio freti, contempsisse artem Logicam dicuntur, eorum tamen qui vel sibi, vel aliis propter ingenium aut judicium natura minus acre ac perspicax utilissi-
5 mam esse sibique diligenter excolendam judicarunt, optime est de ea meritus, ut ego quidem cum *Sidneio* nostro sentio, *Petrus Ramus*. Cæteri fere Physica, Ethica, Theologica Logicis, effrænata quadam licentia, confundunt. Sed Noster dum brevitatem sectatus est nimis religiose, non plane luci,
10 sed ubertati tamen lucis, quæ in tradenda arte, non parca, sed plena & copiosa esse debet, videtur defuisse: id quod tot in eum scripta commentaria testantur. Satius itaque sum arbitratus, quæ ad præcepta artis plenius intelligenda, ex ipsius *Rami* scholis Dialecticis aliorumque commentariis necessario
15 petenda sunt, ea in ipsum corpus artis, nisi sicubi dissentio, transferre atque intexere. Quid enim brevitate consequimur, si lux aliunde est petenda? Præstat una opera, uno simul in loco artem longiusculam cum luce conjungere, quam minore cum luce brevissimam aliunde illustrare; cum hoc non minore
20 negotio multoque minus commode hactenus fiat, quam si ars

PREFACE.

THOUGH many of the philosophers, trusting to their own native abilities, are said to have contemned the art of logic, yet some, thinking their own talent and judgment or that of others naturally less keen and penetrating, judge that it is very useful and that they should study it diligently; of the latter, as I hold with our countryman Sidney, Peter Ramus is believed the best writer on the art. Other logicians, in a sort of unbridled license, commonly confound physics, ethics, and theology with logic. But our author in seeking too earnestly for brevity seems to have fallen short not exactly of clarity but yet of copiousness of clarity, for in the presentation of an art it should not be scrimped but full and abundant; the many commentaries written on him testify to this. So I have decided that it is better to transfer to the body of the treatise and weave into it, except when I disagree, those aids to a more complete understanding of the precepts of the art which must of necessity be sought in the *Scholæ Dialecticæ* of Ramus himself and in the commentaries of others. For why should we insist on brevity if clarity is to be sought elsewhere? It is better by producing one work to put together in one place a rather long exposition of a subject with clarity than with less clarity to explain in a separate commentary a work that is too brief, although this last has up to the present been done with no less trouble and much less convenience than if, as now, the

ipsa ut nunc suapte copia se fuse explicaverit. Quam artis tradendæ rationem uberiorem ipse etiam *Ramus* in Arithmetica & Geometria aliquanto post a se editis, edoctus jam longiore usu, secutus est; suasque ipse regulas interjecto commenta-
5 riolo explanavit, non aliis explanandas reliquit. Quorum cum plerique nescio an nimio commentandi studio elati, certi omnis methodi quod in iis mirum sit, obliti, omnia permisceant, postrema primis, axiomata Syllogismos eorumque regulas primis quibusque simplicium argumentorum capi-
10 tibus ingerere soleant, unde caliginem potius discentibus offundi quam lucem ullam præferri necesse est, id mihi cavendum imprimis duxi ut nequid præriperem, nequid præpostere quasi traditum jam & intellectum, nequid nisi suo loco attingerem; nihil veritus, ne cui forte strictior in explicandis
15 præceptis existimer, dum per pendenda magis quam percurrenda proponere studebam. Nec tamen iis facile assenserim, qui paucitatem regularum objiciunt *Ramo,* quarum permultæ etiam ex *Aristotile* ab aliis collectæ, nedum quæ ab ipsis cumulo sunt adjectæ, vel incertæ vel futiles, discen-
20 tem impediunt atque onerant potius quam adjuvant: ac siquid habent utilitatis aut salis, id ejusmodi est, ut suopte ingenio quivis facilius percipiat, quam tot canonibus me-

treatise itself was so detailed as to furnish its own explanation. Indeed Ramus himself, having profited by longer experience, used the more diffuse method of teaching a subject in the *Arithmetic* and *Geometry* which he issued somewhat later;
5 he explained his own rules with a brief running commentary and did not leave them to be made clear by others. Since many of these expositors, perhaps drawn on by too much zeal for commenting, reveal a neglect of all proper method astonishing in them by mixing everything together,
10 the last with the first, and are accustomed to heap up the axioms, syllogisms, and their rules in the early chapters that deal with simple arguments, thus necessarily covering students with darkness rather than furnishing them light, I have decided first of all to take care that I treated nothing
15 prematurely, that I mentioned nothing before its proper time as though it were already explained and understood, and that I dealt with nothing except in its place, without fear that any one might judge me too narrow in my explanation of the precepts of Ramus, while I was trying to set them forth
20 by lingering over rather than rushing through them. Yet I should not easily agree with those who object to the paucity of rules in Ramus, since a great number even of those collected from Aristotle by others as well as those which they have themselves added to the heap, being uncertain or futile,
25 impede the learner and burden rather than aid him, and if they have any usefulness or show any wit, it is of such a sort as any one might more easily understand by his native ability than learn by means of so many memorized canons. And I

moriæ mandatis, addiscat. Multoque minus constitui, canones quidvis potius quam Logicos, a Theologis infercire; quos illi, quasi subornatos in suum usum, tanquam e media Logica petitos, depromant de Deo, divinisque hypostasibus & sacra-
5 mentis; quorum ratione, quo modo est ab ipsis informata, nihil est a Logica, adeoque ab ipsa ratione, alienius.

Prius autem quam opus ipsum aggredior, quoniam ars Logica omnium prima est suisque finibus latissime patet, præmittam quædam de arte generalia, deque artium dis-
10 tributione; artem deinde ipsam persequar: ad extremum, Analytica quædam exempla, sive usum artis, exercitationis causa, iis quibus opus est, & in eo genere exercere se libet, exhibebo: Quibus opus est inquam; quibus enim ingenium per se viget atque pollet, iis ut in hoc genere Analytico cum
15 labore nimio ac miseria se torqueant, non sum author. Ad id enim ars adhibetur, ut naturam juvet, non ut impediat: adhibita nimis anxie nimisque subtiliter, & præsertim ubi opus non est, ingenium per se jam satis acutum, obtundit potius quam acuit; ita plane ut in medicina remediorum usus vel
20 nimius vel non necessarius, valetudinem debilitat potius quam roborat. Quod autem *Aristotelis* aliorumque veterum auctoritatem ad singulas fere Logicæ regulas adjungimus, id quidem in tradenda arte supervacuum fuisset, nisi novitatis sus-

have determined that still less will I cram in those canons of the theologians which are anything but logical; for the theologians fetch out as though from the heart of logic canons about God and about divine hypostases and sacraments as if 5 these had been furnished for their use; yet nothing is more alien from logic or in fact from reason itself than the ground of these canons, as prepared by the theologians.

But before I enter upon the work itself, considering that the art of logic is the first of all the arts and spreads its terri- 10 tories widely, I shall make some general prefatory remarks on art and the distribution of the arts. I shall next treat the art of logic itself. Last of all I shall give some analytic examples or make some application of the art for the sake of practise for those who have need and opportunity to exercise 15 themselves in this way. For those who have need, I say, for I do not require that those whose native abilities are active and strong should torture themselves in this analytic sort of exercise with too much labor and misery. For art is used for the purpose of aiding nature, not of hindering it; when it is 20 employed too anxiously and too subtly, and especially where it is unnecessary, it blunts rather than sharpens capacities which are already of themselves acute enough, just as surely as in medicine the use of excessive and unnecessary remedies weakens the health rather than builds it up. Our common 25 addition of the authority of Aristotle and other old writers to the separate rules of logic would be wholly superfluous in the teaching of the art, except that the suspicion of novelty which until now has been strongly attached to Peter Ramus

picio, quæ *Petro Ramo* hactenus potissimum obfuit, adductis ipsis veterum authorum testimoniis, esset amolienda.

Artium omnium quasi corpus & comprehensio ἐγκυκλοπαιδεία Græce, i.e. eruditionis circuitus quidam in se redeuntis, ad-
5 eoque in se absolutæ atque perfectæ, vel Philosophia dicitur. Hæc cum sapientiæ studium proprie significat, tum vulgo artium omnium vel doctrinam, vel scientiam: doctrinam, cum præcepta artium tradit; scientiam, cum ars, quæ habitus est quidam mentis, præceptis illis percipitur, quasique possi-
10 detur. Eodem modo & artis significatio distinguitur: cum doctrinam significat, de qua nobis potissimum hic est agendum, est ordinata præceptorum exemplorumque comprehensio sive methodus, qua quidvis utile docetur.

Artis materia præcepta sunt: quæ qualia esse debeant, artis
15 Logicæ, quam nunc tradimus, proprium est suo loco præscribere.

Forma sive ipsa ratio artis, non tam est præceptorum illorum methodica dispositio, quam utilis alicujus rei præceptio: per id enim quod docet potius, quam per ordinem docendi,
20 ars est id quod est: quod ex cujusque artis definitione perspicitur, ut infra ostendetur.

Præceptorum artis tria genera sunt: duo præcipua *definitiones* & *distributiones;* quarum doctrinam generalem Logica etiam loco idoneo sibi vendicat; tertium, minus principale,
25 *consectarium* nominatur; estque proprietatis alicujus explicatio, ex definitione fere deducta.

ought to be removed by bringing up these testimonies from ancient authors.

The body and full extent of all the arts is called in Greek the ἐγκυκλοπαιδεία, that is the completed circuit of erudition, quite absolute and perfect in itself, or philosophy. The study of this body of knowledge, or vulgarly of all the arts, is properly known as doctrine or science: doctrine when it teaches the precepts of the arts; science, when the art, which is a sort of habit of the mind, is learned from those precepts, and as it were possessed. The meaning of the word *art* is given in the same way; when it means doctrine — the meaning with which we are especially concerned here — it is the orderly body or scheme of precepts and examples, by which something useful is taught.

The materials of an art are precepts; it is proper to set down in its place the sort of precepts dealt with in the art of logic, which we are now teaching.

The form or true cause of an art is not so much the methodical arrangement of those precepts as it is the teaching of some useful matter; for an art is what it is rather because of what it teaches than because of its method of teaching; this may be seen from the definition of any art, as will be shown below.

The precepts of an art are of three kinds: definitions and distributions are the two foremost types; in a suitable place logic claims as its own the general doctrine of these. The third kind, less important, is called a consectary; it is the explication of some property, usually deduced from a definition.

Exempla sunt quibus præceptionum veritas demonstratur, ususque ostenditur: suntque, ut scite *Plato,* quasi obsides sermonum: quod enim præcepto in genere docetur, id exemplo in specie confirmatur.

5 Efficiens artis primarius neminem reor dubitare quin sit Deus, author omnis sapientiæ: id olim Philosophos etiam non fugit.

Causæ ministræ fuerunt homines divinitus edocti, ingenioque præstantes; qui olim singulas artes invenerunt. Inveni-
10 endi autem ratio eadem prope fuit quæ pingendi: ut enim in pictura duo sunt, exemplum sive archetypus, & ars pingendi, sic in arte invenienda, archetypo respondet natura sive usus, & exemplum hominum peritorum, arti pictoris respondet Logica; saltem naturalis, quæ facultas ipsa rationis in mente
15 hominis est; juxta illud vulgo dictum, Ars imitatur naturam.

Ratio autem sive Logica, primum illa naturalis, deinde artificiosa, quatuor adhibuit sibi quasi adjutores, *teste Aristot.* Metaphys. 1. c. 1, sensum, observationem, inductionem, & experientiam. Cum enim præcepta artium generalia sint, ea
20 nisi ex singularibus, singularia nisi sensu percipi non possunt: sensus sine observatione, quæ exempla singula memoriæ committat, observatio sine inductione, quæ singularia quam plurima inducendo generalem aliquam regulam constituat, inductio sine experientia, quæ singulorum omnium coveni-

Examples are the things by which the truth of precepts is demonstrated and their use shown. They are, as Plato wisely says, as it were the hostages of lectures, for what is taught by precept in the genus is confirmed by an example in the species.
5 I suppose no one doubts that the primal mover of every art is God, the author of all wisdom; in the past this truth has not escaped philosophers.

The assisting causes were the men divinely taught and eminent for ability who in the past discovered the individual
10 arts. The method of discovering these was much like the method of painting; for as there are in a picture two things —the subject or archetype and the art of painting—so in the discovery of an art, nature or practice and the example of skillful men corresponds to the archetype, and logic to
15 the art of the painter—natural logic at least, which is the very faculty of reason in the mind of man, according to that common saying: Art imitates nature.

Reason or logic—first the natural reason just spoken of, then trained reason—attaches to itself, according to Aristotle
20 (*Metaphysics* 1.1), four helpers: sense, observation, induction, and experience. For since the precepts of the arts are general, these cannot be gathered except from specific instances, and specific instances can be observed only by the senses; without observation, which commits individual ex-
25 amples to memory, the senses avail nothing; without induction, which by working on individuals rather than on large numbers sets up some general rule, observation is useless; without experience, which judges the conformity with one

entiam in commune & quasi consensum judicet, nihil juvat. Hinc recte *Polus* apud *Platonem* in *Gorgia, experientia artem peperit, imperitia fortunam,* i.e. præcepta fortuita, adeoque incerta. *Et Aristot. Prior.* 1. *c.* 30. *cujusque rei principia*
5 *tradere, experientiæ est: sic Astrologica experientia, illius scientiæ* principia suppeditavit. *Et Manilius;*

Per varios usus artem experientia fecit,
exemplo monstrante viam . . . .

Et Cicero; omnia quæ sunt conclusa nunc artibus, dispersa
10 *quondam & dissipata fuerunt, donec adhibita hæc ars est, quæ res dissolutas divulsasque conglutinaret & ratione quadam constringeret.* Ea ars Logica est, vel hæc saltem naturalis, quam ingenitam habemus, vel illa artificiosa, quam mox tradimus: hæc enim præcepta artis invenit ac docet. Hactenus de
15 efficientibus causis artium.

Forma artis, ut supra dixi, non tam præceptorum dispositio est, quam præceptio ipsa rei alicujus utilis, eademque est finis. Quemadmodum enim non tam præceptorum Logicorum methodica dispositio quam ipsum bene disserere, &
20 forma Logicæ & finis est, ut infra docebitur, ita in genere non solum præceptorum dispositio, sed ipsa rei utilis præceptio, forma artis & simul finis est: quod autem præcipitur, id esse

another and as it were agreement of all individuals, induction is useless. Hence Pole comments correctly on Plato's *Gorgias:* "Experience has brought forth art; inexperience fortune," that is fortuitous and indeed unreliable statements. And 5 Aristotle says (*Prior Analytics* 1.30): "It is for experience to furnish the first principles of anything; thus astrologic experience has furnished the principles of that science." And Manilius writes:

> Experience by varied practice has wrought art,
> 10 The example pointing out the way.

And Cicero: "All things which now are summed up by the arts formerly were dispersed and scattered, until this art was applied to bring together and bind by some reason things scattered and separate." He means the art of logic, 15 either that merely natural logic with which we are born, or that artificial logic which we learn later, for logic finds and teaches the precepts of the art. So much for the efficient causes of the arts.

The form of an art, as I said above, is not so much an 20 arrangement of precepts, as the actual teaching of something useful, and the end is the same. For as the form and end of logic is not so much the methodical arrangement of logical precepts as it is good debating itself, as will be explained below, so in the genus not merely the arrangement of pre- 25 cepts but the actual teaching of a useful thing is at once the form and the end of an art. All agree, besides, that what is

utile in hominum vita debere, quod *Græci*, βιωφελὲς vocant, omnes consentiunt; indignamque esse artis nomine, quæ non bonum aliquod sive utile ad vitam hominum, quod idem quoque honestum sit, sibi proponat, ad quod omnia præcepta
5 artis referantur; adeoque formam artis esse rei alicujus utilis præceptionem, per quam scilicet ars est id quod est, necessario sequitur. Verum ad hunc finem perveniri non potest, nisi doctrinam natura commode percipiat, exercitatio confirmet, utræque simul doctrina & exercitatio artem quasi alteram natu-
10 ram reddant. Sed ingenium sine arte, quam ars sine ingenio plus proficere censetur: proficere autem non admodum utrumque, nisi accesserit exercitatio: unde illud *Ovidii:*

solus & artificem qui facit, usus erit.

Exercitatio duplex est; analysis & genesis. Illa est, cum ex-
15 empla artis in sua principia quasi resolvuntur, dum singulis partibus ad normam, i. e. ad præcepta artis examinantur: hæc, cum ex artis præscripto efficimus aliquid aut componimus.

Hactenus causæ artium: sequuntur species. Artes sunt generales vel speciales: generales, quarum materia subjecta est
20 generalis. Materia autem illa vel artificis est, vel artis. Artificis materia generalis generalibus cunctis artibus est communis;

taught should be useful in the life of men, should be βιωφελές as the Greeks put it, and that anything is unworthy the name of art which does not make its aim something good or useful for human life, and honorable as well, to which are referred all the precepts of the art. From this indeed it necessarily follows that the form of the art is the teaching of some useful thing, because of which the art evidently is what it is. Certainly this end cannot be attained unless nature is adapted to receiving instruction, and practice establishes what has been received, and unless both instruction and practice make art as it were a second nature. Yet natural ability without art is thought to avail more than art without natural ability; but neither one can function adequately unless supplemented by practice. As Ovid says:

> Practice alone is the giver of skill.

There are two kinds of practice, analysis and production. The first appears when the examples of an art are as though resolved into their principles, while in their single parts they are examined with respect to a norm, that is with respect to the precepts of the art. The second appears when according to the direction given by the art we do or make something.

So much for the causes of the arts; the species follow. Arts are general or special. The general arts are those of which the subject matter is general. That matter belongs either to the artisan or to the art. The general matter of the artisan is common to all the general arts; the general matter

artis autem, singularum est propria: estque artificis quidem generalis materia, omne id quod revera est, aut esse fingitur; artis, quod in eo omni efficiunt singulæ. Id omne vel ratio complectitur, vel oratio: generalium itaque artium materia
5 generalis, vel ratio est, vel oratio: versantur enim in excolenda vel ratione ad bene ratiocinandum, ut Logica; vel oratione, eaque vel ad bene loquendum, ut Grammatica, vel ad dicendum bene, ut Rhetorica. Omnium autem prima ac generalissima, Logica est; dein Grammatica, tum demum Rhetorica;
10 quatenus rationis usus sine oratione etiam magnus, hujus sine illa potest esse nullus. Grammaticæ autem secundum tribuimus locum, eo quod oratio pura esse etiam inornata; ornata esse nisi pura sit prius, facile non queat.

Artes speciales sunt, quæ materiam habent specialem;
15 nempe naturam fere vel mores: earum enim accuratior distributio non est hujus loci.

of art is the special matter of the single arts. The general material of the artisan is all that which really is or is feigned to be; the general material of art is what the single arts effect upon it all. Reason or speech embraces all this. Hence the general matter of the general arts is either reason or speech. They are employed either in perfecting reason for the sake of proper thinking, as is logic, or in perfecting speech, and that either for the sake of the correct use of words, as is grammar, or the effective use of words, as is rhetoric. Of all the arts the first and most general is logic, then grammar, then last of all rhetoric, since there can be much use of reason without speech, but no use of speech without reason. We give the second place to grammar because correct speech can be unadorned; but it can hardly be adorned before it is correct.

Arts which have special matter, commonly nature or conduct, are special; but this is not the place for a more accurate classification of them.

J. MILTONI ANGLI
ARTIS LOGICÆ
Plenior Institutio, &c.

LIBER PRIMUS.

CAPUT I.

Quid sit Logica?

LOGICA est ars bene ratiocinandi. Eodémque sensu Dialectica sæpe dicta est.

Logica autem, *i.e.* ars rationalis, à *λόγῳ* dicitur: quæ vox Græcè rationem significat; quam excolendam Logica
5 sibi sumit.

Ratiocinari autem est rationis uti facultate. Additur bene, i. e. rectè, scienter, expeditè; ad perfectionem artis ab imperfectione facultatis naturalis distinguendam.

Logicam potius, quàm cum *P. Ramo* Dialecticam, dicen-
10 dam duxi, quòd eo nomine tota ars rationis aptissimè significetur; cùm Dialectica à verbo Græco *διαλέγεσθαι*, artem po-

A fuller institution &c.

OF THE

ART OF LOGIC

BY

JOHN MILTON

AN ENGLISHMAN.

THE FIRST BOOK.

CHAPTER I.

What is Logic?

LOGIC is the art of reasoning well. In the same sense the word *dialectic* is often used.

Logic however, that is the rational art, is so named from λόγῳ, a word which in Greek means reason, the sub-
5 ject which logic takes for explanation.

And to reason is to use the faculty of reason. In order to distinguish the perfection of the art from the imperfection of the natural faculty, the word *well,* that is rightly, skilfully, promptly, is added to the definition.

10 I have thought it proper to use the word *logic* rather than, with Peter Ramus, *dialectic,* because by logic the whole art of reasoning is aptly signified; while dialectic, derived from the Greek word διαλέγεσθαι, indicates rather the art of ques-

tius interrogandi & respondendi, i. e. disputandi significet; ut ex *Platonis Cratylo,* ex doctrina *Peripateticorum* & *Stoicorum, Fabio, Suida,* aliisque docetur. Et tamen *Plato* in Alcibiade primo idem vult esse τὸ διαλέγεσθαι, quod ratione uti. Prior 5 significatio ad rationis usum nimis angusta est; posterior, si inter authores de ea non convenit, nimis incerta.

Ratiocinandi autem potius dico quàm disserendi, propterea quòd ratiocinari, non minus late quàm ipsa ratio, idem valet propriè quod ratione uti; cùm disserere, præterquam quod 10 vox non planè propria, sed translata sit, non latius plerumque pateat, quam disputare.

Addunt nonnulli in definitione subjectum Dialecticæ, i. e. de re qualibet: sed hoc cum Grammatica & Rhetorica commune Dialecticæ fuit, ut in prooemio vidimus; non ergo hîc 15 repetendum.

CAPUT II.

De partibus Logicæ, déque Argumenti Generibus.

RATIOCINATIO autem fit omnis, rationibus vel solis & per se consideratis, vel inter se dispositis; quæ argumenta etiam sæpius dicta sunt.

Logicæ itaque partes duæ sunt; rationum sive argumen-20 torum inventio, eorumque dispositio.

Secutus veteres *Ramus, Aristotelem, Ciceronem, Fabium,* Dialecticam partitur in inventionem & judicium. Verùm non

tioning and answering, that is of debating, as is shown in the *Cratylus* of Plato, in the doctrine of the Peripatetics and Stoics, and by Fabius, Suidas and others. And still Plato in the first *Alcibiades* expresses the belief that τὸ διαλέγεσθαι is the
5 same as to use the reason. The first meaning is too narrow to signify the use of the reason; the second, if there is not an agreement between authors about it, is too uncertain.

In the definition I say *reasoning* rather than *debating* because *to reason,* not less extensive in meaning than the reason
10 itself, properly means the same as to use the reason, while *debating,* in addition to being a word not obviously fitting but having a transferred meaning, would not commonly have any wider significance than that of disputing.

Some add to the definition the subject of dialectic, that is,
15 concerning anything; but dialectic has this in common with grammar and rhetoric, as we saw in the preface; therefore it need not be repeated here.

CHAPTER II.

Of the parts of logic and the kinds of argument.

ALL reasoning is made up of reasons either considered alone and for themselves or related to each other; they are more often called arguments.

Hence there are two parts of logic: the invention of reasons or arguments and the disposition of them.

Ramus follows the ancients, Aristotle, Cicero, and Fabius, in dividing dialectic into invention and judgment. But in

inventio, quæ nimis lata est quocunque modo sumatur, sed argumentorum inventio, pars prima Logicæ dicenda est: dispositio autem eorum, cur sit secunda, non judicium, secundi libri initio respondebimus. Sed neque hæc partitio suis auc-
5 toribus vel ijsdem vel aliis caret: *Plato,* in Phædro, dispositionem inventioni addidit; *Aristoteles* *τάξιν*; *Top.* 8. 1. quod idem est. *Et Cicero,* de Orat. fatetur, inventionem & dispositionem, non orationis esse, sed rationis.

Inventionem autem & dispositionem quarum tandem
10 rerum nisi argumentorum.

Argumentorum itaque inventio *Topica Græcè* nominatur; quia *τόπους* continet, i.e. locos unde argumenta sumuntur, viámque docet & rationem argumenta bene inveniendi, suo nimirum ordine collocata; unde vel ad genesin expromantur,
15 vel in analysi explorentur, inventorúmque simul vim atque usum exponit.

Argumentum est quod ad aliquid arguendum affectum est. Id est, quod habet affectionem ad arguendum; vel ut Cic. in Top. quod affectum est ad id de quo quæritur: id est, ut inter-
20 pretatur *Boethius,* refertur, vel, aliqua relatione respicit id de quo quæritur.

Ista affectione sublatâ, argumentum non est; mutatâ, non est idem; sed ipsum quoque mutatur.

Ad arguendum autem, i. e. ostendendum; explicandum,

truth not invention, which however taken is too broad a term, but the invention of arguments should be called the first part of logic. But the question why the second part should be the arrangement of these arguments, not judgment, we shall
5 answer at the beginning of the second book. But this arrangement does not lack its authorities—either the same or others: Plato, in the *Phædrus,* adds disposition to invention; Aristotle (*Topics* 8. 1) adds τάξιν which is the same; and Cicero (*De oratore*) says that invention and arrangement per-
10 tain not to oratory but to reason.

Indeed to what except arguments can invention and disposition pertain?

So in Greek the invention of arguments is called *topica,* since it contains τόπους, that is places whence arguments are
15 taken, and teaches the way and the method of inventing arguments well, when they have been arranged in their proper order. Then it shows at the same time the force and use of what have been invented, whether they are displayed as to their origin or examined in analysis.

20 *An argument is that which has a fitness for arguing something.* That is, it is that which has a natural bent for arguing; or as Cicero says in the *Topics,* it is what is affected to that of which there is question; Boethius interprets this as meaning that it is referred to or has some relation to that of which there
25 is question.

If this natural bent is removed, there is no argument; if it is changed, the argument is not the same, but is itself changed.

For arguing something, that is for showing, explaining, or

probandum aliquid. Sic juxta illud tritum, *degeneres animos timor arguit, Æneid.* 4. *&* *illud Ovidii; Apparet virtus, arguiturque malis.* Explicare autem & probare etiam simplicis argumenti propria atque primaria vis est, unde aliud ex alio
5 sequi, vel non sequi, i. e. uno posito, alterum poni vel non poni primitus judicatur: quod de inductione quidem recte monuit *Baconus* noster, de Augment. scient. *l.* 5. *c.* 4. *uno eodémque mentis opere, illud quod quæritur, & inveniri & judicari:* sed hoc de singulis argumentis simplicibus non minus verum
10 est.

Ex quo etiam sequitur, judicium non esse alteram Logicæ partem, sed quasi effectum utriúsque partis communem & ex utraque oriundum; ex syllogismo in re presertim dubia clarius quidem at secundario tamen contra ac plerique docent.

15 Aliquid autem, est id quodcunque arguitur: quicquid enim est, aut esse fingitur, subjectum est Logicæ, ut supra demonstravimus. Argumentum autem propriè neque vox est neque res; sed affectio quædam rei ad arguendum; quæ *ratio* dici potest ut supra.

20 Tractat igitur Logica neque voces, neque res. Voces quidem, quamquam & sine vocibus potest ratiocinari, tamen, quoties opus est, distinctas & tantùm non ambiguas, non improprias, ab ipso usu loquendi videtur jure sanè postulare: res ipsas artib. quasque suis relinquit; arguendi duntaxat inter se
25 quam habeant affectionem sive rationem considerat.

proving something. Thus we have the well-known quotation: "Fear argues degenerate souls" (*Æneid* 4), and that of Ovid: "Virtue is made manifest and argued by afflictions." But the proper and primary potency of a simple argument is to ex-
5 plain and prove how one thing follows or does not follow from another; that is, it is judged that when one thing has been laid down as true something else is or is not also laid down originally. Our Bacon (*De augmentis scientiarum* 5. 4) rightly suggests the same thing about induction: "By one and
10 the same operation of the mind the thing in question is both invented and judged"; but this is not less true of simple, single arguments.

From this it follows that judgment is not the second part of logic, but an effect common to both parts and springing
15 from both, from the syllogism, especially in a doubtful case, more clearly though in a secondary way. Nevertheless many teach the contrary.

Something: that is, whatever is argued; for whatever is or is feigned to be is the subject of logic, as we demonstrated
20 above. An argument in the proper sense of the word is not a word or a thing, but a certain fitness of something for arguing; this, as is shown above, can be called *reason.*

Logic, therefore, treats neither words nor things. Although it is possible to reason without words, yet from the very neces-
25 sity for speaking, logic seems with perfect right to demand that whenever it is necessary words should be employed that are distinct and certainly not ambiguous and not inappropriate. Logic leaves things themselves to their appropriate

Ratio autem dicitur, voce à Mathematicis petita, qua terminorum proportionalium inter se certa habitudo significatur.

Argumentum est artificiale aut inartificiale. Sic Aristot. Rhet. 1. 2. quem *Fabius* sequitur, *l.* 5. *c.* 1. *Cicero* in *insitum*
5 & *assumptum* dividit. Artificiale autem dicitur, non quo inveniatur arte magis quàm inartificiale, sed quòd ex sese arguit, i. e. vi insita ac propria.

Artificiale est primum, vel à primo ortum. Primum, quod est suæ originis. Id est, affectionem arguendi non modò in se
10 habet, sed etiam à se; quod infrà clarius patebit, cùm quid sit à *primo ortum* docebitur.

Primum est simplex aut comparatum.

Simplex, quod simpliciter & absolutè consideratur. Id est, simplicem habet affectionem arguendi id quod arguitur, sine
15 quantitatis aut qualitatis cum eo comparatione.

Simplex est consentaneum aut dissentaneum.

Nam quæ sine comparatione considerantur, necesse est vel consentient inter se, vel dissentiant.

Consentaneum est quod consentit cum re quam arguit. Id
20 est, ponit, sive affirmat esse rem quam arguit.

Estque consentaneum absolutè aut modo quodam. Absolutè, i. e. perfectè; absolvere enim est perficere. *Aristotelis* quoque hæc distributio est. Quæ autem absolutè consentiunt,

arts; it considers merely what affect or ratio for arguing they have among themselves.

This word *ratio,* taken from the mathematicians, signifies a certain condition of terms proportional to each other.

5 *An argument is either artificial or inartificial.* Thus Aristotle (*Rhetoric* I.2), followed by Fabius (book 5, chap. I). Cicero divides it into the *innate* and the *assumed.* But it is called artificial not because it is found out by art more than is the inartificial, but because it argues of itself, that is from 10 innate and peculiar force.

The artificial is either primitive or sprung from what is primitive. The primitive is itself original. That is, it has the tendency for arguing not merely in itself, but also of itself, as will appear more clearly below, when the expression *sprung* 15 *from what is primitive* will be explained.

The primitive is either simple or comparative.

The simple is what is considered simply and absolutely. That is, it has a simple affect for arguing what is argued, without comparison of quantity or quality with it.

20 *The simple is either consentany or dissentany.*

For things which are considered without comparison must necessarily either consent or dissent.

A consentany argument agrees with what it argues. That is, it establishes or affirms the being of the thing which it 25 argues.

It is consentany either absolutely or after a fashion. Absolutely means perfectly, for to absolve is to make perfect. This distribution is also used by Aristotle. But of things which

eorum alterum alterius vi existere intelligitur; & sic consentiunt causa & effectus. Atque hæ sunt argumentorum distributiones generales ex affectionum differentiis desumptæ; suóque nunc ordine singulatim tractandæ: argumentorum
5 autem omnium primum *causa* est; id quòd per se quivis intelligere potest.

CAPUT III.

De Efficiente, procreante, & conservante.

C*AUSA est, cujus vi res est.* Vel, si ex capite superiore, quod intelligi memoriáque teneri potest, repetito est opus, causa est argumentum artificiale, primum,
10 simplex, absolutè consentaneum, cujus vi, vel facultate, res, i. e. effectum, arguitur esse vel existere. Nec male definiatur causa *quæ dat esse rei.*

Cujus autem vi vel facultate, i.e. à quo, ex quo, per quod, vel propter quod res est, id causa esse dicitur. *Res* etiam, idem
15 quod *aliquid* in definitione argumenti, vox generalis adhibetur, quæ significaret causam, sicut & reliqua argumenta, esse rerum omnium quæ vel sunt, vel finguntur: nam quæ revera sunt veras; quæ finguntur, fictas causas habent.

Hinc intelligitur *causam sine qua non,* quæ vulgò dicitur,
20 impropriè causam, & quasi fortuitò, dici, ut cùm amissio rei alicujus dicitur causa recuperationis; quamvis amissio recu-

absolutely agree one is known to exist by force of the other; and thus cause and effect agree. So these are the general distributions of arguments founded on differences in their affects. Now they are to be treated one by one in their order.
5 The first of all arguments is *cause*—as anyone can know for himself.

CHAPTER III.

Of the efficient cause as procreant and conserving.

A *CAUSE is that by the force of which a thing exists.* Or if there is need of repetition from a preceding chapter which can be understood and remembered,
10 a cause is an artificial argument, primitive, simple, absolutely consentany, by the force or capability of which a thing, that is an effect, is argued to be or to exist. A cause is not badly defined as *that which gives being to a thing.*

By the force or capability *of which,* that is the thing by
15 which, from which, through which, or on account of which a thing is, is said to be a cause. The word *thing,* the same as *something* in the definition of an argument, is used as a general word which signifies that there is a cause, as well as the other arguments, for all things that exist or are feigned to
20 exist; for true things have true causes, and feigned things have feigned causes.

Hence it is understood that the cause *sine qua non,* as it is commonly called, is improperly and as though fortuitously considered a cause, as when the loss of something is called
25 the cause of its finding, since loss of necessity precedes find-

perationem necessariò præcedat. Neque enim causa sic intelligi debet, id quod & *Cicero* docuit, l. de Fato, ut quod cuique antecedat, id ei causa sit, sed quod cuique efficienter antecedat; i.e. ita ut res vi ejus existat. Hinc causa propriè dicta, 5 *principium* quoque nominatur à *Cic.* 1. de Nat. deor. sed frequentiùs apud Græcos.

Causa autem est cujus vi res non solùm est, verùm etiam fuit, vel erit. Ut enim præcepta Logica de omni re, sic omnium præcepta artium de omni tempore intelligenda sunt; 10 unde & æterna esse, veritatisque æternæ dicuntur.

Ex definitione autem causæ tertium illud artis præceptum, de quo in præfatione diximus, consectarium hoc oritur: *primus hic locus inventionis, fons est omnis scientiæ; scirique demum creditur cujus causa teneatur.*

15 Neque aliud est *Aristotelis* decantata illa demonstratio, quàm qua effectum arguitur, probatur, cognoscitur, ponitur, ex causa posita; quodcunque illud demum causæ genus sit: ut cùm risible probatur ex rationali, quippe, omnis homo est risibilis, quia rationalis: eóque erit clarior demonstratio, quo 20 causa certior, propior, præstantior.

Causa est efficiens & materia, aut forma & finis. Cur sic causa dividatur quasi in duo genera anonyma, infrà in doctrina distributionis facilius intelligetur.

ing. For, as Cicero (*De fato*) teaches, cause ought not so to be understood that what precedes anything is considered its cause, but what efficiently precedes something; that is in such a way that the thing exists by the power of it. Hence the
5 cause in the true sense of the word is also called *principium* by Cicero (*De natura deorum* I), and more frequently among the Greeks.

The cause, moreover, is not merely that by force of which the thing is, but also has been or will be. For just as the pre-
10 cepts of logic are to be understood as applying to everything, so the precepts of all the arts are to be understood of every time; therefore they are said to be eternal and of eternal truth.

From the definition of cause that third precept of art, a consectary, of which we spoke in the preface, arises as fol-
15 lows: *This first place of invention is the fount of all knowledge; and in fact if the cause of something can be comprehended it is believed to be known.*

That often-mentioned demonstration of Aristotle is nothing else than that by which an effect is argued, proved, rec-
20 ognized, established, from an established cause, of whatever sort that genus of cause may be, as when the ability to laugh is proved from rationality; to wit, every man is able to laugh because he is rational. The demonstration will be the clearer as the cause is more certain, nearer, more important.

25 *The cause is efficient and matter, or form and end.* Why cause is thus divided into two nameless genera will be more easily comprehended when explained below in the section on distribution.

Quot autem modis alicujus vi res est, tot esse species causæ statuendum est. Modis autem quatuor alicujus vi res est; ut rectè *Aristot. Phys.* 2. 7. & nos suprà diximus; vel enim à quo, vel ex quo, vel per quod, vel propter quod res una quæque
5 est, ejus vi esse rectè dicitur. His modis nec plures inveniuntur, nec pauciores esse possunt: rectè igitur causa distribuitur in causam à qua, ex qua, per quam, & propter quam, i.e. efficientem & materiam, aut formam & finem.

Efficiens est causa, à qua res est, vel efficitur. Ab efficiente
10 enim principium movendi est; ipsa tamen effecto non inest.

Ciceroni omnis causa *efficiens* nominatur: sic enim in Topicis; *primus est locus rerum efficientium, quæ causæ appellantur:* & de Fato; *causa est quæ id efficit, cujus est causa.* Hinc fit ut *causatum,* à causis licet omnib. ortum habens,
15 *effectum* tantummodo vocitetur: unde hoc solum intelligitur, efficientem esse causam præcipuam atque primariam; omnem autem causam aliquo modo efficere.

Efficientis etsi, vera genera nulla sive species nobis apparent, ubertas tamen permagna modis quibusdam distinguitur.
20 *Primò, quòd procreet, aut tueatur.*

Sic pater & mater procreant; nutrix tuetur. Huc quoque omnium rerum inventores, auctores, conditores, conservatores referendi sunt. Procreare igitur & tueri duo sunt modi quibus

It may be laid down that there are as many species of cause as of modes by the force of which a thing is. But in four modes a thing exists by the force of something, as Aristotle (*Physics* 2. 7) rightly says and as we have mentioned above; 5 for a thing is correctly said to be through the power of that by which, from which, through which, or on account of which it is. Neither more than these four modes can be found nor can there be fewer; cause is therefore rightly classified into cause by which, from which, through which, and on account 10 of which, that is efficient and matter, or form and end.

The efficient is the cause by which the thing is or is brought about. For by the efficient is brought about the beginning of moving, yet the efficient is not within the effect.

By Cicero every cause is called *efficient;* thus he writes in 15 *Topics:* "The first place is given to efficient things, which are called causes;" and in *De fato:* "A cause is that which effects that of which it is the cause." This is the reason why *the thing caused,* though it has its origin from all the causes, is so commonly called *the effect.* It means merely that the efficient is 20 the special and primary cause, for every cause in some way effects something.

Although no true genera or species of the efficient appear to us, yet the exceeding richness of it is distinguished in various ways.

25 *First, because it procreates or maintains.*

Thus father and mother procreate; the nurse maintains. Here also are to be put the inventors of everything, the authors, the founders, and the preservers. Hence to procreate

idem sæpe efficiens efficere solet: procreando quidem id quod nondum est, ut sit; conservando autem id quod jam est, ut porrò sit.

CAPUT IV.

De Efficiente sola, & cum aliis.

SECUNDÒ, *causa efficiens sola efficit, aut cum aliis. Earúmque omnium sæpe alia principalis, alia minus principalis, sive adjuvans & ministra.* Quam *Cicero,* in Partit. *causam conficientem* vocat: & cujus, inquit, generis vis varia est, & sæpe aut major aut minor; ut & illa quæ maximam vim habet, sola sæpe causa dicatur. Hinc, Æneid. 9. *Nysus* ab
10 *Eurialo* socio transfert in se factæ cædis & culpam & pœnam; quasi solus auctor fuerit, quia fuit præcipuus. Et solitaria causa cum plerisque & principalibus & sociis, pro *Marcello,* variè adhibetur. Sed hæc duo exempla vide post finem in praxi analytica.

15 Causa minus principalis (ut quidam volunt) vel est impulsiva, quæ principalem quoquo modo impellit ac movet, vel est instrumentalis.

Impulsiva duplex est Græcisque vocibus receptis, *proegumena* dicitur, vel *procatarctica.* Illa intus, hæc extrinsecus

and to maintain are two modes in which often the same efficient cause is in the habit of working, procreating that which not yet is that it may come into being, and conserving what now is that it may continue to be.

CHAPTER IV.

Of the efficient cause singly and with others.

SECONDLY, the efficient cause works alone, or with others. And of all these last often one is principal, another less principal or a helping and servant cause. Cicero, in *De partitione oratoria,* gives to all of this type the name of *conficient cause;* and the force of this kind is, he
10 says, various, and often either greater or less, so that the one having greatest force is often called the sole cause. Thus in *Æneid* 9 Nysus shifts from his comrade Euryalus to himself the blame and penalty for the slaughter that has been made, as though he were the single author, since he was the chief
15 one. And a solitary cause with many both principal and associated causes is variously exhibited in *Pro Marcello.* But see these two examples in the analytic praxis at the end of the present work.

A principal cause of the lower order, as some put it, is
20 either impulsive, in some way impelling and moving the principal, or it is instrumental.

The two sorts of impulsive cause are called by accepted Greek names either *proegumenic* or *procatarctic.* The first moves the principal from within, the second from without;

movet principalem: & vera si est, *occasio,* si ficta, *prætextus* dicitur.

Sic causa proeg. quæ intus movebat infideles ad persequendum Christianos (exemplis enim receptis hîc utemur) erat
5 eorum ignorantia aut impietas, causa procat. erant nocturni conventus, vel potius quæ vis conventicula Christianorum. Olim interficiendi Christi causa proeg. erat Judæorum zelus ignarus: procat. objecta sabbathi violatio concionésque seditiosæ. Notandum autem est ubi causa proegumena, sive in-
10 terna, non est, ibi causæ procatarcticæ, sive externæ, vim nullam esse.

Ad causam autem procatarcticam, ea sæpe referenda videtur, si omnino est in causis numeranda, quæ suprà dicta est *causa sine qua non;* siquidem quovis modo causam extrinse-
15 cus movere principalem dici potest.

Instrumenta etiam in causis adjuvantibus connumerantur. Quo argumento *Epicureus,* apud *Cic.* 1. de Nat. deor. disputat mundum nunquam esse factum. Hoc etiam exemplum ad praxin retulimus. Instrumenta autem propriè non agunt, sed
20 aguntur aut adjuvant. Et qui causam adjuvantem nullam nisi instrumenta habet, potest rectè *solitaria causa* dici: quanquam lata admodum instrumenti significatio admittitur; ut apud *Aristot. Polit.* 1. 3. *instrumenta sunt animata, vel inanimata.* Quo sensu omnes ferè causæ adjuvantes & ministræ possunt
25 *instrumentales* nominari.

Ad hunc locum referendus commodissimè videtur causa-

if it is genuine it is called the *occasion,* if feigned the *pretext.*

Thus the proegumenic cause which from within moved the infidels to persecute the Christians (for we use here the received examples) was their ignorance or impiety; the pro-
5 catarctic cause was the nocturnal meetings, or rather the capacity to hold meetings, of the Christians. Long ago the proegumenic cause of the death of Christ was the ignorant zeal of the Jews; the procatarctic cause was the violation of the sabbath and the seditious assemblies with which he was
10 charged. It should be noted, however, that where a proegumenic or internal cause is lacking, there the procatarctic or external cause has no power.

To the procatarctic cause, if in any way it can be counted among the causes, often seems to be assigned that which
15 above is called the cause *sine qua non,* if in any way it can be said externally to move the principal cause.

Instruments are also reckoned among the helping causes. By this argument Epicurus, according to Cicero's *De natura deorum,* book 1, maintains that the world never has been
20 made. This example too we have put in the praxis. Instruments, however, do not act of themselves, but are used or help. And a cause which has no helping cause except an instrument can properly be called a *solitary cause,* however wide the significance given to the word instrument, as accord-
25 ing to Aristotle (*Politics* 1.3) "instruments are either animate or inanimate." In this sense almost all helping and servant causes can be called *instrumental.*

To this place it seems may be assigned most conveniently

rum ordo, quo alia dicitur *prima,* ídque vel absolutè, ut Deus, vel in suo genere; ut sol, & ejusmodi quippiam; alia *secunda;* & sic deinceps, quæ à prima vel à prioribus pendet, & quasi effectum est. Alia deinde *remota* dicitur, alia *proxima:* quò
5 spectat illud vulgo dictum; *quicquid est causa causæ, est etiam causa causati.* Quæ regula in causis duntaxat necessariò inter se ordinatis valet. Sed hæ causarum divisiones in Logica non magnopere sectandæ sunt; quandoquidem tota vis arguendi in causa proxima continetur; déque ea sola generalis defi-
10 nitio causæ intelligitur.

CAPUT V.

De Efficiente per se, & per accidens.

TERTIÒ, *causa efficiens per se efficit, aut per accidens.* Tertium hoc par modorum efficiendi est, ab *Aristotele* etiam & veteribus notatum.

Per se efficit causa, quæ sua facultate efficit. Id est, quæ ab
15 interno principio effectum producit.

Vt quæ natura vel consilio faciunt. Naturalis efficientia est elementorum, fossilium, plantarum, animalium. Consilii exemplum est illa *Ciceronis* de se ad *Cæsarem* confessio: *nulla vi coactus, judicio meo ac voluntate, ad ea arma profectus sum,*
20 *quæ erant sumpta contra te.*

Naturæ, appetitum; consilio, artem nonnulli adjungunt. Sed appetitus aut naturalem, aut ad naturam, aut ad naturæ

the order of causes in which one is called *first,* either absolutely, as God, or in its genus, as the sun and anything of the sort; others, called *secondary* and so forth, depend on the first or the prior causes, and each is a kind of effect. Others are
5 called *remote,* others *proximate,* where applies the common saying that *whatever is the cause of a cause is the cause of what is caused.* This rule applied to causes so far as necessarily related among themselves. But these divisions of causes in logic need not be zealously followed out, for the whole
10 force of arguing is contained in the proximate cause; and from this alone the general definition of cause is understood.

CHAPTER V.

Of the efficient cause by itself and by accident.

THIRDLY, the efficient cause works of itself or by accident. This is the third pair of the modes of working, as indicated by Aristotle and the ancients.

15 *A cause works of itself which works by its own power,* that is, which produces an effect from an internal principle.

Such as those that work by nature or according to a plan. Natural efficiency is possessed by elements, minerals, plants, and animals. An example of operation by thought is that
20 confession of Cicero about himself to Caesar: "Not constrained by any, but of my judgment and will, I came forth to those wars which were undertaken against thee."

To nature some join appetite, and to planning they join art. But appetite is referred either to what is natural, or to

vitium; ars ad consilium sine incommodo referetur: ars n. & consilium quatenus aliquid efficiunt, non illa ab intellectu, hoc à voluntate; sed ut utrumque ab utroque proficisci videtur: etenim ars ferè non invita, non proximè saltem invita; &
5 consilium prudens sciénsque agit. Hi quatuor modi efficiendi per se, ad eundem nonnunquam effectum concurrunt: ut cùm quis loquitur, naturâ; hoc vel illud, consilio simul & appetitu; eleganter, arte.

Videtur itaque huc proprie referenda etiam causa impul-
10 siva, sive ea proegumena, sive procatarctica sit, de quibus capite superiore diximus; quæ non tam causæ sunt principali sociæ aut ministræ quam modi efficientis, quibus vel affectu aliquo impulsus, vel ex occasione aliqua oblata, consilio adductus hoc vel illud agit, ut ex allatis ibi exemplis intelligi
15 potest.

Quæ autem naturâ necessariò, quæ consilio, libere agunt, necessariò agit quæ aliter agere non potest, sed ad unum quidpiam agendum determinatur, idque solum sua propensione agit quæ necessitas naturæ dicitur; ex hypothesi nimirum.
20 Nisi Deus aliud voluerit, aut externa vis aliorsum impulerit, ut Lapidem sursum. Libere agit efficiens non hoc duntaxat ut naturale agens, sed hoc vel illud pro arbitrio idque abso-

nature, or to a vice of nature; art is without difficulty to be referred to planning; for as far as art and thought effect anything, the first does not seem to set out from the intellect, the second from the will, but either one seems to set out from the
5 other, for art is not commonly against the will, not at least in a strict sense against the will; and the prudent and well-informed man makes use of thought. These four modes in which a cause works of itself sometimes concur to the same effect, as when any one speaks it is by nature, yet he says this
10 or that as a result of both consideration and desire, and puts it elegantly by means of art.

It seems too that this is the proper place for the impulsive cause, whether proegumenic or procatarctic, of which we spoke in the chapter above; these are not so much causes
15 associated with or aiding the principal cause, as modes of the efficient cause, through which either impelled by some affect, or because some occasion has been furnished, under the guidance of thought a man does this or that, as can be understood from the examples there brought forward.

20 What men do by nature they do of necessity; what they do after planning they do freely. By necessity anyone does what he cannot do otherwise than as he does it, but he is bound to the doing of the one thing, and does this thing only through the impulse which is called the necessity of
25 nature, *ex hypothesi* certainly, unless God wishes otherwise, or external force impels in some other direction, as a stone upward. The efficient cause does not work freely to this extent as working naturally, but as doing this or that

lute vel ex hypothesi. Absolute solus Deus libere agit omnia; id est quicquid vult; & agere potest vel non agere; testantur hoc passim sacræ literæ. Libere ex hypothesi, illae duntaxat causæ quæ ratione & consilio faciunt, ut angeli &
5 homines; ex hypothesi nimirum divinæ voluntatis, quæ iis Libere agendi potestatem in principio fecit. Libertas enim potestas est agendi vel non agendi hoc vel illud. Nempe nisi Deus aliud voluerit, aut vis aliunde ingruat.

Per accidens efficit causa, quæ externa facultate efficit. Id
10 est, non sua; cùm principium effecti est extra efficientem, externúmque principium interno oppositum: sic. n. efficiens non efficit per se, sed per aliud. Hinc vere dicitur, *omne effectum causæ per accidens potest reduci ad causam per se.*

Vt in his quæ fiunt coactione, vel fortuna. Duo n. hæc sunt
15 externa principia internis, naturæ nempe & voluntati sive consilio, opposita. Sic *Aristot.* Rhet. 1. 10. cùm dixisset, homines facere quædam non per se, quædam per se; subjungit, *eorum quæ non per se, alia per fortunam, alia ex necessitate.* Sed *necessitas* vox nimis lata est, ut ex supra dictis de efficiente
20 naturali patebit.

Coactione fit aliquid, cum efficiens vi cogitur ad effectum. Ut cum lapis sursum vel recta projicitur qui suapte natura

according to judgment and so doing it either absolutely or *ex hypothesi*. Absolutely, God alone freely does all things, that is whatever he wishes, and is able to act or not to act. The Bible frequently asserts this. Those causes merely which
5 work according to reason and thought, as angels and men, act freely *ex hypothesi*—on the hypothesis of the divine will, which in the beginning gave them the power of acting freely. For liberty is the power of doing or not doing this or that, except, to be sure, God wished otherwise, or force from some
10 other quarter assailed them.

A cause works by accident which works by some external power, that is by a power not its own, when the beginning of the effect is without the efficient and is an external principle opposed to the internal, for thus the efficient cause acts
15 not through itself, but through another. Thence it is truly said that *all effect of cause through accident can be reduced to cause of itself.*

This is true of those things which are done by coercion or fortune, for these two are external principles opposed to the
20 internal ones, namely, nature and will or thought. Thus Aristotle (*Rhetoric* I. 10) when he said that men do certain things not of themselves and certain things of themselves, adds: "Of those things done not of themselves, some they do through fortune, some from necessity." But the word
25 *necessity* is too extensive, as will be plain from what is said above on the efficient natural cause.

Something is done by coercion when *the efficient cause is driven by force to the effect,* as when a stone is thrown up-

deorsum fertur. Hæc necessitas coactionis dicitur & causis etiam liberis nonnunquam accidere potest. Sic necesse est mercatori in tempestate merces ejicere, siquidem salvus esse vult. Hæc itaque necessitas mixtas quasdam actiones pro-
5 duxit, quas facit quis volens nolente animo, quod aiunt.

Fortuna sive fortuitò fit aliquid, cùm præter scopum efficientis accidit. Non enim fortuna, sed efficiens, quæ per fortunam sive fortuitò agit, est propriè causa per accidens rerum fortuitarum: eò quòd earum principium, occulta nimirum
10 illa causa quam *fortunam* dicimus, extra illam efficientem est: fortuna autem est eventuum eorum principium, etsi occultum, non per accidens tamen, sed per se. Fortuna itaque apud veteres aut nomen sine re esse existimabatur, quo usi sunt homines, teste alicubi *Hippocrate,* cùm secundarias contin-
15 gentium causas ignorarent, aut est ipsa latens causa: ut *Cicero* in Top. *cùm enim nihil sine causa fiat, hoc ipsum est fortuna, eventus obscura causa, quæ latenter efficit.* Inter fortunam & casum hæc volunt interesse *Aristot. Phys.* 2.6. Et *Plutarch.* de Placit. & de Fato, ut casus quàm fortuna latius pateat: for-
20 tuna in iis duntaxat qui ratione utuntur; casus in omnibus tam animantibus quàm inanimatis dominetur: sed loquendi ferè usus fortunæ sub nomine casum etiam complectitur, quoties-

ward or horizontally which by its nature is borne downward. This is called the necessity of coercion and is able sometimes to happen even to free causes. Thus it is necessary for a merchant in a storm to throw overboard his goods if he wishes 5 to be safe. So this necessity produces certain mixed actions, which, as they say, a willing man does with an unwilling heart.

Something is done by fortune or fortuitously when it happens beside the intent of the efficient cause. For not fortune 10 but the efficient cause which works through fortune or fortuitously is properly the cause through accident of fortuitous things, for the reason that the origin of these, that occult cause which we call *fortune,* is in addition to the efficient cause; but fortune, though it is the occult cause, is the prin- 15 cipal cause of those events, not through accident, however, but of itself. So among the ancients fortune was thought to be either a name without a substance—which men used, as Hippocrates bears witness, when they were ignorant of the secondary causes of contingent things—or fortune is the latent cause 20 itself, as Cicero says in the *Topics,* "since nothing can be done without cause, at this very point fortune appears as the obscure cause of the effect and one that works under cover." Aristotle (*Physics* 2.6) and Plutarch (*De placitis philosophorum* and *De fato*) make some difference between fortune 25 and chance, namely that chance has wider influence than fortune, since fortune effects only those who use reason, but chance rules all animate as well as inanimate beings; but ordinary speech includes chance under the name of fortune when-

cunque præter scopum sive finem efficientis aliquid accidit. *Sic casu fortuito,* ait *Tullius,* 3. de nat. deor. *Pheræo Jasoni profuit hostis, qui gladio vomicam ejus aperuit, quam medici sanare non poterant.*

5 *In hoc genere causarum imprudentia connumerari solet.* Sic etiam *Aristot. Ethic.* 3. 1. *videntur non voluntaria esse, quæ per vim aut ignorantiam fiunt. Et Ovid.* 2. *Trist.*

Cur aliquid vidi? cur noxia lumina feci?
Cur imprudenti cognita culpa mihi est?
10 *Inscius Actæon vidit sine veste Dianam:*
Præda suis canibus nec minus ille fuit.
Scilicet in superis etiam fortuna luenda est:
Nec veniam, læso numine, casus habet.

Durum id esse queritur poeta: *nam cæteroqui hinc sumitur* 15 *plerumque deprecatio; & excusationi etiam nonnunquam locus hîc est.* Deprecationis exemplum est apud *Cic.* pro *Ligario: ignosce pater: erravit; lapsus est: non putavit:* Et

ever anything happens beyond the scope or end of the efficient cause. As Tully says (*De natura deorum* 3): "So the case chanced that an enemy was profitable to Jason of Pheræ, who opened his impostume with his sword; which the physicians 5 could by no means heal."

To this genus of causes lack of foresight is commonly assigned. Thus Aristotle (*Ethics* 3. 1) says: "Things done through force or ignorance seem not to be voluntary." And Ovid writes (*Tristia* 2):

10 Why did I see or yet beholde with eye?
What was the cause, I did by sight offend,
And unto me unwise and foolish why
Was ever the fault by any manner kend?
Although by chance that Acteon did see
15 The nude Diane upon the hairy bent,
Yet for all this she did make him a prey
To his own dogs which him in pieces rent.
Wherefore I see that hap or negligence
Among the gods no mercy hath at all,
20 But whoso doth by fortune or by chance
Offend the gods, they shall in trouble fall.

The poet complains of this as hard; and under other conditions *prayer for pardon* is for the most part *rested on lack of foresight,* and surely there is sometimes room for excuse 25 here. An example of prayer for pardon is to be found in Cicero (*Pro Ligario*): "Pardon, O father, he hath erred, he is slipped, he thought not." And a little later he says: "I have

paulò pòst; *erravi: temerè feci: pœnitet; ad clementiam tuam confugio.*

Fortunæ autem nomen, ut suprà dictum est, ignoratio causarum confinxit: cùm enim aliquid præter consilium spémque contigerit, fortuna vulgò dicitur. *Unde Cicero,* apud *Lactantium,* Instit. 3. 29. *ignoratio rerum atque causarum fortunæ nomen induxit.* Nec inscite *Juvenalis:*

Nullum numen abest, si sit prudentia: sed te
Nos facimus, fortuna, deam; cœlóque locamus.

Certè enim & cœlo locanda est; sed, mutato nomine, *divina providentia* dicenda. Unde *Arist. Phys.* 2. 4. *sunt nonnulli quibus fortuna quidem videtur esse causa, sed ignota humanæ intelligentiæ, tanquam divinum quiddam. Et Cic.* Acad. 1. *providentiam Dei quæ ad homines pertinet, nonnunquam quidem fortunam appellant, quod efficiat multa improvisa nec opinata nobis propter obscuritatem ignorationémque causarum.* Sed providentia rerum omnium prima causa est, sive notæ sive ignotæ sint earum causæ secundariæ: & providentiæ si necessitatem adjungas, *fatum* dici solet. Verùm de providentia meliùs Theologia quàm Logica disceptabit. Hoc tantùm obiter; fatum sive decretum Dei cogere neminem malefacere; & ex hypothesi divinæ præscientiæ certa quidem esse

erred, I have done rashly, it repenteth me, I fly to thy clemency."

As was said above, *ignorance of causes has fabricated the name of fortune,* for when anything happens contrary to
5 plan and expectation, it is commonly said to happen by fortune. Whence, according to Lactantius (*Institutiones* 3.29), Cicero said: "Ignorance of things and causes has brought up the name of fortune." Nor did Juvenal unwisely say:

If wisdom present be,
10 There is no god absent;
But Fortune, we thee set on high,
And eke a goddess vaunt.

Certainly fortune should be placed in heaven, but should be called by the different name of *divine providence*. Whence
15 Aristotle (*Physics* 2.4) says: " There are some to whom fortune indeed seems to be a cause, but unknown to human intelligence as something divine." And Cicero (*Academic Questions* 1) writes: "The providence of God which pertains to men they sometimes call fortune, because it brings about
20 many things unforeseen and unimagined by us on account of the obscurity of causes and our ignorance of them." But providence is the first cause of all things, whether their secondary causes are known or unknown, and if necessity is joined to providence it is usually called *fate*. But certainly
25 theology will discuss providence better than will logic. Yet this by the way: fate or the decree of God forces no one to do evil; and on the hypothesis of divine prescience all things are

omnia, non necessaria. Non excusandus itaque *Cicero,* pro *Ligario,* cùm ait, *fatalis quædam calamitas incidisse videtur & improvidas hominum mentes occupavisse; ut nemo mirari debeat humana consilia divina necessitate esse superata.* Multo
5 rectius alibi, *datur quidem venia necessitati; sed necessitati, quæ instituto efficientis repugnat, & voluntati.*

CAPUT VI.

De Materia.

M*ATERIA est causa ex qua res est.* Efficientem ordine naturæ sequitur materia; & efficientis effectum quoddam est; præparat enim efficiens mate-
10 riam, ut sit apta ad recipiendam formam. Ut autem efficiens est id quod primum movet, ita id materia quod primum movetur, hinc efficiens, agendi; materia, patiendi principium appellatur. Hæc autem definitio materiæ apud omnes eadem ferè occurrit. *Est causa:* materiæ enim vi effectum est. Illa
15 autem vis particulà *ex qua* significatur: quanquam hæc vulgò non materiæ solùm nota est, sed nunc efficientis, ut, *ex ictu vulnus:* nunc partium, ut, *homo constat ex anima & corpore;* nunc mutationis cujusvis, ut, *ex candido fit niger. Res:*

certain though not necessary. So Cicero (*Pro Ligario*) is not to be excused when he says: "Some fatal calamity seems to have fallen on and so occupied the unforeseeing minds of men that no one ought to wonder that human counsels are over-
5 thrown by divine necessity." Much more properly elsewhere he says: "Indulgence is indeed given to necessity, but that is granted to necessity which is repugnant to the order of the efficient cause and the will."

CHAPTER VI.

Of matter.

M*ATTER is the cause from which a thing is.* In the order of nature matter follows the efficient cause, and is a sort of effect of the efficient cause; for the efficient cause prepares the matter that it may be fit for receiving the form. As the efficient cause is that which first moves, so the matter is that which is first moved; hence
15 the efficient cause is called the principal cause of acting, matter the principal cause of being acted on. This definition of matter is the same in almost all writers. *Matter is the cause,* for the effect comes by force of the matter. That force is signified by the words *from which,* since these popularly are
20 the sign not of the matter alone, but sometimes of the efficient cause—as in the words: *from the blow a wound*—, sometimes of the parts—as in the statement: *Man consists of spirit and body*—, sometimes of the change of something—as in the saying: *Black is made from white. A thing:* that is

nempe quam arguit; effectum scilicet materiatum; ut intelligamus materiam etiam esse omnium entium & non entium communem; non rerum sensibilium & corporearum propriam. Quales autem res ipsæ sunt, talis materia earum esse
5 debet; sensibilium sensibilis, æternarum æterna; & ita in reliquis. Sic artium materia sunt præcepta. *Est.* i.e. efficitur & constat: unde *Cic.* 1. Acad. *materia ea causa est, quæ se efficienti præbet, ut ex sese non modò effectum fiat, sed etiam postquam effectum est, constet.* Hoc argumento ficto, apud
10 *Ovid.* 2. Metam. solis domus auro, pyropo, ebore, argento componitur. *Regia solis erat* &c. Sic *Cæsar* 1. Bell. civil. navium materiam describit: *carinæ primum ac statumina ex levi materia fiebant* &c.

Dividitur vulgo materia in primam & secundam; secunda
15 in proximam & remotam. Verùm hæc distributio Physica potius est. Id enim solum Logicus in materia spectat, ut res ex ea sit; & potissimum quidem ut proximè ex ea sit; proxima enim potissimum arguit.

the thing which the matter makes evident, to wit, the effect produced by the matter, since we know that matter is common to all entities and nonentities, not peculiar to sensible and corporeal things. But of whatever sort these things are, such the matter of them ought to be; the sensible should be composed of sensible things, the eternal of eternal things, and so in the rest. Thus the matters of the arts are precepts. *Is,* that is, is effected and consists; whence Cicero (*Academic Questions* 1) says: "This matter is the cause which furnishes itself to the efficient cause, that through itself not merely may the effect be produced, but after it is effected may endure." Ovid (*Metamorphoses* 2) used this argument fictitiously, saying that the house of the sun is composed of gold, bronze, ivory and silver: "The palace of the sun was" etc. Thus Caesar (*Civil War* 1) describes the matter of the ships: "The keel and ribs of the ship were made of light material" etc.

Matter is commonly divided into primary and secondary; the secondary into proximate and remote. This distinction is indeed rather suitable to physics. The logician is concerned with the material only as the thing is from it, and especially as it is proximately from it, for the proximate argues with the greatest strength.

CAPUT VII.

De Forma.

C*AUSÆ primum genus ejusmodi est in efficiente & materia: secundum sequitur in forma & fine.* Quia scilicet ordine temporis est posterius. Efficiens enim & materia sub genere priore continentur, quòd in
5 effecto producendo præcedunt; forma & finis sub posteriore, quòd efficientem & materiam sequntur effectúmque ipsum comitantur: positis enim efficiente, & materiâ, non continuò sequntur forma & finis: efficiens enim etsi materiæ suppetit, forma tamen & fine suo nonnunquam frustratur; forma &
10 finis si adsit, necesse est efficientem & materiam fuisse. Qui autem in usu observatur ordo causarum, idem debet in doctrina quoque observari. Nec tamen ordo iste ad constituenda causarum genera satis valet, sed aliud quiddam quod nomine caret. Unde meritò non satis accurata videtur illa causarum
15 distributio, quæ affertur *Aristotelis,* in causas vel effectum præcedentes, ut efficientem & materiam; vel cum effecto simul existentes, ut formam & finem: tam etsi enim hæc distributio ordinem causarum servat, naturam tamen earum non distinguit; immo causæ neque convenit, neque propria est: non
20 convenit, quia causa quælibet, ut causa, non præcedit, sed cum effecto simul est. Præcedunt autem utcunque efficiens

CHAPTER VII.

Of form.

SUCH *is the first kind of cause containing the efficient and the matter; the second follows consisting of the form and the end,* since evidently in the order of time it is posterior. For the efficient and the matter are included
5 in the prior genus, because they precede in producing effect; form and end are included under the posterior, because they follow the efficient and the matter and accompany the effect itself. For when the efficient and the matter are given, the form and end do not directly follow, for albeit the efficient
10 cause fits with the matter, yet form is sometimes frustrated by its end. If form and end are present, the efficient and the matter must have preceded. But there should be observed in presentation the same sequence of causes as in practice. Yet indeed this sequence does not avail sufficiently for consti-
15 tuting the genera of causes, but there is another that lacks a name. For these reasons it may properly be said that there does not seem to be enough accuracy in Aristotle's commonly used distribution of the causes into causes either preceding the effect, as efficient and matter, or existing with the effect,
20 as form and end. Although this arrangement preserves the order of causes, it does not distinguish their nature; nay more, it does not befit the cause and is not proper to it. It is not fitting, since any cause, as cause, does not precede, but is simultaneous with the effect. But in one way or another the

& materia effectum vel naturæ ordine, vel temporis: si naturæ, id & cum reliquis causis & cum subjectis omnibus commune habent; si temporis, hoc efficienti & materiæ neque omni commune est (quædam enim cum effecto non nisi simul sunt) 5 neque solis iis proprium; nam & subjecta pleraque adjunctis suis tempore priora sunt. Nec fœliciùs ab eodem *Aristotele* dividuntur causæ in externas, efficientem & finem; & internas, materiam & formam: hæc enim distributio etsi usus ejus aliquis esse potest, ad leges tamen artis minus accommodata est: 10 esse enim externum vel internum, non est causis proprium, sed effecto etiam & adjuncto commune. Deinde materia & forma cùm intra effectum sunt, non tam causæ quàm partes effecti sunt: quid? quòd finis, quæ perfectio rei est aptitudóque ad usum, interna potius causa diceretur. Postremò, hæc 15 distributio turbat ordinem causarum, methodi proinde legem: efficiens enim est principium motus & causarum prima; finis, ultima est: si igitur internum externo præmittitur, materia & forma, quæ efficientis quodammodo effecta sunt, efficienti præponentur; si externum interno, finis efficienti, i.e. ultima 20 primæ, adjungetur; mediis, materiæ nempe & formæ, præmittetur. Cautius itaque *Ramus* atque arti convenientiùs, causarum genera anonyma reliquit: quod ut ostenderemus, longiuscule cum venia digressi, nunc ad alterum genus causarum, formam & finem, redeamus. Formæ autem est prior locus

efficient and the matter precede the effect either in the order of nature or of time; if in the order of nature, they have it in common with the rest of the causes and with all subjects, if in the order of time, this is not common to every efficient and 5 to all matter (for some efficients and matter are only simultaneous with the effect) nor is it proper to these alone, for many subjects also are prior to their adjuncts in time. Neither again has Aristotle more happily divided causes into external —namely, efficient and end—, and internal—namely, mat- 10 ter and form—; for although some use can be made of this distribution, it is little accommodated to the laws of art, for to be external or internal is not proper to causes, but is common to the effect and the adjunct. Then matter and form, since they are within the effect, are not so much causes as parts 15 of the effect. Why? Because the end, which is the perfection of the thing and its aptitude for use, rather is called the internal cause. Finally, this distribution disturbs the order of causes, and therefore the law of method; for the efficient is the beginning of motion and the first of causes; the end is the last; if 20 therefore the internal is put before the external, matter and form, which in some sense are effects of the efficient, are put before the efficient; if the external is put before the internal, the end is joined to the efficient, that is the last to the first, and is put before the middle ones, that is matter and form. So 25 Ramus cautiously and more suitably to the art leaves the genera of causes nameless. In order to show this we have with your permission digressed at some length; now we may return to the other genus of causes, the form and end. To form

concedendus, cùm finis nihil aliud sit quàm fructus quidam formæ.

Forma est causa per quam res est id quod est. Hæc definitio *Platonicam* & *Aristotelicam* conjunxit: ille enim definit
5 formam esse causam per quam, hic, quod quid est esse. Ut autem materia, sic etiam forma effectum quoddam efficientis quidem est. Formam enim efficiens & producit nondum existentem, & inducit in materiam: forma autem effecti & causa est, & præcipua quidem, soláque effectum arguit, quòd vi
10 formæ potissimum existit. Efficiens enim frustrari formâ, forma effecto non potest. *Per quam* itaque particula eam causam significat eamque vim, quæ rem sive effectum informat atque constituit. Res enim nulla est quæ suam non habeat formam, nobis licet incognitam.

15 Res etiam singulæ, sive individua, quæ vulgò vocant, singulas sibíque proprias formas habent; differunt quippe numero inter se, quod nemo non fatetur. Quid autem, est aliud numero inter se, nisi singulis formis differre? Numerus enim, ut rectè *Scaliger,* est affectio essentiam consequens. Quæ igi-
20 tur numero, essentiâ quoque differunt; & nequaquam numero, nisi essentiâ, differrent. *Evigilent hîc Theologi.* Quòd si quæcunque numero, essentiâ quoque differunt, nec tamen materiâ, necesse est formis inter se differant; non autem communibus, ergo propriis. Sic anima rationalis, forma hominis
25 in genere est; anima *Socratis,* forma *Socratis* propria. *Per quam res est id quod est;* i.e. quæ dat proprium esse rei. Cùm

the first place is to be conceded, since end is nothing other than a sort of product of form.

Form is the cause through which a thing is what it is. This definition joins those of Plato and Aristotle. For Plato defines 5 form as the cause through which, Aristotle as that which is. As the matter, so also the form is a kind of effect of the efficient. For the efficient produces the form not yet existing and induces it into the matter; but the form is also the cause of the effect and especially and alone argues the effect, which 10 exists chiefly by the strength of the form. For the efficient cannot be frustrated by the form, the form by the effect. *Through which:* the phrase signifies that cause and that force which informs and constitutes the thing or effect. For there is nothing that does not have its form, though unknown to us.

15 Single things, or what are commonly called individuals, have form single and proper to themselves; certainly they differ in number among themselves, as no one denies. But what is differing in number among themselves except differing in single forms? For number, as Scaliger rightly says, is 20 an affection following an essence. Therefore things which differ in number also differ in essence; and never do they differ in number if not in essence.—*Here let the Theologians awake.*—Because if whatever things differ in number differ also in essence, but not in matter, necessarily they differ among 25 themselves in forms, but not in common forms, therefore in proper ones. Thus the rational soul is the form of man generically; the soul of Socrates is the proper form of Socrates. *Through which a thing is what it is:* that is, which gives the

enim cujusque ferè rei essentia partim sit communis, partim propria; communem materia constituit, forma propriam. Et per alias quidem causas *esse* res potest dici; per solam formam *esse id quod est.*

Ideóque hinc à cæteris rebus omnib. res distinguitur. Id est, distinctione, quam vocant essentiali: ex sola enim forma est differentia essentialis. Immo quæcunque inter se quovis modo, eadem etiam formis differunt; fónsque omnis differentiæ forma est; nec aliis argumentis inter se res, nisi formis primariò discreparent. Et hoc quidem consectarium ex definitione est primum, sequitur alterum.

Forma simul cum reipsa ingeneratur. Hinc illud verissimum: *positâ formâ, res ipsa ponitur; sublatâ, tollitur.* Ad exempla nunc veniamus. Anima rationalis est forma hominis, quia per eam homo est homo, & distinguitur à cæteris omnibus naturis: geometricarum figurarum in triangulis, quadrangulis sua forma est: Physicarum, cœli, terræ, arborum, piscium sua.

Unde præcipua rerum ut natura est, sic erit explicatio, si possit inveniri. Tertium hoc consectarium est ex definitione formæ. Unde illud quod de causa in communi suprà dictum est, nempe fontem esse omnis scientiæ, formæ potissimum convenire intelligitur. Quæ enim causa essentiam præcipuè constituit, eadem si nota sit, scientiam quoque potissimum

peculiar essence of the thing. For when the essence of almost anything is partly common, partly proper, the matter constitutes what is common, the form what is proper. And through other causes the thing can be said to be; through form alone
5 to be *what it is*.

Therefore by it a thing may be distinguished from all other things, that is, by an essential distinction as they say; for from form alone comes an essential distinction. Still more, whatever things differ among themselves in whatever mode, differ
10 also in forms; and form is the source of every difference; nor do things show discrepancy among themselves by other evidences unless by forms in the first place. And this is the first consectary from the definition; the second follows.

Form is produced in the thing simultaneously with the
15 *thing itself.* Therefore the maxim is altogether true: *When the form is given, the thing itself is given; when the form is taken away, the thing is taken away.* We may now give examples. The rational soul is the form of man, since through this man is man and is distinguished from all other natures;
20 the form of the geometric figures appears in their being triangles or quadrangles; the form of physical things appears in distinguishing between heaven, earth, trees, and fishes.

Therefore as the special nature of things is, so will be the explanation if it can be found. This third consectary is from
25 the definition of form. Whence that said above about cause in common, namely that it is the fount of all knowledge, is understood especially to apply to form. For the cause which especially constitutes the essence, if it is noted, above all brings

facit. Sed formam internam cujusque rei nosse, à sensibus, ut ferè fit, remotissimam, difficile admodum est. In artificiosis autem rebus forma, ut pote externa, sensibúsque exposita, facilius occurrit; ut apud *Cæsarem* de bell. Gall. l. 7. *muri* 5 *autem omnes Gallici hac ferè forma sunt &c.* Sic forma *Virgiliani* portus explicatur, Æneid. 1. *est in secessu longo locus* &c.

Distributio autem formæ nulla vera est. Nam quod nonnulli internam vel externam esse volunt, ea distributio neque 10 ad res omnes, sed tantùm ad corporeas pertinebit; & externa non minus essentialis cuique rei est artificiosæ, quàm interna naturali.

CAPUT VIII.

De Fine.

F*INIS est causa cujus gratia res est.* Sic etiam *Aristoteles, Phil.* 1. 3. *quarta causa est cujus & bonum: hoc enim generationis omnis finis est.* Cùm enim efficiens assecutus est finem, in eo acquiescit, actioníque suæ finem imponit. Finis itaque est causarum ultima. Verùm ut rectè *Aristot. Phys.* 2. 2. *non omne ultimum finalis causa est, sed quod est optimum.* Finis enim vel terminum rei significat, 20 vel bonum rei; sicut & terminus est vel durationis, vel magnitudinis aut figuræ. Finalis autem causa non est nisi bonum

knowledge. But to know the internal form of anything, because it is usually very remote from the senses, is especially difficult. In artificial things, however, the form, as being external and exposed to the senses, is more easily observed,
5 as in the words of Caesar (*Gallic War 7*): "All the French walls are of this form" etc. Thus the form of the port in Virgil (*Æneid* 1) is explained: "There is a place within a spacious recess" etc.

But there is no true distribution of form. For the distri-
10 bution of internal or external which some hold will not apply to all things but merely to the corporeal; and the external is not less essential to each artificial thing than the internal to each natural thing.

CHAPTER VIII.

Of the end.

THE *end is the cause for the sake of which a thing is.* Thus even Aristotle (*Metaphysics* 1. 3) says: "The fourth cause is the good of anything; for this is the end of all generation." For when the efficient cause has led up to the end, it acquiesces in it, and imposes an end to its action. Thus the end is the last of the causes, just as Aristotle
20 (*Physics* 2. 2) truly says: "Not every ultimate is a final cause, but that which is best." For the end signifies either the terminus of the thing, or the good of the thing, as also the terminus is either of duration, or magnitude, or figure. The final cause is not other than some good, and in the same sense
25 it is called an end and a good; whether a true or an apparent

quid; eodémque sensu finis & bonum dicitur; verúmne an apparens, ad vim causæ nihil interest. Sic etiam *Aristot. Phys.* 2. 3. idémque in Eth. passim: mali etiam evitatio habet rationem boni. Nonnulli tamen inter finem & finalem 5 causam ita distinguunt, ut finis sit usus rei, finalis autem causa de usu cogitatio. Atqui non cogitatio, sed res, i.e. finis ipse effecti causa finalis vera est: nam de materia quoque & de forma prius cogitatur, sine hac tamen distinctione: cogitatur etiam de causa impulsiva, eáque movet efficien- 10 tem, nec tamen finalis causa dici potest; cùm eam efficiens non appetat, sed sæpius aversetur, quoties affectus aut habitus aliquis pravus ad bonum aliquod apparens consequendum impellit. Idémque finis in animo efficientis primus, in opere atque effecto est postremus. Dum autem in animo tantum 15 efficientis est, & nondum obtinetur, nondum sanè existit; cùm nondum existit, causa esse qui potest? Cùm itaque vulgò dicitur, finis quatenus efficientem quasi suadendo movet ut materiam paret, eíque formam inducat, non modò effecti, verùm etiam causarum causa earúmque optima est, id im- 20 propriè & per anticipationem quandam dicitur. In opere autem & usu licet sæpe sit ultimus, aptitudine tamen ad usum nisi simul cum forma & tempore & naturâ esse intelligatur, erit posterior effecto per formam jam constituto, & adjunctum potius effecti quàm causa. Sic non habitatio, sed ad habitan- 25 dum, aptitudo, quæ cum inducta forma simul & tempore &

good is of no importance for the force of the cause. Thus also Aristotle (*Physics* 2. 3; *Ethics, passim*), holds that even the avoidance of evil has the nature of good. Some however distinguish between the end and the final cause in this manner,
5 namely, that the end is the usefulness of a thing, but the final cause thought on its usefulness. Yet not thought, but a thing, that is the very end of the effect, is the true final cause; for there is preceding thought on matter and form, but without this distinction; there is also thought on the impulsive cause,
10 and it moves the efficient, but yet it cannot be called a final cause, since the efficient does not seek for this, but more often is averse to it, when some wicked affection or habit impels toward pursuing some apparent good. Likewise the end is first in the mind of the efficient, last in act and effect. But
15 when it is merely in the mind of the efficient and is not yet obtained, it does not yet truly exist; and how can it be a cause when it does not yet exist? When therefore it is commonly said that the end—in so far as by persuading, as it were, the efficient it moves it that it may prepare the matter and endow
20 it with form—is certainly the cause not merely of the effect but also of the causes and is the best of the causes, this is said improperly and by a sort of anticipation. In fact and usefulness indeed it often should be put last, and in aptitude for usefulness, unless it is known to be simultaneous with form
25 and time and nature, it will be posterior to the effect now constituted through form, and an adjunct of the effect rather than a cause. Thus not habitation but aptitude for habitating, which is simultaneous with the induced form in time and

naturâ est, proprius finis domus est statuendus, reíque perfectio & formæ quasi fructus est. Hinc *Græci* non modò τελέω perficio, à τέλος, i.e. *finis* deducunt, sed etiam *perfectum* τέλειον, à fine vocant, teste *Aristotele, Phil.* δ. 24.

5 Vis autem propria qua finalis causa aliis ab causis distinguitur, his verbis, *cujus gratia,* exprimitur; ut & aliis etiam particulis, nempe *cujus causa, ad, ob, pro, propter, quo, quorsum,* & similibus. *Ne* autem est nota illius finis, qui in mali alicujus vitatione versatur. Finis autem dicitur non eorum 10 solùm qui finem sibi proponunt, i.e. efficientium rationalium, sed eorum quæcunque ad finem referuntur, i.e. quorumvis effectorum. Sic Physicis rebus finis homo propositus est, homini Deus. Quod nec ignoravit *Aristoteles,* Phys. 2. 2. *rebus* inquit, *utimur, quasi nostra causa essent omnia: nam* 15 *& nos quodammodo finis sumus.* Deum esse omnium finem docet sapiens *Hebræus, Proverb.* 16. 4. *Deus propter se fecit omnia.* Omnium artium est aliquod summum bonum & finis extremus; quæ & earum forma est: ut Grammaticæ, bene loqui; Rhetoricæ, bene dicere; Logicæ, bene ratiocinari.

20 Quod autem forma finis quoque esse potest, testatur haud semel *Aristoteles,* Phil. δ. 24. & Phys. 2. 7, 8. Et *Plato* in *Philebo,* essentiam sive formam rei, generationis finem statuit: unde *Arist.* de part. 1. 1. idem.

nature, is to be considered more properly the end of a house and the perfection of the thing and as it were the fruit of the form. Thence the Greeks not merely derive τελέω, *I complete,* from τέλος, that is *end,* but also *perfect,* τέλειον, they name
5 from *end,* according to Aristotle (*Metaphysics* 4. 24).

The proper force by which the final cause is distinguished from other causes is expressed by these words, *for the sake of which,* and also by other particles, namely *because of which, toward, because of, on account of, by reason of, whither,* and
10 the like. But *that not* is the sign of the end which is occupied with the shunning of some evil. Yet there is said to be an end not merely of those things which set an end for themselves, that is of efficient rational beings, but of those things which are referred to that end, that is of any effects. Thus man is
15 given as the end of physical things, God as the end of man— something of which Aristotle (*Physics* 2. 2) was not ignorant, saying: "We use things as though all were for our sake; for we too are in a way an end." The wise Hebrew teaches that God is the end of all things in Proverbs 16. 4: "The Lord hath
20 made all things for himself." For all the arts there is something that is their highest good and final end; this is the form of the art; for grammar it is to use words well, for rhetoric to make good speeches, and for logic to reason well.

That the form can also be the end Aristotle testifies not
25 once only (*Metaphysics* 4. 24; *Physics* 2. 7, 8). And Plato in the *Philebus* lays down the essence or form of the thing as the end of generation; and Aristotle (*De partibus* 1. 1) says the same thing.

Ut formæ, ita & finis distributio vera nulla est: quæ vulgò efferuntur, non sunt Logici finis distributiones, sed specialium finium pro varietate effectorum distinctiones. Distinguitur ab *Aristotele*, de Anima, l. 2. 4. *finis cujus*, & finis cui: finis 5 cujus, est finis operæ, sive operandi; finis cui, est finis ipsius operis: e.g. in domo ædificanda; finis cujus, sive operæ, est domus; finis cui, sive ipsius operis, i.e. domus ædificatæ, est aptitudo ad habitationem.

Afferuntur & aliæ distributiones finis, quæ ad finem cui 10 pertinent ut ex *Aristot.* Mag. mor. 1. 2. *finis alius est perfectus, alius imperfectus;* vel, quod idem est, ex aliis, *finis est summus, aut subordinatus.* Summus autem est, qui propter se expetitur: éstque vel universalis, omnib. scilicet rebus communis, vel specialis, cuique speciei peculiaris & proprius. 15 Subordinatius autem non tam finis est, quàm destinatum quiddam ad finem: & esse summum vel subordinatum, esse universale vel speciale, ad alia æque argumenta pertinet, atque ad finem. Postremò, lex distributionis jubet partes distributionis esse oppositas: at inter summum & subordinatum oppo- 20 sitio nulla est. Ad omnes igitur omnium rerum fines intelligendos, unica finis definitio satis est; ut id sit cujus gratia res est: utrum autem sit summus an subordinatus, universalis an specialis, id Logica non spectat, sed inferioribus quibusvis disciplinis relinquit.

As of form so also of end there is no true distribution; those distributions commonly brought forward are not distributions of the end in logic but distinctions of special ends for variety of effects. It is distinguished by Aristotle (*De anima* 2. 4) into the end-of-which and the end-for-which; the end-of-which is the end of work, or of working; the end-for-which is the end of the work itself. For example in building a house, the end-of-which, or of the work, is the house; the end-for-which, or of the work itself, that is of the completed house, is aptitude for habitation.

There are mentioned also other distributions of the end, which pertain to the end-for-which, as from Aristotle (*Magna moralia* 1. 2): "One end is perfect, the other imperfect," or, what is the same thing, from others: "An end is either the highest, or subordinate." But the end is highest, which is sought because of itself; it is either universal, that is common to all things, or special, as peculiar and proper to each species. The more subordinate end is not so much an end, as something aimed toward an end; and to be highest or subordinate, to be universal or special, pertains as much to other arguments as to the end. Finally, the law of distribution orders the parts of distribution to be opposites; but between the highest and the subordinate there is no opposition. Therefore to make clear all the ends of all things, a single definition of the end is sufficient, that it is that for the sake of which a thing is, but whether it may be the highest end or subordinate, universal or special, logic does not consider, but leaves to the various inferior disciplines.

CAPUT IX.

De Effecto.

EFFECTUM *est, quod è causis existit.* Effectum cùm sit vi omnium causarum, à causa tamen principe, scilicet efficiente, effectum denominatur. Sed quoniam, si propriè loquimur, effectum ab efficiente solo efficitur, 5 omnium autem causarum vi est, idcirco non definitur ex denominatione quòd à causis efficitur, sed ex re potius, i.e. ex communi causarum vi, quod è causis est vel existit. Jam illud hîc monendum est, ex cap 2. quod in causa explicanda monuimus, effectum esse argumentem absolute cum causa sive causæ 10 consentaneum, i.e. causam absolutè arguere; ita ut quemadmodum posita causa, ponitur effectum; sic posito effecto, ponatur causa: ut enim causæ dant esse effecto, ita effectum *esse suum* habet à causis, i.e. ab efficiente, ex materia, per formam, propter finem existit. Effectum igitur causas arguit, 15 & ab iis vicissim arguitur; sed non pari ratione: effectum enim arguit causam esse aut fuisse, *Græcis* ὅτι; causa autem,quare sit effectum demonstrat, *Græcis* διότι. Causæ sunt priores & notiores; effectum, ut posterius, ita minus arguit. Sic argentum materia poculi, magis arguit & manifestum reddit natu-

CHAPTER IX.

Of the effect.

THE *effect is that which comes from the causes.* Though the effect is by virtue of all the causes, it is named the effect from the principal cause, that is, the efficient. But though, if we speak properly, the effect is
5 effected by the efficient alone, yet it is by virtue of all the causes; it is therefore not defined by giving its name because it is effected by the causes, but rather from the fact, that is from the common force of the causes, because from causes it is or exists. Now here that must be urged which we urged in
10 chapter two in explaining causes, that the effect is an argument absolutely with the cause or a consentany of the cause, that is that it absolutely argues a cause, so that in whatever way the cause has been laid down, the effect is laid down; thus when the effect has been laid down, the cause is laid
15 down, for as the causes give being to the effect, so the effect has *its being* from causes, that is, it exists by the efficient, from the matter, through the form, for the sake of the end. The effect therefore argues causes and is in turn argued by them, but not on the same ground; for the effect proves that the cause
20 is or has been, in Greek expressed by ὅτι; but the cause demonstrates why the effect should be, in Greek διότι. The causes are prior and clearer; the effect, as posterior, argues less weightily. Thus silver as the matter of a cup proves and makes manifest the nature of the cup, more than does the

ram poculi, quàm poculum argenti. Interdum autem effecta, non per se quidem, sed nobis notiora, clarius causas arguunt, quàm arguuntur à causis. Sic etiam *Aristoteles, Post.* 1. 10. *nihil prohibet eorum quæ se reciprocè arguunt,* ut causa & 5 effectum, *id notius nonnunquam esse quod non est causa.*

Sive igitur gignatur, sive corrumpatur, sive modo quolibet, moveatur quidlibet, hic motus & res motu facta effectum dicitur. Ut causarum modi quidem fuere, ita nunc effectorum quidam his verbis ostenduntur. Modi effectorum generales 10 sunt, vel speciales. Generales sunt vel motus quilibet, quæ *operatio* & *actio* dicitur; vel res motu factæ, quæ sunt *opera.* Modi speciales, sive exempla specialia sunt *generatio, corruptio* & *similia* à Physicis petita. Causa enim corrumpens est causa procreans corruptionis. Notandum autem est hîc *rem* 15 quamlibet, non *motam,* sed *motu factam, Effectum* dici: nulla enim res mota, moventis effectum est, nisi res effecta: res enim corrupta corrumpenti contraria est.

Hujus loci sunt laudes & vituperationes, quarum pleni sunt libri sacri & prophani. A factis enim quisque potissimum lau- 20 datur & vituperatur.

Huc etiam dicta scriptaque referenda sunt; consilia item & deliberationes, etiamsi ad exitum perductæ non fuerint. Neque enim facta solùm, sed etiam consulta & cogitata pro effectis habenda sunt.

cup the nature of silver. But sometimes the effects, not through themselves indeed, but as better known to us, more plainly argue the causes than they are argued by the causes. And thus also Aristotle (*Posterior Analytics* I. 10) writes: 5 "Nothing prohibits that of those things which reciprocally prove each other" as cause and effect, "the one that is not cause is sometimes better known."

If therefore anything is produced or destroyed, or moved, in any way whatever, this motion and thing made by motion 10 *is called an effect.* Just as there were modes of the causes, so now some modes of the effects are revealed by these words. The modes of the effects are general or special. The general comprise motion of any sort, which is called *operation* and *action,* or things made by motion, which are *works.* Special 15 modes or special examples are *generation, corruption, and the like* taken from physics. For the destroying cause is the procreating cause of destruction. But it must here be noted that not *something moved* but *something made by motion* is called an effect, for no object moved is the effect of the mover 20 unless the object is effected; for the thing destroyed is contrary to the thing destroying.

From this place of the effect come praises and dispraises, of which sacred and profane books are full, because for his deeds anyone is especially lauded and vituperated.

25 *Here also are to be put things said and written, also resolutions and plans, although they are not carried into execution.* For not deeds merely, but also things considered and reflected on are to be classed as effects.

Sunt etiam effecta virtutum & vitiorum. Horatius hoc modò ebrietatis effecta describit:

Quid non ebrietas designat? operta recludit, &c.

Volunt hîc plerique *Rami* interpretes motûs doctrinam, 5 utpote rei generalis, ad Logicam pertinere; sed non rectè. Quid enim potest Logica docere de motu, quod naturale & Physicum non sit. *Scientias,* inquiunt, ex *Aristot.* Phys. 8. 3. *& opiniones, motu uti omnes.* Utuntur quidem, sed ex natura, quam Physica docet, petito. Sic Logica ratione utitur, 10 nec tamen rationis naturam, sed ratiocinandi artem docet. Omnis quidem causa movet, effectum movetur; nec tamen quid moveat aut moveatur, sed quid arguat aut arguatur Logicus considerat. Ipsum etiam *arguere & argui* non quatenus motus est, aut res motu facta, sed quatenus relatione 15 quadam arguendi vel facultatem ratiocinandi juvat vel artem tradit, ad Logicam pertinet.

Duos hîc canones causæ & effecti communes, quamvis in Physica potius quàm in Logica tractandos, ut & multa alia quæ *Aristotelici* congerere huc solent, tamen quia sæpe occur- 20 runt & fallaces sunt, appendiculæ in modum libet cum suis cautionibus hîc attingere. Primus est, *qualis causa, tale causatum:* ex *Aristot.* 2 *Top. c.* 9. Quod verum non est primò in causis per accidens: ut, *hic sutor est vir bonus;* at non ergo *bonos consuit calceos;* potest enim esse sutor non bonus. Se-

There are also effects of virtues and vices. Horace describes thus the effects of drunkenness:

> What thing is not through drunkenness commit?
> For hid secrets he maketh come to light, etc.

5 In this matter most interpreters of Ramus are of the opinion that the doctrine of motion, as of a general thing, pertains to logic, but not rightly. For what can logic teach about motion that is not natural and according to physics. "Things known" they say from Aristotle (*Physics* 8. 3) "and opinions, all use 10 motion." Surely they use it, but, as physics teaches, taken from nature. Thus logic uses reason, yet does not teach the nature of reason but the art of reasoning. Every cause moves, an effect is moved, but the logician considers not what moves or is moved, but what argues or is argued. But *arguing or* 15 *being argued* in itself, so far as it is motion or a thing made by motion, does not pertain to logic, but only so far as by some presentation of arguing it aids the power of reasoning or teaches the art.

The two common canons of cause and effect are to be 20 treated in physics rather than in logic, like many other things which the Aristotelians are in the habit of gathering here, yet since they often occur and are fallacious, it is proper to present them here with their cautions in the form of a little appendix. The first is: *Of what sort the cause is, such is what* 25 *is caused,* from Aristotle, (*Topics* 2. 9), which is not true, first, in causes through accident, as *This shoemaker is a good man,* but it cannot be said: *therefore he make good shoes;* he can be

cundò, non in causis universalibus: ut, *sol omnia calefacit;* at non *idcirco ipse est calidus.* Tertiò, non in causis voluntariis, nisi velint. Quartò, si res in qua effectum est producendum, id per naturam suam recipere non potest.

5 Canon secundus est, *propter quod unumquodque est tale, illud est magis tale: Aristot.* 1 Post. c. 2. Scilicet primò rursus in causis per se: ut, *hic est ebrius;* non ergo *vinum magis ebrium.* Secundò, si id à quo tales denominantur utrique insit: ut, *cera fit mollis à sole;* non *ergo sol est mollior.* Tertiò, 10 si causa illa recipiat magis & minus: non *ergo si filius est homo propter patrem, pater propterea magis homo.* Sed canon hic valet præcipuè in causis finalibus: ut, *hic studiis dat operam proper quæstum; quæstui igitur studet magis.*

a shoemaker that is not good. Secondly, it is not true in universal causes, as *The sun warms all things,* but not *hence the sun itself is warm.* Thirdly, not in voluntary causes, unless they are willing. Fourthly, it is not true if the thing in which 5 the effect is to be produced is through its nature not able to receive the effect.

The second canon is *That on account of which a thing is of a certain sort is more of that sort,* from Aristotle *(Posterior Analytics* I. 2). First, this is apparently false again in causes 10 through themselves, as *This man is drunk,* but it is not therefore true that *the wine is drunker.* Secondly, it is false if this from which both are named as they are is within, as *Wax is made soft by the sun,* but not *therefore the sun is softer.* Thirdly, if that cause may receive more and less; for it cannot 15 be held: *Therefore, if the son is a man because of his father, the father for that reason is the more a man.* But this canon applies especially in final causes, as *He gives attention to his studies for the sake of gain; therefore he is more anxious about gain than about study.*

CAPUT X.

De Subjecto.

ARGUMENTUM *modo quodam consentaneum succedit, ut subjectum & adjunctum.* Absoluta enim consensio causæ & effecti hanc modo quodam consensionem subjecti & adjuncti meritò præcessit. Modo quo-
5 dam consentire cum re quam arguunt dicuntur, quæ leviter & extrinsecus tantum consentiunt, i.e. citra rationem essentiæ; cùm non ut causa effecto, ita subjectum det esse adjuncto; neque hoc ab illo essentiam accipiat. De subjecto prius est agendum: etenim subjectum omne suis adjunctis naturâ prius
10 est, & quodammodo se habet ad adjunctum, ut causa ad effectum.

Subjectum est, cui aliquid adjungitur. Hoc argumentum *Cicero rem subjectam* appellat, quia nimirum alicui subjicitur: subjici autem id dicitur, cui, cùm ex causis constitutum
15 jam est, aliquid tanquam additamentum quoddam præter causas adjungitur: adjungitur itaque aliquid, quod alteri, nempe subjecto, perfecto jam suísque causis constituto, extrinsecus sive præter essentiam accedit. Subjectum ergo est quod ad aliquid arguendum est affectum, quod sibi præter illam
20 essentiam, quam è causis habet, insuper accedit.

Ut causa, ita & subjectum suos quosdam habet modos: subjici enim aliquid dicitur vel recipiendo adjuncta vel occu-

CHAPTER X.

Of the subject.

THE *argument follows which is consentany after a sort, as the subject and the adjunct.* For absolute agreement of cause and effect properly precedes this agreement after a sort of subject and adjunct. Things are said
5 to agree after a sort with the thing they prove which merely agree easily and extrinsically, that is, without touching their essence, since the subject does not give being to the adjunct as does the cause to the effect; nor does the adjunct receive its essence from the subject. The subject is first to be dealt with;
10 for every subject is by nature prior to its adjuncts, and in some ways is related to the adjunct as cause to effect.

A subject is that to which anything is adjoined. Cicero calls this argument the thing subjected, since certainly it is subjected to something. A thing is said to be subjected when,
15 after it has already been constituted by its causes, something as a sort of addition besides its causes is adjoined to it; and thus something is adjoined which as extrinsic or in addition to the essence is joined to something else, that is to the subject, which is already perfect and constituted by its causes. A sub-
20 ject therefore is that which is affected toward arguing something which is joined to it in addition to that essence which it has from causes.

As cause, so also subject has its modes after a sort; anything is said to be subjected either in receiving or in occupy-

pando. Unde subjectum distingui potest in *recipiens,* quod *Græci* δεκτικὸν appellant, & *occupans* quod *objectum* dici solet, quia in eo adjuncta occupantur. Recipiens vel in se recipit adjuncta, vel ad se: recipiens in se adjuncta, vel sustinet ea &
5 quasi sustentat, quæ idcirco *insita* & *inhærentia* appellantur, vel continet, ut locus locatum.

Primus ergo modus est cùm subjectum recipit adjuncta insita sive inhærentia. Sic anima est subjectum scientiæ, ignorantiæ, virtutis, vitii; quia hæc animæ adjunguntur, i.e. præ-
10 ter essentiam accedunt: corpus sanitatis, morbi, roboris, infirmitatis, pulchritudinis, deformitatis; quia corpori quidem insunt, sed præter essentiam.

Secundus modus est subjecti adjuncta in se continentis, i.e. *loci.* Sic locus est subjectum rei locatæ, sive in quo res locata
15 continetur. Sic Philosophi divinis entibus, licet parte & magnitudine carentibus, attribuunt locum. Sic Geometræ locum locíque differentias in rebus Geometricis. Physici multo etiam diligentius in rebus Physicis considerant, in mundo, in elementis simplicibus, in rebus compositis. Hinc nonnulli
20 Dialectici suæ artis amplificandæ studio, ut motûs, ita loci doctrinam in Logica tractandam esse contendunt. Verùm cùm locus externa sit affectio cujusvis naturæ sive corporeæ sive incorporeæ, miror quid illis, *Rami* præsertim discipulis,

ing adjuncts. Whence the subject can be distinguished into the *receiving,* what the Greeks call δεκτικόν, and the *occupying,* which is usually called *object,* since in this the adjuncts are occupied. The receiving receives adjuncts either into itself
5 or to itself; receiving adjuncts into itself, either it sustains and as it were maintains these, which therefore are called *ingrafted* and *inherent,* or it contains them, as a place contains what is located.

The first mode, therefore, is when the subject receives
10 ingrafted or inherent adjuncts. Thus the soul is the subject of knowledge, ignorance, virtue, and vice, since these are adjoined to the mind, that is, are added over and above its essence; the body is the subject of health, sickness, strength, infirmity, beauty, and deformity, since these are in the body
15 but aside from its essence.

The second mode is of the subject containing the adjuncts in itself, that is, the mode of *place.* Thus the place is the subject of the located thing, or is that in which the located thing is contained. Thus the philosophers attribute place to divine
20 beings though lacking body and magnitude. Thus the geometers consider place and differences of place in geometric concerns. The physicists also consider place much more diligently in physical things, in the world, in simple elements, and in composite things. Hence some dialecticians in their
25 zeal for increasing the scope of their art contend that the doctrine of place as well as that of motion should be treated in logic. Certainly since place is an external affection of some nature or other, whether corporeal or incorporeal, I wonder

in mentem venerit, ut cùm argumenta, i.e. non res, sed rationes subjectum esse Logicæ doceant; res tamen aut rerum naturalium affectiones, motum, locum, tempus in Logica tractandas esse statuerent. Locus inquiunt omnium omninò rerum communis est: ergo, inquam, ad artem aliquam non corporum duntaxat, sed rerum naturalium omnium sive Physicam, universalem, non ad Logicam pertinet: quæ non quid sit Locus, spatiumne an superficies corporis ambientis, sed quomodo arguat rem locatam, id solùm considerat; nempe ut subjectum arguit adjunctum.

Tertius modus est subjecti ad vel circa se recipientis adjuncta: quæ idcirco *adjacentia* & *circumstantiæ* appellantur. Sic homo est subjectum divitiarum, paupertatis, honoris, infamiæ, vestitus, comitatus, & eorum ferè quæ dicuntur *antecedentia, concomitantia, consequentia,* si quam omninò affectionem inter se habent non necessariam; quæ causarum & effectorum quæque ab his orta sunt argumentum affectio duntaxat esse solet. Hactenus de subjecto recipiente.

Quartus modus est subjecti occupantis, in quo nimirum adjunctum occupatur & exercetur: atque hoc propriè *objectum* dicitur. Sic sensilia sensuum, & res virtutib. ac vitiis propositæ, subjecta vitiorum & virtutum hoc modo nominantur. Color est subjectum visus, sonus subjectum auditus; quia hi sensus in his sensilibus occupantur & exercentur. Virtutes & vitia declarantur in Ethicis hoc argumento: temperantia & in-

what has come into the mind of the logicians, especially the disciples of Ramus, that although they teach that arguments, that is, not things but reasons, are the subject of logic, yet they decree that things or affections of natural things, motion,
5 place, and time, should be treated in logic. Place they say is common to all things of every sort. Therefore I say that it pertains to some universal art concerned not merely with bodies but with all natural things, that is to physics, but not to logic. For logic considers not what place is, whether a
10 limited space or the surface of an encompassing body, but merely in what way place argues a thing located, just as the subject argues the adjunct.

The third mode is that of the subject receiving to or about itself adjuncts, which therefore are called *adjacents* and *cir-*
15 *cumstances.* Thus a man is the subject of riches, poverty, honor, infamy, clothing, companionship, and generally those things which are called *antecedents, concomitants, consequents,* if they have between themselves any affection at all that is not necessary. This affection usually is at least
20 the argument of the causes and effects which rise from these adjuncts. Thus much on the subject as receiving.

The fourth mode is that of the subject as occupying, in which the adjunct truly is occupied and employed; hence this is properly called the *object.* Thus things that can be sensed
25 are in this manner called the subjects of the senses, and things related to virtues and vices the subjects of the vices and virtues. Color is the subject of sight, sound the subject of hearing, since these senses are occupied and exercised on these sensible

temperantia, voluptate; fortitudo & ignavia, periculis; liberalitas & avaritia divitiis. Sic res numerabilis Arithmeticæ; mensurabilis, ut ita dicam, Geometriæ subjicitur. Ejusmodi subjecto *Cicero* 2 Agrar. disputat, inter *Campanos* nullam
5 contentionem esse, quia nullus sit honor: *Non gloriæ cupiditate,* ait, *efferebantur, propterea quòd ubi honos publicè non est, ibi cupiditas gloriæ esse non potest:* &c.

CAPUT XI.

De Adjuncto.

ADJUNCTUM *est cui aliquid subjicitur,* vel quod affectum est ad arguendum subjectum. Doctrina adjuncti doctrinæ subjecti per omnia respondet. *Cicero* hoc argumentum *adjunctum* & *conjunctum* vocat. Ab *Aristotele,* Accidens vocatur, nec male. Quicquid enim ulli subjecto extrinsecus accidit, sive fortuito sive non, adjunctum ejus est. Animi, corporísque & totius hominis bona & mala,
15 quæ dicuntur, adjuncta sunt animi, corporis, hominis.

Cùm igitur adjunctum subjecto præter essentiam accedat, non mutatur ejus accessione vel decessione essentia subjecti, neque aliud inde fit subjectum, sed alio duntaxat modo se habet. Unde & modi, qui dicuntur, in adjunctis numerandi

things. Virtues and vices are made plain in ethics by this argument, temperance and intemperance by pleasure, fortitude and cowardice by perils, liberality and avarice by riches. Thus a numerable thing is subjected to arithmetic, a mensurable, so to speak, to geometry. By using a subject of this mode Cicero tries to show (*Agrarian Law* 2) that among the Campanians there is no strife since there is no honor: "They are not carried with the desire of glory, because where there is no public honor there the desire of glory cannot be" etc.

CHAPTER XI.

Of the adjunct.

AN *adjunct is that to which something is subjected;* or that which is affected to proving the subject. In all points the doctrine of the adjunct corresponds to that of the subject. Cicero calls this argument *adjunct* and *conjunct.* By Aristotle it is called accident, not badly, for whatever happens extrinsic to any subject, whether fortuitous or not, is an adjunct of it. The good and ills, as they are called, of the soul, the body, and the whole man, are adjuncts of the soul, the body, and the man.

Since therefore the adjunct is added to the subject over and above the essence, the essence of the subject is not changed by the accession or removal of it, nor is the subject made something different, but merely exists in another mode. Whence also the modes, as they are called, are to be numbered among

sunt. Sic in causis *procreare* & *tueri,* modi, ut suprà dictum est, sive adjuncta quædam vel efficientis vel efficiendi sunt.

Hoc argumentum etsi subjecto est levius, attamen est copiosius & frequentius. Subjecto suo levius est, quia subjec-
5 tum prius est, & adjuncti sui quoddammodo causa. Id quod de adjunctis non quibusvis verum esse docebitur. Hinc *Aristot.* Phil. ζ. 1. *adjunctum subjecto est posterius ratione, tempore, cognitione & natura:* quod etiam de omni adjuncto ita duntaxat verum est, si de tempore excipias. Exi-
10 stentiam enim Adjuncti non spectat Logica, sed mutuam quam cum subjecto habet affectionem quæ utrobique simul est ita ut Subjectum Adjuncto non magis sit tempore prius quam Adjunctum subjecto. Sublato igitur subjecto, tollitur adjunctum, ut, *mortuus non est; ergo nec miser est.* Hinc
15 strepitur in scholis, *ab* est *secundi adjecti, ad* est *tertii adjecti valet consequentia negando.* Et posito adjuncto, ponitur necessariò subjectum; ut, *si mortuus est miser, certè necessariò mortuus est.* Quod & scholæ sic balbutiunt; *ab* est *tertii adjecti, ad* est *secundi, valet consequentia affirmando.* Est autem
20 adjunctum subjecto copiosius & frequentius, quia unius ejusdémque subjecti plurima adjuncta esse possunt. Itaque quod de ejusmodi signis ait *Ovid.* 2. de Remed.

the adjuncts. Thus among the causes *procreating* and *conserving* are modes, as it is put above, or adjuncts, whether of the efficient or the thing to be effected.

Though this argument is lighter than the subject, yet it is 5 *more copious and commonly used.* It is lighter than the subject, since the subject is prior to its adjunct, and a sort of cause of it—a thing that some will not teach as true of adjuncts. Hence Aristotle (*Metaphysics* 6. 1) says that the adjunct is posterior to the subject " in reason, time, consciousness, and 10 nature;" this is true of every adjunct, provided only you make an exception of time. For logic does not regard the existence of the adjunct but the mutual affect, at the same time for both, which it has with the subject, so that the subject is not in time prior to the adjunct any more than the adjunct is to the sub- 15 ject. Therefore when the subject is taken away, the adjunct is taken too, as *He is not dead, therefore he is not wretched.* Hence it is loudly asserted in the schools: "*Ab est* is valid for denying the consequences of the second adject, *ad est* the consequences of the third adject." And when the adjunct is 20 assumed the subject of necessity is assumed, as *If a dead man is wretched, certainly he is of necessity dead;* which the schools stammer out as follows: "*Ab est* is valid in affirming the consequences of the third adject, *ad est* in affirming the consequences of the second." But the adjunct is more copious and 25 plentiful than the subject, since there can be several adjuncts of one and the same subject. Concerning signs of this sort Ovid remarks (*De remediis* 2):

Forsitan hæc aliquis (nam sunt quoque) parva vocabit
Sed quæ non prosunt singula, multa juvant.

Huc itaque referuntur signa, quæ ad effecta potius referenda sunt; vímque arguendi perinde habent ut eorum causæ
5 certæ sunt & cognitæ. Sic tumor uteri signum est gravidæ; incertum tamen, quia causæ tumoris illius aliæ esse possunt: lac mammarum multo certius, quia causa certior & notior. Ejusdem generis sunt signa physiognomonica, prognostica Astrologorum & Medicorum. Itaque ut causæ & effecta sci-
10 entiam, sic subjecta & adjuncta conjecturam ferè pariunt. Hoc genere argumenti *Fannium Chæream Cicero* pro *Roscio Comœdo* cavillatur; & ab adjuncta corporis habitudine, signa malitiæ colligit: *nónne ipsum caput & supercilia illa penitus abrasa olere malitiam, & clamitare calliditatem videntur?*
15 *nónne ab imis unguibus usque ad verticem summum (si quam conjecturam affert homini tacita corporis figura) ex fraude, fallaciis, mendaciis constare totus videtur?* Sic *Martial. l.* 2. *Zoilum* ludit.

Crine ruber, niger ore, brevis pede, lumine luscus.
20 *Rem magnam præstas, Zoile, si bonus es.*

Subjectorum porrò modis, adjunctorum respondent modi. Quemadmodum igitur subjectum erat recipiens vel occupans,

These things (for so they are) perchance may
small be reputed,
But such as help not singly do jointly profit.

Here also are classed the signs which rather are to be re-
5 ferred to effects; they have the power of arguing something
in proportion as their causes are sure and understood. Thus
swelling of the womb is the sign of a pregnant woman, yet
uncertain, since there can be other causes of that swelling;
milk in the breasts is much more certain, since the cause is
10 more certain and better known. Of the same sort are signs
of physiognomy, and the prognostics of astrologers and physicians. Thus as causes and effects bring forth knowledge, so
subjects and adjuncts for the most part bring forth conjecture.
With this sort of argument Cicero (*Pro Roscio Comœdo*)
15 mocks at Fannius Chærea, and from the adjoined habit of
body gathers the signs of malice: "Do not his head and eye-
brows altogether bald, seem to favor of malice and cry out of
deceit; doth he not seem to be compounded from the foot to
the head (if a man may conjecture by his shape) of frauds,
20 fallacies, lies?" Martial (book 2) makes sport of Zoilus as
follows:

Thy hair is red, thy mouth is black withal,
Thy feet are short, one eye thou hast to see;
Zoyle, if thou be good, we may say all
25 There is no little fact commit by thee.

Furthermore, the modes of the adjuncts correspond to the
modes of the subjects. In whatever mode, therefore, the sub-

ita adjunctum est receptum vel occupatum. Receptum vel in subjectum recipitur vel ad subjectum: quod in subjectum recipitur, vel sustinetur ab eo, vel in eo continetur aut collocatur: quod sustinetur, est adjunctum insitum, sive inhærens.

5 Primus ergo, modus est adjunctorum inhærentium sive insitorum. Omninóque qualitates (qualitas autem est qua res qualis dicitur) subjectis præter causas, i.e. formas externas (quæ etiam in qualitatibus numerantur) adjunctæ; sive propriæ sint, quæ omni solíque subjecto semper conveniunt, ut 10 homini risus, equo hinnitus, cani latratus; sive communes, quæcunque non sunt eo modo propriæ. Propria autem quatuor modis vulgò dicuntur: soli, sed non omni; ut homini proprium est Mathematicum esse, sed non omni: omni, sed non soli; ut bipedem esse homini: omni & soli, sed non sem- 15 per; ut homini canescere in senectute: omni, soli, & semper; ut risibilem esse homini: hoc demum verè proprium est & reciprocum; ita ut omnis homo sit risibilis, & omne risibile, proprie dictum, sit homo. Adjunctum itaque proprium etsi naturâ est posterius subjecto, adeóque levius, tempore tamen 20 simul est, nobísque ferè notius; positóque adjuncto proprio, ponitur subjectum, & contrà: subjectum enim adjuncto proprie est modo quodam essentiale, adjunctumque à forma sub-

ject is receiving or occupying, so the adjunct is received or occupied. The adjunct received is either received into the subject or to the subject; what is received into the subject either is sustained by it or contained in it or collocated with it; what is sustained is an adjunct placed within or an inhering adjunct.

The first mode, therefore, is that of adjuncts inherent or placed within. Qualities (quality is that by which a thing is said to be of what sort it is) are adjoined to subjects altogether in addition to causes, that is external forms (which also are numbered among its qualities); they are either proper, always characterizing every individual subject, as laughter does man, whinnying does a horse, and barking a dog, or they are common, including everything not in this way proper. But proper qualities are commonly classified in four modes: proper to an individual but not to every one, as it is proper to man to be a mathematician, but not to every man; proper to every one, but not to an individual, as for man to be a biped; proper to every one and to an individual, but not always, as for man to grow gray in old age; proper to every one, to the individual, and always, as for man to be able to laugh. This only is truly proper and reciprocal, so that every man is a laughing being, and every laughing being, properly so called, is a man. Thus the proper adjunct though by nature posterior to its subject, and besides less important, yet is temporally simultaneous and to us generally better known. When a proper adjunct is given, a subject is given, and the opposite; for the subject is in a way properly essential to the adjunct, and the adjunct

jecti fluit: habet igitur à forma subjecti, non ab natura sua, quòd subjectum ponit & tollit.

Communis etiam qualitas est separabilis vel inseparabilis: ut aquæ frigus, qualitas est separabilis; humiditas verò insepa-
5 rabilis; utraque autem communis. Atque istæ qualitatum distinctiones, communium & propriarum, separabilium & inseparabilium, ad judicium faciendum valde sunt utiles, ut secundo libro facile perspiciemus. Ad hunc modum refertur etiam quantitas, quâ res magnæ vel parvæ, multæ vel paucæ
10 dicuntur; & passio, quâ res aliquid pati dicitur: adeóque motus, ad rem motam si referatur, hujus loci est. Hactenus de adjuncto quod in subjecto sustinetur.

Secundus modus est adjunctorum quæ continentur in subjecto, ut locatum in loco: atque huc etiam situs locorum re-
15 fertur; nisi si cui ad primum potius modum referendus videatur; cùm situs passio sit quædam rei locatæ, & ad priorem modum sic pertineat. Atque hæc de adjunctis quæ in subjectum recipiuntur.

Tertius modus est adjunctorum quæ recipiuntur ad sub-
20 jectum; quæ vulgò circumstantiæ nuncupantur, quia extra subjectum sunt. Huc *tempus* refertur, duratio nempe rerum præterita, præsens, futura. Sic etiam Deus dicitur qui est, qui erat, & qui futurus est, *Apocal.* 1. 4, & 4. 8. Deo tamen ævum sive æternitas, non tempus attribui solet: quid autem est ævum

arises from the form of the subject; it depends therefore on the form of the subject, not on its own nature, because the subject causes it to be and takes it away.

A common quality is separable or inseparable, as the cold 5 of water is a separable quality, and humidity is inseparable, but both are common. Yet these distinctions of qualities, common and proper, separable and inseparable, are very useful in making judgments, as we shall easily prove in the second book. To this mode is referred quantity also, by which things 10 are pronounced great or little, many or few; and passion, through which a thing is said to suffer something, is likewise of this mode; also motion, if assigned to the thing moved, is to be put here. Thus far of the adjunct which is sustained in the subject.

15 The second mode is of adjuncts which are contained in the subject as located in a place; and here the position of places is to be assigned, unless it seems to anyone that rather it should be referred to the first mode, since position may be a sort of passion of a thing located and thus may pertain to the prior 20 mode. And thus much of adjuncts which are received into the subject.

The third mode is of adjuncts which are received near to the subject, which commonly are called circumstances, since they are without the subject. Here is put *time,* to wit, the 25 duration of things past, present, and future. Thus also God is named, who is, who was, and who is to be (*Apocalypse* 1.4 and 4.8). But to God everlastingness or eternity, not time, is generally attributed, but what properly is everlast-

proprie, nisi duratio perpetua, *Græcè* αἰὼν, quasi ἀεὶ ὂν semper existens. Sed quod superioribus capitibus de motu & loco, idem nunc de tempore monendum est; non pertinere ad Logicam quid sit tempus philosophari, sed quo in genere argu-
5 menti ponendum sit, hîc nempe in adjunctis. Huc etiam referuntur divitiæ, paupertas, honor, infamia, vestitus, comitatus, & ejusmodi quicquid adesse, adjacere, circumstare, aut citra vim causæ antecedere, concomitari, sequi, ut suprà in subjecto diximus, dici potest, vel, ut Cic. in Top. Quicquid
10 ante rem, cum re, post rem, dummodo non necessariò, evenit.

Quo circumstantiæ genere, *Dido venatum proficiscens, magnifice* 4. *Æneid. depingitur:*

> *Oceanum interea surgens aurora reliquit.*
> *It portis, jubare exorto, delecta juventus:*
> 15 *Retia rara, plagæ, lato venabula ferro:* &c.

In hoc exemplo *Dido* est subjectum: cujus adjuncta adjacentia sive circumstantiæ variæ hîc enumerantur: 1. *Tempus, oceanum interea,* &c. 2. *Comitatus,* nimirum *delecta juventus, equites,* principes *Pœnorum*. 3. Instrumenta (quæ qua-
20 tenus ad habentem referuntur) adjuncta; & hujus quidem

ingness except eternal duration, in Greek *αἰών* as though *ἀεὶ ὄν, ever existing*? But what has been said in the earlier chapters on motion and place must now be urged concerning time; it does not pertain to logic to philosophize on what
5 time may be, but in what kind of argument it may be put, here, to wit, among the adjuncts. Here also are to be put riches, poverty, honor, infamy, clothing, attendance, and anything of the sort which is present, adjoins, is round about, or beyond the power of cause can be said to precede, accom-
10 pany, or follow, as we said above in dealing with the subject, or, as Cicero says in the *Topics,* "whatever happens before a thing, with a thing, or after a thing, though not necessarily."

With this sort of circumstance Dido setting out to hunt is magnificently described in Æneid 4:

15 In the mean time while that Aurora bright
Left the main sea, ascending up on height,
And Phoebus' rising brought the light of day,
The chosen lusty youth in best array
Went out the streets toward the port or gate,
20 Having their nets with meshes wide and great,
And hunting staves with iron heads sharp and broad, etc.

In this example Dido is the subject, of whom the adjacent adjuncts or various circumstances are here enumerated: 1, time, by saying "In the mean time" etc. 2, accompaniment,
25 that is the chosen youth, the horsemen, and the princes of Carthage. 3, instruments, which as adjuncts generally are referred to the one possessing, and surely are of this mode,

modi sunt, *retia, plagæ, venabula, canes, sonipes.* 4. Habitus sive vestitus, *Sidonia chlamys, purpurea vestis,* &c. Atque hæc de adjuncto recepto.

Quartus modus est adjuncti occupati. *Est* enim *adjuncto-* 5 *rum ad subjecta, quibus occupantur, usus item magnus.*

Hoc argumento *Plato miseras civitates auguratur, quæ medicorum & judicum multitudine indigeant, quia multam quoque & intemperantiam & injustitiam in ea civitate versari necesse sit.* Quia nempe in effectis intemperantiæ sanan- 10 dis, medici; in effectis injustitiæ vindicandis, judices tanquam adjuncti occupati in subjecto suo occupante versantur.

Sed categoria sive locus argumentorum *consentaneorum sic est, unde quidvis alteri consentaneum, vel idem vel unum dici possit; omnésque modi unitatis & (ut ita dicam) iden-* 15 *titatis huc sunt tanquam ad primos & simplices fontes referendi.*

Ad explicandum consentaneorum in comparationibus usum hæc clausula adjecta est. Námque ut consensionis omnis duorum in uno tertio, ita & unitatis modi hinc sunt petendi. Quot 20 autem modis plura dicuntur inter se consentire, tot etiam modis dicuntur unum & idem: absolute scilicet aut modo quodam: absolute unum vel idem causâ & effecto; modo quodam unum & idem subjecto & adjuncto. Causa vel efficiente vel materia vel forma vel fine. Sic plures statuæ, effici- 25 ente sunt eædem, si ejusdem artificis: materia, si ex eadem,

namely the nets with meshes wide, the hunting staves, the dogs, and a horse. 4, habit or clothing, as a Sidonian cloak and purple clothes, etc. So much on the adjunct received.

The fourth mode is that of the adjunct occupied. For *the service of the adjuncts to the subjects by which they are employed is likewise great.*

By means of this argument Plato conjectures that "those states are wretched which lack a multitude of physicians and judges, since necessarily much intemperance and injustice will be practised in such a state," because the physicians in curing the effects of intemperance and the judges in avenging the effects of injustice are engaged like occupied adjuncts in their occupying subjects.

But the category or place *of consentany* arguments *is such that through it anything agreeing with another can be called either the same or one with it; and all the modes of unity and, so to speak, of identity here are to be assigned as to their first and simple sources.*

For the explanation of the use of consentanies in comparisons these few words are added, for as of all consent of two things in one third thing, so also of unity the modes are here to be sought. In whatever number of modes several things are said to consent among themselves, in so many modes they are called one and the same, absolutely or in some way or other; they are absolutely one or the same by cause and effect, and are in some way one and the same in subject and adjunct, in cause or efficient or matter or form or end. Thus several statues are the same in efficient if by the same artist,

auro scilicet aut ebore; forma si effigies ejusdem, *Alexandri* puta vel *Cæsaris;* fine, si ad eundem ornandum. Sic subjecto idem sunt adjuncta duo vel plura in eodem subjecto; adjuncto idem sunt plura subjecta quibus idem adjungitur: ut duæ vel
5 plures res albæ vel nigræ, albedine vel nigredine idem sunt.

CAPUT XII.

De Diversis.

A*RGUMENTUM consentaneum expositum est* in causa & effecto, subjecto & adjuncto.

Altera species argumenti artificialis, primi, simplicis, dissentaneum, sequitur. Et sequi debet: ut enim affir-
10 matio negatione, sic consensio prior est dissensione; prior autem non natura solum, verùm etiam usu & dignitate. Ab affirmatione enim & consensione, ut scientia omnis, ita ars omnis atque doctrina deducitur.

Dissentaneum est quod dissentit à re quam arguit. Ab
15 altero nempe sui generis ac nominis dissentaneo. Nam in hoc genere argumentorum, argumenta inter se affecta eodem nomine, ideóque plurali numero enunciantur, eadémque definitione & doctrina explicantur.

Sunt autem dissentanea inter se æquè manifesta: alterum-
20 *que ab altero æqualiter arguitur; tametsi sua dissensione clarius elucescant.*

in matter if of the same substance, as gold or ivory, in form if the effigy of the same man, such as Cæsar or Alexander, in end if for adorning the same place. Thus in the case of the subject also there are two or more adjuncts in the same 5 subject; likewise for the adjunct there are several subjects to which the same adjunct can be joined, as two or more things white or black are the same in whiteness or blackness.

CHAPTER XII.

Of diverse arguments.

T*HE consentany argument has been set forth* in cause and effect, subject and adjunct.

There follows another species of argument that is artificial, prime, and simple, namely the dissentany. And it ought to follow, for as affirmation is prior to negation, so consent is prior to dissent, but prior not by nature alone but also in use and dignity. For from affirmation and consent 15 all art and teaching, like all knowledge, are deduced.

A dissentany is what dissents from the thing it argues, that is, from another dissentany of its kind and name. For in this kind of arguments, arguments affected between themselves are called by the same name and also by the same plural 20 number, and are explained by the same definition and teaching.

But dissentany arguments are equally manifested with relation to one another; each is equally argued by the other; yet by their dissent they more evidently appear.

Hæ duæ sunt proprietates dissentaneorum communes. Primum n. in consentaneis causæ effectis, subjecta adjunctis, priora, notiora, firmiora, præstantiora fuerunt: in dissentaneis alterum altero neque prius neque notius; sed natura simul, 5 in illa nempe dissensione, & æquè nota, æquè firma inter se sunt: id quod necesse est cùm eodem nomine ac definitione tractentur.

Secunda quoque proprietas, quam *Aristoteles* contrariis alligat, dissentaneorum est omnium communis; nempe *sua* 10 *dissensione clarius elucescere.* Quod nisi fieret, argumentum dissentaneorum nullius usus esset. Debet enim omne argumentum affectum esse ad aliquid arguendum & illustrandum. Quorum autem hæc est proprietas ut æquè nota & ignota sint, eorum alterum ab altero argui aut illustrari non potest. Priori 15 igitur proprietati secunda hæc subvenit: quamvis enim dissentanea sint inter se æquè manifesta, ita ut unum ab altero tanquam notiori argui non queat, ex dissensione tamen sua, sive, ut alii loquuntur, juxta se posita, clarius elucescunt. Sic bonæ valetudinis commoda adversæ valetudinis incommo-20 dis manifestiora fiunt; virtutum laudes contrariorum vituperatione vitiorum illustrantur.

Utiles itaque sunt hi loci dissentaneorum, teste etiam *Aristotele,* Top. 3. 4. non solùm ad arguendum & illustrandum, verùm etiam ad impellendum ac refutandum: ut enim con-25 sentaneorum loci valent maximè ad arguendum, probandum & confirmandum, sic loci dissentaneorum ad redarguen-

These two are common properties of dissentanies. For first in the consentany effects of a cause, subjects were prior, better known, firmer, more important than adjuncts; in dissentany effects neither is prior to or better known than another, but by nature they are in that very dissent both equally known and equally firm among themselves, as is necessary since they are considered according to the same name and definition.

The second property which Aristotle assigns to contraries is also common to all dissentanies, to wit, *by their dissent to appear more evidently*. And unless this happens the argument of dissentanies is of no use. For every argument ought to be affected toward arguing and clarifying something. But of those having as their property that they are equally known and unknown, one cannot be argued or clarified by another. This second property is therefore subordinate to the first, for however equally manifest dissentanies may be among themselves, so that one cannot be argued from another as better known, yet from their dissent, or as others put it, their juxtaposition, they more evidently appear. Thus the conveniences of good health are made more manifest by the inconveniences of bad health; praises of the virtues are elucidated by censure of the contrary vices.

So these places of dissentanies, as Aristotle (*Topics* 3.4) says, are useful not merely for arguing and explaining, but also for persuading and refuting, for as the places of the consentanies are valuable chiefly for arguing, proving, and confirming, thus the heads of the dissentanies are useful in

dum, impellendum & refutandum: ut qui consentaneo argumento doceri non vult, dissentanei absurda consecutione eò redigatur, ut nolens etiam non possit veritati non assentiri. Hinc *Aristot.* Rhet. 3. 17. *refutantia demonstrativis* anteponit.

5 *Dissentanea sunt diversa vel opposita.*

Diversa sunt dissentanea, quæ sola ratione dissentiunt. Nomen hoc videtur aptissimum ad hanc levissimam dissensionem significandam: hac enim voce ea significantur quæ cùm consensionem quandam inter se habere videantur, pos-
10 sintque per se suáque natura eidem subjecto simul convenire, tamen nec idem sunt, nec ei subjecto competunt cujus ratione dissentire dicuntur: quæ autem dissentiunt in eodem tertio, dissentiunt etiam inter se.

Sola igitur ratione dissentiunt, quia non per se suáque na-
15 tura dissentiunt, sed solummodo ratione attributionis, i.e. ratione ac respectu alicujus subjecti, cui simul non attribuuntur. Distributio itaque dissentaneorum pro ratione dissensionis rectè instituta est: nam ut consensio alia arctior est & absoluta, alia remissior & imperfecta (unde consentanea divisa sunt in
20 ea quæ absolutè vel modo quodam consentiunt) ita dissensio omnis vel remissior est, ut in distinctione sive discretione diversorum, vel acrior, ut in disjunctione oppositorum: ergo

contradicting, overthrowing, and refuting, so that he who does not wish to be taught by a consentany argument is led back to it by the absurd result of a dissentany argument, so that even an unwilling man is unable not to assent to the 5 truth. Hence Aristotle (*Rhetoric* 3. 17) places *refuting* before *demonstrative arguments.*

Dissentanies are diverse or opposite.

Diverse arguments are dissentanies which disagree in a single reason. This name seems very suitable for signifying 10 this the slightest of the dissents. For by this word those are signified which though they seem to have a sort of agreement among themselves, and though they are able through themselves and by their nature to unite in the same subject, yet they are not identical nor do they agree with that subject by 15 reason of which they are said to dissent; but those things which dissent from the same third thing dissent also from each other.

They dissent therefore in a single reason, since they do not dissent through themselves and in their nature, but 20 merely by reason of an attribute, that is by reason and in respect of some subject to which they are not at the same time attributed. Therefore the distribution of dissentanies on the ground of their dissent is rightly made, for as one agreement is rather narrow and absolute, another rather slack and im- 25 perfect (whence consentanies are divided into those which absolutely and those which after a fashion consent) so all dissent is either slacker, as in distinction or separation of diverse things, or more distinct, as in the disjunction of op-

dissentanea aut ratione & modo quodam dissentiunt, ut diversa, aut re & absolute, ut opposita. Verùm quod de consentaneis etiam objici potuit, speciebus æque communicandum est genus (has enim voces etiam communi usu citra artem 5 vulgò intellectus, pace methodi nonnunquam anticipare fas sit) respondetur, quemadmodum consentanea absolute & modo quodam erant æque consentanea, sed non æque consentiebant, sic diversa & opposita æque dissentanea sunt, sed non æque dissentiunt; in diversis tam est dissensio quàm in 10 oppositis, sed non tanta: ut in re simili Cic. de Fin. 4. *æquè contingit omnib. fidibus, ut incontentæ sint; illud non continuò, ut æquè incontentæ.* Diversa autem idcirco priore loco tractantur, quòd propter levissimam dissensionem videntur affinitatem quandam cum consentaneis præ se ferre. Quan- 15 quam autem diversorum doctrina ab omnibus præter *Ramum* Logicis omissa est, constat tamen locum in argumentorum doctrina diversis etiam assignandum, cùm ex arguendi varia affectione argumenta distinguenda sint, affectio autem dissensionis in diversis, ut diximus, levior sit, in oppositis acrior. 20 Cur diversa Logici hactenus omiserint, videtur hoc esse; quod ad unum syllogismum omnia referunt, in quo diversa locum non habent, ut l. 2. ostendetur.

Diversorum autem notæ sunt frequentissimè *non hoc, sed*

posites; therefore dissentanies dissent either in reason and in some fashion, as diverse things, or in fact and absolutely, as opposites. Certainly to the objection to consentanies that genus must be equally communicated to species (for these words that from common use are generally known apart from an art it is sometimes, with apology to method, proper to anticipate) it may be answered that just as consentanies absolutely and in some fashion are equally consentany, but do not equally consent, thus diverse things and opposites are equally dissentanies, but do not equally dissent; in diverse things as in opposites there is dissent, but not so much, as of a similar thing Cicero *(De finibus 4)* writes: "It happens equally to all lyres that they get out of tune, but it does not follow that they are equally out of tune." But diverse things are treated in the first place for the reason that on account of their very slight dissent they seem to exhibit a certain affinity with the consentanies. But though the doctrine of diverse things is omitted by all the logicians except Ramus, yet certainly a place in the doctrine of arguments must be assigned to the diverse, since arguments may be distinguished through their varied affect for arguing, but the affect for dissent in diverse arguments, as we have said, is lighter, and in opposites it is stronger. This seems to be the reason why logicians up to now have omitted the diverse arguments, because they refer all to one syllogism in which the diverse arguments do not have a place, as will be shown in book 2.

The signs of the diverse arguments are most often *not*

illud, quanquam, tamen: ut pro *Pompeio; non victoriam, sed insignia victoriæ reportarunt.* Victoria & victoriæ insignia res admodum affines sunt; possúntque ac debent eidem duci competere: ad *Syllam* autem & *Murænam* si spectas qui non re-
5 portata victoria triumpharunt, dissentanea sunt, & distinguuntur, alteróque affirmato alterum negatur. Sic *Ovid.* 2. de Arte.

Non formosus erat, sed erat facundus Ulisses.

Et *Æneid.* 2.

10 *Hic Priamus quanquam in media jam morte tenetur,*
non tamen abstinuit.

Ut victoria & victoriæ insignia respectu *Syllæ* & *Murænæ,* sic formosum & facundum respectu *Ulyssis,* in media morte teneri non & abstinere à convitiis ratione *Priami,* diversa adeó-
15 que dissentanea sunt. *Paulò* secus in *Eunucho:*

Nam si ego digna hac contumelia
sum maxime: at tu indignus qui faceres tamen.

Sed idem est ac si dictum esset, quanquam ego digna; tamen tu indignus qui mihi hanc contumeliam faceres. Dig-
20 nam se quidem esse contumelia *Thais* affirmat; à *Chærea* tamen negat. Cic. 5. Tusc. *Quanquam sensu corporis judi-*

this . . . but that, although . . . yet, as in *Pro Pompeio:* "They did not bring home the victory but the signs and tokens of the victory." Victory and the signs and tokens of victory are things close akin; they can and should belong 5 to the same leader, but if you consider Sylla and Muræna who did not triumph though they reported a victory, they are dissentanies, and are distinguished, for when one is affirmed the other is denied. Thus Ovid (*Ars amatoria* 2) writes:

10 Ulysses was not fair but he was eloquent.

And in *Æneid* 2:

> Although Priam was in the midst of death yet
> he did not abstain.

Like victory and the signs and tokens of victory for Sylla 15 and Muræna, so to be beautiful and to be eloquent for Ulysses, and to have death all about him and not to abstain from reproaches for Priam, are diverse and certainly dissentany. It is a little otherwise in the *Eunuchus:*

> Although I be most worthy of this contumely,
> 20 yet thou art unworthy to do it unto me.

But this is the same as saying: "Though I am worthy, yet it is unworthy in you to insult me thus." Thais affirms that she is worthy of insult, but denies that she deserves to be insulted by Chærea. Cicero (*Tusculan Disputations* 5) 25 writes: "Though they are judged by sense, they are referred

centur, ad animum tamen referuntur. Hoc affirmato, negatum intelligitur non ad corpus.

Item illa aliusmodi. Pro *Ligario: scelus tu illud vocas, Tubero? cur? isto n. nomine illa adhuc causa caruit: alii enim errorem appellant, alii timorem; qui durius, spem, cupiditatem, odium, pertinaciam; qui gravissimè, temeritatem: scelus præter te adhuc nemo.* In hoc genere exemplorum aliquid conceditur, ut aliud vicinum possit negari: cujusmodi & illud est; veritas premi potest, opprimi non potest; & similia.

Atque hi modi quidam diversorum sunt: in quibus plerunque accidit, ut quæ sua natura sunt opposita, ratione tamen certi alicujus subjecti sint tantùm diversa; ut in exemplo superiore error, timor, spes, cupiditas, pertinacia, scelus. Sic aurum, argentum, æs opposita sunt, ut infrà liquebit: ratione tamen attributionis huic vel illi subjecto, qui unum vel aliqua horum habet, alterum vel reliqua non habet, cùm habere simul possit, diversa sunt.

CAPUT XIII.

De Disparatis.

O*PPOSITA sunt dissentanea, quæ ratione & re dissentiunt.* Opposita respondent nomine quidem iis, qua ab *Aristotele* ἀντικείμενα dicuntur; sed re & significatione latius patent: nam ἀντικείμενα *Aristoteli* (qui dis-

to the mind." This being affirmed, the negative is understood, that is, they are not referred to the body.

Moreover, another type appears, as in *Pro Ligario:* "Callest thou it a mischievous act, Tubero? Why? Surely as yet 5 it was called by no man so; some indeed called it an error, others fear; some, naming it more hard, either hope, desire, hatred, or obstinacy; those that call it most hard name it rashness; a mischievous act no man as yet but thou." In this type of examples something is conceded that another near 10 at hand can be denied; of this kind is the saying: *Truth can be crushed down, it cannot be destroyed;* and the like.

And there are also these modes of diverse arguments, to wit, those in which it often happens that things which are by their nature opposites are in respect to some certain sub-15 ject or other merely diverse, as, in the example above, error, fear, hope, cupidity, pertinacity, and crime. Thus gold, silver, and brass are opposites, as will appear below; nevertheless by reason of attribution to this or that subject who has one or other of them, and does not have the second or the rest 20 of them, when he might have them all at once, they are diverse.

CHAPTER XIII.

Of disparates.

OPPOSITES *are dissentanies which dissent in reason and fact.* In name opposites correspond to what Aristotle calls ἀντικείμενα; but in fact and signifi-25 cance they spread more widely; for the ἀντικείμενα of Aris-

parata non attigit) nihil aliud quàm *contraria* sunt. Possunt etiam *repugnantia* dici; siquidem repugnare ea dicuntur, quæ ejusmodi sunt, ut cohærere nunquam possint; quod Cic. ait in Top. ejusmodi enim sunt opposita. *Re* autem *& ratione,* est non solùm ratione certi alicujus subjecti, cui cùm tribuuntur, simul non conveniunt, verum etiam reipsa, i.e. per se & inter se, sua ipsorum natura dissentire, etiam subjecto cuivis non attributa; cui si attribuuntur, non solùm non conveniunt, sed, servata, quæ sequitur, oppositorum lege, convenire non possunt. Ea lex quæ ex ipsa definitione oritur, & est oppositorum omnium communis, non, ut docuit *Aristoteles,* contrariorum propria, hæc est, *Opposita eidem attribui, secundum idem, ad idem, & eodem tempore non possunt. Eidem,* i.e. eidem numero rei sive subjecto. *Secundum idem,* i.e. eadem parte. *Ad idem,* i.e. eodem respectu; ut, *sol & major est terra & minor;* sed non eodem respectu; in se quidem, major; ut nobis videtur, minor. Extra has tres conditiones possunt eidem subjecto attribui opposita. *Sic Socrates, albus & ater non potest secundum idem, i.e. eadem parte esse; pater & filius ejusdem,* sive ad eundem relatus; *sanus & æger eodem tem-*

totle (who does not touch on disparates) are nothing but *contraries*. They can also be called *repugnants,* if those things may be said to be repugnant which are of such a sort that they would never be able to cohere; for Cicero says in the
5 *Topics* that opposites are of this sort. But *in fact and reason* means not alone by reason of some certain subject which when they are attributed to it they do not at the same time agree with, but that even in reality, that is through themselves and among themselves, by their very nature, they
10 dissent, even when not attributed to any subject. And if they are attributed, not merely are they unfitting, but with preservation of the law of opposites, which follows, they are unable to be fitting. This law which springs from the very definition itself and is common to all opposites, not, as
15 Aristotle teaches, proper to contraries, is as follows: *Opposites cannot be attributed to the same thing if they are supposed to work with respect to the same thing, under the same relations, and at the same time. To the same thing,* that is, to the same thing or subject by number. *With respect*
20 *to the same thing,* that is, in the same part. *Under the same relations,* that is, from the same point of view, as *The sun is both greater and less than the earth.* But it is not from the same point of view, for in itself it is greater, but as it appears to us less. Aside from these three conditions opposites can
25 be attributed to the same subject. *Thus Socrates cannot be black and white as to the same thing, that is, in the same part of his body; nor can he be father and son of the same man,* or as related to the same person, *nor well and sick at*

pore: at albus esse potest alia parte, ater alia; pater hujus, filius illius; sanus hodie, cras æger.

Itaque ex altero affirmato alterum negatur.

Ex quo facile apparet quid intersit inter diversa & opposita: 5 in illis enim *altero affirmato;* in his, *ex altero affirmato* alterum negatur: i.e. ex affirmatione unius, necessariò sequitur negatio alterius. Ut, sumpto ex diversis exemplo, *non victoriam, sed insignia victoriæ reportarunt:* hic insignia victoriæ affirmantur, victoria negatur; non ex his affirmatis negatur 10 illa: at in oppositis, dicta lege servata, *Socrates* est homo, ergo non est equus: juxta illud; *opposita se invicem tollunt.*

Opposita autem *sunt disparata aut contraria.*

Disparata sunt opposita quorum unum multis pariter opponitur.

15 Disparatorum ergo remissior videtur esse oppositio, contrariorum acrior. Disparata etiam à *Boethio* nominantur, *quæ tantum à se diversa sunt, nulla contrarietate pugnantia;* ut vestis, ignis. Apud *Ciceronem* tamen, Invent. 1 & *Fabium, l.* 5. *c.* 10. *contradicentia* significant. Nos verborum inopiâ 20 coacti, *Boethium* sequimur. *Multis:* nempe sine ulla certa oppositionis lege aut numero: nam & infinitæ ferè res hoc

the same time, but he can be white in one part of his body, black in another; father of one man, son of another; well today, sick tomorrow.

So whenever one opposite is affirmed the other is thereby 5 *denied.*

From this easily appears the difference between diverse and opposite things. In the diverse *if one is affirmed,* the other is denied; in opposites *from the affirmation of the one* comes the denial of the other, that is, from the affirmation 10 of the one necessarily follows the negation of the other, as, to take an example from the diverse, "They did not bring home the victory but the signs and tokens of the victory." Here the insignia of victory are affirmed, victory is denied; victory is not denied by the affirmation of the insignia; but 15 in opposites, when the said law is preserved, it may be said: *Socrates is a man, hence he is not a horse.* This is in accord with the saying *Opposites dispose of each other.*

Opposites, moreover, *are disparates or contraries.*

Disparates are opposites one of which is equally opposed 20 *to many.*

The opposition of disparates seems, therefore, slacker, and that of contraries keener. By Boethius "even those things which are merely diverse from each other, not opposing with contrariety, as clothing and fire, are called disparates." 25 But according to Cicero (*De inventione* 1) and Fabius (5.10) disparates mean *contradicting* things. Compelled by scarcity of words, we follow Boethius. *To many:* to wit, without any certain law or number of opposition, for almost

modo opponi inter se possunt: & sic intelligendum est verbum *opponitur,* juxta illud; *Vocabula in artibus facultatem significant:* ut vestis & ignis etsi res duæ, inter se tamen disparata sunt, eò quòd multis pariter opponi possunt. *Pariter:*
5 i.e. æquè pari ratione, eodem dissensionis modo: ut enim disparata sint, non multis tantum, sed pariter opponi debent. Albedo opponitur nigredini, flavedini, rubedini, ut unum pluribus; non autem singulis, ut disparatum quia non pariter: nigredini enim opponitur ut contrarium, cæteris rebus omni-
10 bus ut disparatum. Viride, cineraceum, rubrum media sunt inter album & nigrum, quæ singula extremis, & inter se disparata sunt. Sic liberalitas & avaritia inter se disparantur. Sic homo, arbor, lapis, & ejusmodi res infinitæ disparantur; nec eadem res potest esse homo, arbor, lapis. *Virgil.* 1. *Æneid.*
15 hoc argumento disputat:

O quam te memorem, virgo! namque haud tibi vultus
mortalis; nec vox hominem sonat: o dea certè.

infinite things can surely be opposed among themselves in this way, and the word *opposed* is to be understood according to that saying: *Words in the arts signify efficacy;* as clothing and fire, although they are two things, are never-
5 theless disparate among themselves, in that they can be equally opposed to many things. *Equally:* that is, in like manner with equal reason, with the same mode of dissent, for as they are disparates they ought to be opposed not merely to many but equally. White is opposed to black, yellow, and
10 red, as one to many, but not to the single ones as a disparate, since its opposition is not equal, for it is opposed to black as a contrary, to all the others as a disparate. Green, ash-color, and red are means between white and black, and as individuals disparate to the extremes and to each other. Thus
15 liberality and avarice are disparates between themselves. Thus man, tree, rock, and infinite things of this sort are disparates, nor can the same thing be a man, a tree, and a stone. Vergil (*Æneid* I) employs this argument:

> O virgin, what should I call thee, for thy visage
> 20 and voice declareth that thou art no mortal
> woman. Truly thou art a goddess.

CAPUT XIV.

De Relatis.

C*ONTRARIA sunt opposita, quorum unum uni tantum opponitur.*

Intelligitur autem unum uni in eodem genere opponi contrariorum, ut relatorum unum uni tantum, & sic in reliquis: nam in diversis speciebus contrariorum, plura possunt ut contraria, uni eidémque rei opponi; ut *videnti, non videns, & cæcus; motui, motus contrarius, & quies; servo, dominus & liber.*

Quæ *Aristoteles* ἀντιθέμενα & ἀντικείμενα, *ea Cicero* in *Topicis* (quem *Ramus* sequitur) *contraria* appellat: quas etiam in species quatuor *Aristoteles* ἀντικείμενα, in easdem *Cicero contraria* distribuit.

Prius autem quàm ad contrariorum distributionem in species accedimus, inserenda est distinctio quædam non inutilis, & ad ea quæ diximus capite superiore clarius intelligenda, & ad eas, quæ secundo libro dicentur, disjunctiones necessarias à contingentibus dijudicandas. Dictum est superiore capite, viride, cineraceum, rubrum media esse inter album & nigrum, quæ singula extremis & inter se disparata sunt. Sciendum itaque est contraria, quasi extrema quædam habere, alia medium, alia medio carere: medium vel est negationis vel par-

CHAPTER XIV.

Of relatives.

C*ONTRARIES are opposites, one of which is opposed to one only.*

But it is understood that one of the contraries is opposed to another of the same genus, as of the relatives one to but one, and thus in the rest, for in diverse species of contraries several are able as contraries to be opposed to one same thing; as *to seeing, not-seeing and blind; to motion, contrary motion and quiet; to a slave, a master and a free man.*

What Aristotle calls ἀντιθέμενα and ἀντικείμενα, Cicero (whom Ramus follows) in the *Topics* calls *contraries;* Cicero divides *contraries* into the same four species as Aristotle does ἀντικείμενα.

But before we come to a distribution of contraries into species, there should be inserted a certain distinction not useless both for understanding more clearly what we have said in the preceding chapter and in separating from contingents those necessary disjunctions which are presented in the second book. In the preceding chapter it was said that green, ash-color, and red are means between white and black, and that individually they are disparate to the extremes and to each other. So it should be known that contraries have what may be called extremes, that some have a mean, others lack it; the mean is either of negation or par-

ticipationis; ex *Aristotele, Top.* 4. 3. & *Phil.* γ. 7. Medium negationis est quicquid inter duo contraria dici potest, quod sit neutrum eorum: ut inter præceptorem & discipulum, is qui neque est præceptor neque discipulus. Medium participati-
5 onis est, quod utriusque extremi naturam participat; ut viride inter album & nigrum, tepidum inter calidum & frigidum. Contrariorum igitur quæ medium habent, non est necesse alterutrum affirmari; potest enim affirmari medium: quæ autem medio carent, eorum alterum necesse est affirmari.
10 Quænam autem contraria medium habeant aut non habeant, ex eo dignoscitur quod & *Gellius* tradit *l.* 16. Noct. *Att. c.* 8. Contraria quorum contradicentia, cùm attribuuntur ei subjecto cui propriè possunt attribui, sunt etiam inter se contraria, ea medium non habent. Sanum & ægrum contraria sunt:
15 eorum contradicentia, non sanum non ægrum, si animali attribuas cui soli possunt attribui, contraria etiam reperies: non sanum enim, est ægrum; non ægrum, sanum; sanum ergo & ægrum medio carent: sic nox & dies, non nox & non dies, æquè sunt inter se contraria; non nox enim, est dies; non dies,
20 nox; medio igitur carent: sic visu præditum, & cæcum esse, si homini tribuis. Quorum verò contradicentia non sunt contraria, ea medium habent; ut præceptor & discipulus: non præceptor enim, non est discipulus; neque non discipulus, est præceptor; etenim potest alteruter aliquid esse tertium sive
25 medium. Sic album & nigrum: námque non album & non

ticipation, as may be read in Aristotle (*Topics* 4. 3 and *Metaphysics* 3. 7) The mean of negation is whatever can be said to be between two contraries yet to be neither of them, as between teacher and pupil, he who is neither teacher nor pupil.
5 The mean of participation is what participates in the nature of either extreme, as green between white and black, tepid between hot and cold. It is not necessary that either one of contraries that have a mean should be affirmed, for the mean is able to be affirmed; but when contraries lack a mean it is
10 necessary for one of them to be affirmed. What contraries have a mean or do not have one is discerned from what Gellius (*Noctes Atticæ* 16. 8) presents, when he says that contraries do not have a mean if the things contradicting them, when attributed to the subject to which properly they can
15 be attributed, are contraries to each other. Well and sick are contraries; their contradictions, not-well and not-sick, if attributed to an animal to which alone they can be attributed, you will find also contrary, for not-well is sick, not-sick is well; therefore well and sick lack a mean. Thus night and
20 day, not-night and not-day are equally contraries among themselves, for not-night is day, not-day is night; therefore they lack a mean. The same is true of being provided with sight and being blind, if attributed to a man. But those things whose contradicting things are not contraries have a
25 mean, as teacher and pupil, for not-teacher is not the same as pupil, nor is not-pupil the same as teacher; thus there can be something else as a third or mean. Thus with white and black, for not-white and not-black can be said of any mean

nigrum de quovis colore medio dici possunt. Nunc ad distributionem contrariorum veniamus.

Contraria sunt affirmantia aut negantia.

Affirmantia, quorum utrumque affirmat. Scilicet rem, sive
5 veram sive fictam; vel quorum vox utraque rem certam ponit atque significat; quorúmque unum alteri ut res rei opponitur; ut pater filio, calor frigori. Contraria itaque affirmantia, quod hic notandum est & distinguendum, sunt quorum utrumque affirmat rem, non affirmatur de re sive subjecto
10 eodem, id enim supradictæ oppositorum regulæ, qua ex altero affirmato alterum negatur, planè repugnaret. Quæ igitur affirmat rem aut negat, topica affirmatio aut negatio dicitur; qua res de alio affirmatur aut negatur *axiomatica,* de qua lib. 2.

Contraria affirmantia sunt relata aut adversa.

15 *Relata sunt, quorum alterum constat ex mutua alterius affectione.*

Atque ita quidem ut ex eorum illa mutua affectione, contrarietas ipsa nascatur, ut infra demonstrabitur. Quid ergo? num idcirco relata nunc consentanea nunc dissentanea sunt?
20 Nequaquam, ut relata quidem: sed ea tamen quæ relata sunt, aliis atque aliis argumentorum generibus possunt subjici; ipsa interim argumentorum genera inconfusa & distincta manent. Sic causa & effectum, quæ arguendo inter se relata sunt, adeóque dissentanea & æque manifesta, suam ta-

color. Now let us come to the distribution of contraries.

Contraries are affirmative or negative.

They are affirmative when both of them affirm, affirm a thing, that is, whether it is true or feigned; or they are af-
5 firmative when each of the two words lays down and signifies a certain thing of which one is opposed to the other as thing to thing, as father to son or heat to cold. Affirming contraries, as is here to be observed and distinguished, are those of which both affirm a thing, and the affirmation is
10 not about the same thing or subject, for this is plainly opposed to the rule of opposites given above, according to which the affirming of one is the denying of the other. Therefore what affirms or denies a thing is called topic affirmation or negation; that by which a thing is affirmed
15 or denied concerning another is called *axiomatic* affirmation or negation; it will be treated in book two.

Affirming contraries are relatives or adverses.

Relatives are those of which one exists from the mutual affect of the other.

20 So in this way, as from their mutual affect, contrariety itself may spring, as will be demonstrated below. What then? Is it true here that relatives are sometimes consentany, sometimes dissentany? Not at all, as relatives, but those things which are related can be subjected to other arguments and
25 other genera of arguments. Meanwhile the genera themselves of the arguments remain without confusion and distinct. Thus cause and effect, which in arguing with each other are relatives, and to that extent dissentany and equally

men vim propriam arguendi retinent, qua & consentanea sunt, & causa prior notiorque effecto. Relata esse contraria ex definitione & consectariis contrariorum liquet; sunt enim opposita, quorum unum uni tantum opponitur, ut pater &
5 filius. At, inquis, unus multis, pater filiis, frater fratribus, præceptor discipulis, herus famulis, opponi potest. Respondetur, opponi patrem filio ut relatum; neque aliud quicquam patri quàm filium, neque filio quàm patrem; & sic de cæteris: sed hunc patrem & hunc filium, hunc præceptorem & hunc
10 discipulum, &c. non esse relata, sed disparata: neque enim horum alter ex mutua alterius affectione constat; neque natura simul sunt, & alter sine altero existere potest. Itaque primæ substantiæ, sive individua & singularia, ut ait *Aristoteles,* Categor. 5. *non sunt relata.* Et *Categor.* 6. ait multa genera
15 *relata esse, singularia verò nulla.* Sed non video cur relata, quemadmodum & alia argumenta, etiam in singularibus considerari non possint; singularia enim exempla sunt ferè omnia. Nec magis video cur in uno relato singulari non possit ad correlata multa esse multiplex relatio; dummodo relatio una
20 numero inter bina tantummodo sit, totiésque consideretur quot sint correlata; patris nimirum toties quot sunt filii; filii, quot sunt parentes, pater nempe & mater; fratris, quot sunt

manifest, retain their proper force of arguing, in so far as they are consentany, and the cause is prior to and better known than the effect. It is apparent that relatives are contraries from the definition and consectaries of contraries, 5 for they are opposites of which one is opposed to one only, as father and son. But, you say, one can be opposed to many, the father to his children, the brother to brothers, the teacher to pupils, the master to the servants. The answer is that I have opposed the father to the son as a relative, and nothing 10 else to the father than the son, nor anything else to the son than the father, and so as to the others. But this particular father and this son, this teacher and this pupil, and so on, are not relatives, but disparates. For neither of these exists because of the mutual affect of the other, nor are they by 15 nature simultaneous, and one can exist without the other. So first substances or individual and single things, as Aristotle (*Categories* 5) says, "are not relatives." And in *Categories* 6 he says that "many genera are relatives but no single things." But I do not see why relatives in the same way as 20 other arguments are unable to be considered even in single things, for almost all examples are single things. Nor do I see further why in one related single thing there cannot be a multiplex relation to many correlated things; if there may be only one relation by number between two things, it 25 should be considered as many times as there are correlatives; as many times of the father as there are sons; as many times of the son as there are parents, to wit father and mother; of the brother as many times as there are brothers and sisters,

fratres & sorores; nam nisi quicquid de relatis in genere dici solet de singulis quoque Relatis vere dicatur, id ne toto quidem de genere verè dici posset. Si reponas ex *Aristot. Philos.* ϛ. Relata non Significare existentiam, ne cetera quidem argumenta id significant. Sed mutuam tantummodo affectionem. Sunt *affirmantia,* i.e. ut duæ voces sunt, ita etiam duæ sunt res inter se oppositæ; ut pater, filius. Constare autem alterum ex mutua alterius affectione, est nullam aliam habere essentiam, quatenus relata sunt, præter mutuam illam unius affectionem ad alterum & alterius ad illud. *Atque inde nominata sunt relata,* quòd ad se invicem referuntur, totáque illorum natura in relatione consistit. Sic patrem esse, est habere filium; filium esse, est habere patrem. Hinc illud; Omnia relata convertuntur: ut pater est filii pater; filius est patris filius. Hujus mutuæ affectionis ratione relata sunt mutuæ sibi causæ & mutui effectus, nam quòd quis pater est, id habet à filio; quòd filius, à patre: & tamen hujus mutuæ affectionis vi ita sibi invicem opponuntur, ut neque unum de altero nec ambo de tertio dici possint; ut *Æneas* est pater *Ascanii,* ergo non est *Ascanii* filius; *Ascanius* est filius *Æneæ,* ergo non est *Æneæ pater*. Sed quoniam relatorum unum constat ex mutua alterius affectione, mutuæque sibi, ut diximus, causæ atque effecta sunt, consectarium hoc inde est quod sequitur.

for unless whatever is commonly said generically about relatives is truly said also about single relatives, it cannot be said aright of the whole genus. If you should reply from Aristotle (*Metaphysics* 6) that related things do not signify
5 existence, it may be answered that the other arguments likewise do not signify this, but merely a mutual affect. *They are affirmatives,* that is, as there are two words, so there are two things opposed between themselves, as father, son. But for one to depend on the mutual affect of the other, is to have no
10 other essence, so far as they are related, aside from that mutual affect of one for the other and of the other for that. *And thence the named things are related* because they are mutually connected, and all their nature consists in relation. Thus to be a father is to have a son, to be a son is to have a
15 father. Hence the saying: *All relatives can be transposed;* as the father is the father of the son, the son is the son of the father. By reason of this mutual affect, mutual causes and mutual effects are related to each other, for that some one is a father he has from his son, and that some one is a
20 son he has from his father. And nevertheless by force of this mutual affect they are so reciprocally opposed to each other that it is not possible for one of them to be affirmed about the second, or both of them about a third, as *Æneas is the father of Ascanius, therefore he is not the son of As-*
25 *canius; Ascanius is the son of Æneas, therefore he is not the father of Æneas.* But since one of the related things exists from the mutual affect of the other, the causes and effects are, as we have said, mutual, whence this consectary follows.

Relata simul sunt natura: ut qui alterum perfectè norit, norit & reliquum.

Relata autem simul esse natura docuerunt & veteres Logici, *Aristoteles, Damascenus,* & alii; relatáque se mutuò inferre 5 mutuóque tollere; ut posito patre, ponatur filius; sublato, itidem tollatur: etiamsi enim ille manet qui filius fuit, non tamen filius manet. Neque solùm unum existere nequit sine altero, sed ne intelligi quidem. Necesse est igitur, quod & meminit *Aristot. Top.* 6.4. *Ut alterum in alterius definitione compre-* 10 *hendatur;* útque alterum perfecte, i.e. definite, qui norit, norit continuò alterius definitionem; quæ sicuti & essentia eorum, reciproca est. Supra itaque *Ramus* definivit subjectum, *cui aliquid adjungitur;* non, *quod alteri subjicitur,* ut alii malebant; etiamsi his verbis non modò essentia subjecti, sed etiam 15 notatio contineri videatur: deinde adjunctum definivit, *cui aliquid subjicitur,* non quod alteri adjungitur quia subjectum & adjunctum relata sunt; & subjectum adjuncti, adjunctum subjecti, ex qua alterum alterius mutua affectione constat, eâ erat definiendum, quæ ipsorum essentia est. Ad exempla 20 nunc veniamus.

Pro Marcello: Ex quo profectò intelligis quanta in dato beneficio sit laus, cùm in accepto tanta sit gloria. Hic dare &

Relatives are by nature simultaneous, so that he who perfectly knows one knows also the rest.

The old logicians, Aristotle, Damascenus, and others, teach that related things are simultaneous by nature, and
5 that related things mutually assume and remove each other, as when the father is assumed the son also is assumed, when the father is removed the son also is removed, for even though he who was the son remains, he does not remain as son. Not merely cannot one exist without the other, but it
10 cannot even be understood. It therefore is necessary—something Aristotle (*Topics* 6.4) has mentioned—"that one should be included in the definition of the other," so that he who knows one perfectly, that is definitely, immediately knows the definition of the other, which, like their essence,
15 is reciprocal. In an earlier chapter Ramus defined the subject as *that to which something is joined,* not as *what is subjected to another,* as others prefer to put it, although in these words not merely the essence of the subject but also the etymological significance of the word seem to be contained. Then he
20 defines the adjunct as *that to which something is subjected,* not as what is adjoined to another, since subject and adjunct are relatives, and the subject of the adjunct and the adjunct of the subject are both to be defined by that mutual affect of either one by which the other exists and which is their
25 essence. Now let us come to the examples.

Pro Marcello: "By which thou truly understandest how much praise there is for the benefit given, whenas for the receiving is so much glory." Here to give and to receive are

accipere relata sunt, quorum unius consequens ex consequente alterius intelligi ait *Cicero. Martialis in Sosibianum. l.* 1.

Tum servum scis te genitum, blandéque fateris;
Cùm dicis dominum, Sosibiane, patrem.

5 Arguebat se servum esse genitum *Sosibianus,* dum negare videbatur, quia dominum vocabat patrem. Sic apud *Quintilianum, l.* 5. *c.* 10. *Si portorium Rhodiis locare honestum est, & Hermacreonti conducere.* Quomodo & in Oratore perfecto *Tullius: Num igitur est periculum, ait, ne quis putet in* 10 *magna arte & gloriosa turpe esse docere alios id quod ipsi fuerit honestum discere?* Apud *Ovidium* in ætatis ferreæ descriptione, *Metam.* 1. varia relatorum exempla afferuntur:

——Non hospes ab hospite tutus,
Non socer à genero: fratrum quoque gratia rara est.
15 *Imminet exitio vir conjugis, illa mariti:*
Lurida terribiles miscent aconita novercæ:
Filius ante diem patrios inquirit in annos.

Atqui argumentum talis relationis contrarium nihil habet, immo arguit mutuas causas: ut sum tuus pater; tu es igitur 20 meus filius. *At quum dico,* sum tuus pater, non igitur sum tuus filius, *tum contraria verè sunt;* atque ex ipsa quidem hac mutua relatione.

relatives, and Cicero says that the consequent of one of them is to be understood from the consequent of the other. Martial (*In Sosibianum,* book 1) writes:

> When that thy master thou dost father call,
> 5 Thou dost confess thyself a slave and thrall.

Sosibianus argues himself born a servant, while he seems to deny it, since he calls his master father. Thus in Quintilian (book 5, chapter 10) we read: "If it be honest to the Rhodians to set out the custom, it is honest also for Hermac-10 rion to hire it." In the same manner Tully writes in *The Perfect Orator:* "Is there any danger lest some should think it filthy to teach others a glorious and excellent art, the which to learn was most honest?" By Ovid (*Metamorphoses* 1) in his description of the iron age various examples of 15 relatives are presented:

> Ne doth the guest safe in his inn remain,
> His host him troubles who doth him retain;
> Sisters e'en from their brethren are not free;
> The husband longs the death of's wife to see,
> 20 She hateth him and gainst him doth conspire;
> The cursed stepdam's always in an ire;
> The son before his time doth's father's years inquire.

So an argument of such a relation has nothing contrary in it, rather it argues mutual causes; as, I am your father, 25 *you therefore are my son. But when I say, I am your father, therefore I am not your son, then the contraries are present,* and result from the very mutual relation itself.

CAPUT XV.

De Adversis.

ADVERSA *sunt contraria affirmantia, quæ inter se velut è regione absolutè adversantur.*

Sic etiam à Cicerone appellantur in Topicis. *Sunt contraria,* quia eorum unum uni tantum opponitur; ut hones-
5 tum turpi: duo n. duntaxat possunt sibi invicem è regione adversari. *Sunt affirmantia;* quia unum uni opponitur, ut res rei; quod supra demonstratum est, & infra clarius patebit. His autem verbis *è regione absolutè adversantur,* nihil aliud quàm directa oppositio, adeóque maxima, intelligitur; qualis est
10 inter duo puncta diametri in eodem circulo. His etiam verbis distinguuntur adversa à suis mediis, quæ inter se & cum extremis disparantur. *Absolutè;* i.e. omninò, perfectè; ut in *Consentaneis,* quæ absolutè consentiebant. *Ramus perpetuo* dixerat: sed assentior aliis, qui *absolutè* malunt: nam *perpetuò*
15 opponi, omnib. oppositis, etiam relatis, commune est, quatenus opposita sunt, i.e. ratione & re dissentiunt. *Absolutè* autem additur, ut hac particula distingui adversa possint à relatis, in quibus consensio quædam est, quatenus alterum ex mutua constat alterius affectione, cujusmodi hîc omninò
20 nulla est. Sic albor & nigror, calor & frigus opponuntur.

CHAPTER XV.

Of adverses.

A*DVERSES are affirming contraries, which are absolutely diagonally adverse to each other.*

Thus they are also named by Cicero in the *Topics. They are contraries,* since one of them is opposed
5 to one only, as honorable to base, for only two can mutually be directly opposed. *They are affirming,* since one is opposed to one, as thing to thing, as has been demonstrated above and below will appear more clearly. But by the words *are absolutely diagonally adverse,* nothing other than direct op-
10 position, the most complete, is to be understood, such as that between two points of the diameter of the same circle. By these words adverses are distinguished from their means, which are disparate among themselves and with their extremes. *Absolutely,* that is, in every way, perfectly, as in
15 consentany things which absolutely consent. Ramus used the word *perpetually,* but I agree with others who prefer *absolutely,* for to be opposed perpetually is common to all opposites, and even related things, so far as they are opposed, that is, dissent in reason and fact. *Absolutely* is added, that
20 by this particle adverses may be distinguished from relatives, in which there is a certain agreement, so far as one exists from the mutual affect of the other; in the present instance there is nothing at all of the sort. Thus whiteness and blackness, heat and cold are opposed.

Aristoteles, contraria (sic enim *adversa* vocat *Categ.* 6.) definit, *quæ plurimum inter se distant in eodem genere:* & rursus *Categ.* 8. *Contraria sunt vel in eadem specie, vel in eodem genere.* Quem *Cic.* est secutus in *Top.* & *Galen* de *Opt.* 5 secta. Verùm adversa, ut docet idem *Aristot.* cap. de Contrariis, non in eodem solùm genere plurimum differunt, ut album & nigrum, verum etiam in contrariis, ut justitia & injustitia; vel ipsa genera, ut bonum & malum, virtus & vitium. Quid quod in eodem genere differre, commune videtur ad- 10 versis cum relatis: pro eodem igitur genere, rectius in definitione ponitur *è regione,* prout *Cicero* interpretatur.

Æneid. 11.

Nulla salus bello; pacem te poscimus omnes.

Libertas & servitus apud *Tibullum, l.* 2.

15 *Sic mihi servitium video, dominámque paratam;*
Tu mihi libertas illa paterna vale.

Sic consilium & casus; pro *Marcello: nunquam enim temeritas cum sapientia commiscetur, nec ad consilium casus admittitur.* Et Parad. 1. contra *Epicureos: illud tamen arctè* 20 *tenent accuratéque defendunt, voluptatem esse summum*

Aristotle defines contraries (as he calls *adverse* things in *Categories* 6) "as things in the same genus which are as distant as possible from each other" and again in *Categories* 8 he says that "contraries are either in the same species or
5 the same genus." Cicero follows him in the *Topics* and Galen in *De optima secta*. But as Aristotle nevertheless teaches in his chapter on contraries, certainly adverses differ very much not merely in the same genus, as white and black, but also in contrary genera, as justice and injustice,
10 or the genera themselves may be adverse, as good and evil, virtue and vice. And furthermore difference in the same genus seems common to both adverses and relatives. Hence instead of *in the same genus* the words *diagonally opposite* are more properly put in the definition, as Cicero explains.
15 In the *Æneid* 11 is the example:

No health in war; we all desire peace.

Liberty and servitude appear in Tibullus, book 2:

Hard servitude I see to me prepared
In time to come my mistress for to be.
20 Farewell therefore thou which hast me decored,
Freedom and eke paternal liberty.

Thus counsel and chance appear in *Pro Marcello:* "For temerity is never joined with wisdom, neither is chance admitted to counsel." And in *Paradox* 1, *Against the Epi-*
25 *cureans,* we read: "They hold this opinion stoutly, and diligently do defend that pleasure is felicity, which appears to

bonum: quæ quidem mihi vox pecudum videtur, non hominum, &c. Pecudem & hominem adversa *Cicero* opposuit: voluptas pecudis bonum est, non igitur hominis. Usus enim hujus argumenti non in qualitatibus duntaxat, ut
5 vulgò putant, verùm in substantiis etiam & quantitatibus, immo omnibus in rebus versatur: id quod *Aristot.* non diffitetur, cùm ait *Phil.* κ. 3. *Contraria etiam ad primas entis differentias referri:* & rursus; *in omni genere contrarietatem esse.* Contrarietas deinde argumentum esse Logicum ab om-
10 nibus agnoscitur: nihil ergo obstat quominus ad quævis rerum genera pertineat. Quædam denique formæ vel maximè substantiæ sunt: formas autem specificas omnes sibi invicem adversas esse, apud omnes receptissimum est: immo verò major videtur esse formarum contrarietas quàm qualitatum; quali-
15 tates enim commisceri facile possunt, formæ vix unquam. Quod ergo idem *Aristot.* alibi docet, substantiæ & quantitati nihil esse contrarium, id non ratione tantùm, sed ipsius etiam testimonio suprà citato refellitur; non substantiarum autem pugna etsi non Physica, Logica tamen est, dum ex altera sub-
20 stantia singulari affirmata, negatur altera.

me to be the voice of brute beasts, and not of men" etc. Cicero opposes a beast and a man as adverse; pleasure is the good of the beast, therefore not of the man. The use of this argument is not limited to qualities, as is commonly thought, or even to substances and quantities, but it is applicable to all things, as Aristotle does not deny when he says in *Metaphysics* 10. 3: "Contraries are to be assigned to the first differences of being." And again he says: "In every genus there is contrariety." Contrariety is then acknowledged by all as a logical argument; nothing therefore obstructs it from pertaining to any of the genera of things. Then there are certain forms or, especially, substances, but it is fully received by all that all specific forms are mutually adverse; still further, there seems to be more contrariety of forms than of qualities, for qualities can easily be mixed together, forms hardly ever. Likewise therefore the doctrine that nothing is contrary to substance and quantity, elsewhere taught by Aristotle, is refuted not merely by reason but by his own testimony cited above; but the war over the substances, though not the concern of physics, is not that of logic either, though by one discipline substance is assigned to the single thing, and by the other denied to it.

CAPUT XVI.

De Contradicentibus.

CONTRARIA *negantia sunt, quorum alterum ait, alterum negat idem.* Ab altero negante sic nominantur: in puris enim negantibus, ut loquuntur, nullus est rationis usus. Atque hinc demum nunc clarius patet, quænam essent contraria affirmantia: de quibus cùm dictum est, de negantibus quoque est dictum quod satis sit.

Ea sunt contradicentia aut privantia.

Contradicentia sunt contraria negantia, quorum alterum negat ubique: ut justus, non justus, animal, non animal; est, non est.

Contradicentia sunt contraria, quia una negatio uni affirmationi opponitur, & contrà; immo sine medio. Sic etiam *Aristot. Post.* 1. 2. *Contradictio est oppositio cujus nullum est medium per se.* Quorum alterum negat ubique; *i.e.* in re qualibet: negare enim ubique est de re qualibet dici, de qua affirmatum non dicitur: ut de quo *videt* non dicitur, de eo *non videt* dicitur. unde illud vulgò dictum, *contradicentia sunt omnia:* & illud *Aristot.* 1 *Post.* 1. 2. *quodvis veré est vel affirmare vel negare: verè affirmare et negare simul, impossibile est.* & Top. 6. 3. *de qualibet re vel affirmatio vel negatio veré*

CHAPTER XVI.

Of contradictories.

DENYING *contraries are those one of which affirms, the other denies the same thing.* From negating each other they are so named, for in pure negatives, as they say, there is no use of reason. And
5 from this it now more clearly appears of what sort are affirming contraries. When they have been discussed, the negative contraries have also been sufficiently treated.

They are either contradictories or privatives.

The contradictories are denying contraries, both of which
10 *universally deny, as just, not just; animal, not animal; is, is not.*

The contradictories are contraries, since one negation is opposed to one affirmation, and the opposite, without any mean. Thus Aristotle (*Posterior Analytics* 1.2) writes: "A
15 contradiction is an opposition for which nothing is of itself a mean." *Both of which universally deny,* that is, in any affair whatever; for to deny universally is to be said of anything whatever of which an affirmative is not stated: for example, if it is not said of any one that *he sees,* it is said
20 that *he does not see;* thence comes the common saying that *all things are contradictories,* and that of Aristotle (*Posterior Analytics* 1. 1): "Anything can truly be affirmed or denied;" "truly to affirm and deny at the same time is impossible." He also says in *Topics* 6.3: "Of anything what-

dicitur. Alterum autem negare ubique dicitur, vel expressè vel implicitè. Expressè ut suprà, cum negandi particula: implicitè, cùm reipsa non minus contradicit & repugnat alteri, quàm si verbo negaret; ut corpus infinitum, proprietas communis. Vulgò vocatur contradictio in adjecto; quia id subjecto adjungit quod subjectum planè tollit; atque ita contradictionem implicat. Atque hinc etiam est quòd contradicentia medio carent non solùm participationis verùm etiam negationis, quia necesse est affirmare vel negare unum quodvis de altero. Sic etiam *Boethius* in Topicis: *inter affirmationem & negationem nulla est medietas.* Contradicentium porrò exempla hæc sunt. In defensione *Murænæ* contradicitur sententiis *Catonis* & *Ciceronis*; illius Stoici, hujus Academici. Dialogus est his verbis: *nihil ignoveris: immo aliquid, non omnia. Nihil gratiæ causa feceris: immo ne resistito gratiæ, cùm officium & fides postulabit. Misericordia commotus ne sis; etiam in dissolvenda severitate: sed tamen est aliqua laus humanitatis. In sententia permaneto: enim verò nisi sententia alia vicerit melior.* In hoc exemplo quadruplex contradictio est: nihil ignoveris; nonnihil ignoveris; nihil gratiæ causa feceris; nonnihil gratiæ causa feceris, &c. *Martial. l.* I.

ever either affirmation or negation is truly spoken." One thing is said to deny another everywhere either expressly or implicitly: expressly as explained above, with a word of denying; implicitly when in fact not less it contradicts and 5 opposes another than if it verbally denied, as in speaking of an infinite body, or a common peculiar possession. Generally it is called contradiction in the adject, since it adjoins to the subject what the subject plainly takes away; thus it implies contradiction. And thence it is that contradictories 10 lack a mean not merely of participation but also of negation, since it is necessary for one to affirm or deny something about the other. Thus also Boethius writes on the *Topics:* "Between affirmation and negation there is no middle ground." The following are examples of contradictories. In 15 the defence of Muræna there is contradiction in the opinions of Cato and Cicero, one a Stoic, the other an Academic. The dialogue is as follows: "Thou shalt forgive nothing; yes, something, not all. Grace shall have no place; yes, when office and duty requireth. Be not moved with mercy; yes, 20 in dissolving of severity; yet there is some praise of humanity. Stand to thine opinion; yea surely, without a better opinion get the victory." In this example there is a quadruple contradiction: you should forgive nothing, you should forgive something; you should do nothing for the sake of 25 kindness, you should do something for the sake of kindness, etc. Martial writes in book 1:

Bella es; novimus: & puella; verum est:
Et dives; quis enim potest negare?
Sed dum te nimium, Fabulla, laudas,
Nec dives, neque bella, nec puella es.

5 *Cicero* in *Tusc.* cogit hoc argumento *Atticum* Epicureum fateri mortuos miseros non esse, si omnino non sint, ut Epicurei credebant. *Quem esse negas; eundem esse dicis: cùm enim miserum esse dicis, tum eum qui non sit, esse dicis. Sic Terentianus Phædria Dori eunuchi* dictum elevat, quòd affir-
10 masset prius, quæ pòst inficiaretur: *modò ait, modò negat.*

Sunt qui contradictionem nullam esse statuunt, nisi axiomaticam; de qua *lib.* 2. Verùm si affirmatio & negatio Topica datur, ut suprà demonstravimus, necesse est dari quoque Topicam contradictionem: qualis est illa *Rom.* 9. *Vocabo non*
15 *populum meum, populum meum; & non dilectam, dilectam.* In distinctionibus etiam frequentissimus est hujus contradictionis usus; præsertim ubi alterum distinctionis membrum apta voce exprimi non potest: ut Dialecticæ materia est ens, & non ens; lex est scripta, vel non scripta. Sic ad *Critonem*

We know, Fabulla, thou art fair,
A maid also, true, thou so are,
And rich withal, who may withstand?
But when thou dost too much prepare
5 Thyself with praises to upbear,
Then neither art thou rich nor fair,
Nor virgin, I dare take in hand.

Cicero in his *Tusculan Disputations* by this argument forces Atticus the Epicurean to say that the dead are not 10 miserable if they do not exist at all, as the Epicureans believed: "The same which thou deniest to be, thou admittest to be . . . For when thou sayest that the dead be in misery, that thing which is not thou admittest to be." Thus in Terence, Phædria disparages the speech of Dorus the eunuch, 15 because first he had affirmed what later he denied: "This fellow sometime affirmeth and sometime denieth."

There are those who hold that there is no contradiction except the axiomatic, which will be discussed in the second book. Certainly if there is topic affirmation and negation, 20 as we have demonstrated above, it is necessary that there is also topic contradiction, such as that of Romans 9: "I will call them my people which were not my people, and her beloved which was not beloved." In distinctions the use of this contradiction is very frequent, especially where the other 25 member of the distinction cannot be expressed with an apt word, as that the matter of dialectic is being and not-being, law is written or unwritten. Thus Socrates said to Crito:

Socrates; videris opportunè quidem non excitasse me. In his exemplis axiomatica contradictio nulla est: uti neque in illo quod suprà in hoc capite ex *Martiale* allatum est: *Bella es; novimus, & puella,* &c. Non enim verbum est sive copulatio
5 negatur, sed partes. Fabulla est bella & puella & dives; Fabulla est & non bella, & non puella, & non dives. Axiomatica enim contradictio hujusmodi fuisset: Fabulla non est & bella & puella & dives: quod lib. 2. clarius intelligetur.

CAPUT XVII.

De Privantibus.

PRIVANTIA *sunt contraria negantia, quorum alterum negat in eo tantum subjecto, in quo affirmatum suapte natura inest.* Atque hîc affirmatum dicitur habitus, quo quis quid habet, negatum autem privatio, quâ quis ea re privatur aut caret: ut visus & cæcitas, motus & quies in iis rebus quæ motu conservantur. Sunt contraria, quòd unum uni op-
15 ponitur, habitus privationi; qua ex parte *negantia* quoque dicuntur: nam & hîc rei alicujus affirmationi ejusdem negatio,

"You seem to have been most opportune in not awakening me." In these examples there is no axiomatic contradiction, as there is not in that which is quoted above in this chapter from Martial:

5 We know, Fabulla, thou art fair,
A maid also, etc.

For not the word *is* or the connection is denied, but the parts. *Fabulla is fair and a maid and rich; Fabulla is not fair and not a maid and not rich.* For an axiomatic contradiction 10 would be of this sort: *Fabulla is not at once both fair and a maid and rich,* as will be understood more plainly from the second book.

CHAPTER XVII.

Of privatives.

PRIVATIVES *are negative contraries, one of which denies only in that subject in which the affirmative by its very nature is present. And here what is affirmed is called the habit,* by which anyone has what he has, *but the thing denied is called the privation,* by which anyone is deprived of or lacks this thing, as sight and blindness, motion and quiet in those things which are preserved by 20 motion. Contraries are the habit of privation, because one thing is opposed to one; from this function they are also called *deniers,* for here the denial of anything is opposed to the affirmation of it, that is, not-being to being; for priva-

i.e. enti non ens opponitur: privatio enim, ut inquit *Aristot. Phys.* 1. 8. *per se est non ens:* & *Plut.* de primo frigido; *privatio est essentiæ negatio; habituíque opponitur, non ut natura quædam aut essentia per se existens, sed ut ejus corruptio & 5 ademptio.* Quorum alterum negat in eo tantum subjecto, in quo, &c. His verbis forma privantium qua distinguuntur à contradicentibus, exprimitur. In contradicentibus enim negatio infinita est, affirmatum suum ubique, i.e. qualibet in re negans; ut quicquid non est justum, est non justum; in privan- 10 tibus verò finita est negatio, atque in eo tantum subjecto affirmatum sive habitum negans, in quo affirmatum suapte natura inest: aut inesse potest, ut etiam *Aristot.* in Categor. Sic cæcitas est negatio visus, non ubique & in re qualibet, sed in qua solùm visus inesse natura debuit: nam privari aliquid 15 tum demum dicitur, cùm eo caret quod natum est habere: non ergo quicquid non videt, propriè cæcum dicitur. Deinde in contradicentibus negatum contradicendo negat, & est pura negatio; ut videns, non videns: in privantibus negat privando; nec solùm negatio est, sed privans negatio & extinctio habitus 20 alicujus qui inesse naturâ subjecto debuit aut potuit; ut videns, cæcus. Hinc illæ privationis proprietates ex *Plut.* de primo frigido, non inutiles: *privatio iners & agendi impos est: non suscipit magis aut minus;* neque enim quis dixerit hunc illo cæciorem; aut tacentem, magis minúsve tacere; aut defunc-

tion, as Aristotle (*Physics* 1.8) says, "through itself is not-being." And Plutarch *(De primo frigido)* writes: "Privation is the negation of essence, and is opposed to habit, not as a sort of nature or essence existing through itself, but as the corruption and removal of it." *One of which denies merely in that subject in which,* etc. By these words the form of the privatives by which they are distinguished from contradictories is expressed. For in contradictories negation is infinite, denying its affirmative everywhere, that is, in anything whatever, as *whatever is never just is as not-just.* In privatives, however, the denial is finite, and denies the affirmative or habit merely in that subject in which the affirmative by its nature resides or can reside, as Aristotle explains in the *Categories.* Thus blindness is the denial of sight, not everywhere and in anything whatever, but in that alone where sight by nature should be present, for anything is said to be deprived only when it lacks what it is born to have; therefore it is not proper to say that anything that does not see is to be called blind. Then in contradictories the thing denied denies the contradicting thing, and is pure denial, as *seeing* and *not-seeing.* In privatives it denies by depriving; it is not merely denial, but a depriving denial and extinction of some habit which by nature ought to be or is able to be within the subject, as seeing, blind. Hence those properties of privation mentioned by Plutarch (*De primo frigido*) are not valueless: "Privation is inert and incapable of acting; it does not recognize more or less," for one may not be called blinder than another, or when he is

tum, magis minúsve esse mortuum: habitûs enim gradus esse possunt, non entis non item. Illa autem *Aristot. à privatione ad habitum non datur regressus,* incertior est: cùm enim habitus quo quis habere quid dicitur duo modi sint, potentia &
5 actus, à privatione potentiæ vel facultatis, ídque naturâ duntaxat, regressus negatur. Contradicentia denique medio carent non solùm participationis, verùm etiam negationis: privantia verò carent quidem medio participationis, nulla enim est habitus cum privatione permixtio; non carent autem me-
10 dio negationis; multa enim sunt, quæ neque vident, neque cæca sunt; ut lapis, arbor, &c. nisi cùm ei subjecto attribuuntur, cui natura inesse debuerunt: tum enim negationis etiam medio carent; quippe omnis homo aut videns est aut cæcus, gnarus aut ignarus. Exempla porrò privantium sunt dives &
15 pauper: *Martial. l.* 5.

Semper eris pauper, si pauper es, Æmiliane:
Dantur opes nullis nunc, nisi divitibus.

Vita & mors, ut in *Miloniana: hujus mortis sedetis ultores, cujus vitam, si putetis per vos restitui posse, nolitis.* Item loqui
20 & tacere: 1 *Catil. quid expectas auctoritatem loquentium, quorum voluntatem tacitorum perspicis.* Cætera exempla quæ *Ramus* attulit, minus quadrant: ut ebrius & sobrius, mortalis

silent said to be more or less silent, or when he is defunct to be more or less dead, for there can be grades of habit, but not of not-being. More uncertain is the saying of Aristotle: "There is no regress from privation to habit," for 5 since there are two modes of habit by which any one is said to have something, namely potency and act, regress is denied by privation of potency or capacity, and that by their nature. Contradictories, then, lack a mean not merely of participation but also of denial; privatives lack a mean of 10 participation, for there is no mixture of habit with privation, and they do not lack a mean of denial—for there are many which neither see nor are blind, as a stone, a tree, etc.—except when they are attributed to that subject in which by nature they should be, for then they lack also a mean of 15 denial, since every man is either seeing or blind, knowing or ignorant. The rich man and the pauper are examples of privatives, according to Martial, book 5:

> Poor shalt thou be, Emilian, if poor;
> Wealth's never given but to the rich before.

20 So are life and death, as in the *Miloniana:* "Sit you still, O revengers of this man's death, whose life, if you thought it might be restored, ye would not." The same is said of speaking and being silent in the first *Oration against Catiline:* "Why dost thou wait for the authority of the speakers, 25 whose silence thou beholdest to be their pleasure?" Other examples which Ramus suggests are less fitting, as drunk and sober, mortal and immortal, which are rather adverse.

& immortalis, quæ potius adversa sunt. Neque enim *in* præpositio in compositis privationem semper, sed adversum habitum sæpe significat; unde nec peccatum privationem esse dixerim; siquidem hoc vel illud peccatum sive vitium, privatio 5 non est. Atque hæ quidem species contrariorum sunt. Sed quæri hic solet, quænam earum sint maximè inter se contrariæ. *Aristoteles* maximam contrarietatem nunc adversis tribuit, nunc contradicentibus. Sed videtur maximam esse dissensionem inter privantia: deinde inter adversa; minorem adhuc 10 inter contradicentia; minimam inter relata: nam relata propter illam mutuam affectionem, partim consentanea sunt: contradicentia purè quidem contraria negantia sunt, sed tamen propter infinitam illam negationem, pro mediis & disparatis crebro accipiuntur, ut non calidum non tam opponitur calido 15 quàm frigidum; quoniam non calidum potest tepidum esse; sic non bonum, medium quiddam esse potest & adiaphorum: non album de rubro dici aut intelligi potest: adversa è regione quidem adversantur; non ita tamen, quin commisceri queant: privantia verò mixtionem non admittunt; & privatio ferè est 20 habitûs extinctio atque ereptio aut saltem deficientia; habitúsque est ens, privatio non ens; enti autem nihil, æquè ac non ens, contrarium est.

Sed dissentaneorum categoria sic est, unde quidvis ab altero differre quolibet modo possit.

25 Quanquam enim causa omnis essentialis differentiæ forma primitus est, reliquarum, argumenta reliqua consentanea, ut

For the prefix *in* in compound words does not always signify privation, but often an adverse habit. For that reason I should not say that a sin is a privation; if this or that is a sin or a vice, it is not a privation. And still these are cer-
5 tainly species of contraries. But it is usual for those that are specially contrary to each other to be considered here. Aristotle assigns the greatest contrariety sometimes to adverses, sometimes to contradictories. But there seems to be the greatest dissent among the privatives, the next greatest
10 among the adverses, less still among the contradictories, the least among the relatives, for the relatives on account of that mutual affect are partly consentany. Contradictories are certainly denying contraries, but nevertheless on account of that infinite negation they are frequently received for means
15 and disparates, as not-hot is not so much opposed to hot as is cold, since not-hot can be tepid. Thus not-good can be a sort of mean and indifferent; not-white can be said or understood about red. Adverses are indeed directly opposed, yet not in such a way but that they are able to be mingled, but
20 privatives admit of no mixture, and privation commonly is the extinction and taking away, or at least deficiency, of habit. Habit is being, privation is not-being, but nothing and not-being are equally contrary to being.

But such is the category of dissentany arguments, accord-
25 *ing to which anything may differ from something else* in any way.

For although the cause of every essential difference is originally form, and the remaining consentany arguments—

quot modis consentire totidem dissentire res dicantur, causa nempe vel effecto, subjecto vel adjuncto, modi tamen omnes, quib. res inter se differunt vel ratione scilicet vel re, non tractantur nisi in dissentaneis, vel si comparantur, in comparatis. 5 Unde illud genere vel specie differre, nihil aliud est quàm communi vel propria forma, quarum illa symbola sunt, ut infra dicetur.

CAPUT XVIII.

De Paribus.

A*RGUMENTA simplicia ita fuerunt in consentaneis & dissentaneis.*

Comparata sunt argumenta prima, quæ inter se comparantur.

Simplex rerum affectio comparatione prius tractanda fuit: hanc enim si removes, comparata omnia aut consentanea erunt aut dissentanea. *Platonis* doctrina & *Xenophontis* ante 15 adjuncta utrique erat, quàm comparata. *Sunt argumenta* prima non orta, eo quòd orta, ut patebit infra, eandem habent affectionem cum primis unde orta sunt; comparata etsi simplicia prius fuere, simplicium tamen affectionem non habent. *Inter se comparantur;* nimirum quæ sunt ejusdem generis:

as that things are said to dissent in as many manners as they consent, to wit, in cause or effect, subject or adjunct—are the causes of the remaining differences, yet all the modes by which things differ among themselves in reason or in
5 fact are treated only among the dissentanies or, if they are compared, among the comparatives. Whence to differ in genus or species is nothing else than to differ in common or proper form, of which the genera and species are symbols, as will be shown below.

CHAPTER XVIII.

Of equals.

SIMPLE arguments, both consentany and dissentany, are as I have said.

Comparatives are primary arguments which are compared among themselves.

The simple affect of things is properly treated before com-
15 parison, for if you remove the latter all comparatives are either consentanies or dissentanies. The doctrines of Plato and of Xenophon are adjuncts of either philosopher before the two doctrines are comparatives. *They are primary arguments* and not derived, because the derived, as will ap-
20 pear below, have the same affect as the primaries whence they are derived; comparatives, although they first were simple, yet do not have the affect of simple arguments. *They are compared among themselves:* certainly those which are of the same genus, and distribution will afterwards teach

genera autem distributio mox docebit. Nunc proprietates comparatorum sunt dicendæ.

Comparata etsi ipsa comparationis natura æque nota sunt; attamen alterum altero alicui notius & illustrius esse debet.

5 Ubi hoc advertendum, non sua sed comparationis natura dici æquè nota esse comparata. Ita sunt, inquis, & relata vi relationis; immo argumenta omnia quæ etiam relata sunt. At, inquam, relatio & comparatio non sunt idem; & reliqua argumenta, & si quatenus relata sunt notione Logica, æque nota
10 sunt, suâ tamen naturâ, prout quæque est, vel æquè vel non æquè sunt manifesta; dissentanea quidem æquè, consentanea non æquè, ut jam supra est dictum. Debet autem ei quicum disputamus comparatorum id quod arguit sua natura & priusquam comparatio instituitur, notius esse atque illustrius eo
15 quod arguitur; æque enim obscurum nihil argueret. Unde insignis comparatorum usus elucet; quo fit ut inæqualis rerum notitia comparationis vi æqualis reddatur. Sic consentanea ad probandum, dissentanea ad refellendum, comparata ad illustrandum aptissima sunt.

20 *Comparata autem sæpe notis brevius indicantur; aliquando partibus plenius distinguuntur, quæ propositio redditióque nominantur.*

Duplex ergo est comparationis forma: altera contracta,

the genera. Now the properties of comparatives are to be discussed.

Though by the very nature of comparison comparatives are equally known, yet one must be better known and more
5 *evident to some one than another is.*

Here it should be mentioned that comparatives are said to be equally known not by their own nature but by that of comparison. So are, you may say, relatives by the force of relation, and indeed all arguments that are related. But, I
10 answer, relation and comparison are not the same, and the remaining arguments, so far as they are related in logical notion, are equally known, but by their nature, as everything is, they are manifest equally or not equally, and are dissentany equally, and consentany not equally, as has just
15 been said above. Before comparison is begun that which the comparatives argue by their nature should be better known and clearer to him with whom we discuss a comparative than is the thing argued, for something equally obscure would make nothing plain. Hence the extraordi-
20 nary usefulness of comparatives stands out, for by this it comes about that an unequal knowledge of things by force of comparison is made equal. Thus the consentanies are fittest for proving, the dissentanies for refuting, the comparatives for making plain.

25 *Comparatives often are indicated rather briefly by signs, and sometimes are more fully distinguished by their parts, which are named the proposition and the reddition.*

Hence the form of comparison is duplex, one form con-

altera explicata. Contracta est quæ uno verbo concluditur, ut infra cap. 21. Explicata, quæ partibus distinguitur; partésque istæ propositio & redditio nominantur. Propositio præcedit sæpe, & argumentum est: redditio sæpe sequitur, éstque id 5 quod arguitur; si secus occurrit, inversio est. Omnis autem forma comparationis contracta, suis partibus explicari potest.

Atque omnino comparata etiam ficta arguunt fidémque faciunt.

Arguunt scilicet rem veram; in quo cæteris argumentis 10 præcellunt; quæ ficta si sunt, rem fictam duntaxat arguunt; ut materia ficta, fictam solis domum. At comparata etiam ficta, non sua quidem natura, sed comparationis vi, res veras arguunt fidémque faciunt.

Comparatio est in quantitate vel qualitate.

15 *Quantitas est qua res comparatæ quantæ dicuntur.*

Estque parium vel imparium. Non hic loquimur de quantitate solùm mathematica, quæ magnitudinis est aut numeri, sed de quantitate Logica, quæ ratio quælibet sive affectio est, qua res quæcunque inter se comparatæ quantæ, i.e. æquales 20 vel inæquales, pares vel impares dici possunt.

Paria sunt, quorum est una quantitas.

Sic etiam definit *Aristoteles, Phil. δ.* 15. Quod idem valet

tracted, the other full. The contracted form is that given in one word, as will appear below in chapter twenty-one. The full form is that which is divided into parts, and these parts are called proposition and reddition. The proposition often precedes and is the argument; the reddition often follows, and is what is argued; if it is otherwise, there is inversion. But every contracted form of comparison can be given in full in its parts.

And so even feigned comparisons certainly argue and produce confidence.

They evidently argue that the thing is true, and in this are more excellent than other arguments, which, if feigned, argue that the matter in question is merely feigned, as fictitious materials argue that the house of the sun is fictitious. But even feigned comparisons argue not by their nature but by force of comparison that things are true and produce confidence.

Comparison is in quantity or quality.

Quantity is that by which things compared are said to be great or small.

It can be used of either equals or unequals. We are not here speaking of mathematical quantity alone, which is of magnitude or number, but of logical quantity, which is any reason or affect by which things of any sort when compared can have relative quantity assigned to them, that is, can be called equals or unequals, likes or unlikes.

Equals are those things that have the same quantity.

So Aristotle defines them in *Metaphysics* 4. 15. This means

acsi diceretur, quorum par ratio est. *Una,* i.e. eadem, æqualis: unde in plurali numero eodem nomine ac definitione explicantur.

Argumentum igitur paris est, cùm par illustratur à pari.

5 Ad exempla veniamus; atque ad ea primùm quæ in forma, ut diximus, contracta notis brevius indicantur. Hæ autem notæ præcipuæ sunt *par, æquale, æquare;* ut in his: *Æneid.* 2.

—— *Par levibus ventis.*

Ubi levitas *Creusæ* umbræ comparatur levitati ventorum.
10 *Æneid.* 3.

Et nunc æquali tecum pubesceret ævo.

Æneid. 6.

En hujus nate auspiciis, illa inclyta Roma
Imperium terris, animos æquabit Olimpo.

15 His notis aliæ sunt affines, *pariter, æquè, æqualitas, æqualiter, perinde ac si,* & id genus alia.

Sequitur forma explicata; in qua propositio & redditio distinguuntur, quæ in contracta forma erant implicitæ. In hac autem forma explicata par quantitas vel notis apertè indicatur,
20 vel sine notis mente & ratione concipitur. Notæ istæ sunt vel propriæ parium, vel negationes imparium: parium propriæ,

the same thing as if he had said things of which the ratio is equal. *One:* that is, the same, equal, so that in the plural number it is explained by the same name and definition.

The argument of the equal, therefore, is used when equal 5 *is illustrated by equal.*

Let us come to the examples, and first to those which in contracted form are indicated rather briefly by signs. These signs are especially *equal to, equal, to equate,* as in the following: *Æneid* 2:

10 Equal with light winds.

Here the lightness of the shade of Creusa is compared with the lightness of the winds. *Æneid* 3:

And now should grow in equal age with thee.

Æneid 6:

15 Behold this thing. Great Rome with earth is even,
The spirit of man shall also equal heaven.

Other signs are akin to these, as *on a level with, equally, equality, uniformly, in like manner as though,* and others of that sort.

20 The full form follows, in which are distinguished the proposition and reddition which were implicit in the contracted form. But in this full form equal quantity is either openly indicated by signs, or without signs is understood by the mind and reason. The signs are either those proper to 25 equals, or are negations of unequals; the proper signs of

idem, quod; tam, quàm; tanto, quanto; tot, quot. In quibus singulis notarum paribus prior quæque redditioni inservit, posterior verò propositioni. *Catil.* 4. *Cujus res gestæ atque virtutes iisdem, quibus solis cursus, regionibus ac terminis*
5 *continentur. Æneid.* 4.

Tàm ficti pravíque tenax quàm nuntia veri.

Catull. 4.

Tantò pessimus omnium poëta,
Quantò tu optimus omnium patronus.

10 *Ovid.* 4. *Trist.*

Littora quot conchas, quot amœna rosaria flores
Quótque soporiferum grana papaver habet, &c.
Tot premor adversis.——

Negationes imparium sunt; vel majoris & minoris seorsim
15 vel utriusque simul *non magis, non minus. Philippic.* 9. *Neque enim ille magis Jurisconsultus quàm justitiæ fuit,* &c. *Neque constituere litium actiones malebat, quàm controversias tollere. Ovid.* 2. *de Arte.*

Non minor est virtus, quàm quærere, parta tueri.

20 *Utriusque simul pro Muræna: Paria cognosco esse ista in L. Muræna, atque ita paria, ut neque ipse dignitate vinci potu-*

equals are *the same . . . which, so . . . as, by so much . . . by how much, as many . . . so many.* In using any one of these pairs of signs, the first member of the pair is attached to the reddition, the second to the proposition. For
5 example, *Against Catiline* 4: "Whose great deeds and virtues have the same confines and bounds as the course of the sun." *Æneid* 4:

> As well a bruiter of things false that be,
> As messenger of truth and verity.

10 Catullus 4:

> By so much I am worst of poets all,
> By how much thee men best of patrons call.

Ovid, *Tristia* 4:

> As many shells on shore, as roses sweet,
> 15 As many sleeps as men by poppy seeds do get,
> So many griefs me press.

Negations of unequals, either of greater and less separately or of both at the same time are *not more, not less,* as in *Philippics* 9: "Neither had he more skill of the law than of
20 justice, etc. Neither had he rather approve actions of strife than take away controversies." Ovid (*Ars amatoria* 2):

> 'Tis no less virtue for to keep than get.

An example of both together is found in *Pro Muræna:* "I acknowledge this to be equal for Lucius Muræna, and so

erit, neque te dignitate superarit. Observandum est autem negationem majoris vel minoris seorsim non semper esse notam parium: neque enim si *servus non est major domino, ergo est æqualis;* nec si *dominus non est minor servo, ergo par.*

5 Hactenus cum notis; nunc sine notis hæc quæ sequuntur. Atque in hoc potissimum genere exemplorum sine notis, apparet vis eadem arguendi in utramque partem; adeo ut si unum, alterum quoque sit; si non sit unum, neque alterum. Itaque ex uno eorum affirmato, alterum affirmatur; ex negato,
10 negatur: 2 *Philip. Quorum facinus commune, cur non eorum præda communis? Ter. in Adel.*

Quando ego non curo tuum, ne cura meum.

Hujus loci, parium nempe sine notis, *sunt consectaria illa è contrariis quidem orta, sed parium collatione tractata. Ut*
15 ex adversis ista; *Cicero* pro *Sylla: neque verò quid mihi irascare intelligere possum; si, quòd eum defendo quem tu accusas, cur tibi quoque ipse non succenseo, qui accuses eum quem ego defendo? Inimicum, inquis, accuso meum: & amicum, inquam, ego defendo meum. Sic 5. Tusc. quod cùm*

equal that neither he shall be overcome by dignity neither by dignity shall overcome thee." But it should be observed that the negation of the greater or the less separately is never the sign of equals, for it cannot be held that *if the slave* 5 *is not greater than his master, therefore he is equal,* nor can it be held that *if the master is not less than the slave, he is therefore equal.*

Thus far of equals with signs, now without the signs these which follow. And chiefly in this kind of examples without 10 signs the same power of arguing appears in either part, so that if one thing is, the other also is; if one is not, neither is the other. So if one of these is affirmed the other is affirmed; if one is denied, the other is denied, as in *Philippics* 2: "Since their crime is common, why is not their prey common?" 15 Similarly Terence in the *Adelphi:*

Whenas I care not for thine, care not thou for mine.

To be considered here, that is, as equals without signs, *are those consectaries sprung indeed from contraries,* but 20 treated by the laying together of equals, as these from adverses. Cicero says in *Pro Sulla:* "Neither may I perceive wherefore thou art moved against me. If because I defend him whom thou accusest, why am I not moved with thee also that accusest him whom I defend. If thou say I accuse 25 mine enemy, I answer alike, I defend my friend." Similarly *Tusculan Disputations* 5: "Whenas they grant that there is force enough in naughtiness to make men unhappy, must they not also yield that there is the same force in goodness

fateantur, satis magnam vim esse in vitiis ad miseram vitam; nónne fatendum est eandem vim in virtute esse ad beatam vitam? Contraria enim contrariorum sunt consequentia.

Quæ tamen regula non est perpetuo vera primò nisi col-
5 latio sit verè parium: non ergo sequitur, *mala opera damnant; ergo bona justificant.* mala n. opera omnino mala, bona imperfectè bona sunt; illa nostra, hæc non plane nostra. *Secundo,* sed in iis duntaxat paribus, contrariorum ex loco petitis, quorum parium propositio reciprocatur. Quod in relatis quidem
10 fit frequentissimè: ut apud *Martialem.*

Tum servum scis te genitum, blandéque fateris,
Cùm dicis dominum, Sosibiane, patrem.

Pater est filii dominus, & filii dominus est pater: pariter ergo filius est patris servus. Sic ex adversis: *bonum est appe-*
15 *tendum; pariter ergo malum est fugiendum.* Nempe quia propriè adeóque reciprocè, omne appetendum est bonum. Et ex privantibus: *Ovid.* 1. Fast.

In pretio pretium nunc est, dat census honores,
Census amicitias: pauper ubique jacet.

20 Dives est in pretio, & quisquis est in pretio, est dives; ergo omnis pauper jacet.

Quoties autem collationis propositio non reciprocatur, vel quoties uni parium id quasi proprium tribuitur quod utrisque

to make men happy? For contraries are the consequences of contraries."

But this rule is not perpetually true unless, first, there is really a laying together of equals; it does not follow that *because evil works damn, good works therefore justify,* for evil works are in every way evil, good works are imperfectly good; the first are our own, the latter not wholly ours. *Secondly,* it is not perpetually true in those equals merely that are taken from the place of the contraries, and whose proposition is reciprocated, something very frequently done among related things, as we read in Martial:

> When that thy father thou dost master call,
> Thou dost confess thyself a slave and thrall.

The father is master of the son, and the master of the son is the father; equally, therefore, the son is the servant of the father. The same is true of adverses, as in the argument: *Good is to be desired; equally, therefore, evil is to be fled from,* since beyond doubt properly and therefore reciprocally: *Everything that is to be desired is good.* And it is true also of privatives, as is illustrated by Ovid (*Fasti* 1):

> Price is in price; the censor honor gives,
> He giveth friends; contemned the poor man lives.

The rich man is in esteem and whoever is in esteem is rich, hence every poor man is despised.

As often as the proposition of the comparison is not reciprocated, or to one of the equals is attributed as proper to

commune est, eorum consequentia contraria non sunt, sed sæpe eadem. Fallit ergo hoc ex relatis: *pater est dives; ergo filius est pauper:* quia propositio non est reciproca; omnis enim dives non est pater. Et hoc etiam ex adversis: *homo est* 5 *sensu præditus; bestia igitur sensu caret. Homo mortalis; bestia igitur immortalis:* quippe nec sensu præditum, nec mortale est homini proprium; sed utrique contrario commune, & homini & bestiæ. Hoc etiam ex contradicentibus: *homo est animal; ergo non homo est non animal.* Hoc denique ex pri- 10 vantibus: *videns vivit; ergo cæcus est mortuus:* vivere enim & videnti & cæco commune est. *Non enim idem non dici de contrariis, sed contraria de eodem dici non possunt: immo quod suscipit unum contrariorum, suscipit alterum; & quod unum non suscipit, neque alterum;* ut, *in quo est amor, in eo* 15 *potest esse odium. Quibus nullum est jus, jis nulla fit injuria.*

Est & alius parium sine notis modus, *quo interdum lacessiti, par pari reponimus.* Qualis est *Virgil.* Ecl. 3. In illa pastorum alterna contentione repetitum illud; *Dic quib. in terris,* &c. Cujusmodi est & illud *Mat.* 21. 23. &c. *Qua authoritate* 20 *facis ista,* &c. *Interrogabo vos ego etiam quiddam: Baptisma Joannis unde erat?* Affine est illud *Cic. Off.* 2. *Cato, cùm ab*

it what is common to both, the consequences of these are not contraries, but often the same. This then, taken from the relatives, is false: *The father is a rich man, therefore the son is a pauper.* It is untrue because the proposition is not
5 reciprocal, for every rich man is not a father. And false also is this from the adverses: *Man is gifted with sense, a beast therefore lacks sense; man is mortal, a beast therefore immortal.* These are incorrect because to be gifted with sense and to be mortal are not proper to man, but on the contrary
10 common to both man and beast. This also from the contradictories is incorrect: *Man is an animal, therefore not-man is not an animal.* And this from the privatives: *The seeing man lives, therefore the blind man is dead,* for life is common to the seeing and the blind. In fact something not
15 the same is unable not to be said of contraries, but contraries cannot be said of the same thing, rather what acknowledges one of the contraries acknowledges the other, and what does not acknowledge one does not acknowledge the other, as *If there is love in a person, in him can also be hate. To those*
20 *who have no law, no injury can be done.*

There is also another mode of equals without signs, by which sometimes when assailed we pay like for like. Of this sort is Vergil's *Third Eclogue,* where in the alternate contest of the shepherds is repeated: "Tell in what place"
25 etc. Of the same sort is Matthew 21.23, etc.: "By what authority doest thou these things? etc. I also will ask you one thing: The baptism of John, whence was it?" Allied to it is a passage in Cicero (*De officiis* 2): "Cato, when he was

eo quæreretur, quid esset fœnerari? respondit, quid hominem occidere.

Paria verò ficta quorum esse proprium suprà diximus rem veram arguere, sunt illa apud *Ciceronem,* Invent. 1. ex
5 *Æschine Socratico;* ubi *Aspasia* cum *Xenophontis* uxore & *Xenophonte* ipso sic inducitur locuta: *dic mihi, quæso, Xenophontis uxor, si vicina tua melius habeat aurum quàm tu habes, utrum illius an tuum malis? Illius, inquit. Et si vestem? Illius verò respondit. Age verò, si virum illa meliorem,*
10 *an illius malis.* Hîc mulier erubuit. Comparatio sic se habet: si aurum, si vestem vicinæ meliorem habere malles quàm tuam, malle etiam meliorem vicinæ virum argueris. Non dicit vicinam habere aurum aut vestem meliorem, sed fingit aut ponit, eámque si mallet *Xenophontis* uxor, arguitur malle
15 virum quoque vicinæ si melior sit.

asked: 'What of putting out money to usury?' replied: 'What of murder?'"

The feigned equals, of which as we said above it is the property to represent a thing as true, are those in Cicero
5 (*De inventione* 1), from Æschines the Socratic, where Aspasia is brought in speaking as follows with the wife of Xenophon and with Xenophon himself: "'Tell me, I pray thee, thou wife of Xenophon, if thy neighbor should have better gold than thou, whether hadst thou rather have hers
10 or thine?' 'Hers,' said she. 'And if she have a gown and other women's garments of a greater price than thou, whether hadst thou rather have hers or thine?' 'Hers,' said she. 'Go to, then, if she have a better husband than thou, hadst thou rather have hers?' Here the woman blushed."
15 Thus goes the comparison: If you prefer to have the better gold and garments of your neighbor rather than your own, you are inferred to prefer also her better husband. She does not say that the neighbor has better gold or garments, but feigns or posits it, and if the wife of Xenophon should pre-
20 fer them, she is inferred also to prefer the husband of the neighbor if he is better.

CAPUT XIX.

De Majoribus.

I*MPARIA sunt, quorum quantitas non est una.*

Non una, i.e. non eadem; quorum par ratio non est: contrariorum enim contraria ratio est.

Impar est majus vel minus.

5 *Majus est cujus quantitas excedit.*

Major autem vel minor quantitas æstimanda est ex rerum quæ comparantur, elatione vel summissione, ut inquit *Cic.* in *Top.* i.e. excessu vel defectu; quæ vel notis indicantur, vel, si desunt notæ aliis vocibus, quæ excessum vel defectum signi-
10 ficant, intelliguntur. Ex eo autem quod suprà de Logica quantitate diximus, intelligendum est id Logicè majus quoque esse, cujus non solùm magnitudo, mensura, aut numerus, sed etiam auctoritas, potentia, præstantia, probabilitas, difficultas, aut quid hujusmodi majus est; vel brevius, quod quavis ratione
15 excessum habet, id majus est; ídque non solùm rei ipsius natura, sed vel opinione disserentis. Majus igitur est cujus quantitas excedit id quod minus est: majus enim hîc adhibetur ad arguendum minus.

Quemadmodum autem parium, ita argumenti à majore,

CHAPTER XIX.

Of greaters.

UNEQUALS are things of which the quantity is not one.

Not one, that is, not the same; of which the ratio is not equal, for of contraries there is a contrary ratio.

5 *The unequal is either greater or less.*

The greater is that of which the quantity exceeds.

But greater or smaller quantity is to be estimated from the elevation or depression of the things which are compared, as Cicero puts it in the *Topics,* that is, by excess or 10 defect, which are either indicated by signs or, if signs are lacking, are understood from other words which signify excess or defect. But from what we have said above about logical quantity, it must be understood that that is logically greater which is greater not merely in magnitude, measure, 15 or number, but also in authority, potency, distinction, probability, difficulty, or anything else of the sort; or, briefly, what according to any idea exhibits excess is greater, and that not merely by the nature of the thing, but as it were in the opinion of the one who is thinking. The greater thing 20 therefore is that which surpasses in quantity what is less, for the greater is here brought forward to demonstrate the smaller.

Like the argument of equals, the argument from the greater has one short form which is rather briefly indicated

forma alia contracta est, quæ notis brevius indicatur; alia explicata, quæ partibus plenius distinguitur.

Contractioris formæ notæ sunt vel nomina comparativa & superlativa suos casus regentia, vel verba quædam; & ea qui-
5 dem utraque, non solùm quæ excessum significant, ut *major, melior, pejor; præstare, superare, vincere, excedere, præferri,* cùm referuntur ad id quod arguit, verùm etiam ea cùm nomina tum verba quæ defectum significant, ut *minor, inferior, posthabeo, cedo, vincor, superor,* si referuntur ad id quod
10 arguitur.

Explicata autem forma nunc est cum notis, nunc sine notis. Notæ sunt *non solùm, sed etiam; non tam, quam,* & comparationes, verbáque, ut suprà non modò elationem significantia cum particula *quàm,* si ea particula tribuatur ei semper
15 quod arguitur, sed etiam ea quæ summissionem significant, si modò particula *quàm* referatur ad id quod arguit: ut, *minus est amicum pulsare, quàm patrem.* Sed hoc exemplum arguit potius à minori quàm grave scelus sit pulsare patrem, quàm à majori non admodum grave esse pulsare amicum. Idem de
20 cæteris hujusmodi est dicendum.

Exemplum primæ notæ: *Cic.* pro *Muræna: Tollitur è medio non solùm ista verbosa simulatio prudentiæ, sed etiam illa domina rerum sapientia. Spernitur orator non solùm odiosus in dicendo aut loquax, verùm etiam bonus.* In hujus-
25 modi exemplis *sed etiam* est propositio, &, ut majus, arguit redditionem *non solum,* ut minus.

by signs, and another full form which is fully distinguished into parts.

The signs of the shorter form are either comparative and superlative words governing their cases, or certain verbs, 5 and both these not merely those which signify excess, as *greater, better, worse, surpass, overcome, conquer, exceed, be preferred,* when they are referred to what argues, but also when these comparative words and verbs signify a defect, as *less, inferior, postpone, yield, give up, surrender,* 10 if they are referred to what is argued.

The full form sometimes has the signs, sometimes is without them. The signs are *not merely . . . but also, not so . . . as,* and comparatives, and, as above, verbs not merely signifying superiority with the particle *than,* if this particle 15 is always assigned to that which is argued, but also those which signify inferiority, if only the particle *than* is referred to that which argues, as *It is less to strike a friend than a father.* But this example argues rather from the minor how grave an offense it is to strike a father than from the major 20 that it is not very serious to strike a friend. So it may be said of the others of this sort.

There is an example of the first sign in Cicero's *Pro Muræna:* "There is taken from amongst us not only that verbal counterfeit of prudence, but also that lady of things, 25 Wisdom herself. Not only the orator hateful in pleading or the pratler, but also the truly good is despised." In examples of this kind *but also* is the proposition, and, as a greater, argues a reddition *not only,* as the less.

Huic nota affinis est *immo*, vel *immo verò*. Cujusmodi est illud apud *Terent. Thr. Magnas verò agere gratias Thais mihi? Gn. Ingentes. Thr. Ain tu? læta est? Gn. Non tam ipso quidem dono, quàm abs te datum esse: id verò seriò tri-
5 umphat.* Hîc facilè intelligitur *immo ingentes* & *immo id seriò triumphat.* Ingentes gratiæ arguunt magnas; & triumphare, lætam esse. *Sic Catil.* 1. *Hic tamen vivit, vivit? immo verò in senatum venit. Et illud Ver. 3. Non furem, sed raptorem; non adulterum, sed expugnatorem pudicitiæ,* &c.

10 Exemplum secundæ notæ, comparativorum scilicet & verborum cum particula *quàm*, est ex *Cic.* pro *Marcello: Plus admirationis habitura, quam gloriæ.* Sed ambiguum: aut enim plus admirationis arguit minus gloriæ, & sic argumentum est à majori, aut minor gloria si magna sit, arguit maximam ad-
15 mirationem.

Verborum elationem significantium cum particula *quàm* exemplum hoc erit; *mendicare præstat, quàm furari.* Hîc mendicare, quanquam inhonestum, ut magis tamen & potius faciendum, arguit multo minus esse furandum.

20 Sic *malo illud,* scilicet quod arguit, *quàm hoc,* scilicet quod

A sign akin to this is *yes indeed,* or *nay rather.* Of this sort is the passage in Terence:

Thraso. But doth Thais give me many thanks for it?
Gnatho. Enormous.
5 *Thr.* Sayest thou so? is she glad?
Gn. Not so much for the gift itself as that it was given by thee; for that she triumpheth in good earnest.

Here easily can be understood *Yes indeed, enormous,* and *Nay rather, she triumphs in good earnest. Enormous thanks*
10 argue *many thanks,* and *to triumph* argues *to be glad.* Thus in the first *Against Catiline:* "Yet this man lives. Does he live? Nay rather, he comes into the senate." And in *In Verrem* 3: "Not a thief but a pillager, not an adulterer but a raper of chastity" etc.
15 An example of the second sign, that is, of comparatives and verbs with the particle *than,* is from Cicero's *Pro Marcello:* "They may gain more wonder than glory." But it is ambiguous, for either more wonder argues less glory, and thus the argument is from the major, or less glory if it is
20 great argues the greatest admiration.

The following is an example of the word signifying superiority with the particle *than: It is better to beg than to steal.* Here begging, though disgraceful, as nevertheless sooner and rather to be done, argues that by so much the less one
25 should steal.

Of the form *I prefer that rather than this,* to wit, what

arguitur: ut *Juvenal.* satyra 8. adversus gloriosum nobilem.

Malo pater tibi sit Thersites, dummodo tu sis
Æacidæ similis, Vulcaniáque arma capessas,
Quàm te Thersitæ similem producat Achilles.

5 Quod malit ignobilem fortem, quod tamen non est ita optandum, ex eo arguit atque ostendit à majori sive à potiori quàm minime velit nobilem ignavum. *Cæsar: Malo modestiam in milite, quàm virtutem.* Modestia, judicio *Cæsaris,* præstantior & major, arguit virtutem sive fortitudinem in 10 milite minus esse quàm modestia requirendam: vel potius à minori exaggerat modestiæ laudem in milite præ virtutis laude.

Sequitur majorum tractatio sine notis.

Atque in hoc solùm genere id majus est cujus probabilitas 15 aut difficultas est major. Hîc etiam Logici regulas consequentiæ tradere solent non solùm negando, ut vult *Aristot.* Rhet. 2. 23. verùm etiam affirmando, pro quantitatis diversa vi & consideratione, in exemplis diversis: ejusdem enim exempli una tantum ratio est. Si majus est probabilius, duntaxat ne-20 gando, in hunc modum: *quod non valet in majore, non valebit in minore.* Si majus est difficilius aut incredibilius, dun-

argues rather than what is argued, there is an example in Juvenal's eighth *Satire* against the boastful noble:

> Thersites I'd rather thy sire should be,
> Whil'st that Æacides is like to thee,
> And that thou shouldst with Vulcan armor make,
> Than for Achilles' son men should thee take
> And yet thy feature like Thersites' be.

In that he prefers the courageous man even when ignoble, something not very desirable, he argues and shows from the greater or stronger how much less he wishes the noble man to be cowardly. Cæsar declared: "I choose modesty in a soldier before virtue." In Cæsar's opinion modesty, when regarded as superior and greater, argues that virtue or fortitude is less required in a soldier than modesty; or rather by the minor he exaggerates the esteem of modesty in a soldier before that of courage.

Now follows the treatment of the majors without signs.

And in this genus alone that is greater of which the probability or difficulty is greater. For here logicians are accustomed to teach the rules of consequence not merely in denying, as Aristotle prefers in *Rhetoric* 2.23, but also in affirming, through the diverse force and consideration of quantity in diverse examples, for there is one reason alone for the same example. If the greater is more probable, this genus appears merely in denying, in this manner: *What is not valid in the greater will not be valid in the less.* If the greater is more difficult or more incredible, this genus of

taxat affirmando: *quod in re majore valet, valet in minore,* ut inquit *Cic.* in *Top.* Hujus exemplum est *Æneid.* 1.

O socii (neque enim ignari sumus ante malorum)
O passi graviora! dabit Deus his quoque finem.

5 Si gravioribus malis dedit Deus finem, dabit his certè. *Sic Cic.* pro *Muræna: Noli tam esse injustus, ut cùm tui fontes vel inimicis tuis pateant, nostros rivulos etiam amicis putes clausos esse oportere.*

Ficta etiam majora idem valent in suis consequentiis vel 10 *refutandis vel probandis.*

Refutandi exemplum est *Terent. Heaut.*

——Satrapes si siet
amator, nunquam sufferre ejus sumtus queat:
nedum tu possis.

15 quasi diceret, finge satrapam esse.

Et Æneid. 5.

Magnanime Ænea, *non si mihi Jupiter auctor*
Spondeat, hoc sperem Italiam contingere cœlo:
Mutati transversa fremunt, &c.
20 *Nec nos obniti contrà, nec tendere tantùm*
Sufficimus.

i.e. multo nunc minus Jove non spondente.

argument appears only in affirming: *What is valid in the greater thing is valid in the less,* as Cicero says in the *Topics*. *Æneid* 1 furnishes an example of this:

> O fellows, we these evils knew before;
> 5 God will them end, we greater far have bore.

If God has given an end to greater evils, he certainly will to these. Thus Cicero says in *Pro Murœna:* "Be not so unjust as to hold that whenas thy fountains lie open to thy enemies, our rivers should be forbidden to our friends."

10 *Feigned greaters are of the same value either in refuting or in proving their consequences.*

An example of refuting is found in the *Heautontimorumenos* of Terence:

> A satrap if he should become a lover could never
> 15 undergo the charges; much less thou then.

It is as though he said: Feign to be a satrap. And there is an example in *Æneid* 5:

> Then, to his fearless chief: "Not heaven," said he,
> "Though Jove himself should promise Italy,
> 20 Can stem the torrent of this raging sea.
> Mark how the shifting winds, etc.
> Nor can our shaken vessels live at sea,
> Much less against the tempest force their way."

That is, it is now much less possible since Jove denies Italy.

CAPUT XX.

De Minoribus.

MAJUS & minus inter se affecta & relata sunt: adeóque unius definitionem qui norit, norit alterius. Ut igitur majus est cujus quantitas excedit, *ita minus est cujus quantitas exceditur.* Quantitas autem ut ma-
5 joris erat in qualibet rerum elatione sive excessu, ita nunc minoris est in qualibet rerum summissione sive defectu. Sententiarum enim minor probabilitas aut difficultas locum non habet, nisi in minorum forma explicata; quod ex majorum quoque explicata forma intelligi potest. Minus igitur est
10 cujus quantitas exceditur à majore: argumentum itaque à minore est, cùm id quod minus est, adhibetur ad arguendum id quod est majus.

Minora etiam vel brevius indicantur notis, vel plenius distinguuntur partibus. Hujus utriusque formæ vel propriæ
15 sunt minorum notæ, vel negationes parium.

Propriæ notæ contractioris formæ sunt primùm, voces comparativæ Grammaticæ, cùm nomina tum verba, elationem utraque significantia, si modò attribuantur ei quod arguitur. *Ovid.* 3. de Trist. *Sævior es tristi Busiride.* Hîc minor sævitia

CHAPTER XX.

Of lessers.

GREATER and less are affected and related among themselves in such a way that whoever knows the definition of one knows that of the other.

As therefore the greater is that the quantity of which ex-
5 ceeds, thus *the less is that the quantity of which is exceeded.* But as the quantity of the greater was in some superiority or excess of things, thus that of the lesser is in some inferiority or defect. For a lesser probability or difficulty of ideas has no place, unless it is set forth in the form of the lessers, as
10 can be understood from the full form of the greaters. The lesser therefore is that the quantity of which is exceeded by the greater; hence the argument is from the lesser when that which is less is applied to arguing what is greater.

The lessers also are either briefly indicated by signs or
15 more fully distinguished by parts. The forms of either of these are either the peculiar signs of the lessers, or the negations of equals.

The peculiar signs of the shorter form are, first, the comparative words of grammar, nouns as well as verbs, both
20 indicating superiority if only they are assigned to what is argued. Ovid (*Tristia* 3) writes:

> Thou art more fierce than the harsh Busiris.

Here the less cruelty of Busiris argues the greater cruelty of

Busiridis arguit majorem illius in quem poeta invehitur. *Præstat sapientia divitiis. Sævior* & *præstat* elationem significant, & notæ sunt majoris; sed quia tribuuntur ei quod arguitur, argumentum utrobique est à minori. Atque hoc sedulò adver-
5 tendum est, ut argumentum majoris à minori dijudicare possis: majora enim & minora, contractæ præsertim formæ, easdem plerumque notas præ se ferunt; idémque exemplum utramvis in partem vel à majori vel à minori arguere potest: ut, *sævior es tristi Busiride.* Hoc si ad sævitiam cujusvis ex-
10 aggerandam dicatur, ut hoc loco, à minori est: si ad *Busiridis* extenuandam, à majori. Si igitur illa quæ elationem significant, referantur ad id quod arguitur, sunt illa quidem notæ majoris, argumentum autem est à minori; quoniam majus, cujus illa notæ sunt, est id quod arguitur: sin illa quæ summis-
15 sionem significant, referuntur ad id quod arguitur, sunt illa quidem notæ minoris, sed argumentum est à majori; quoniam id quod arguitur, minus est.

Secundò, comparationes Grammaticæ verbáque summissionem significantia, ut minor, inferior, &c. Posthabeo, post-
20 pono, cedo, vincor, superor, &c. Si modò ad id quod arguit, referatur: ut *cedant arma togæ.* Hîc togæ dignitas arguitur à minori armorum dignitate, quæ cedit.

Atque hæ sunt notæ affirmantes contractæ formæ: quibus

him against whom the poet inveighs. Another example is found in the assertion: *Wisdom is better than riches. More fierce* and *is better than* signify superiority, and are signs of the greater, but since they are assigned to that which is
5 argued, the argument of either is from the lesser. And this must be carefully noticed, that you may be able to distinguish the argument of the greater from the less, for the greater and the less, especially the contracted forms, to a great extent present the same signs, and the same example can be
10 argued in either direction either from the major or the minor, as "Thou art more fierce than the harsh Busiris." If this is spoken for exaggeration of the savageness of some one, as here, it is argued from the lesser, but if for the extenuation of Busiris, from the greater. If therefore the things that sig-
15 nify superiority are assigned to what is argued, they are, it is true, the signs of the greater, but the argument is from the lesser, since the greater, of which these are the signs, is that which is argued. If those which signify inferiority are assigned to that which is argued, they are, it is true, signs of
20 the lesser, but the argument is from the greater, since what is argued is less.

Secondly, the signs of the contracted form are the grammatical comparatives and words signifying inferiority, as *less, inferior,* etc., *esteem less, put after, yield, am conquered,*
25 *am overcome,* etc., if only the reference is to what argues, as *Arms yield to the toga.* Here the dignity of the toga is argued from the lesser dignity of arms, which yield.

And these are the affirming signs of the short form, with

annumerandæ sunt etiam istæ formulæ, quæ fiunt negatione parium. *Philip.* 9. *Omnes ex omni ætate, qui in hac civitate intelligentiam juris habuerunt, si unum in locum conferantur, cum S. Sulpitio non sunt conferendi.* i.e. non æquandi, quæ
5 nota parium fuit. Hactenus contracta forma.

Explicata forma vel cum notis est, vel sine notis. Propriæ notæ sunt primò, *non modo non, sed ne. Cic.* 2 *Catil. Nemo non modò Romæ, sed ne ullo in angulo totius Italiæ oppressus ære alieno fuit, quem non ad hoc incredibile sceleris fœdus*
10 *asciverit.* Hîc posterior nota *sed ne,* est propositionis, & nota minoris; arguitque *non modò non,* quæ redditionis est, & nota majoris, quod arguitur. Ne ullo in angulo Italiæ non fecit, quod minus utile sibi erat, non modò non igitur vel multo magis Romæ fecit, quod majus erat, vel sibi magis utile. Pro
15 *Fonteio: Non modò nullum facinus hujus protulerunt, sed ne dictum quidem aliquod reprehenderunt.* Ne minus quidem fecerunt ut dictum aliquod reprehenderent, quæ propositio est & arguit non modò non majus, i.e. ergo non majus, ut facinus aliquod proferrent, quæ redditio est, & arguitur.

20 Verùm in hujus notæ exemplis propositionis nota *sed ne,* aliquando omittitur. *Ad Lent. Nullum meum minimum*

which are to be numbered also those formulas which are made by the denial of equals. An example is furnished by Cicero (*Philippic* 9): "All in all ages who have had the understanding of the law in this city, if they might be brought
5 together into one place are not to be equaled with Servius Sulpitius." That is, they are not to be equated, which was the sign of equals. So much for the shorter form.

The full form is either with signs or without signs. The proper signs are first, *not merely not . . . but not even,* as
10 illustrated by Cicero (*Against Catiline* 2): "There was no man not only in Rome, but in no corner of Italy overlaid with debt whom he had not associate to the incredible league of that mischievous enterprise." Here the posterior sign *but not even* is of the proposition and the sign of the lesser; it
15 argues *not merely not,* which is of the reddition, and the note of the greater, which is argued. In no corner of Italy did he not do what was less useful to himself; not merely therefore did he not do, or rather much more he did do, at Rome what was greater or more useful to him. An example is found in
20 *Pro Fonteio:* "Not merely did they not accuse him of any crime, but they did not even reprehend any word of his." The proposition is that they did not do the lesser thing of reprehending any speech, and argues *not merely not the greater,* that is, therefore they did not do the greater thing
25 of making an accusation of crime; this is the reddition and is argued.

It is true that in examples of this sign *but not even* as the sign of the proposition is sometimes omitted, as in *Ad Lentu-*

dictum, non modò factum pro Cæsare intercessit. i.e. nullum non modò factum, sed ne dictum quidem. Huic notæ affinis est illa formula, *tantum abest ab hoc, ut ne illud quidem.* Pro *Marcello: Tantum abes à perfectione maximorum operum,* 5 *ut fundamenta, quæ cogitas, nondum jeceris.* Ne hoc quidem fecisti quod minus est, abes ergo longe ab illo quod est majus.

Secundæ notæ sunt comparationes Grammaticæ & verba quædam cum particula *quàm* quæ vel elationem significant, ut *potius hoc quàm illud, malo hoc quàm illud,* vel summis-10 sionem, ut *minor, inferior,* ita ut *quàm* utrobique referatur ad id quod arguitur. *Catil.* 1. *Ut exul potius tentare, quàm consul vexare remp. possis.* Quod potius erat *Ciceroni* ut exul tentaret remp. quàm consul vexaret, illud ut minus malum arguit hoc esse majus. Hîc comparatio Grammatica *potius,* 15 ad id quod arguit, refertur, nempe ad minus malum; particula *quàm* ad id refertur quod arguitur, nempe ad majus malum. *Sic maluit Metellus de repub. quàm de sententia sua dimoveri.* Hîc *maluit,* verbum elationis, refertur ad id quod arguit, nempe ad minus malum, judicio *Metelli,* de rep. dimoveri; 20 particula *quàm* ad id refertur quod majus malum arguitur,

lum: "I have not spoken the least word, not merely no action of mine in behalf of Cæsar has occurred." That is, not only nothing done, but not even anything said. Akin to this sign is that formula: *He is so far from this that he is not even that,* as illustrated in *Pro Marcello:* "Thou art so much wanting from the perfection of great works that the foundation thou hast not as thou thinkest, yet laid." You have not even done that which is less, hence you are far from that which is greater.

The second signs are grammatical comparisons and certain verbs with the particle *than* which signify either superiority, as *rather this than that, I prefer this to that,* or inferiority, as *less, inferior,* provided that *than* in either case is applied to what is argued. An example appears in the first *Against Catiline:* "Thou canst rather as an exile tempt than as a consul vex the commonwealth." When it is said that it is preferable for Cicero that an exile should assail the commonwealth than that a consul should vex it, the first as the less evil argues that the second is the greater. Here the grammatical comparative *preferable* is referred to that which argues, namely to the lesser evil; the particle *than* is assigned to what is argued, namely to the greater evil. An example of the verb in a comparison is the statement: "Metellus preferred to be removed from the republic rather than from his opinion." Here *preferred,* a verb of superiority, is referred to what argues, to wit to the lesser evil, in the judgment of Metellus, of removal from the republic; the particle *than* is referred to what argues the greater evil, namely to be moved

dimoveri de sententia. Sic in iis notis quæ summissionem significant, particula *quàm* refertur semper ad majus quod arguitur, non secus atque in iis quæ significant elationem: ut, *minus est accipere, quàm dare. inferior est Cæsar quàm* 5 *Scipio.*

His notis affinis est *antequam,* i.e. potius quam. Pro *Milone: Utinam Clodius dictator esset, antequam hoc spectaculum viderem.*

Tertia nota est *cùm tum:* 2 Agr. *Quæ cùm omnib. est diffi-* 10 *cilis & magna ratio, tum verò mihi præter cæteros.*

Sequuntur negationes parium in hac forma explicata. *Non tam, quàm.* Catil. 2. *Quanquam illi qui Catilinam Massiliam ire dictitant, non tam hæc queruntur, quàm verentur.* Sic *non tot, quot:* pro *Muræna; Quod enim fretum, quem* 15 *Euripum tot motus, tantas, tam varias habere putatis agitationes fluctuum; quantas perturbationes & quantos æstus habet ratio comitiorum?* In hoc exemplo interrogatio fortius negat paria.

Nunc ad exempla formæ sine notis explicatæ veniamus. 20 *Cic. Off.* 1. *Ergo histrio hoc videbit in scena, non videbit sapiens in vita.* Atque hinc etiam consequentiæ ducuntur non solùm affirmando & probando, ut vult *Arist.* Rhet. 2. 23. & *Cic.* in *Top.* sed etiam negando & refutando: si quidem hoc de exemplo non eodem intelligitur: sin de eodem, tum qui-

from his opinion. Thus among those signs which signify submission the particle *than* is always assigned to the greater which is argued, and not otherwise among those which signify superiority, as when it is said that *it is less to receive than*
5 *to give,* or that *Cæsar is inferior to Scipio.*

Akin to these signs is *before,* that is, *rather than,* which appears in *Pro Milone:* "I prefer to have Clodius as dictator rather than to see this spectacle."

The third sign is *if . . . then,* as in *De lege agraria* 2:
10 "Which if to all it is very hard and a great reason, then truly it is to me above the rest."

There follow the negations of equals fully given in the form *not so . . . as,* as in the second *Against Catiline:* "Although those which say that Catiline is gone to Massilia
15 do not so much complain of it as fear it." Similarly *not so many . . . as many,* as in *Pro Muræna:* "What channel of the sea, what Euripus has movements and disturbances of its waters so many and great and varied as are the passions and agitations of the reason of assemblies?" In this example
20 the question strongly denies the equals.

Now we come to examples of the full form without signs, as Cicero, *De officiis* 1: "Shall a player see to this in choosing his part, and shall a wise man not see to it in life?" And the consequences are obtained from these not merely by affirm-
25 ing and proving, as Aristotle would have it in the *Rhetoric* 2.23 and Cicero in the *Topics,* but also in denying and refuting, if this is understood of an example not the same; but if of the same, then the right procedure is in affirming alone

dem vel solum affirmando, vel solùm negando rectè proceditur. Affirmandi exemplum est *Ovid.* 1. de Remed.

Ut corpus redimas ferrum patieris & ignes, &c.
Ut valeas animo quicquam tolerare negabis?

5 Si corporis causa, multo magis animi quidvis tolerabis; animus enim dignior. Item pro *Archia: Bestiæ sæpe immanes cantu flectuntur: nos non poetarum voce moveamur? Sic illud Mat.* 6. 26. *Passeres curat Deus: multo magis ergo homines.* At negando, nulla ex his consequentia deducitur: non
10 ergo sequitur, *si corporis causa quicquam non tolerabis ergo nec animi;* & sic de cæteris. Rectè igitur, si hoc modo intelligitur *Aristoteles,* à minore ad majus affirmando solùm proceditur. Verùm exempla non desunt, in quib. à minore arguitur etiam solùm negando: cujusmodi est illud suprà citatum,
15 pro *Marcello; fundamenta nondum jecisti, certè ergo non perfecisti.* Nec tamen idem affirmando; *fundamenta jecisti; ergo perfecisti.* Hîc modò cavendum est, ne ponatur negatio quæ affirmationi æquipolleat: ut, *Deus non negligit passeres,* idem est quod *curat.* Sic enim utriusque consequentiæ idem
20 exemplum prout sententia eadem vel affirmando vel negando

or in denying alone. An example of affirming is given by Ovid (*De remediis* 1):

> Thy body to redeem bear fire and sword, etc.
> To save thy soul wilt thou not all forbear?

5 If you will tolerate anything for the sake of the body, much more you will for the sake of the soul, for the soul is worthier. The same thing is exemplified in *Pro Archia:* "Wild beasts are tamed and subdued by singing; shall not then the words of the poets move us?" Similar is Matthew 6.26: God feed-10 eth the fowls of the air; much more, therefore, he feedeth men. But in denying no consequence is deduced from these examples; it does not therefore follow that *if you will not tolerate something for the sake of the body, therefore you will not tolerate it for the sake of the soul;* and thus of the 15 others. Therefore, if in this way Aristotle is understood, in affirming one can rightly proceed from the lesser to the greater only. Examples certainly are not lacking in which it is argued from the lesser in denying only. Of this type is that above cited from *Pro Marcello: You have not yet laid* 20 *the foundations; certainly, therefore, you have not finished the work*. But it is not the same in affirming, as appears in *You have laid the foundations, therefore you have finished the work*. In arguments of this kind the laying down of denial equivalent to an affirmative should be avoided, for 25 when it is said that *God does not neglect the sparrows* it is meant that *He cares for them*. Thus the same example can be given with either consequence according as the same idea

variatur, dari posset: ut, *si fures plectendi, multo magis sacrilegi. Si furib. non parcendum, multo minus sacrilegis.* Hîc *plectere* & *non parcere* idem est; & minus sit nota majoris: non igitur notæ, sed rerum elatio vel summissio majus vel
5 minus efficit. Atque hæc de consequentiis minorum sine notis.

Verùm eædem consequentiæ ducuntur ab explicata forma, quæ etiam cum notis est, ut ex iis exemplis quæ suprà ponuntur, intelligas licet. In hac forma explicata sine notis est ubi occurrit minorum quædam gradatio: ut *Ver.* 7. *Facinus est*
10 *vincire civem Romanum; scelus verberare; propè parricidium necare: quid dicam in crucem tollere?*

Finguntur etiam minora: Virgil. Ecl. 1.

> *Antè leves ergo pascentur in æthere cervi,* &c.
> *Quàm nostro illius labitur pectore vultus.*

15 Philip. 2. *Si inter cœnam in tuis immanibus illis poculis hoc tibi accidisset, quis non turpe duceret? In cœtu verò populi R. negotium publicum gerens, magister equitum,* &c.

is varied in affirming or denying, as in the example: *If thieves are to be punished, much more the sacrilegious; if thieves are not to be spared, much less the sacrilegious.* Here *to punish* and *not to spare* are the same, and *less* is the sign
5 of the greater. Hence not the signs but the superiority or inferiority of the things produces the greater or the less. So much for the consequences of lessers without signs.

The same consequences are indeed deduced from the full form, which occurs also with signs, as you may understand
10 from those examples which are given above. In the full form without signs there may be a certain gradation of lessers, as in *In Verrem* 7: "It is a crime to put a Roman citizen in chains, a heinous offence to scourge him, almost a parricide to put him to death; what can I say that it is to crucify him?"
15 *Lessers are also feigned,* as by Vergil (*Eclogues* 1):

The light held hinds in th' air shall feed therefore, etc.
Ere his dear lovely face shall from my bosom slide.

There is another instance in the second *Philippic:* "If it had happened to thee amongst thine inhumane pots, who
20 would not have accounted it filthy? But in the assembly of the Romans about public affairs, the master of the horse" etc.

CAPUT XXI.

De Similibus.

HACTENUS comparatio in quantitate fuit. Sequitur *comparatio in qualitate, qua res comparatæ quales dicuntur.*

Qualitas enim Logica non solùm est habitus, aut dispositio,
5 aut potentia, vel impotentia naturalis, aut denique figura aut forma exterior, quæ *Aristot.* species qualitatis sunt, & in aliis artibus tractandæ, sed est affectio quælibet sive ratio, quâ res inter se comparatæ quales, nempe similes aut dissimiles dicuntur. Nulla autem res est, quæ si alteri qualitate conferatur,
10 non sit ei similis vel dissimilis.

Similia sunt quorum eadem est qualitas.

Sic etiam definit *Aristoteles,* Phil. *δ.* 15. & *Boëthius,* l. 2. in *Cic. Top. similitudo,* inquit, *est unitas qualitatis.* Argumentum igitur similitudinis est, quando simile explicatur à
15 simili. Magna quidem est affinitas parium cum similibus; verùm ut ex definitionibus eorum perspicere licet, in hoc maximè differunt, quòd paria non admittunt elationem aut summissionem, similia admittunt: possunt enim etiam simillima majora esse vel minora; quod paria non possunt.

20 Similitudo proportio dicitur, Græcè ferè *analogia;* & similia proportionalia, Græcè *analoga.* Proportio autem nihil aliud est quàm duarum rationum similitudo: ratio autem est duo-

CHAPTER XXI.

Of likes.

THUS *far comparison has been in quantity. There follows comparison in quality, by which the things compared are said to be of a certain sort.*

For logical quality is not merely habit, or disposition, or
5 natural potency or impotency, or finally figure or exterior
form, which are the Aristotelian species of quality, and to
be treated in other arts, but is a certain affect or ratio by
which things compared among themselves are said to be of
a certain sort, namely, like or unlike. But there is nothing
10 which when compared with another in quality is not either
like it or unlike it.

Like things are those that have the same quality.

For thus Aristotle (*Metaphysics* 4.15) defines it and
Boethius (*On the Topics of Cicero,* book 2) says: "Simili-
15 tude is unity of quality." It is, therefore, an argument of
similitude when like is explained by like. There is, it is true,
great affinity of equals with likes, yet as may be seen from
their definitions they differ especially in that equals do not
admit superiority or inferiority, but likes admit it, for even
20 the things most alike can be greater or less, but equals cannot.

Similitude is called proportion, in Greek usually *analogy,*
and *similars are called proportionals,* or, in Greek, *analogues.*
But proportion is nothing other than similitude of two proc-
esses of reasoning. But a process of reasoning is the compari-

rum inter se terminorum sive rerum collatio. * Monendum autem est similia sive contractæ formæ sive explicatæ urgenda non esse ultra eam qualitatem quam in utrisque eandem esse propositum assimilanti erat ostendere: sic magistratus assimi-
5 latur cani, sola nimirum fidelitate custodiæ: unde illa in scholis, *nullum simile est idem, simile non currit quatuor pedibus, omne simile claudicat.*

Similia nunc notis brevius indicantur, nunc partibus plenius distinguuntur; hoc enim comparatis omnibus commune
10 est. Notæ similitudinis contractæ *quæ uno verbo concluditur,* sunt vel similium propriæ vel dissimilium negationes. Propriæ similium sunt vel nomina, ut *similis, effigies, imago, more, ritu, instar, in modum;* vel adverbia, *tanquam, veluti, quasi, sicuti;* vel verba, *imitari, referre,* &c. 1 *Æneid. Os hu-*
15 *merósque Deo similis.* Philip. 9. *Quanquam nullum monumentum clarius Servius Sulpitius relinquere potuit, quàm effigiem morum suorum, virtutis, constantiæ, pietatis, ingenii, filium.* 1 Trist.

Namque ea vel nemo, vel qui mihi vulnera fecit,
20 *Solus Achilleo tollere more potest.*

In Pis. *Unus ille dies mihi quidem instar immortalitatis fuit, quo in patriam redii. Verr.* 1. *Sed repente è vestigio ex*

son of two terms or things among themselves.* Warning, however, should be given that likes whether of short or full form are not to be urged beyond that quality which the man making the comparison intended to show as the same in
5 both. Thus a magistrate is likened to a dog, yet merely in the fidelity of his guardianship, whence came the sayings of the schools: "Nothing similar is identical; likeness does not run on four feet; every likeness hobbles."

Similars are sometimes briefly indicated by signs, some-
10 times more fully distinguished with parts, for this is common to all comparatives. Short signs of likeness *which are comprised in one word* are either properties of similar things or the denial of dissimilars. The proper signs of similars are either nouns, as *like, effigy, image, in fashion of, in the way*
15 *that, in the likeness of, in the manner of,* or adverbs, as *like as, just as, as if, as it were,* or verbs, as *imitate, reproduce,* etc., as in the *Æneid* I:

> In countenance and shoulders like a god.

Philippics 9: "Although Servius Sulpicius could leave no
20 clearer monument than his son, the effigies of his manners, virtues, constancy, piety, and wit." *Tristia* I:

> For he or none, even he that made the wound,
> Now in Achilles' mode can make me sound.

In Pisonem: "There was one day which was to me the like-
25 ness of immortality, wherein I returned to my country." *Divinatio in Verrem:* "But in a moment of time from the

homine, tanquam aliquo poculo Circæo, factus est Verres. Pro lege *Manil. Itaque omnes quidem nunc in his locis Cn. Pompeium, sicut aliquem, non ex hac urbe missum, sed de cœlo delapsum intuentur.* Negationes dissimilium sunt, *haud* 5 *secus, non aliter, non absimilis,* &c. *Æneid.* 3. *Haud secus ac jussi faciunt. Terent. in Phor. Ego isti nihilo sum aliter, ac fui.*

Ad contractam similitudinis formam pertinet etiam metaphora: metaphora enim, ut docent Rhetores, est ad unum verbum contracta similitudo sine notis quidem, quæ tamen intel-10 liguntur. Pro *Sest. Cujus ego patrem Deum atque parentem statuo fortunæ nominísque mei.* i.e. *tanquam Deum.*

Similitudinis partes deinceps explicantur, & quidem disjunctè vel continuè.

Similitudo disjuncta est, quando termini sive res *quatuor* 15 *reipsa distinguuntur.* i.e. quando duo termini sive res distinctæ in propositione comparantur duobus terminis sive rebus distinctis in redditione. Occurrit autem hæc forma & cum notis & sine notis. Notæ sunt, *qualis, talis;* illa propositionis, hæc redditionis nota est. Item *quemadmodum, ut, sicut,* proposi-20 tionis; quibus respondent, *sic, eodem modo, similiter,* redditionis. *Ecl.* 5.

likeness of a man, as it were by some Circean cup, he is made a boar." *Pro lege Manilia:* "Therefore all in these places do behold Cnæus Pompeius not as one sent from the city but fallen from heaven." Negations are of dissimilars, as *not*
5 *otherwise, not in another way, not unlike,* etc., as *Æneid* 3:

> No otherwise they do than they are commanded.

Terence, in the *Phormio:*

> I am not, neither have been otherwise than he.

To the short form of similitude pertains the metaphor,
10 for, as the rhetoricians teach, the metaphor is a similitude contracted to one word without signs, which, however, are understood. This is illustrated in *Pro Sestio:* "Whose father I hold the god and parent of my fortune and name," that is, *as the god.*

15 *The parts of a similitude are sometimes laid out in full,* and that *either disjunctly or continuously.*

A similitude is disjunct when the four terms or things *are distinguished in fact,* that is, when two terms or distinct things in the propositions are compared with two terms or
20 distinct things in the reddition. This form also occurs with signs and without signs. The signs are *such as . . . so,* the first the sign of the proposition, the second of the reddition. Likewise signs of the proposition are *in whatever way, as, just as,* to which answer *so, in the same way, similarly* in the
25 reddition. Examples follow. *Eclogues* 5:

Tale tuum carmen nobis, divine poëta
Quale sopor fessis in gramine.

Carmen ad auditorem, ut soper ad fessum, termini quatuor distincti sunt. *Ad* Frat. 1. *Quemadmodum gubernatores optimi vim tempestatis, sic sapientissimi viri fortunæ impetum persæpe superare non possunt.* Hîc quatuor sunt item termini, ut gubernator ad tempestatem, sic sapiens ad fortunam. 1 *Trist.*

Scilicet ut fulvum spectatur in ignib. aurum,
Tempore sic duro est inspicienda fides.

Cicero 2 Phil. Sed nimirum ut quidam morbo & sensus stupore suavitatem cibi non sentiunt; sic libidinosi, avari, facinorosi, veræ laudis gustum non habent. In vita *Virgil.*

Hos ego versiculos feci, tulit alter honores:
Sic vos non vobis nidificatis aves:
Sic vos non vobis mellificatis apes: &c.

In hoc exemplo redditio sine nota præcedit. Particula autem *Sic* quæ nota solet esse redditionis hîc propositioni attribuitur.

Aliquando nulla prorsus est nota. Virgilius Ecloga 2.

What thing that sleep and rest on grass
To weary men appear,
The same to me of thy sweet verse
The melody so clear.

5 Poetry is to the hearer as sleep to the tired: the four terms are distinct. *Ad fratrem* 1: "As the best governors of ships oftentimes may not overcome the strength and rage of the tempest, so the most wise man may not always vanquish the invasion and violence of fortune." Here there also are four 10 terms, for as the pilot is to the tempest so is the wise man to fortune. *Tristia* 1:

As tawny gold is tried in fire,
In time of need must faith be tested.

Cicero (*Philippics* 2): "But even as those who in a great sick- 15 ness do not taste the sweetness of meat, so the lustful, covetous, and wicked have not the taste of true praise." In the *Life* of Vergil we read:

I made these rimes, another had the land;
So, birds, you nests not for yourselves have made,
20 So you, O bees, make honey not for you, etc.

In this example the reddition without a sign precedes. But the particle *so* which is usually the sign of the reddition is here attributed to the proposition.

Sometimes there is absolutely no note, as in the second 25 *Eclogue* of Vergil:

O formose puer nimium ne crede colori,
Alba ligustra cadunt, vaccinia nigra leguntur.

Continua similitudo est, quando est ut primus terminus ad secundum, ita secundus ad tertium. Leg. 3. *Ut magistra-*
5 *tibus leges, ita populo præsunt magistratus.* Hîc termini sunt tres; lex, magistratus, populus. Sed medius bis adhibetur, & in omni proportione continua continuatur; éstque posterior terminus propositionis, prior redditionis. In omni enim proportione termini esse debent ad minimum quatuor. Ordo
10 hujus sic est: ut leges magistratibus, ita magistratus populo præsunt.

Quanquam autem similia magis ad illustrandum quàm ad probandum accommodata sunt, & *Plato in Phædone, Ego,* inquit, *sermones qui ex similibus demonstrationes sumunt,*
15 *probè novi ad ostentationem comparatos esse; & nisi quis caveat ab iis, facile imponunt.* Quod ad regulas tamen consequentiarum attinet, ex definitione similium perspicitur, similium similem esse rationem; valere igitur similia in utramque partem. *Unde Aristot.* Top. 2.10. *Quod in aliquo simili valet,*
20 *in aliis quoque similibus valebit; & quod non in aliquo, nec in cæteris.*

Quoniam autem similitudo non solùm est propositionis & redditionis, sed terminorum etiam inter se, idcirco si quædam similia sunt, inversè quoque similia erunt, & alternè. Et in-

Ah my fair boy, trust not thy hue too much,
Hurtles though black by every handsome hand
Are plucked, while daisies none vouchsafe to touch;
Albe they white, yet shed they as they stand.

5 *A continued similitude occurs when as the first term is to the second, so the second is to the third,* as in *De legibus* 3: "As the laws do govern the magistrates, so the magistrates do rule the people." Here the terms are three: law, magistrate, people. But the middle one is twice brought forward, 10 and is continued in every continued proportion; it is the posterior term of the proposition, the prior term of the reddition, for in every proportion the terms should number at least four; the order here is as follows: as the laws govern the magistrates, so the magistrates govern the people.

15 Sometimes, however, similars are more fitted for making plain than for proving, and Plato says in the *Phædo:* "I have known speeches which receive their demonstrations from similars opportunely compared for display, and unless one bewares of them, they easily impose on one." As to the 20 rules of consequences, it is seen from the definition of likes that likes are alike in nature; therefore likes are valid on either side. Hence Aristotle (*Topics* 2.10) writes: "What is valid for one like, will be valid also for the other likes, and what is not valid for one will not be valid for the others."

25 Since there is likeness not merely in the proposition and the reddition, but also in the terms among themselves, therefore if they are similar, they are also similar inversely and

versè quidem duobus modis; inversione scilicet vel propositionis & redditionis, quæ aliorum comparatorum communis est; vel terminorum, quæ videtur similium propria. Exempli gratia; ut gubernator ad tempestatem, sic sapiens ad fortu-
5 nam: inversè ergo; ut sapiens ad fortunam, sic gubernator ad tempestatem. Hæc propositionis & redditionis inversio est. Rursus, ut tempestas ad gubernatorem, sic fortuna ad sapientem: hæc inversio est terminorum. Alternatio est quando antecedens propositionis antecedenti redditionis & consequens
10 consequenti comparatur. Regula ergo hîc est; si quædam similia fuerint, alternè similia erunt. Ut gubernator ad tempestatem, sic sapiens ad fortunam: ergo, alternè; ut gubernator ad sapientem, sic tempestas ad fortunam. Inversionum hujusmodi & alternationum in Mathematicis proportionibus usus
15 maximus est: sed proportio non Mathematica solùm verùm etiam Logica est, ut supradiximus, rerum omnium communis; ejus ergo regulæ non erant hîc omittendæ.

Ficta similitudo parem vim habet superioribus illis, sed præcipuè in hac explicata similitudine Æsopici apologi ex-
20 *cellunt.*

Horat. 1. Epist.

> *Quod si me populus Romanus fortè roget, cur*
> *non ut porticibus, sic judiciis fruar iisdem,*
> *nec sequar aut fugiam quæ diligit ipse vel odit?*
> 25 *Olim quod vulpes ægroto cauta leoni*

alternately. Inversely in two manners, obviously by inversion of the proposition and reddition, which is common to other comparatives, or of the terms, which seems proper to similars. For example, *As the pilot is to the tempest, so is the wise*
5 *man to fortune;* inversely, therefore, it will be *As the wise man is to fortune, so is the pilot to the tempest.* This is inversion of the proposition and reddition. Again, *As is the tempest to the pilot, so is fortune to the wise man;* this is inversion of the terms. Alternation is when the antecedent of
10 the proposition is compared with the antecedent of the reddition, and the consequent to its consequent. The rule here, therefore, is that if things are similar they are alternately similar. *As is the pilot to the tempest, so is the wise man to fortune;* therefore, alternately, *As is the pilot to the wise man,*
15 *so is the tempest to fortune.* The greatest use of inversion and alternation of this sort is in mathematical proportions. But as we said above, proportion not merely mathematical but also logical is common to all things; hence its rules could not be omitted here.

20 *The fictitious similitude has equal force in argument with those mentioned above, but the apologues of Æsop especially excel in this explicated similitude.*

This is illustrated from Horace (*Epistles* I):

> But if Rome's people ask me happily,
> 25 Why not 'mongst judges on the bench sit I,
> And do that which they love, fly that they hate.
> I answer as the crafty fox of late,
> When tooth-sick lion he this message sent,

respondit, referam; quia me vestigia terrent
omnia te adversum spectantia, nulla retrorsum.

Huc etiam refertur parabola *Socratica* vulgò dicta; quæ est inductio similium interrogationib. ferè constans. Illa autem, 5 inquit *Fabius, hanc habuit vim; ut cùm plura interrogasset Socrates, quæ fateri adversario necesse esset, novissime id, de quo quærebatur inferret, cui simile adversarius concessisset.* Vide pag. 194. ad *.

CAPUT XXII.

De Dissimilibus.

HACTENUS similia, quorum qualitas est eadem. *Dissimilia sunt comparata, quorum qualitas est diversa.*

Contrariorum enim eadem scientia est. Et *Cic.* in *Top. ejusdem est,* inquit, *dissimile & simile invenire.* In hoc differunt dissimilia à diversis, quod dissimilitudo sit differentia 15 comparata, & non eidem, eodem saltem tempore, sed diversis plerumque subjectis attribuatur. Itaque diversorum uno negato, alterum affirmatur; dissimilia sive diversa sive opposita, simul affirmari aut negari possunt. Diversa autem qualitas est non eadem; sive diversa sit sive opposita: quasi dicas dissimi-

"Fain would I come, to that thing was I bent,
But that I saw the steps of many feet
That way to go, none back again to get."

Under this head is also what is commonly called the Socratic parable, which is a well-nigh constant induction of similar things by interrogations. But that, says Fabius, has this force, that when Socrates had asked many things which it was necessary for his adversary to acknowledge, he finally would infer about the subject of his questions a conclusion the like of which had already been conceded by his adversary. See page 195, at the asterisk.

CHAPTER XXII.

Of unlikes.

THUS far I have treated likes, of which the quality is the same. *Unlikes are comparatives the quality of which is diverse.*

Of contraries, certainly, the theory is the same, and in the *Topics* Cicero says that *the process of finding unlike and like is the same.* Unlikes differ from diverse things, in that unlikeness is a difference arising from comparison, and is not attributed to the same subject, at least at the same time, but commonly to diverse subjects. So of diverse things, if one be denied, the other is affirmed; but unlikes, whether diverse or opposite, can be at the same time affirmed or denied. But diverse quality is quality not the same, whether it is diverse

lium dissimilis est ratio. Argumentum igitur dissimilitudinis est, quando dissimile arguitur à dissimili.

Contractæ dissimilitudinis notæ sunt *dissimile, dispar, differens, aliud, secus:* Pro *Planc. Dissimilis est debitio pecuniæ 5 & gratiæ. Ennius: O domus antiqua, heu quàm dispari dominare domino.* dispar autem est non impar, sed dissimilis. *Cæsar* 1. *bell. Gal. Hi omnes linguâ, institutis, legibus inter se differunt.* 2 *Agrar. Alio vultu, alio vocis sono, alio incessu esse meditabatur. Cic.* 2. *Nat. Quoniam cœpi secus agere,* 10 *atque initio dixeram.*

Dissimilitudinis notæ etiam sunt per negationem similium, ut non similis, non talis, non idem, non tanquam, &c. 3 de *Orat. Non est Philosophia similis artium reliquarum.* 2 Æneid.

15 *At non ille, satum quo te mentiris, Achilles,*
talis in hoste fuit Priamo.——

Horat. 1. *Epist. Non eadem est ætas, non mens.* 1. ad *Frat. Sit annulus tuus, non tanquam vas aliquod, sed tanquam*

or opposite; you may as it were say that the nature of unlikes is unlike. The argument therefore of unlikeness appears when unlike is argued from unlike.

The signs of the short form of dissimilitude are *unlike, unequal, different, other, otherwise,* as in the following examples. *Pro Plancio:* "The paying of money and thanks is unlike." Ennius:

> O ancient house, alas, how far unlike
> The lord that ruleth thee.

But the disparate is not unequal but unlike. Cæsar (*Gallic War* 1): "All these differ in their tongues, institutions, and laws." *De lege agraria* 2: "He designed to be marked out by another countenance, another tone of voice, another gait." Cicero (*De natura deorum* 2): "Because I have begun to do otherwise than I said in the beginning."

The signs of unlikeness are also to be found in the denial of likes, as *not like, not such, not the same, not just as,* etc., as in *De oratore* 3: "Philosophy is not like the other arts." *Æneid* 2:

> Not he, whom thou and lying fame conspire
> To call thee his—not he, thy vaunted sire,
> Thus used my wretched age.

Horace (*Epistles* 1):

> Not the same is the age, not the same the mind.

Ad fratrem 1: "Let thy ring be not as it were a mere utensil

ipse tu. Hoc argumento pastor ille errorem suum confitetur *Eclog.* 1.

> *Urbem, (quam dicunt Romam) Melibœe, putavi,*
> *stultus ego huic nostræ similem.*———

5 Et mox,

> *Sic canibus catulos similes, sic matrib. hœdos*
> *noram, sic parvis componere magna solebam.*

Ut nec canibus catuli, nec matribus hœdi, sic nec *Mantua Romæ* similis est. In hoc exemplo erroris confessio pro nega-10 tione similium est.

Explicata dissimilitudo itidem cum notis est vel sine notis. Notæ sunt hîc etiam negationes similium. 3. *Philip. Certus dies non ut sacrificii sic consilii expectari solet.*

Nota plerumque nulla est, cum dissimilitudo plenius 15 *explicatur.*

Quintil. l. 5. *c.* 11. *Brutus occidit liberos proditionem molientes. Manlius virtutem filii morte mulctavit.* Catullus.

> *Soles occidere & redire possunt:*
> *Nobis cùm semel occidit brevis lux,*
> 20 *Nox est perpetua una dormienda.*

Dissimilitudo est diei & vitæ nostræ. Redditio est vitam semel amissam non restitui. Illustratur à dissimili, quæ propositio est, soles occidere & redire possunt.

but as it were thyself." By this argument the shepherd confesses his error in the first *Eclogue:*

> Fool that I was, I thought imperial Rome
> Like Mantua.

5 And later:

> So kids and whelps their sires and dams express,
> And so the great I measured by the less.

As neither puppies are like dogs, nor kids like their mothers, so Mantua is not like Rome. In this example the confes-
10 sion of error is in place of denial of likes.

The explicated dissimilitude is also either with signs or without signs; the signs are denials of likes, as in the third *Philippic:* "This certain day is wont to be expected not so much for sacrifice as for counsel."

15 *Commonly when the unlikeness is fully developed there is no sign.*

An example occurs in Quintilian, book 5, chapter 11: "Brutus slew his children who were attempting treason; Manlius did punish by death the virtue of his son." Catullus
20 writes:

> Suns that set may rise again;
> But if once we lose this light,
> 'Tis with us perpetual night.

The unlikeness is between day and our life; the reddition
25 is that life once lost is not restored; it is made plain by the unlike, which is the proposition, namely

> Suns that set may rise again.

CAPUT XXIII.

De Conjugatis.

HACTENUS prima argumenta sunt exposita: quorum tria genera fuere; consentanea, dissentanea & comparata.

Sequuntur *orta de primis; quæ ad id quod arguunt perinde* 5 *sunt ut prima unde oriuntur: ut conjugata & notatio, distributio & definitio.*

In se itaque habent vim arguendi ut argumenta artificialia, & eandem quidem cum iis unde oriuntur: non autem à se, quia non prima, ut in capite secundo jam dictum est. Definitionem 10 autem vix aliam requirunt præter ipsum nomen quod naturam eorum satis per se explicat: unde illud consectarium, *Orta argumenta perinde esse ad id quod arguunt, ut sunt prima unde oriuntur.*

Quatuor hæ species ortorum, in duo genera, anonyma licet, 15 distinguuntur, cùm propter dichotomiæ studium, tum quia conjugata & notatio sub eodem genere continentur, propter illam quæ inter ea intercedit communionem. *Cicero* itaque in *Top.* locum ex conjugatis notationi finitimum esse dixit. Et in multis exemplis conjugata à notatione & nomine nihil 20 aut parum differunt. Communio autem illa duplex est: primò quòd sunt argumenta nominalia sive à nomine petita. Sed in

CHAPTER XXIII.

Of conjugates.

T*HUS far primitive arguments have been set forth,* of which there are three genera, namely consentany, dissentany, and comparative.

There follow those derived from the primitive arguments,
5 *which are to that which they argue as are the primitives from which they are derived. Their kinds are conjugates and notation, distribution and definition.*

So in themselves they have the power of arguing as artificial arguments, and the very same power as those whence
10 they are derived, but not by themselves, since they are not primitive, as has already been said in the second chapter. They scarcely require any other definition than their name alone, which in itself sufficiently explains their nature; thence comes the consectary: *Derived arguments are to that which*
15 *they argue just as are the primitive arguments whence they are derived.*

These four species of derived arguments are distinguished into two, though anonymous, genera, both on account of love for dichotomy and since the conjugates and notation are in
20 the same genus because they have much in common. So Cicero in the *Topics* says that the place of the conjugates is very close to notation. And in many examples conjugates differ not at all or little from notation and name. They have something in common in two ways: first, because they are

hoc differunt, ut etiam tradit *Boet. l.* 4. in *Top. Cic.* quod notatio expositione nominis, conjugatio similitudine vocabuli ac derivatione perficitur. Neque idcirco ad Grammaticam pertinent: ex vi enim nominum argumenta petere, Logici est,
5 non Grammatici. Secunda communio est, quòd sunt orta simplicia: neque enim ex pluribus primis simul conjunctis, sed ex uno aliquo argumento primo singula eorum exempla oriuntur, nisi in nominibus compositis: compositorum enim nominum composita interdum ex pluribus argumentis notatio est.
10 Distributio autem & definitio sunt argumenta realia, i.e. in rerum explicatione versari solent, & composita, i.e. ex pluribus argumentis primis simul conjunctis originem suam trahunt. Si ergo ortorum genera, quæ anonyma esse diximus, nominibus distinguere lubet, orta erunt vel nominalia & simplicia, ut
15 conjugata & notatio, vel realia & composita, ut distributio & definitio: nisi hoc fortè excipiamus, quod definitio ex uno primo, i.e. ex sola forma nonnunquam constare potest. Ex his autem duobus generibus prius tractandum est illud cui conjugata & notatio subjiciuntur, quia ferè simplicius est. Atque in
20 hoc genere conjugata priorem sibi locum vendicant, quod ex solis consentaneis oriantur, cùm notatio ex quovis argumento primo petatur. *Fabius l.* 5. *c.* 10. conjugata nihili facit: *Aris-*

nominal arguments, or those obtained from a name. But, as Boethius (*On the Topics of Cicero* 4) explains, they differ in that notation is carried through by the exposition of the name, conjugation by the likeness of word and derivation. Nor do they therefore pertain to grammar; to get arguments from the force of nouns is the business of the logician, not of the grammarian. The second thing they have in common is that they are simple derivatives, for they are derived not from several primitives joined together at one time, but the single examples of them are derived from some one primitive argument, except in compound nouns, for sometimes the notation of composite nouns is composed of several arguments. But distribution and definition are realistic arguments, that is, they are commonly employed in the explanation of things, and are composite arguments, that is, take their origin from several primitive arguments joined together at one time. If therefore anyone is disposed to distinguish by names the genera of derived arguments, which we have said are anonymous, the derived arguments can be called either nominal and simple, as conjugation and notation, or realistic and composite, as distribution and definition, unless indeed we make the exception that definition sometimes can rest upon one primitive, that is, upon a single form. Of these two genera the first to be treated is that containing conjugates and notation, since it is usually the more simple. And in this genus conjugates claim for themselves the prior place because they spring from single consentanies, while notation is obtained from any prime argument. Fabius (5. 10) makes

toteles autem & *Cicero* in *Topicis suis* aliter sentiunt: quorum ille, *l.* 3. *c.* 4. & *l.* 7. *c.* 2. locos ex dissentaneis, conjugatis & casibus plurimum ait valere; & ad plurima esse utiles.

Conjugata sunt nomina ab eodem principio variè deducta. 5 *Ut* justitia, justus, justè. *Aristoteles* & *Cicero* conjugata, ille, nomina ejusdem conjugationis; hic, ejusdem generis esse definiunt: sed neque ille quasi jugum ipsum conjugatorum, neque hic genus, neque noster principium ipsum sive originem & thema conjugatorum numero excludit. Conjugata autem 10 sunt omnia non solùm nomina tam substantiva quàm adjectiva, sed etiam verba, &, quæ *Aristoteles casus* vocat, adverbia, cùm paronuma, i.e. derivata, tum ipsa themata, servatis tamen istis conditionibus. 1. Si ut idem sonant, sic idem etiam significant. 2. Si in eadem significationis ratione sumantur. Nam 15 si unum significat potentiam sive facultatem aut habitum, alterum verò actum & ex potentia sive habitu arguatur actus aut contra, captio est. 3. Si in iis symbolum sit consentaneorum argumentorum, i.e. si à consentaneis orta sunt: quorum vim & affectionem in arguendo aliis nominibus iísque conju-20 gatis referant: quorum etiam ad inventionem nominalis hujusce conjugationis indicio ducamur: unde elucet non contemnendus hujus loci usus, præsertim in definitionibus.

Sequuntur exempla; ut justitia, justus, justè. Cujusmodi in exemplis observandum est, abstractum quod vocant, cau-

conjugates of no importance, but Aristotle and Cicero in their *Topics* judge otherwise; Aristotle (3.4; 7.2) says that points of proof from dissentanies, conjugates, and cases are of much value and useful for most arguments.

5 *Conjugates are words variously derived from the same root, as justice, just, justly.* Aristotle and Cicero define conjugates, the first as words in the same set of paronyms, the second as words of the same genus. But Aristotle does not exclude from the number of the conjugates their yoke itself
10 as it were, nor does Cicero exclude their genus, nor Ramus their very root, or origin and theme. But conjugates are not merely all nouns, both substantive and adjective, but also verbs and—what Aristotle calls cases—adverbs, both *paronuma,* that is derivatives, as well as the roots themselves, if
15 the following conditions are preserved: 1, if as they sound the same, they also signify the same; 2, if they are to be taken with the same type of significance, for if one signifies potency or faculty or habit but the other signifies act and the act is argued from potency or habit or the reverse, there is a falla-
20 cious argument; 3, if in these there is a symbol of consentany arguments, that is, if they have sprung from consentanies the force and affect of which in arguing they reproduce by other words which are conjugates, to the discovery of which we are led by the indication of this nominal conjugation;
25 from this it is clear that the employment of this place is not to be despised, especially in definitions.

There follow examples, as *justice, just, justly.* In examples of this sort it should be observed that what they call abstract

sam esse concreti, & concretum adverbii. Ut justitia est causa, cur aliquis sit justus: & quia justus est, idcirco justè agit. Quod tamen non est ubique verum: sanum enim, i.e. quod efficit aut conservat sanitatem, causa est sanitatis, concretum scilicet
5 abstracti, *ut notat Aristot. top.* 2. 3. *Propert. lib* 2.

Libertas quoniam nulli jam restat amanti,
Nullus liber erit, siquis amare velit.

Hîc libertas quæ causa est cur sis liber, quia non restat, ergo nullus, &c. *Cicero* 3. de *Nat. deor.* cùm de *Dionysio* tyranno
10 loquitur: *Jam mensas argenteas de omnibus delubris jussit auferri, in quibus quòd more veteris Græciæ inscriptum esset* bonorum deorum, *uti eorum bonitate velle se dicebat: dii boni sunt: eorum igitur bonitate est utendum.* Hîc ex effectis ad causas est disputatum; ut vult *Ramus:* ut mihi quidem videtur
15 à causis ad effecta. *Terent. Homo sum, humani à me nihil alienum puto.* Ex subjecto est ad adjunctum. *In Pison. Cùm esset omnis illa causa consularis & senatoria, auxilio mihi opus fuerat & consulis & senatus.* Ex adjunctis est ad subjectum. *Phil.* 2. *Non tractabo ut consulem, ne ille quidem*
20 *me ut consularem.* Ex effecto est ad causam: nam esse con-

is the cause of the concrete, and the concrete is the cause of the adverb, for justice is the cause why any one is just, and since he is just, therefore he does justly; but this is not everywhere true, for what is healthful, that is, what produces or 5 preserves health, is the cause of health, the concrete indeed of the abstract, as Aristotle observes in *Topics* 2. 3. Propertius writes in book 2:

> Because in love there is no liberty,
> Whoever loves, e'en he can ne'er be free.

10 According to these lines, since liberty—the cause why you should be free—does not remain, therefore no one, etc. Cicero in *De natura deorum* 3 says of Dionysius the tyrant: "Now he chargeth that there should be taken out of the temples all the golden tables in the which (after the fashion 15 of the Grecians) it was written 'Of the good gods,' saying he would use their goodness." *The gods are good, therefore their goodness is to be used. Here the argument is from the effects to the causes,* as Ramus holds; to me it seems from the causes to the effects. Terence writes:

20 I am a man, no human thing is strange to me.

This is from the subject to the adjunct. From *In Pisonem* we have: "Whenas all the cause was of a consul and a senator, I had need of the help of both a consul and a senate." This is from the adjuncts to the subject. *Philippics* 2: "I will not 25 handle him as a consul, lest he should handle me as of consular rank." This is from the effect to the cause, for being con-

sulem, causa est ut quis postea sit consularis: unde sic arguitur: non agnoscit is in me effectum, non agnoscam ergo in eo causam. Notandum est nonnulla sensu duntaxat, non sono esse conjugata: ut, *somnus, dormiens; morbus, æger.*

CAPUT XXIV.

De Notatione.

NOTATIO *est nominis interpretatio.* i.e. reddita ratio cur quidvis ita nominatum sit. Definitio autem hæc est *Boëthi, l.* 1. *in Cic. Top. Notatio* inquit *Cic. in Top. Græcis* etymologia *dicitur,* i.e. verbum ex verbo veriloquium: *nos autem novitatem verbi non satis apti*
10 *fugientes, genus hoc* notationem *appellamus, quia sunt verba rerum notæ.* Hæc ille. Ex iis igitur quæ supradicta sunt, intelligi potest, notationem esse argumentum ortum adeóque symbolum alicujus primi; esse nominale, i.e. ut *Cicero* loquitur, argumentum ex vi nominis elicitum.

15 *Quippe nomina sunt notæ rerum & cujuslibet nominis vel derivati vel compositi, siquidem notatione vera nomen inditum fuit, ratio reddi potest ex aliquo argumento primo.*

Ut homo ab humo. Hæc à materia est notatio. Sed linguæ,

sul is the cause why one afterwards should be of consular rank; from this is argued thus: *He does not recognize in me the effect, therefore I should not recognize in him the cause.* It should be noted that some things are conjugates in sense
5 merely and not in sound, as *sleep, dormant; sick, ill.*

CHAPTER XXIV.

Of notation.

N*OTATION is the interpretation of a name,* that is, a reason given why anything is named as it is. But this definition is that of Boethius (*On the Topics of Cicero* 1). "Notation," says Cicero in the *Topics,*
10 "is called by the Greeks etymology, that is, word from word, true-speaking, but we, to escape the novelty of a word not sufficiently appropriate, call this genus notation, since words are the signs of things." That is what Cicero says. From what has been already said, therefore, it can be understood
15 that notation is a derived argument, and therefore a symbol of some primitive argument; it is a nominal argument, that is, as Cicero says, an argument elicited from the power of a name.

Names are truly the signs of things, and a reason for any
20 *name whether derived or composite, if the name was bestowed with true notation, can be given from some primitive argument.*

For example, homo from humo. Here the notation is

cùm prima illa quam *Adamus* in Edene, tum illæ variæ atque à prima fortassis ortæ, quas conditores turris Babelicæ subito acceperunt, divinitus proculdubio datæ sunt; unde vocum primitivarum ratio si ignoretur, mirum non est: quæ autem 5 voces derivatæ sunt aut compositæ, vel earum origines ex aliis linguis antiquis jamque obsoletis petendæ sunt, vel ipsæ vetustate aut infimæ plebis inquinata fere pronuntiatione ita immutatæ, mendosè etiam scribendi consuetudine ita quasi obliteratæ, ut vera vocum notatio raro admodum teneatur. Unde 10 argumentum à notatione, nisi ea fortè manifestissima sit, fallax admodum & sæpe ludicrum est.

Nunc reliqua exempla videamus. *Ovid.* 6 *Fast.*

Stat vi terra sua; vi stando Vesta vocatur.

Terra dicitur *Vesta* ab effecto suo naturali, propterea quod 15 vi sua stat.

At focus à flammis & quod fovet omnia dictus.

Ex effectis est notatio. Item *Verr.* 4. *O Verrea præclara! Quò enim accessisti, quo non attuleris tecum istum diem? Etenim quam tu domum, quam urbem adiisti, quod fanum* 20 *denique, quod non eversum atque extersum reliqueris? Quare*

from the matter. But languages, both that first one which Adam spoke in Eden, and those varied ones also possibly derived from the first, which the builders of the tower of Babel suddenly received, are without doubt divinely given; hence
5 it is not strange if the reason of primitive words is unknown. But as to those words that are derived or composite, either their origins are to be sought in other languages ancient and now obsolete, or by their own antiquity and the usually corrupt pronunciation of the lower classes are so changed, and
10 by the habit of writing them falsely are so obliterated as it were that a true notation of words very seldom may be had. Therefore unless a notation chances to be very obvious, an argument from it is quite false and often ludicrous.

Now let us see the remaining examples. Ovid (*Fasti* 6)
15 writes:

> By her own force the earth stands; from standing
> by force *(vi stando)* Vesta has her name.

The earth is called Vesta from her natural effect, since she stands by her own force.

20
> But the hearth *(focus)* is so called from flames and
> because it warms *(fovet)* everything.

The notation is from the effects. Likewise in *In Verrem* 2. 2: "O trim sweepings! for to what place didst thou ever come to the which thou didst not bring with thee this day? To
25 what house, to what city, yea and shortly to what church? which thou didst not leave spoiled, clean swept behind thee?

appellentur sanè ista Verrea, quæ non ex nomine, sed ex moribus naturáque tua constituta esse videantur. Ex effectis item est notatio. *Ovid.* 1. *Fast.*

Prima dies tibi, Carna, datur, dea cardinis hæc est,
5 *numine clausa aperit, claudit aperta suo.*

Notatio hæc è subjecto est, cardine scilicet, in quo versando dea illa exercebatur. Hinc illa cavillatio in *Antonium* generum: *Tuæ conjugis, bonæ fœminæ, locupletis quidem certè, Bambalio quidam pater, homo nullo numero, nihil illo con-*10 *temptius; qui propter hæsitantiam linguæ stuporémque cordis, cognomen ex contumelia traxerit.* Ex adjunctis est notatio hæc *Bambalionis,* quia balbus & stupidus. E dissentaneis autem sunt illa apud *Quintil. l.* 1. *c.* 6. *Lucus, quia umbra opacus, parum luceat: & ludus, quia sit longissimè à lusu:* 15 *& Dis, quia minimè dives.* Est etiam è comparatis notatio pyropi, quòd ignis quondam speciem præbeat.

Atque hactenus de notatione: nunc aliquid de nomine adjiciendum est. *Est enim ut notationi ad suum nomen, sic nomini ad notationem sua affectio.* Hoc est, ut notatio arguit 20 nomen, sic nomen vicissim arguit notationem. Ut animi

Therefore these thy doings may well be called sweepings, not so much for thy name (although thou be named Verres, which may signify a sweeper) as for thy manners and nature." The notation here is likewise from the effects. In
5 *Fasti* 1 Ovid writes:

> O Carna, goddess of the hinge *(cardo)*, the first
> day is for you;
> By power divine the closed you ope, the open close.

The notation here is from the subject, the hinge to wit, in
10 turning which the goddess is engaged. Hence that censure of Antonius the son-in-law: "Bambalio was father to thy wife, a man of no estimation, and above all things contemned, who for his stutting and stammering of his tongue and dullness of spirit had this surname Bambalio, for a re-
15 buke and a taunt." This notation of Bambalio comes from the adjuncts, since he is stammering *(balbus)* and stupid. But from the dissentanies are those in *Quintilian* 1.6: "A grove *(lucus)* is so called because when thick with shade it can be light *(luceat)* but little, a school *(ludus)* since it is
20 very far from play *(lusus)*, and Dis since he is to the least extent rich *(dives)*." The notation of bronze, called by the Greeks fire-metal, is from comparatives, since it presents a sort of appearance of fire.

So much for notation; now something on name must be
25 added. *For as is the affect of the notation to its name, so is that of the name to the notation*. This means that as the notation argues the name, so the name in its turn argues the nota-

plenus, ergo animosus, & contrà, animosus, ergo animi plenus. Nam & nomen quoque ortum argumentum est; ex quo autem fonte oriatur, notatio declarat. Hæc autem appendicula de nomine idcirco est adjecta, quia cum alia argumenta inter se 5 affecta, quot quidem eodem nomine ac definitione non sunt comprehensa, sua seorsum capita sibi habuerint, & tantillum esset quod de nomine dicendum erat, non videbatur caput novum ob id esse instituendum. In hoc igitur capite duo loci inventionis continentur, notationis & nominis: inter quos si 10 comparatio fiat, potior videtur nominis. Unde tota hæc categoria ab *Aristotele locus à nomine* dicitur. Sæpiúsque & firmius à nomine quàm à notatione argumentum ducitur: ut homo est, ergo ex humo; focus est, ergo fovet. At non eadem vi argumentum à notatione deducitur; ex humo est, homo 15 igitur; fovet omnia, ergo focus est.

CAPUT XXV.

De Distributione.

RELIQUUM est ex ortis aliunde argumentis argumentum distributionis & definitionis.

In qua utraque affectio reciprocationis est, illic partium omnium cum toto, hic definitionis cum definito.

tion, as it may be said that one is full of spirit, therefore spirited, and contrary-wise, spirited, therefore full of spirit. For name is also a derived argument, and from which source it is derived the notation declares. But this little appendix on
5 name is added because, though other arguments related among themselves which are not comprehended under the same name and definition have separate chapters for themselves, so little was to be said on name that it did not seem that a new chapter should be made for it. In this chapter,
10 then, two points of invention are contained, notation and name; if comparison is to be made between them, it seems that name should have the first place. Therefore all this category is called by Aristotle the logical place of name. Argument is carried on oftener and more firmly by name than by
15 notation, as in saying *He is a man, therefore he is from the earth (humo); it is a hearth (focus), therefore it warms (fovet).* But argument is not derived from notation with the same force, as in the examples *He is from the earth, therefore he is a man; it warms everything, therefore it is a hearth.*

CHAPTER XXV.

Of distribution.

OF THE derived arguments there is now left the argument of distribution and definition.

In either of these there is an affect of reciprocation, in the first of all the parts with the whole, in the second of definition with what is defined.

Reciprocatio autem hoc loco est qua prorsus idem, eadémque, ut ita dicam essentia utrinque significatur: nam partes omnes simul sumptæ, i.e. rite compositæ, idem sunt quod totum, & definitio idem quod definitum; quod de nullo præ-
5 terea genere argumentorum dici potest. Unde nascitur hæc regula utrique huic argumento communis, ut in distributione ac definitione *nequid desit, nequid redundet:* nam ubi reciprocatio, ibi quoque æqualitas requiritur. Hinc eximia illa distributionis & definitionis laus effloruit; ex iis nempe artium
10 institutiones maxima ex parte constare. Cùm n. omnia artium præcepta constare debeant ex argumentis reciprocis, reciprocatio autem nusquam alibi reperiatur nisi inter formam, (quæ ipsa in definitionibus comprehendi solet) & formatum, inter subjectum & proprium adjunctum; hinc
15 factum est ut præcepta omnia vel definitiones sint vel distributiones vel regulæ quædam sive consectaria, quæ proprietatum explicationes dicuntur.

Distributio est, cum totum in partes distribuitur.

Totum est, quod continet partes.

20 *Pars est, quæ continetur à toto.*

Totum Logicè & generaliter dicitur, quicquid quocunque modo distribuitur & partes continet: pars, quæ quocunque modo continetur à toto.

Atque ut distinctio totius in partes, distributio; sic collectio
25 *partium ad constituendum totum, inductio dicitur.*

Reciprocation is here what signifies absolutely the same thing, and the same—as I might say—essence in either one, because all the parts taken at once, that is, properly put together, are the same as the whole, and definition is the
5 same as what is defined—something that can be said of no other genus of arguments. From this springs the rule common to both these arguments that in distribution and definition *nothing is lacking and nothing redounds,* for where there is reciprocation, there also equality is required. For
10 that reason flourishes the extraordinary reputation of distribution and definition; of them, indeed, the precepts of the arts for the greatest part consist. For though all the precepts of the arts ought to consist of reciprocal arguments, reciprocation is found in no other place than between form (which
15 indeed is usually comprehended in definitions) and the thing formed, and between a subject and its proper adjunct. By this it is caused that all the precepts or definitions are either distributions or rules of some sort or consectaries, which are called explanations of properties.

20 *There is distribution when the whole is distributed into parts.*

The whole is that which contains the parts.

That is a part which is contained by the whole.

Logically and generally that is called a whole which is in
25 any manner distributed and contains parts, and that is called a part which in any manner is contained by a whole.

And as the division of the whole into parts is called distribution, so the collection of the parts to make up the whole is called induction.

Inter hanc autem inductionem & distributionem nullum aliud discrimen est, nisi quod distributio à toto ad partes, hæc verò à partibus ad totum progreditur. Quamobrem, ut supra, nomen ad notationem, ita hîc inductio ad distributionem referenda est; non ad syllogismos, ut plerique volunt; cùm non alio modo ab inductione argumentemur atque à distributione: siquidem eadem est via *Thebis Athenas* quæ *Athenis Thebas*. Inductionis autem auctorem *Aristoteles* agnoscit *Socratem:* ejúsque necessitatem tantam esse testatur, ut cùm scientia universalium sit, universalia cognoscere nequeamus nisi per inductionem. Inductionis ergo ope præcepta artium inventa sunt; ut in proœmio monuimus.

Distributio sumitur ex argumentis toti quidem consentaneis, inter se autem dissentaneis.

Sed dissensio illa non est distributionis dissensio (nunquam n. dissentaneum in dissentaneum distribuitur) sed partium distributarum.

Itaque tanto accuratior erit distributio, quanto partium & cum toto consensio & inter se dissensio major fuerit.

Hinc efficitur, eam distributionem accuratissimam esse, quæ in duas partes fit; eáque *dichotomia* dicitur: dissensio enim inter duo maxima est; & contrariorum unum uni tantum opponitur. *Platonis* itaque regula est: *oportet in quàm proxi-*

But between this induction and distribution there is no other discrimination than that distribution moves from the whole to the parts and that induction moves from the parts to the whole. Therefore, as in the preceding chapter name
5 was properly classed with notation, so here induction is to be classed with distribution, not with syllogisms as many hold, for we do not argue by induction in one way and by distribution in another, if it is true that the way from Thebes to Athens is the same as from Athens to Thebes. Aristotle
10 recognized Socrates as the author of induction, and testified that the necessity of induction was so great that, since science deals with universals, we are unable to know universals except through induction. By means of induction, therefore, the precepts of the arts have been found, as we have suggested
15 in the preface.

Distribution is taken from arguments consentany with the whole but dissentany among themselves.

But that dissent is not the dissent of distribution (for a dissentany is never distributed into a dissentany) but of dis-
20 tributed parts.

So the distribution will be the more accurate in proportion as the parts have more consent with the whole and more dissent among themselves.

It is thus brought about that the distribution which is
25 made into two parts is the most accurate, and this is called *dichotomy,* for the dissent between two things is the greatest, and one of the contraries is opposed to one alone. So runs the rule of Plato: "It is best so far as it can be done

mum fieri potest numerum semper dividere. Quod si dichotomiam invenire non queamus, difficile n. est eam semper invenire, species bisbinas ponere interdum præstat, quasi sub duobus generibus, licet anonymis, quàm quatuor sub uno.
5 Hæc n. distributionis forma, licet non sit optima, est tamen optimæ proxima. Hac ratione suprà cap. 3. *Ramus* divisit causas, in duo genera anonyma nempe *efficientem & materiam, aut formam & finem.* Ubi autem dichotomia nullo modo commodè adhiberi potest, *multis protinus differentiis*
10 *res dividenda est,* ut *Aristoteles* monet. Neque enim propter dichotomiæ studium distributio vel mutilanda vel implicanda aut confundenda est.

CAPUT XXVI.

De Distributione ex causis.

DISTRIBUTIO *prima est ex absolutè consentaneis, causis nempe & effectis. Distributio ex causis est, quando partes sunt causæ totius.*

Hîc distributio integri in sua membra præcipuè laudatur.

Integrum est totum, cui partes sunt essentiales. i.e. quod ex partibus totam suam essentiam complectentibus constituitur; ideóque symbolum est effecti ex materia per formam
20 existentis.

Membrum est pars integri.

always to divide number." Because if we are unable to gain dichotomy, for it is difficult always to attain it, it is better in the meanwhile to reckon four species, as though under two genera, even though anonymous, than four under one genus. 5 For this form of distribution, though not the best, is nevertheless next to the best. For this reason in chapter three, above, Ramus divided causes into two anonymous genera, the *efficient and the matter, or form and end.* But where dichotomy can in no manner conveniently be employed, "a 10 thing is to be immediately divided according to many specific differences," as Aristotle advises. For distribution should not be either mutilated or entangled or confused because of zeal for dichotomy.

CHAPTER XXVI.

Of distribution from the causes.

THE first distribution is through arguments absolutely consentany, to wit, causes and effects. The distribution is by the causes when the parts are causes of the whole.

Here distribution of the integer into its members is especially commended.

20 *The integer is the whole to which the parts are essential,* that is, what is constituted from the parts making up its whole essence; hence it is a symbol of the effect existing from the matter through the form.

A member is part of an integer.

Nimirum integro suo essentialis. Sive ut *Aristot. Phil. δ.* 25. *Membra sunt ex quibus integrum componitur.* Et membra quidem symbola sunt causarum essentialium, materiæ nimirum & formæ, in quibus tota integri essentia consistit:
5 singula n. membra materiam continent; cuncta simul, ipsam quoque formam. *Sic Grammatica in etymologiam & syntaxin: Rhetorica in elocutionem & actionem; Logica in inventionem & dispositionem argumentorum dividitur. Ab his n. partib. artes illæ constituuntur;* non tanquam ex causis, sed
10 tanquam ex causarum symbolis. Cùm enim essentia Dialecticæ partim communis sit materia scilicet, i.e. præcepta, & forma etiam, nempe methodica illorum præceptorum dispositio; partim propria, quæ in bene disserendo posita est, tota hæc Dialecticæ essentia in inventione & dispositione compre-
15 henditur. Nec tamen partes istæ sunt ipsa materia, i.e. præcepta, nec ipsa forma communis, i.e. methodica præceptorum dispositio, nec propria, i.e. ipsa facultas disserendi; sed ex præceptis methodicè dispositis conflatæ sunt, & ipsa facultas disserendi inventionis & dispositionis finibus continetur.

20 Quæ sequuntur apud authorem nostrum exempla duo, alterum ex *Virgilio, Georg.* 1. Alterum ex *Cicerone* pro *Muræna,* objectis utraque distinguuntur, non causis; ideóque ad cap. 28. ad distributionem nempe è subjectis, ad quam etiam præmissa illa annotatio de usu pertinet.

It is indisputably an essential part of its integer. Or as Aristotle writes (*Metaphysics* 4.25): "The members are those from which the integer is composed." And the members are symbols of the essential causes, of matter and form, 5 in which consists the whole essence of the integer, for the single members contain the matter, and when taken together also the form itself. *Thus grammar is divided into etymology and syntax, rhetoric into elocution and action, logic into the invention and disposition of arguments, for from these* 10 *parts those arts are made up,* not as if from causes, but as if from the symbols of causes. The essence of dialectic is partly common, to wit, the matter, that is, precepts, and the form also, which is the methodical disposition of those precepts, and this essence is also partly proper, and as such consists in 15 arguing well; hence all the essence of this discipline of dialectic is comprehended in invention and disposition. But these parts are not themselves matter, that is, precepts, nor are they the common form itself, that is, the methodical disposition of precepts, nor are they proper, that is, the faculty 20 itself of arguing, but they are made up of the precepts methodically disposed, and the very faculty of arguing is contained within the limits of invention and disposition.

Here in our author follow two examples, one from Vergil (*Georgics* 1), the other from Cicero *(Pro Muræna),* and 25 both are distinguished by objects, not by causes, and hence should be referred to distribution from subjects in chapter twenty-eight, to which pertains also the prefixed illustration from use.

Quinetiam aliter tractatur hoc argumenti genus, vel à partibus ad totum, vel à toto ad partes.

Hac de re *Aristoteles, Top.* 6. 6. regulas quasdam tradit. Primo à partibus: *affirmatis partibus cunctis, affirmatur totum:* & contrà; *sublatis partibus cunctis, tolli totum.* Item ab una parte: *una parte sublata, totum tolli.* Secundo à toto ad partes: *toto affirmato, affirmantur partes.* Verùm hæc omnia ex illa reciprocationis regula superioris capitis initio tradita satis intelliguntur. Nam quæ reciprocantur, eorum alterum ex altero vicissim & necessariò affirmatè & negatè concluditur. Hoc verò, ut *Aristoteles* etiam notavit, non sequitur; sublato integro, partes tolluntur.

Utriusque generis (nempe affirmationis & negationis à partibus ad totum) exemplum habemus apud *Catullum*.

Quintia formosa est multis: mihi candida, longa,
recta est: hæc ego sic singula confiteor:
Totum illud, formosa, nego. Nam nulla venustas,
nulla in tam magno est corpore mica salis.
Lesbia formosa est: quæ cùm pulcherrima tota est,
tum omnibus una omnes surripuit veneres.

Est & alia distributio ex causis & meritò quidem imperfectior dicta, cùm non tam ipsius rei quàm ejus causarum distributio sit: ut ab efficiente, testimonium est divinum vel huma-

Yea, more, this sort of argument is otherwise handled, either from the parts to the whole or from the whole to the parts.

On this matter Aristotle (*Topics* 6. 6) gives certain rules.
5 First from the parts: "If all the parts are affirmed, the whole is affirmed," and on the contrary, "If all the parts are removed, the whole is taken away." The same is true of one part, for "If one part is taken away, the whole is taken away." Secondly, from the whole to the parts: "If the whole is af-
10 firmed, the parts are affirmed." Certainly all these are sufficiently understood from that rule of reciprocation treated at the beginning of the chapter above. For if things are reciprocated, either one in turn and necessarily is concluded affirmatively and negatively by means of the other. But, as
15 Aristotle notes, it does not follow that if the whole is taken away the parts are taken away.

We have in Catullus an example of both kinds, namely of affirmation and negation from the parts to the whole:

> Quintia is handsome, fair, tall, straight, all these
> 20 Very particulars I grant with ease:
> But she all ore's not handsome; here's her fault,
> In all that bulk, there's not one corne of salt,
> Whilst Lesbia fair and handsome too all ore
> All graces and all wit from all hath bore.

25 There is also another distribution from causes properly called less perfect, since there is distribution not so much of the thing itself as of its causes, as when in distribution from

num. Sic statuæ veteres aliæ factæ erant à *Phydia,* aliæ à *Polycleto,* &c. Distributio hæc quædam est totius in partes; ubi tamen non tam partes ipsæ ponuntur quàm pro iis earum efficientes, quibus inter se distinguuntur. Sic statuæ aliæ erant
5 aureæ, aliæ argenteæ, aliæ æneæ, aliæ eburneæ, &c. Distributio est ex materia. Aliæ ad hominum, aliæ ad brutorum effigiem factæ; est distributio à forma externa. Aliæ factæ sunt ad usum religiosum, aliæ ad civilem; est distributio à fine.

CAPUT XXVII.

De Distributione ex effectis, ubi de genere & specie.

DISTRIBUTIO ex effectis est, quando partes sunt effecta.

Distributio generis in species hic excellit.

Nonnulli ex Cicerone distributionem integri in membra, *partitionem* vocant; generis in species *divisionem.* Nec de nihilo sanè: membra enim copulari, species disjungi solent.

15 *Genus est totum partibus Essentiale.*

In quo contrarium est integro: illic enim toti partes, hîc totum partibus est essentiale: unde constat, illam ex causis,

the efficient there is divine or human testimony. Thus some ancient statues were made by Phidias, others by Polyclitus, etc. This sort of distribution is of the whole into parts, where not so much the parts themselves are given as the efficient
5 causes of them, by which they are distinguished among themselves. Thus some statues were golden, some silver, some bronze, some ivory, etc. This is distribution from the matter. Some are made in the likeness of men, others of brutes; this is distribution from external form. Some are
10 made for religious use, others for civil use; this is distribution from the end.

CHAPTER XXVII.

Of distribution from the effects, and also of genus and species.

THERE is distribution from the effects when the parts are effects.

The distribution of a genus into species is here
15 *most important.*

Some, following Cicero, give the name of *partition* to distribution of the whole into members; and that of *division* to that of the genus into species. Not at all properly, for members are accustomed to be connected, species to be disjoined.
20 *A genus is a whole essential to the parts.*

In this it is contrary to the integer, for all the parts are essential to that, but here the whole is essential to the parts, whence it is certain that the first is rightly to be called dis-

hanc ex effectis distributionem rectè dici. *Genus* autem *est totum partibus essentiale,* quia illam essentiam nempe materiam & formam, quæ speciebus omnibus æquè communis est, significatione sua complectitur: vel brevius, quia symbolum est communis essentiæ. Neque enim genus propriè essentiam speciebus communicat (cùm in se extra species revera nihil sit) sed earum duntaxat essentiam significat. Quod enim essentiale est & speciebus omnibus commune, ejus notio *genus* dicitur, et idea sæpe à *Græcis,* non separata quidem à rebus illa, ut velunt *Platonica,* quæ nugæ sunt, teste *Aristot. Phil.* 1. 7. & *μ.* 5. sed quod cogitatione & ratione unum & idem est specieb. multis commune in quibus re & natura est singulatim, ut *Plato* in Menone. *Stoici* etiam Ideas, ut refert *Plut.* de Placit. 1. 10, nostras notiones esse dixerunt.

Species est pars generis.

Sic etiam *Aristoteles, Phil. δ.* 25. Et *Cicero,* Invent. 1. *Pars quæ generi subest.* Ex definitione autem generis intelligimus speciem ejusmodi partem esse cujus essentia communis in generis significatione contineatur. Propriam autem essentiam species, per quam est id quod est, à propria forma habet, quæ generis significatione minime continetur. Sic etiam *Aristot. Phil. ζ.* 12. *Genus non videtur particeps esse differentiarum: simul n. contrariorum idem particeps esset; differentiæ n. contrariæ sunt.* Unde illud; Plus est in specie quàm in

tribution from causes, the second distribution from the effects. But *genus is the whole essential to the parts,* since in its signification it embraces that essence, namely matter and.form, which is equally common to all species, or more briefly, since
5 it is a symbol of the common essence. For genus does not properly communicate essence to species (since in itself it is in truth nothing outside the species) but merely signifies their essence, for the notion of what is essential and common to all species is called *genus,* and by the Greeks often *idea,* but not
10 separated from things, as they think the Platonic ideas are, which are clouds, according to Aristotle (*Metaphysics* 1.7; 12.5), but what in thought and reason is one and the same thing common to many species in each of which in fact and nature it appears singly, as Plato says in the *Meno*. The Stoics,
15 however, as Plutarch reports (*De placitis philosophorum* 1.10), said that ideas were our notions.

A species is part of a genus.

Thus Aristotle says (*Metaphysics* 4.25), and Cicero (*De inventione* 1) calls it "the part which is subordinate to the
20 genus." But from the definition of the genus we know that the species is a part of such a sort that its common essence is contained in the significance of the genus. The species has its proper essence, through which it is what it is, from its proper form, which is not at all contained in the meaning of genus.
25 Thus also Aristotle writes (*Metaphysics* 7.12): "Genus does not seem to be a participator in differences, for the same thing would be at the same time participator in contraries, for differences are contraries." From this comes the assertion that

genere: & illud *Porphyrii; differentia est qua species superat genus.* Tota igitur generis essentia singulis æqualiter inest speciebus; at tota essentia speciei non est in genere, nisi potentia, ut inquit *Porphyrius.* Hinc ut species est pars generis, ita genus
5 pars esse speciei quodammodo videtur: quod & *Plato* in Politico notavit. Sic animal genus hominis & bestiæ dicimus. Animal enim est totum, cujus essentia, nempe corporea, animata, sentiens, ad hominem & bestiam communiter attinet. Sic dicimus hominem & bestiam species animalis; quia partes sunt
10 animali subjectæ, quæ animalis essentiam communem habent.

Genus est generalissimum aut subalternum.

Species subalterna aut specialissima.

Genus generalissimum, cujus nullum est genus.

Ut in Logica inventione argumentum est genus generalissi-
15 mum artificialium & inartificialium.

Subalternum genus, ut subalterna item species, quod species hujus, illius autem genus est.

Id est, quod nunc genus est, nunc species: genus, si ad species sibi subjectas referatur; species, si ad suum genus.
20 Sic causa, genus est materiæ & formæ; species, argumenti absolutè consentanei. Sic homo est genus subalternum, sive species subalterna: species quidem, si ad animal referas; genus, si ad singulos homines.

there is more in species than in genus, and that saying of Porphyry: "A difference is that by which a species exceeds its genus." The entire essence, therefore, of a genus is equally present in its species, but the whole essence of the separate
5 species is not in the genus, unless by potency, as Porphyry says. Hence, as the species is part of the genus, so the genus seems in some way or other to be part of the species, as Plato has indicated in the *Politicus*. Thus we say that animal is the genus of both man and beast. For animal is the whole of
10 which the essence, namely the corporeal, animated, and sentient, pertains in common to man and beast. Thus we say that man and beast are species of animal, since the parts which have the common essence of animal are subject to animal.

Genus is wholly general or subordinate.

15 *Species is subordinate or very special.*

A genus is wholly general which belongs to no higher genus.

So in logical invention argument is a wholly general genus of artificials and inartificials.

20 *A subordinate genus, as likewise a subordinate species, is the species of one thing but the genus of another.*

That is, a thing can be now genus, now species; genus, if it is referred to the species subject to itself, species if it is referred to its genus.

25 Thus cause is the genus of matter and form, and a species of argument absolutely consentany. Thus man is a subaltern genus, or subaltern species; a species if you refer to animal, a genus if you refer to single men.

Species specialissima est, quæ individua est in species alias.

Ut materia & forma quæque singularis. Sic homines singuli sunt species specialissimæ hominis, & singuli leones leonis.

Logicorum quidem pars maxima hominem speciem spe-
5 cialissimam, singulos homines individua vocant, non species. Verùm ut animal est totum cujus essentia communis, nempe corporea, animata, sentiens, ad hominem & bestiam communiter attinet; sic homo est totum, cujus communis essentia rationalis communiter ad singulos attinet homines: atque ut
10 homo & bestia species sunt animalis, quia partes sunt animali subjectæ, quæ animalis essentiam communem habent; ita singuli homines species sunt hominis, quia partes sunt homini subjectæ, quæ hominis essentiam communem habent: ergo homo non minus est singulorum hominum genus quàm ani-
15 mal hominis; homines singuli non minus sunt hominis species, quàm homo animalis. Singuli enim homines propria forma differunt: quæ autem forma differunt propria, differunt & specie; teste *Aristot. Phys.* 1. 7. Deinde, quicquid differt, aut genere differt aut specie; teste eodem *Aristot. Phil.*
20 10. 3. differre autem genere singulos homines nemo dixerit; differunt ergo specie. Nam quod aiunt hominem esse speciem singulorum hominum, id planè absurdum est: species enim pars est ejus cujus est species; ut ex ejus definitione constat: genus porrò & species cùm relata sint, genus utique erit speciei
25 genus; species, generis erit species. Si igitur homo, ut vulgò

The lowest species is that which is indivisible into other species.

An example is furnished by the matter and form of any single thing. Thus single men are the lowest species of man, and single lions of lion.

Most logicians call man the lowest species and single men individuals, not species. But as animal is a whole of which the common essence, namely corporeal, animate, and sentient, pertains in common to man and beast, so man is a whole, of which the common rational essence pertains in common to single men, and also as man and beast are species of animal, since the parts which have the common essence of animal are subject to animal, so single men are species of man, since the parts which have the common essence of man are subject to man; therefore man is not less the genus of single men than animal is of man, and single men are not less species of man than man is of animal. Yet single men differ in their proper form, but things that differ in proper form differ also in species, according to Aristotle (*Physics* 1.7). Then whatever things differ have their difference in genus or species, according to the same Aristotle (*Metaphysics* 10.3), but no one says that single men differ in genus; hence they differ in species. For as to the saying that man is the species of single men, it is plainly absurd, for a species is part of that of which it is a species, as is plain from its definition; therefore when genus and species are related, genus will always be the genus of the species, and species will be the species of the genus. If therefore man, as they commonly

volunt, est species singulorum hominum; singuli homines erunt genus hominis; quod nimis absurdum est. At inquiunt singuli homines numero tantum differunt, non forma. Verùm quæ numero differunt, forma quoque differre, jam supra ca-
5 pite de Forma satis ostendimus; etsi formæ cujusque propriæ differentia nobis non nisi per externa quædam effecta, & accidentia, quæ vocant, dignosci potest. Deinde, singuli homines inter se disparantur, ergo opponuntur: quæ autem inter se opponuntur, eorum eadem forma esse non potest; forma ergo
10 differunt non numero tantum. Itaque apud *Laërtium,* in *Zenone, Stoici* docent, *Socratem* esse speciem specialissimam. Immo *Aristot.* de *Part.* 1. 4. *Socratem* & *Coriscum* species infimas vocat. Sic jurisconsulti, hominem genus appellant; *Stichum* & *Pamphilum* species.

15 *Genus verò & species notæ sunt causarum & effectorum.*

In animali n. est essentia corporea, quæ materia est ad species communiter attinens: tum facultas vitæ & sensus, quæ forma item communiter ad species spectat. Quare *genus continet causas, quæ communiter ad ipsius species attinent: contra*
20 *itaque etiam species effecta generis sui continent.*

Hinc universale est insigne ac præstabile: quia causam declarat.

Idem ait *Aristot. Poster.* 1. 24.

Distributio generis in species valdè quidem excellit, sed
25 *difficilis est & rara inventu.*

will have it, is a species of single men, single men will be the genus of man—something altogether absurd. But they say that single men differ in number merely, not in form. But things that differ in number differ also in form, as we have
5 adequately shown above in the chapter on form, though the diversity of the proper form of anything cannot be known to us except through certain external effects and accidents, as they call them. Then single men show disparity among themselves, therefore they are opposed; but things opposed among
10 themselves cannot have the same form; hence they differ in form and not merely in number. So according to Laërtius (*In Zenone*) the Stoics teach that Socrates is the lowest species; still more Aristotle (*De partibus* 1.4) calls Socrates and Coriscus the lowest species. Thus the jurisconsults call man
15 the genus, and make Stichus and Pamphilius species.

Genus and species are signs of causes and effects.

For in an animal there is corporeal essence which is matter commonly pertaining to the species, and also the faculty of life and sense, which form also commonly is connected with
20 species. Therefore *genus contains causes which pertain in common to its species, and on the contrary the species also contain the effects of their genus.*

Hence genus as universal excels in dignity because it indicates the cause.

25 Aristotle says the same thing in the *Posterior Analytics* 1.24.

The distribution of a genus into its species is of very great value but is difficult and rarely met with.

Excellit quidem quia quicquid in artibus ex causis & effectis sumitur, id totum ferè generis & speciei notionibus comprehenditur: difficilis est, cùm quia formæ, unde species oriuntur, difficiles itidem inventu sunt; tum etiam propter vocum 5 penuriam, quibus genera & species apte nominentur.

Attamen illustrationis & exempli gratia afferemus quod poterimus. *Ovidius.* I. *Metam.* dividit animal in quinque species, stellas, aves, bestias, pisces, homines: stellis animam tribuens, ut etiam quidam Philosophi tribuerunt.

10 *Neu regio foret ulla suis animalibus orba,*
Astra tenent cæleste solum formæque deorum: &c.

Sic *Cic. Offic.* I. virtutem dividit in species quatuor, prudentiam, justitiam, fortitudinem, temperantiam; quæ tamen ipsæ non ponuntur in distributione, sed, quod idem est, earum 15 formæ. *Sed omne quod honestum est, id quatuor partium oritur ex aliqua: aut enim in perspicientia veri solertiáque versatur, aut in societate hominum tuenda, tribuendóque suum unicuique, & rerum contractarum fide; aut in animi excelsi atque invicti magnitudine ac robore; aut in omnibus quæ 20 fiunt, quæque dicuntur, ordine & modo, in quo inest modestia & temperantia.*

It is of value since whatever in the arts is taken from causes and effects is almost all comprehended under notions of genus and species; it is difficult because the forms whence the species are derived are difficult to light upon, and also because of the
5 scarcity of words by which genus and species may aptly be called.

Yet for the sake of illustration and example we shall bring forward what we can. Ovid (*Metamorphoses* 1) divides animal into five species, namely, stars, birds, beasts, fishes, and
10 men, attributing soul to the stars as some philosophers have done:

> That no kind, place, or region should be
> Of living things left void or else empty,
> The gods do make their habitation
> 15 Among the stars, etc.

Thus Cicero in *De officiis* 1 divides virtue into four species, prudence, justice, fortitude, and temperance, which indeed are not themselves placed in distribution, but—what comes to the same thing—their forms: "All things that are honest
20 do rise of one of these four parts. Either it consisteth in the perfect knowledge of the truth and quickness of wit, or in the defending of the society and fellowship of man by giving to every man his right and fulfilling of things promised, or in the noble courage and strength of a valiant and mighty
25 spirit, or, last, in observing a good manner and order in all things either done or said, in the which modesty and temperance consisteth."

Hæc quidem, ut dixi, est *distributio generis in specierum formas;* quæ perinde est ac si in ipsas species esset; *quia formæ cum genere constituunt suas species.*

Genus & species non solum tractantur hac simplici divi-
5 *sionis formula, sed etiam separatim alterum ex altero.*

Hoc est, quod de toto genere, id de omnibus etiam speciebus rectè affirmatur. *Sic Cicero,* pro *Archia,* poëticam cum eloquentia comparans, quæ sunt species artis, cognatas esse ait inter se, quia idem de artibus in genere, humanioribus præ-
10 sertim, affirmatur. *Etenim omnes artes, quæ ad humanitatem pertinent, habent quoddam commune vinculum, & quasi cognatione quadam inter se continentur.*

Contra genus tractatur per species.

Hoc est, quod de omnibus speciebus, id de genere quoque
15 rectè affirmatur. Sic *Ovidius* probat, virtutem in rebus adversis clariorem esse, per inductionem specierum: quoniam scilicet virtus militis, nautæ, medici, rebus adversis spectatur. 4 *Trist.*

Hectora quis nosset, felix si Troia fuisset?
20 *Publica virtutis per malafacta via est:*
ars tua Tiphy *jacet, si non sit in æquore fluctus:*
si valeant homines, ars tua, Phœbe, *jacet.*
Quæ latet, inque bonis cessat non cognita rebus,
apparet virtus arguitúrque malis.

25 Cùm itaque genus tractetur etiam per species, ut superiore

This certainly, as I have said, is *distribution of the genus into the forms of the species;* which is the same as distribution into the species themselves, *since forms with genus constitute their species.*

5 *Genus and species are treated not merely by this formula of simple division, but also separately one from the other.*

This means that what can be affirmed of the whole genus is also rightly affirmed of all the species. Thus Cicero, in *Pro Archia,* comparing the arts of poetry and eloquence, which 10 are species of art, says that they are cognate among themselves, since the same is affirmed of the arts in general, especially the more humane ones: "For all arts which pertain to humanity have a certain common band and are contained (as it were) in a certain kinship among themselves."

15 *Conversely, the genus is treated through the species.*

That is, what is affirmed of all the species is properly affirmed of the genus also. Thus Ovid (*Tristia* 4) proves that virtue is the more shining in adverse circumstances by induction of the species; since evidently the virtue of the soldier, 20 sailor, and physician is seen in adverse conditions:

While Troy had peace, brave Hector was not known;
In public troubles virtue's force is shown.
If seas be calm, what need we Tiphys' skill?
What's Phœbus' art when men are healthful still?
25 While Fortune smiles brave virtue hidden lies,
But when she frowns it shines in all men's eyes.

Since in this way the genus is treated through the species,

regula docemur, & exempla specialia species eorum sint, quorum exempla sunt; hinc sequitur, *exempla specialia suo generi accommodata, hujus esse loci;* sive unum solum, sive per inductionem plura adhibeantur: specialia inquam, exempla
5 enim vel similia sunt, quæ similia arguunt; vel specialia, quæ arguunt suum genus; qualia fuerunt in singulis argumentorum capitibus ex poëtis & oratoribus desumpta. Exemplorum autem specialium, non solum in artib. cùm inveniendis tum tradendis usus planè est necessarius (nam inductione exem-
10 plorum præcepta colliguntur, & eorum usu illustrantur) verùm etiam in omni sermone, quoties res lucem desiderat. Cujusmodi est illud *Cic.* ad *Atticum: Urbem tu relinquas? Ergo idem si Galli venirent. Non est, inquit, in parietibus respub. at in aris & focis: fecit idem Themistocles: fluctum enim*
15 *totius barbariæ ferre urbs una non poterat. At idem Pericles non fecit, annum ferè post quinquagesimum, quum præter mœnia nihil teneret: nostri olim urbe reliqua capta, arcem tamen retinuerunt.* Hîc ab exemplo speciali in utramque partem disseritur. *Themistocles* deseruit *Athenas;* ergo urbem
20 deserere licet. *Pericles* non deseruit *Athenas;* nec *Romani Gallis* venientibus *Romam;* ergo urbs non est deserenda. Quod si hoc modo argumentaretur, *Themistocles* urbem reliquit, ergo mihi licet; argumentum esset à simili: nam exempla,

as we learn by the rule above, and special examples are the species of those of which the examples are given, it thence follows that *special examples fitted to their genus belong under this head,* whether one alone or through induction several
5 are brought up. I use the word *special* because examples are either similar, which argue similar things, or special, which argue their genus, such as have been taken from the poets and orators in single points of arguments. But not merely in discovering and teaching the arts is the use of special examples
10 obviously indispensable (for by induction from examples precepts are collected and by the use of examples they are illustrated) but even in every speech, as often as something needs to have light thrown on it. Of this sort is that of Cicero (*Ad Atticum*): "Wilt thou leave the city? Wouldst thou
15 have done the same when the Gauls came? 'The commonwealth,' he saith, 'is not in walls.' But it is in altars and religion. 'Themistocles did the same.' True, for one city could not bear up against the torrent of almost all Scythia. But Pericles did not do so about fifty years later when he kept
20 nothing but the walls; our forefathers, when the other parts of the city were taken, notwithstanding kept the fort." Here from a special example it is debated on either side: *Themistocles deserted Athens, hence it is permitted to desert the city; Pericles did not desert Athens nor did the Romans desert*
25 *Rome when the Gauls came, therefore the city should not be deserted.* If it should be argued in the form *Themistocles abandoned the city, therefore I may,* the argument would be from the like, for examples, when they are accommodated to

cùm ad alia specialia accommodantur, similia sunt vel dissimilia. Hujus autem loci ea demum sunt, quæ generi suo accommodantur.

Est & alia imperfectior distributio ex effectis, quando partes
5 non sunt propriè effecta totius, sed ipsarum partium. *Ut Cic.* de *Senect. Nautarum alii malos scandunt, alii per foros cursitant, alii sentinam exhauriunt; gubernator autem clavum tenet in puppi.* In hoc exemplo totum est nauta, quod est singulorum nautarum genus; partes, malum scandere, cursitare,
10 &c. Quæ tamen nautæ ut totius sive generis partes sive species non sunt, sed specierum, i.e. singulorum nautarum effecta sive officia, quibus ipsæ species, i.e. singuli nautæ inter se distinguuntur. Verùm quanto hæc distributio imperfectior est, tanto est frequentior. Usus autem illius præcipuus est, ut per-
15 fectioris raritatem suppleat; cùm distributio generis in species, ut supradictum est, tam difficilis inventu sit.

CAPUT XXVIII.

De Distributione è subjectis.

R*ELIQUA distributio est modo quodam consentaneorum, ut subjectorum & adjunctorum.*

Distributio è subjectis est, cùm partes sunt sub-
20 *jecta.* Id est quando veræ partes intellectæ subjectis distinguuntur vel adumbrantur.

Ut apud *Catullum:*

other specials, are likes or unlikes. But those certainly belong under this head which are accommodated to their genus.

There is another and less perfect distribution from effects when the parts are not properly effects of the whole, but of 5 the parts themselves. Cicero (*De senectute*) writes: "Some of the mariners climb the masts, others run up and down the gangways, some do make the pump empty, but the governor in the hinder part of the ship guideth the rudder." In this example the whole is sailor, which is the genus of the single 10 sailors, the parts are climbing the mast, running, etc. Yet these sailors are not parts or species of the whole or the genus, but effects or offices of species, that is, of single sailors, by which the species themselves, that is, the single sailors, are among themselves distinguished. Certainly, in propor- 15 tion as this distribution is more imperfect, it is the more frequent. But its use is special, in order that it may supplement the scarcity of the more perfect, since the distribution of the genus into species, as has been said above, is so difficult to come upon.

CHAPTER XXVIII.

Of distribution from subjects.

THE remaining distribution is of the consentanies after a fashion as subjects and adjuncts.

There is distribution from the subjects when the parts are subjects, that is, when the genuine parts that have been recognized are distinguished or set forth by their sub- 25 jects, as in Catullus:

Virginitas non tota tua est: ex parte parentum est.
tertia pars matri data, pars data tertia patri:
tertia sola tua est: noli pugnare duobus,
qui genero sua jura simul cum dote dederunt.

5 Virginitas puellæ vel jus potius virginitatis in tres partes dividitur subjectis distinctas, matre, patre & ipsa puella. Alterum exemplum ex cap. 26. huc transfertur, *Virgil.* 1. Georg. Ubi poëta exorditur opus suum à divisione in quatuor partes, subjectis suis occupantibus distinctas, segetes, arbores, pecora, 10 apes.

Quid faciat lætas segetes, quo sidere terram
vertere, Mæcenas, ulmísque adjungere vites
conveniat: quæ cura boum, quis cultus habendo
sit pecori, atque apibus quanta experientia parcis,
15 *hinc canere incipiam.*——

Tertium exemplum ex eodem etiam capite huc transfertur. *Cic.* pro *Muræna: Intelligo Judices, tres totius accusationis partes fuisse: & earum unam in reprehensione vitæ, alteram*

Thy maidenhead's not wholly thine I ween;
One part thy father gave, the part between
Thou of thy mother hadst; so that to thee
None but the third remaineth for to be.
5 Therefore resist not two, cast not away
The thing thy parents gave to thee I say.

The virginity of the girl, or rather the right of virginity, is divided into three parts distinguished by their subjects, mother, father, and the girl herself. Another example is 10 transferred here from chapter twenty-six, that in which Vergil (*Georgics* 1) introduces his work by division into four parts, distinguished by their occupying subjects, cornfields, trees, sheep, and bees:

Here first I will describe what is the cause
15 Doth make the corn so plentiful to rise,
Under what sign and moneth of the sun
Thou shalt begin to till thy field and ground,
Eke at what time thou may unto the elms
Set to the vines, and so shortly after this
20 What care thou ought to have of thy oxen,
And of thy cattle the food and husbanding,
And last of all how great experience
The sparing bees have into their science.

A third example from the same chapter is transferred here; 25 Cicero writes in *Pro Murœna:* "I understand, honorable judges, that there were three parts of the accusation, one in

in contentione dignitatis, tertiam in criminibus ambitûs esse versatam. Hîc tota accusatio in tria membra distribuitur, subjectis suis occupantibus distincta: atque in his tribus exemplis totum est integrum. Quartum exemplum est generis in species ex *Cic.* 5. *Tuscul. Sint sanè illa tria genera bonorum, dum corporis & externa jaceant humi, & tantummodo quia sumenda sunt, appellentur bona. Alia autem, divina illa, longè latéque se pandant, cælúmque contingant.* Hîc *Cicero* bona in tres species, quas ille genera vocat, dividit, subjectis suis distinctas; nempe animi, corporis & fortunæ.

CAPUT XXIX.

De Distributione ex Adjunctis.

DISTRIBUTIO *ex adjunctis est, quando partes sunt adjuncta.*

Ut hominum alii sani, alii ægri: alii divites, alii pauperes.

Sic *Virgil.* 1. *Georg.* mundum dividit in quinque partes; mediam torridam, duas extremas frigidas, & reliquas duas temperatas:

> *Quinque tenent cœlum zonæ, quarum una corusco*
> *semper sole rubens, & torrida semper ab igni:* &c.

rebuke and blaming of his life, another in contention and strife of dignity, the third to consist in the crimination of unlawful suit for offices." Here the whole accusation is distributed into three members, distinguished by their occupy-
5 ing subjects; and in these three examples the whole is an integer. A fourth example is of division of the genus into species, from Cicero (*Tusculan Disputations* 5): "There are truly those three kinds of good things; though the external goods of the body are but earthy, yet because they are to be
10 undertaken they are called goods. But those others are divine, they spread through the elements and touch the sky." Here Cicero divides goods into three species, which he calls genera, distinguished by their subjects; to wit, goods of mind, body, and fortune.

CHAPTER XXIX.

Of distribution from adjuncts.

THERE is distribution from adjuncts when the parts are adjuncts.

For example, some men are healthy, others sick; some are rich, others poor.

Thus Vergil (*Georgics* 1) divides the world into five
20 parts; the middle is torrid, the two extremes frigid, and the other two temperate:

> Five zones the heavens do hold, the middle hot;
> The sun there burns, cold in it there is not, etc.

Cæsar 1. *Belli Gall. Gallia est omnis divisa in tres partes: quarum unam incolunt Belgæ, aliam Aquitani, tertiam, qui, ipsorum lingua Celtæ, nostra, Galli appellantur.*

In distributionibus hujusmodi imperfectis advertendum est
5 id quod videtur distribui. Nam si id totius rationem habet, integri vel generis, distributio est; si non habet rationem totius, sed simplex aliquod argumentum est, ut causa, effectum, subjectum, adjunctum, non est distributio sed enumeratio potius, vel causarum plurium ejusdem effecti, vel effectorum
10 plurium ejusdem causæ, vel subjectorum plurium ejusdem adjuncti, vel denique adjunctorum plurium ejusdem subjecti. Hoc genere distributionis imperfecto argumenta sæpe quorum veræ species nullæ apparent, modis quibusdam distinguuntur, modos autem supra in adjunctis posuimus. Sic
15 in causis, *procreans* & *conservans, modi* efficientis, non *species,* dicuntur: quia non differunt inter se ut species per differentias oppositas, sed ita ut uni & eidem efficienti convenire queant; quandoquidem quæ causa procreat, eadem ferè conservat; potéstque efficere idem vel solus, vel cum aliis; non-
20 nulla vel per se, vel per accidens.

Cæsar illustrates it in his *Gallic War* I: "Gallia is parted into three parts, whereof the people called Belgi do hold one, the Aquitani another part, and the third those who in their tongue are called Celts, in our language the Gauls."

5 In imperfect distributions of this sort that which seems to be distributed must be observed. For if this holds the reason for being of the whole, there is distribution of the integer or the genus; if it does not hold the reason for the whole, but is some simple argument, as cause, effect, subject, adjunct, there 10 is no distribution but rather enumeration either of several causes of the same effect or of several effects of the same cause or of several subjects of the same adjunct or finally of several adjuncts of the same subject. In this imperfect kind of distribution often arguments of which no true species appear 15 are distinguished by certain modes, but we have set forth the modes above among the adjuncts. Thus among the causes *procreant* and *conserving* are called *modes* of the efficient, not *species,* since they do not differ among themselves as species through opposite differences, but in such a way that they are 20 able to agree in one and the same efficient, since the same cause which procreates also usually conserves, and is likewise able to produce an effect either alone or with others, and can cause some things either through itself or through an accident.

CAPUT XXX.

De Definitione.

DEFINITIO in tradendis artibus est usu quidem prior distributione (prius enim definitur unaquæque res quàm distribuitur) natura tamen & inveniendi ordine est posterior: genus enim, quo non adhibito, si quod sit, nulla definitio constitui potest, à distributione, qui proprius generis est locus, mutuum accipit.

Definitio est, cum explicatur quid res sit.

Definitio vocatur, eo quòd rei cujusque essentiam definit, eámque suis quasi finibus circumscribit.

Atque ut definitio arguit sive explicat definitum, sic vicissim à definito argui potest. Quæ quanquam argumentorum omnium affectio communis est arguere inter se vicissim & argui, hîc tamen eandem ob causam facta mentio est definiti, ob quam in capite notationis facta est nominis; ne argumentorum numero excludi videatur, cùm neque ejusdem sit nominis cum definitione quam arguit, neque caput sibi peculiare obtineat; sicut alia argumentorum paria, quæ nominis ejusdem non sunt. Ad reciprocationem autem quod attinet, quæ definitioni cum distributione communis est, ea definitionis & definiti manifestissima est: Logica enim est ars bene ratiocinandi; & vicissim, ars bene ratiocinandi est Logica. Atque ad hunc modum omnis definitio, ut nonnulli rectè monue-

CHAPTER XXX.

Of definition.

IN treating of the arts definition is to be used before distribution (for anything whatever is defined before it is distributed), but by nature and the order of discovery it is posterior, because genus is borrowed from distribution,
5 which is its proper place, by definition, and when genus is not used, if that is possible, no definition can be constituted.

We have a definition when it is explained what a thing is.

It is called definition in that it defines the essence of a thing, and circumscribes it as though by its boundaries.

10 And as the definition argues or explains what is defined, thus *in turn it can be argued from the thing defined.* Though it is a common affect of all arguments to argue and be argued among themselves in turn, here nevertheless mention is made of the thing defined for the same reason as in the chapter on
15 notation the name is mentioned, lest it should seem to be excluded from the number of the arguments, when it is not of the same name with the definition which it argues, and does not obtain a class peculiar to itself, as do other counterparts of arguments which are not of the same name. As to recipro-
20 cation, which is common to definition and distribution, that of the definition and the thing defined is most manifest, for logic is the art of thinking well, and in turn the art of thinking well is logic. So according to this mode every definition, as some rightly advise, should be examined by conversion,

runt, conversione examinanda est: unde *Boëthius, Top. 5. omnis definitio, rei, quam definit, adæquatur.*

Definitio est perfecta aut imperfecta: illa propriè definitio, hæc descriptio dicitur.

5 *Definitio perfecta est, quæ constat è solis causis essentiam constituentibus.* Redundat ergo in definitione perfecta quicquid præterea ponitur.

Causæ autem illæ genere & forma comprehenduntur.

Genus enim & forma (quæ sunt quasi corpus & anima defi-
10 nitionis) totam rei essentiam constituunt. Non ita tamen necessariò requiritur in definitione perfecta genus, ut perfecta non sit nisi genus habeat: primùm enim, summorum generum, ut argumenti in Logica inventione, genus nullum est; sed tota eorum essentia sub ipsa forma continetur; quæ etiam
15 materiam iis convenientem complectitur; deinde fieri potest ut ipsæ causæ facilius occurrant quam earum symbolum genus. Itaque si ex ipsis causis definitio constat, perfecta erit; si ex genere, succinctior tantum. Genus autem proximum, non remotum, in definitione semper est ponendum: qui enim
20 proximum ponit, remotiora etiam posuit: nisi proximum fortè anonymum sit; tum enim & quotiescunque generis, sive anonymum sit sive non, paulo ante facta mentio est, abesse genus in definitione, & rectè subintelligi potest: ut in hac ipsa

whence Boethius (*Topics* 5) writes that "every definition is equalled to the thing which it defines."

A definition is perfect or imperfect; the first is properly called a definition, the second a description.

5 *A perfect definition is that which depends only on the causes constituting the essence of the thing defined.* Whatever goes beyond this, therefore, is redundant in a perfect definition.

But such causes are comprehended in genus and form.

10 For genus and form (which are as it were the body and mind of the definition) constitute the whole essence of the thing. But not so necessarily is the genus required in a perfect definition that it cannot be perfect without the genus, for, first, there is no genus for the highest genera, such as the ar-
15 gument in logical invention, but their whole essence is contained in the form itself, which also includes the matter suitable to them; then it can be true that the causes themselves occur more easily than the genus which is their symbol. Hence if the definition is made up from the causes themselves, it will
20 be perfect; if from genus, it merely will be more succinct. But the nearest genus, not the remote one, must always be stated in a definition—for he who states the nearest one has stated also the remote one—except when the nearest genus may happen to be anonymous; then, just as often as mention has
25 a little before been made of genus, whether anonymous or not, the genus can be lacking in the definition and can be rightly supplied in thought, as in this definition of definition the

definitionis definitione, genus remotum, nempe ortum argumentum; tum etiam proximum, nempe reale & compositum, subintelligitur. Quam autem hîc formam in definitione appellamus, plerique differentiam vocant. Sed differentia formæ fructus est: & nisi in rerum collatione, quæ in definitione nulla est, non apparet; & forma ipsa est unde præcipua rerum explicatio sumitur; præcipuum ergo in definitione locum habet.

Atque hoc modo definitur homo, animal rationale: nempe genere, *animal,* intelligimus, ut dictum est, essentiam corpoream plenam vitæ & sensus, quæ materies hominis est, & pars formæ: cui si addas *rationale,* totam formam hominis comprehendes, vitæ, sensus, rationis facultate.

Itaque *perfecta definitio nihil aliud est, quàm universale symbolum causarum essentiam rei & naturam constituentium.*

Tales definitiones sunt artium. Grammatica est ars bene loquendi. Rhetorica bene dicendi. Logica bene ratiocinandi. Arithmetica bene numerandi. Geometria bene metiendi. Nam genere *ars* intelligimus præceptorum ordine dispositorum comprehensionem, quæ materies est cujusque artis & pars formæ, sive forma communis, cui si addas formam cujusque artis propriam (quæ finem quoque sub se comprehendit, ut dictum est cap. 8.) habes totam artis essentiam explicatam, quæ perfecta definitio est.

remote genus, that is, the derived argument, as well as the proximate, that is the actual and complex argument, is supplied in thought. But what we here call form in definition many call difference. But difference is the fruit of form, and
5 except in the comparison of things, of which there is none in definition, does not appear, and the form itself is that whence the special explanation of things is taken; it has, therefore, a special place in definition.

And so in this mode man is defined as a rational animal;
10 that is, we understand by the genus *animal,* as has been said, a corporeal essence full of life and sense, which is the matter of man and part of his form. If to this you add *rational* you comprehend the whole form of man, by the capacity for life, sense, and reason.

15 *And so a perfect definition is nothing else than a universal symbol of the causes constituting the essence and nature of a thing.*

Such are the definitions of the arts. The art of grammar is the art of using words well; rhetoric is the art of speaking
20 well; logic is the art of thinking well; arithmetic of numbering well; geometry of measuring well. For by the genus *art* we understand the uniting into a whole of precepts disposed in order, which is the matter of any art and part of its form, or its common form, to which if you add the form proper to
25 any art (which also, as is said in chapter eight, comprehends under itself its end), you have the entire essence of the art explicated, which gives a perfect definition.

Ad regulas consequentiæ quod attinet, nempe à definitione ad definitum; & contrà, affirmatè vel negatè; hæc omnia reciprocatio, quæ distributionis quoque fuit, satis clarè suo loco exposuit.

CAPUT XXXI.

De Descriptione.

DEFINITIONES perfectæ propter causarum & præsertim formarum obscuritatem, difficiles inventu sunt: ad supplendam igitur earum raritatem, *descriptio* inventa est.

10 *Descriptio est definitio imperfecta, ex aliis etiam argumentis rem definiens.* Id est, ex quibusvis aliis rem quoquo modo explicans.

Ubi itaque forma haberi non potest (nam genera ferè notiora sunt) proprietas loco formæ seu differentiæ accipienda 15 est: ut, *angelus est substantia incorporea: equus est animal hinnibile,* &c. Adjuncta sive accidentia, quæ vocantur (quia substantiæ solæ, ut inquit *Aristot. l.* 6. *Metaph. c.* 5. primariò definiuntur, accidentia secundariò tantùm) propria quidem genere, subjecto, causáque proxima vel efficiente, vel finali, 20 vel utrâque definiuntur. Genere & subjecto solo; ut, *simitas est curvitas nasi:* subjecto & efficiente; ut, *tonitru est sonus fractæ nubis, ob ignem oppressum; quantitas continua est adjunctum corporis, ab extensione materiæ:* finali; ut, *sensus est*

All that pertains to the rules of consequence, namely from definition to the defined, and the opposite, affirmatively or negatively, reciprocation, which also pertains to distribution, has clearly enough explained in its place.

CHAPTER XXXI.

Of description.

BECAUSE of the obscurity of causes and especially of forms, perfect definitions are difficult to come upon. *Description* has been devised to supply their scarcity.

Description is an imperfect *definition, defining a thing through other arguments,* that is, explaining the thing in
10 some way from whatever is available.

So where form cannot be had (for the genera are commonly better known) a property must be accepted in place of form or distinguishing difference, as when it is said *An angel is an incorporeal substance;* or *A horse is an animal that*
15 *whinnies,* etc. Adjuncts or accidents, which are called proper (for substances alone, as Aristotle says in the *Metaphysics* 6. 5, are primarily defined, accidents only secondarily) are defined by genus, subject, proximate or efficient cause, or final cause, or both. Definition by genus and subject alone
20 appears in the example: *Simitas is crookedness of the nose.* That by subject and efficient is illustrated in *Thunder is the sound of a cloud broken by compressed fire,* and in *Continuous quantity is an adjunct of body from the extension of*

facultas naturalis in animali, ad judicandum de singularibus: vel utrâque; ut, *respiratio est attractio & expulsio aëris reciproca à pulmonibus facta, ad cordis refrigerationem.* Omittitur enim sæpe subjectum in definitione propriorum, quippe 5 quòd ex genere vel ex causa intelligitur: ut, *memoria est sensus internus conservans imagines rerum cognitarum.* Non dicitur *sensus internus animalis,* addito nempe subjecto, quia id mentione *sensûs* intelligitur. Potentiæ naturales actione sua & causa efficiente definiuntur: ut, *risibilitas est facultas ri-* 10 *dendi, orta ab anima rationali.* Habitus vel fine vel objecto quæ sæpe coincidunt definiuntur: fine; ut, *Logica est ars bene ratiocinandi:* objecto; ut, *Physica est scientia rerum naturalium.* Qualitates patibiles definiuntur subjecto & efficiente: ut *color est qualitas corporis mixti, orta ex contemperatione* 15 *lucidi & opaci.* Actiones ferè subjecto, efficiente & fine definiuntur. Relationes relatis inter se & fundamento sive causa: ut, *paternitas est relatio patris ad filium, ex procreatione orta.*

Adjuncta communia objecto, efficiente, finali, vel ex his quot sunt ex usu, definiuntur: ut, *albedo est color, ortus ex* 20 *lucido opacum superante.*

Illud modo generatim in descriptionib. cavendum, ne causa pro genere habeatur: ut cùm dubitatio describitur, æqualitas rationum; sanitas, symmetria humorum; dolor, solutio con-

matter. Definition is by final cause in *Sense is a natural faculty in an animal, for judging individual things*. Both causes appear in *Respiration is the reciprocal attraction and expulsion of air made by the lungs for the cooling of the heart*. The
5 subject is often omitted in the definition of things proper to it, being understood from genus or from cause, as when it is said: *Memory is an internal sense conserving the images* of things that have been recognized. It is not specified as the *internal sense of an animal,* that is, with the addition of the
10 subject, since that is understood on the mention of *sense*. Natural powers are defined by their action and efficient cause, as *Risibility is the capacity to laugh, sprung from a rational soul*. Habits are defined either by end or object, which often coincide. Definition is by end in *Logic is the art of thinking*
15 *well;* by object in *Physics is the knowledge of natural things*. Qualities that can be experienced are defined by subject and efficient, as *Color is the quality of a mixed body, sprung from a proper mixture of lucid and opaque*. Actions are usually defined by subject, efficient, and end. Relations are defined
20 by the things related among themselves and by foundation or cause, as *Paternity is the relation of father to son, derived from procreation*.

Common adjuncts are defined by object, efficient, final, or by as many of these as are applicable, as *Whiteness is a color*
25 *produced by the lucid overcoming the opaque*.

But generally in descriptions, the taking of cause for genus should be avoided, as when doubt is described the taking of equality of reasons as the genus; when health, equality of the

tinui; eclipsis lunæ, interpositio terræ: aut subjectum; ut, ventus est aër motus; justitia est voluntas constans; vulnus est pars carnis dilacerata; peccatum originis est natura corrupta, & similia.

5 Cæterum in his certæ regulæ dari non possunt. Aliquando enim ex remoto solùm contrario fit descriptio: ut,

> *Virtus est vitium fugere, & sapientia prima*
> *Stultitia caruisse.—*

Aliquando planè arbitraria est.

10 Hinc etsi unica rei definitio, plures tamen descriptiones esse possunt.

Ut autem definitio definito, quod suprà monuimus, ita etiam descriptio descripto vicissim argui potest. Verùm non affectio solùm hæc mutua inter descriptionem & rem descrip-15 tam intercedit, sed etiam reciprocatio; juxta communem illam distributionis ac definitionis regulam, suprà, cap. 25. traditam; quâ descriptio quoque propria rei descriptæ & reciproca esse debet. Quamvis enim in descriptionibus, multa sæpe congeruntur, quorum aliqua fortè latius patent, quàm id quod 20 describitur, juncta tamen æquantur descripto, descriptionémque propriam reddunt; sin minus, vitiosa atque inutilis de-

humors; when pain, the breaking up of a unit; when eclipse of the moon, interposition of the earth. Likewise the subject must not be taken for the genus, as in the statements: *Wind is air moved; justice is a constant will; a wound is a part of* 5 *the flesh torn away; original sin is nature corrupted,* and the like.

Otherwise fixed rules cannot be given in these instances. For sometimes a description is made from a remote contrary alone, as

10 Virtue is flight from vice, and wisdom begins
When folly's gone.

Sometimes it is clearly arbitrary.

Therefore, though there is but one definition of a thing, there can be many descriptions.

15 But as the definition can be argued from the thing defined, as we have shown above, so also the description can in turn be argued from the thing described. But there is not merely this mutual affect alone between the description and the thing described, but also a reciprocation, according to that common 20 rule of distribution and definition set forth in chapter twenty-five, above, according to which a description ought to be proper to the thing described and reciprocal. For sometimes in various descriptions many things are brought together of which some perhaps extend more widely than that which is 25 described, but when joined together they are made equal with the thing described and render the description proper; if less is done, the description must be held vicious and useless.

scriptio censenda est. *Ut, homo est animal mortale, capax disciplinæ.* Hîc cum aliqua causa (materia scilicet & communi forma, quæ sub genere *animal* continetur) miscentur duæ circumstantiæ sive adjuncta, alterum commune, scilicet
5 *mortale,* alterum proprium, *capax disciplinæ.* At quorsum, inquis illud *mortale,* cùm nullum animal non sit mortale? Quia nempe *Aristot.* cujus hæc descriptio est, *Top.* 5. 1. animalia quædam ait esse immortalia, *Top.* 4. 2. & in eodem capite, Deum ipsum ζῶον ἀθάνατον, i.e. *immortale animal*
10 vocat.

Sed hæc succincta brevitas non est in hac specie perpetua; quæ sæpe illustriorem & copiosiorem explicationem desiderat.

Succinctæ descriptiones quæ perfectas æmulantur defini-
15 tiones, usum habent præcipuè in artibus tradendis ac disputationibus. Prolixiores illæ, utpote ad aures vulgi magis accommodatæ, apud oratores ac poëtas frequentiùs occurrunt.

Sic gloria describitur in *Miloniana: sed tamen ex omnibus præmiis virtutis, si esset habenda ratio præmiorum, amplissi-*
20 *mum esse præmium gloriam: hanc unam, quæ brevitatem vitæ posteritatis memoria consolaretur; quæ efficeret, ut absentes, adessemus; mortui, viveremus: hanc denique esse, cujus gradibus etiam homines in cœlum videantur ascendere.* Descriptio hæc gloriæ constat ex genere, *præmio* nempe *vir-*
25 *tutis;* adjuncta amplitudine, eáque aucta à minore, quod sit omnium amplissima; quatuor deinde effecta ejus adjiciuntur.

It may, for example, be said: *Man is a mortal animal with a capacity for science.* Here with some cause (to wit, the matter and the common form which are contained in the genus *animal*) are mingled two circumstances or adjuncts, one com-
5 mon, that is, *mortal,* the other proper, namely, *with a capacity for science.* But why, you ask, is the word *mortal* used, when there is no animal that is not mortal? The answer is that Aristotle (*Topics* 5.1), whose description this is, says that certain animals are immortal (*Topics* 4.2), and in the same
10 chapter calls God himself ζῶον ἀθάνατον, that is an *immortal animal.*

But this succinct brevity is not invariable in this species, which often asks clearer and more copious explanation.

Succinct descriptions which emulate perfect definitions
15 have especial use in treating the arts and in disputations. Those of longer form, as they are more fitted to the ears of the many, occur more frequently in the orators and poets.

Thus glory is described in the *Milonian Oration:* "Yet of all the rewards of virtue, if there were a respect to be had of
20 rewards, I judge glory to be the most great, which only doth comfort the shortness of this life with the memory of the posterity to come, which doth make us when we be absent to be as present, and when we be dead doth make us to live. And likewise fame is that by whose occasion and mean men seem
25 to ascend and mount up to the heavens above." This description of glory depends on the genus, namely on the *reward of virtue;* amplitude is adjoined and increased by the minor that it is most ample of all; then four effects of it are added.

Sic 4 *Æneid.* fama describitur:

Ex templo Libiæ *magnas it fama per urbes,*
fama malum; quo non aliud velocius ullum
mobilitate viget, virésque acquirit eundo. &c.

5 Describitur fama, 1. à genere, *malum.* 2. ab adjuncta velocitate, quæ illustratur à majore negato, *quo non aliud velocius:* tum duplici effecto aliarum rerum dissimili, quòd,

mobilitate vigit, virésque acquirit eundo.

3. Ab adjuncta varietate, quæ ostenditur ex aliis adjunctis,
10 quòd sit primò *parva,* ídque arguitur causa, scilicet *metu,* & circumstantia temporis, *primò* nempe; tum subitò grandior facta incremento exigui temporis incredibili, ídque ostenditur trib. effectis, quæ singula subjectis suis illustrantur,

——*mox sese attollit in auras:*
15 *ingreditúrque solo, & caput inter nubila condit.*

4. A causa procreante, *illam terra parens,*—mater scilicet gigantum, & efficiendi modo, consilio nempe sive impetu naturali, *ira irritata deorum,* qui gigantes occiderant; causa autem procreans communis illustrata tempore adjuncto, & com-
20 muni testimonio,

In *Æneid* 4 Fame is thus described:

From Libia's temple cometh forth great Fame,
Nought swifter than ill news which bears this name,
Moving she grows, by going strength she gets, etc.

5 Fame is described, 1, by her genus, as *an evil thing.*

2, She is described by her adjunct of *swiftness,* which is illustrated by the major which is denied, *nought swifter,* and then by an effect, with two unlike parts, of other things, because

10 Moving she grows, by going strength she gets.

3, By the adjunct of variety, which is shown by the other adjuncts, because first she may be *little,* and this is argued by the cause, to wit, *fear,* and by the circumstances of time, namely, *at first;* then quickly she becomes greater, increasing 15 in a way that seems incredible in so scant a time, and this is shown by three effects, which are illustrated one by one by their subjects:

Anon with winds she fleets,
Walks on the earth, her head she lifts to th' sky.

20 4, She is further described by her procreating cause, *Earth brought her forth*—that is the mother of the giants—, and by its mode of working, namely by counsel or natural force, *exasperated with anger against the gods* who had killed the giants; but the common procreating cause is explained by the 25 adjunct of time and by common testimony:

extremam, ut perhibent, Cæo Enceladóque sororem
progenuit;

rursus illustratam ab adjunctis,

——pedibus celerem, & pernicibus alis,
5 *monstrum horrendum, ingens.——*

Deinde à partibus corporis & membris, iisque paribus,

——cui quot sunt corpore plumæ,
tot vigiles oculi subter, mirabile dictu,
tot linguæ, totidem ora sonant, tot subrigit aures:

10 Tum ab effectis nocturnis, iisque partim affirmatis quæ subjectis locis illustrantur,

nocte volat cœli medio, terræque per umbram
stridens,

partim negatis,

15 *nec dulci declinat lumina somno:*

Tum diurnis, eáque illustrantur & subjectis locis, & adjuncto situ sedendi,

luce sedet custos, aut summi culmine tecti,
turribus aut altis & magnas territat urbes.

Of Cæus and Enceladus I ween
She was the last-born sister.

5, She is further explained by her adjuncts:

Her feet were swift, her wings most hurtful were,
5 A horrid monster, wicked, full of fear.

6, Then comes illustration from the parts of her body and her members, which are equal in number:

As many feathers as upon her are,
So many eyes attend her everywhere,
10 So many tongues, so many mouths do sound,
So many ears do listen her around.

7, Then she is described by her nocturnal effects; such of these as are affirmed are explained by the mention of places subject to them:

15 In night she flies through heaven, and in the shade
About the earth she goes.

Others are denied:

Nor does she close her eyes in sweet repose.

And there follow the diurnal effects, which are explained by
20 subjected places and by the adjunct of the position of her seat:

She sitteth in the light on houses high,
And causeth towns to quiver fearfully.

Ab adjunctis denique paribus;

tam ficti pravíque tenax quam nuntia veri.

Tales sunt descriptiones plantarum, animalium in Physicis; item fluminum, montium, urbium apud Geographos & Historicos; personarum denique apud Poetas & Oratores.

CAPUT XXXII.

De Testimonio divino.

E*XPOSITO artificiali argumento, sequitur inartificiale. Argumentum inartificiale est quod non sua natura, sed assumpta artificialis alicujus argumenti vi arguit. Id uno nomine* Testimonium *dicitur.* Nempe, ut inquit *Cic.* in *Top. quòd ab aliqua externa re sumitur ad faciendam fidem.*

Inartificiale autem dicitur, non quòd artis ope & auxilio non inveniatur (siquidem de eo inveniendo, ut inquit *Cicero,* Partit. in arte præcipitur) sed quod ex se suaque natura artis hujus & facultatis arguendi expers sit. Potest etiam assumptum dici, quod assumpta vi arguit, non sua. Argumentum enim inartificiale naturam rei non attingit, nedum arguit, ut

8, Finally from her equal adjuncts:

As well a bruiter of things false that be
As messenger of truth and verity.

Such are the descriptions of plants and living creatures by
5 naturalists, likewise of rivers, mountains, and cities by geographers and historians, and finally of persons by poets and orators.

CHAPTER XXXII.

Of divine testimony.

S*INCE the artificial argument has been set forth, the inartificial follows.*

The inartificial argument is one which argues not by its own nature, but by the force which it takes from some artificial argument.

In one word this is called testimony, that is, as Cicero says in the *Topics,* what is taken from some external thing to
15 produce faith.

But it is called inartificial not because it is not found out by means of the resources and aid of the art of logic (if indeed, as says Cicero in *De partitione,* this finding out is taught in the art) but because in itself and its nature it has no share in
20 this art and in the faculty of arguing something. It can also be called an assumed argument, because it argues by assumed force, not by its own. For an inartificial argument does not touch the nature of the thing, nor does it argue as the artificial

artificiale solet, neque rei affectio, sicut artificiale, est; sed est nuda cujuspiam aliqua de re attestatio, sive attestantis affirmatio aut negatio. Res autem neque propter affirmationem sunt, neque propter negationem non sunt: testimonium igitur ex se 5 suáque natura non arguit; *sed assumpta artificialis alicujus argumenti vi.* Vis autem hæc est testantis auctoritas, à qua omnis testimonii fides pendet. Auctoritas autem variis in argumentis consistit, sed in effectis testantis & in adjunctis præcipuè cernitur.

10 *Itaque cum exquisita rerum veritas* sive natura *subtiliùs exquiritur, perexiguam probationis vim testimonium habet.*

Hinc *Cic.* I de Nat. *Non tam auctores,* inquit, *in disputando, quàm rationum momenta quærenda sunt.*

In civilibus autem & humanis rebus, ubi de facto quæritur, 15 *plerumque hoc argumentum præcipuam fidem è moribus arguentis efficit, si prudentia, probitas & benevolentia affuerint.*

Horum unum aliquod si deest, vel per imprudentiam testis, vel propter improbitatem, vel inimicitiarum denique aut ni-20 miæ gratiæ causa, falsum sæpe pro testimonio dicitur.

Testimonium est divinum vel humanum.

Et rectè quidem in species efficientibus suis causis distinctas dividitur. Ab efficientibus enim maximè testimonium suas vires assumit. Effectum itaque est, si ad testem spectas; testi-

argument is accustomed to, nor is it an affect of the thing as is the artificial, but is a mere attestation by some one concerning something, or the affirmation or denial of a witness. But things do not exist because of affirmation nor are they with-
5 out existence because of denial; therefore testimony from itself and its nature does not prove anything, but *through the assumed force of some artificial argument.* This force, however, is the authority of the witness, on which depends all the reliability of testimony. Authority depends on various argu-
10 ments, but is especially to be discerned in the effects of the one bearing witness and in adjuncts.

Hence when the deepest truth or nature *of things is carefully sought out, testimony has little force for proof.*

Cicero (*De natura deorum* 1) therefore writes: "In de-
15 bating one should not search for authors so much as for the power of reasons."

Yet commonly *in civil and human affairs,* where a fact is sought for, *this argument gains especial credit from the character of the man arguing, if he is a person of prudence, probity,*
20 *and benevolence.*

If one of these is lacking, falsehood is often given for testimony, either through the imprudence of the witness, or because he lacks probity, or because of some feelings of enmity or of too much gratitude.

25 *Testimony is divine or human.*

It is rightly divided into distinct species by its efficient causes. For from the efficients especially testimony gains its strength; thus it is effect if you look upon the witness, and

monium, si ad rem testatam. Perexiguam autem vim probationis in exquisita veritate & natura rerum pervestiganda communiter tribui testimonio quod tam ad divinum quàm ad humanum pertinere videatur, id cur quempiam offendat, non 5 video: testimonium enim sive divinum sit sive humanum, peræque vim omnem ab authore, nullam in se habet. Et divinum quidem testimonium affirmat vel negat rem ita esse, facitque ut credam; non probat, non docet, non facit ut sciam aut intelligam cur ita sit, nisi rationes quoque adhibeat.

10 *Testimonium divinum est quod Deum habet authorem.*

In divinis testimoniis numerantur non solum deorum oracula, sed etiam responsa vatum & fatidicorum.

Vera hæc sint an ficta, veri numinis an falsi, Logicus non laborat, sed quam modò vim arguendi unumquodque habeat. 15 Itaque in civilib. etiam & humanis rebus testimonium divinum perinde vim probationis habet, ut ejus author verus est aut falsus Deus.

Hujusmodi sunt ista *Catilin.* 3. *Nam ut illa omittam, visas nocturno tempore ab occidente faces, ardorémque cœli; ut* 20 *fulminum jactus, ut terræ motus, cæteráque, quæ ita multa, nobis consulibus, facta sunt, ut hæc, quæ nunc fiunt, canere dii immortales viderentur.*

testimony if you look at the thing testified. Yet I commonly attribute to testimony very little power for proof in investigations of the deepest truth and nature of things; this would seem to apply to divine as well as human testimony, and I
5 do not see why it should offend any one, for testimony whether human or divine equally gets all its force from the author, and has none in itself. And divine testimony affirms or denies that a thing is so and brings about that I believe; it does not prove, it does not teach, it does not cause me to
10 know or understand why things are so, unless it also brings forward reasons.

Divine testimony is that which has God as an author.

In divine testimony is included not merely the oracles of the gods, but also the responses of prophets and soothseers.

15 Whether these are true or false, or by a true god or a false one, the logician does not consider, but merely what force for arguing each one has. Thus in civil and human affairs divine testimony has the power of proof, in proportion as its author is a true or a false god.

20 Of this sort are the testimonies given in *In Catilinam* 3: "And to omit the lightning torches which did appear by night in the occident, the vehement and parching heat of the heavens, as thraws of lightnings and fire breaking out of the clouds, earthquakes, and many other such tempests which, I
25 being consul, did appear, so that the gods with a loud voice seemed to sing those things which now be present."

CAPUT XXXIII.

De Testimonio humano.

TESTIMONIUM humanum est, quod authorem habet hominem.

Estque commune aut proprium.

Distributio hæc proponitur, non ut accurata aliqua divisio
5 (neque enim testimonio propria est) sed ut distinctio qualiscunque subalternarum specierum, ad quas inferiores species testimonii & exempla possint revocari. Atque, ut superior illa distinctio in divinum & humanum, ab efficiente quoque sumitur, qui sit persona publica sive communis, aut propria sive
10 privata.

Testimonium commune est, ut lex & illustris sententia.

Hæc enim duo exempla sunt potius quàm species: quibus adjungi potest *Fama;* quam *Cic.* in *Top.* quoddam multitudinis testimonium appellat; alii, consensum civitatis & publi-
15 cum testimonium vocant.

Legis autem & non scriptæ & scriptæ testimonium est pro Milone: Est enim, judices, non scripta, sed nata lex; quam non didicimus, accepimus, legimus; verùm ex natura ipsa arripuimus, hausimus, expressimus: ad quam non docti, sed facti;
20 *non instituti, sed imbuti sumus: ut, si vita nostra in aliquas insidias, si in vim, in tela, aut latronum aut inimicorum inci-*

CHAPTER XXXIII.

Of human testimony.

TESTIMONY which has a man as its author is human testimony.

It is common or proper.

This distribution is made not as a really accurate division
5 (for it is not proper to testimony) but as a sort of distinction of the subaltern species; to these inferior species of testimony examples can also be referred. So, like that distinction made in the preceding chapter into divine and human, it is also determined from the efficient, who is a person public or com-
10 mon, or proper or private.

There is common testimony, as a law or a famous maxim.

These two are examples rather than species; to them may be added *Fame,* which Cicero in the *Topics* calls a sort of testimony by the multitude; others call the agreement of the
15 state public testimony.

Moreover, according to Pro Milone testimony is found in both unwritten and written law: "There is a law, honorable judges, not written but naturally sprung up, which we have not learned, read, nor received of others but taken, received,
20 and drawn from nature itself, the which to attain we are not taught but made, not instructed by others, but taught by nature, to wit, that if our life should fall into an ambush or conspiracy, into the power and weapons either of robbers or of our enemies, that we should by all honest means deliver our-

disset, omnis honesta ratio esset expediendæ salutis. Et ibidem, *Quod si duodecim tabulæ nocturnum furem quoquo modo, diurnum autem, si se telo defenderit, interfici impunè voluerunt, quis est, qui* &c.

5 Restat illustris sententia; cujus generis sunt proverbia. Ut pares cum paribus facillime congregantur. Spartam nactus es, hanc exorna. Tum dicta sapientum: ut, Nosce teipsum. Ne quid nimis. Sponde, præsto est detrimentum. Quanquam enim hæc dicta singula à singulis fortasse auctoribus orta sunt, 10 tamen quia omnium in ore versantur, quasi omnium fiunt, & ad commune testimonium rectè referuntur.

Proprium testimonium est: ut *Platonis* illud, 1 ad Q. fratrem: *Atque ille quidem princeps ingenii & doctrinæ,* Plato, *tum denique fore beatas respub. putavit, si aut docti & sapi-* 15 *entes homines eas regere cœpissent, aut qui regerent, omne suum studium in doctrina ac sapientia collocassent.*

Talia sunt in poëtis. *Æneid.* 6.

Discite justitiam, moniti; & non temnere divos.

Sic *Homericis* illis versibus,

20 *Αἴας δ' ἐκ Σαλαμῖνος ἄγεν δυοκαίδεκα νῆας,*
Στῆσε δ' ἄγων ἵν' Ἀθηναίων ἵσταντο φάλαγγες,

Ajax autem ex Salamine duxit duodecim naves,
Constituit verò ducens, ubi Atheniensium stabant
phalanges,

selves from all danger." And in the same work: "If the Twelve Tables would a thief taken in the night to be killed by any means and a thief taken in the day, if he by weapon defended himself, to be killed also without danger, who is he
5 that" etc.

There remains the famous saying; proverbs are of this type, as the following: *Birds of a feather flock together. You were born in Sparta, adorn that city*. Then there are the sayings of wise men, as *Know thyself. Nothing in excess. Make your*
10 *vow, danger is upon you.* Although these individual sayings perhaps were produced by single authors, yet since they are in the mouths of all, as though they were made by all, they are properly to be referred to common testimony.

Proper testimony is illustrated by the opinion of Plato
15 quoted in *Ad Quintum fratrem* I: "And surely that prince of engine and knowledge, Plato, had this opinion that the commonwealths should then be most happy and blessed when that either learned and wise men began to govern them, or that those who had the care over them should give themselves
20 to wisdom and knowledge."

Examples of proper testimony are found also in the poets, as *Æneid* 6:

Learn righteousness, and dread the avenging deities.

Testimony likewise appears in these Homeric verses:

25 And out of Salamine
Great Ajax brought twelve sail, that with th'
Athenians did combine.

victi sunt in judicio *Megarenses,* quo contenderunt cum *Atheniensibus* de *Salamine* insula, utrique fortè civitati æquè vicina.

Atque hæc veterum fuere & absentium testimonia, & ferè
5 mortuorum; quæ de jure potissimum afferuntur.

Viventium & præsentium, quæ de facto plerunque testantur, non tantum sunt *cùm quæritur de fundo aut cæde & ejusmodi negotio aliquo, sed etiam obligationis, confessionis, jurisjurandi testimonia sunt.*

10 Obligationis exemplum est *Philipp.* 5. *Promitto, recipio, spondeo, P. C. Cæsarem talem semper fore civem, qualis hodie sit, qualémque eum maximè velle & optare debemus.*

Pignus etiam obligatio quædam est: ut apud *Virgil. Ecl.* 3.

Vis ergo inter nos quid possit uterque vicissim
15 *experiamur? Ego hanc vitulam (ne forte recuses,*
bis venit ad mulctram, binos alit ubere fœtus)
depono: tu dic, mecum quo pignore certes.

Confessio est vel libera, in qua cujusvis testimonium pro se levissimum contra se gravissimum censetur. Vel est expressa
20 *tormentis, quæ propriè quæstio dicitur.*

Because of these verses the Megareians lost the judicial decision when they strove with the Athenians over the island of Salamis, which was equally near to either of the two states.

And these were testimonies of ancient and absent men, and indeed of the dead, which of right are employed with great effect.

The *testimonies* of men living and present, which in practice are commonly used, appear not merely *when there is an investigation of a farm, or a murder, or something of the sort, but also in matters of obligation, confession, and oath.*

An example of obligation is found in *Philippics* 5: "I promise, I undertake, I bind myself, honorable judges, that Cæsar shall be at all times such a citizen as he is this day, and such a one as you ought to wish and desire him to be."

A pledge is also a sort of obligation, as appears in Vergil (*Eclogues* 3):

> Wilt then by turns we hand to hand do try
> What either can, and prove each by our deed?
> I'll pawn this heifer (which lest thou deny,
> She twice hath come already to the pail,
> And two twins suckles at this time). Now say
> What pawn thou'lt gage with her to countervale.

Confession is either free, in which the testimony of a man, though little regarded when for himself, is thought very important when against himself, *or it is extracted by tortures, a process properly called the inquisition.*

Tale fuit argumentum contra *Milonem, quod à Cicerone* deridetur: quia cruciatus non sæpius veritatem quàm mendacium exprimit atque extorquet. *Age verò, quæ erat aut qualis quæstio? Heus, ubi Ruscio? ubi Casca? Clodius insidias fecit* 5 Miloni? *Fecit. certa crux. Nullas fecit. sperata libertas.*

Huc etiam referri potest argumentum, quo utimur cùm affirmationis nostræ approbationem & experientiam adversario proponimus.

Verr. 4. *Ecquis Volcatio, si sua sponte venisset, unam libel-* 10 *lam dedisset? veniat nunc, experiatur: tecto recipiet nemo.*

Terent. Eunuch.

> ——*Fac periculum in literis,*
> *fac in palæstra, in musicis; quæ liberum*
> *scire æquum est adolescentem, solertem dabo.*

15 3. Trist.

> *Quod magis ut liqueat, neve hoc ego fingere credar*
> *ipse velim pœnas experiare meas.*

Jusjurandum etiam testimonium est. Quale est *Æneid.* 6.

> *Per superos, & siqua fides tellure sub ima est,*
> 20 *invitus, regina, tuo de littore cessi.*

Such was the argument against Milo which was derided by Cicero, since torture brings out and extorts the truth no more often than it does falsehood: "Go to then, what or how was the question? 'Ho, ho, where was Roscius? where was Casca? Hath Clodius laid snares for Milo?' 'He hath done so.' Surely the gallows for him. 'He hath done nothing.' There is a hope of his liberty."

Here also is to be classed the argument we use when we set forth to an adversary proof through experience of our affirmation.

An example occurs in *In Verrem* 4: "Is there anybody that would have given to Volcatius, if he had come of himself, the tenth part of a denier? Let him come now and see; there is no man that will receive him within his house." There is also one in Terence (*Eunuchus*):

> Examine in knowledge and learning, in wrestling and fighting at the barriers. I shall give you one cunningly learned in all things which is decent for a gentleman to know.

In *Tristia* 3:

> The which that thou maist better credit me,
> Try thou my pains, believe it then to be.

An oath is also a testimony, as that one in *Æneid* 6:

> I swear by heav'n and all in earth unseen,
> Unwilling I have left thy shore, O queen.

Quamvis autem in juramentis divinum quodammodo testimonium invocetur, juramenti tamen fides authoritate & moribus jurantis nititur.

Reciprocatio hîc obscurior est ad rem testatam, quod est hîc 5 *alterum argumentum affectum; ut quia testatum verum sit, testis sit etiam verax.*

Ut autem non sua vi testimonium, sed auctoritas testis arguit rem testatam; ita vicissim res testata non arguit ipsum testimonium, sed authoritatem testis.

Though in oaths divine testimony is in some way invoked, yet confidence in the oath depends on the reputation and morals of the one swearing.

Reciprocation, in saying that since the thing testified to is 5 *true the witness is veracious, is here rather obscure* as to the thing testified to, which is the other argument affected here.

For as the testimony does not by its own force argue what is testified to, but rather the authority of the witness does so, so in turn the thing testified to does not argue the testimony 10 itself, but the authority of the witness.

J. Miltoni Angli.

ARTIS LOGICÆ

ad Petri Rami methodum concinnatæ.

Liber Secundus.

De Argumentorum dispositione.

CAPUT I.

Quid sit argumentorum dispositio?

ADHUC prima artis Logicæ pars fuit in argumentorum inventione: pars altera sequitur in eorum dispositione.

Quemadmodum Grammaticæ pars prima est de singulis
5 vocibus, secunda de syntaxi earum; sic Logicæ pars prima de argumentis inveniendis fuit, secunda est de disponendis, i.e. quæ doceat argumenta rectè disponere: ita dispositio quasi syntaxis quædam argumentorum est; non tamen ad bene judicandum duntaxat, ut vult *Ramus,* quod nimis angustum est,
10 sed ad bene ratiocinandum, qui finis est Logicæ generalis, ad quem unum finem omnia artis præcepta referenda sunt. Jis itaque non assentior, qui judicium secundam esse partem Logicæ volunt: cùm ipsorum sententia judicium sit secundæ hujus

THE ART OF LOGIC

arranged after the method of Peter Ramus

by John Milton, an Englishman.

The Second Book.

Of the disposition of arguments.

CHAPTER I.

What is the disposition of arguments?

UP to this point has been treated the first part of the art of logic, which deals with the invention of arguments; the second part which now follows deals with their disposition.

5 Just as the first part of grammar deals with single words, the second part with their syntax, so the first part of logic has dealt with the finding of arguments, and the second is concerned with disposing them, that is, it teaches rightly to dispose arguments; disposition is thus the syntax as it were of 10 the arguments, not merely for judging well, as Ramus holds, for that is too narrow, but for thinking well, which is the general end of logic, to which as to a single end all the precepts of the art are directed. I do not therefore agree with those who hold that judgment is the second part of logic, 15 since according to their opinion judgment is the end and

partis nempe dispositionis finis & fructus: non potest autem res eadem esse finis & id cujus est finis, fructus quod effectum est & ejus fructus causa, quæ dispositio est. At inquiunt, judicium ut doctrina est pars Logicæ; finis est ut habitus bene judi-
5 candi. Immo verò inquam, dispositionis doctrina suam operam confert non solùm ad bene judicandum, sed ad bene ratiocinandum; judicium autem & dispositionem pro eodem non dixerim cum *Ramo:* si enim certa, ut ipse *Ramus* ait, dispositionis regula unumquodque judicatur, dispositio utique
10 ac judicium si idem erunt, idem erit & regula, & id cujus regula est: doctrina deinde judicii docet nihil aliud quàm bene judicare; doctrina dispositionis pro sua disponendi parte, etiam bene ratiocinari: sive id sit intelligere, sive judicare, sive disputare, sive meminisse. Certa enim dispositionis regula
15 unumquodque munus ratiocinandi excolitur.

Cum itaque simplicem argumentorum inter se affectionem aliquid per se conferre ad judicium rectumque ratiocinium initio proposuerim, nunc eorum dispositionem aliquanto plus, adeoque clariùs ad idem conducere propono.

20 Prius autem quàm ad partes dispositionis accedimus, generalis quædam dispositionis affectio, quæ *Crypsis* dicitur, attingenda est; ut quæ ad omnes species dispositionis communiter pertineat. Crypsis autem sive occultatio ista, est triplex; dispositarum scilicet partium vel defectus, vel redundantia, vel

product of this second part, to wit, of disposition. For the end and that of which it is the end cannot be the same thing, nor can the fruit, which is the effect, and the cause of that fruit, which is disposition, be the same. But they say that 5 judgment as a doctrine is part of logic; it is the end as a habit of judging well. But I say the more that the doctrine of disposition employs its effort not merely that we may judge well, but also that we may think well, but I will not with Ramus say that judgment and disposition are the same; for, as Ramus 10 himself says, if by a certain rule of disposition anything whatever is judged, surely if disposition and judgment are the same, the rule and that to which the rule applies will also be the same. Then further the doctrine of judgment teaches nothing else than to judge well; the doctrine of disposition 15 by its function of disposing teaches also to think well, whether this is understanding, or judging, or debating, or remembering. For by an established rule of disposition any advantage of thinking is improved.

So while at the beginning I laid down that the simple affect 20 of arguments among themselves through itself gave some assistance to judgment and right thinking, now I lay down that the disposition of them somewhat more and more clearly conduces to the same end.

But before we come to the parts of disposition, a certain 25 general affect of disposition, which is called *crypsis,* must be touched on, as something that pertains in common to all species of disposition. But this crypsis or concealment is threefold, to wit, the defect or redundance or inversion of parts

inversio. Quod itaque semel hîc monendum est, siqua propter has crypses dubitatio contingit, explenda quæ desunt, amputanda quæ supersunt, & pars quæque in suum restituenda est locum.

CAPUT II.

De Axiomatis affirmatione & negatione.

D*ISPOSITIO est axiomatica vel dianoetica.*

Axioma est dispositio argumenti cum argumento, qua esse aliquid aut non esse indicatur.

Axioma sæpe *Aristoteli* significat propositionem sive sententiam ita claram, ut quasi digna sit cui propter se fides ha-
10 beatur. Aliàs axioma & propositionem sive sententiam quamlibet pro eodem is habet: & rectè quidem: ut enim sententia à sentio, i.e. existimo vel arbitror, ita axioma à verbo *Græco* quod idem significat, derivatur. Atque hujus vocis generalem hanc significationem apud veteres Dialecticos receptam
15 fuisse, ex *Cicerone, Plutarcho, Laertio, Galeno, & Gellio lib.* 16. *c.* 8. *constat.*

Latinè *enuntiatum, enuntiatio; pronuntiatum, pronuntiatio, effatum,* & Varroni profatum, & proloquium, apud Gellium Lib. 16. id est sententia in qua nihil desideratur. Ex
20 *Græco* etiam *oratio* & *propositio* dicitur.

Cur ergo, inquis, Græcanica, & hæc præ aliis, vox placita

disposed. So the caution may here be given once for all that if on account of these crypses there is uncertainty, what lacks must be supplied, what is superfluous must be cut off, and any part must be restored to its place.

CHAPTER II.

Of the affirmation and denial of an axiom.

DISPOSITION is axiomatic or dianoetic.

An axiom is a disposition of one argument with another, by which something is shown to be or not to be.

In Aristotle an axiom often signifies a proposition or idea
10 so clear that it is as though worthy that confidence should be put in it for itself. Otherwise he holds axiom and proposition or *sententia* of any sort for the same thing, and properly, for as *sententia* is derived from *sentio,* that is, *I conclude* or *judge,* so *axiom* is derived from a Greek word of the same meaning.
15 And that this general signification of the word was received by the ancient dialecticians, is made certain by Cicero, Plutarch, Laertius, Galen, and Gellius (16. 8).

In Latin the word *axiom* is rendered by *enuntiatum, enuntiatio, pronuntiatum, pronuntiatio,* and *effatum,* and
20 by Varro, according to Gellius (book 16) *profatum* and *proloquium,* that is a statement in which nothing is lacking. From the Greek it is also called *oratio* and *proposition.*

But why, therefore, you say, has a word of Greek origin,

est? Quia, inquam, commodissima. Nam *oratio* & *sententia* voces latiores sunt; ideóque Græci qui λόγον sive *rationem* vocant, addunt ferè *primam, brevissimam* aut *enuntiativam*. Deinde *propositio* ambigua vox est; significat enim nunc priorem partem plenæ comparationis, nunc primam partem syllogismi. Latina autem illa, *enuntiatum, enuntiatio,* &c. orationis exterioris videntur magis quàm rationis interioris esse: cùm dispositio hæc Logica rationis omnino sit tam mente conceptæ quàm ore prolatæ; útque voces symbola sunt & notæ simplicium notionum, ita enuntiatum videtur esse symbolum axiomatis mente concepti. Sic tamen retineri possunt voces Latinæ *enuntiatum, enuntiatio,* &c. Si distinguimus cum *Aristotele* sermonem in exteriorem, qui ore profertur; & interiorem, qui mente solùm concipitur.

Genus autem axiomatis rectè statuitur dispositio, non judicium, quod ut supra retuli, dispositionis effectum est, & hic quidem specialiter quo aliquid esse aut non esse judicatur.

Argumentum autem est id quod arguit cum eo quod arguitur.

Finis dispositionis est, ut per eam esse aliquid aut non esse indicetur, sive ut aliquid de aliquo dicatur aut non dicatur. Hinc illud *Aristot.* Phil. ϑ. 10. *esse est componi, & unum esse; non esse autem est non componi, sed plura esse.* Et simplicia quidem argumenta per se considerata significant ali-

and the word *axiom* rather than any other, seemed best? Because, I answer, it is most suitable. For *oratio* and *sententia* are more general words; hence the Greeks who say *λόγον* or *reason,* usually add first, shortest, or enunciative. Then *proposition* is an ambiguous word, for it signifies sometimes the prior part of a full comparison, sometimes the first part of a syllogism. But those Latin words *enuntiatum, enuntiatio,* etc., seem to apply to external speech rather than to internal reason, while logical disposition is entirely a matter of the reason as well conceived in the mind as uttered by the voice, and as words are symbols and signs of simple notions, so *enuntiatum* seems to be a symbol of the axiom conceived in the mind. But yet we can retain the Latin words *enuntiatum, enuntiatio,* etc., if with Aristotle we distinguish between exterior speech, which is uttered with the mouth, and internal, which is conceived in the mind alone.

The genus of the axiom is properly considered to be disposition, not judgment, which as I have mentioned above, is the effect of disposition, and here especially is that by which something is judged to be or not to be.

An argument is that which argues as well as that which is argued.

The end of disposition is that through it may be shown that something is or is not, or that something may be said or not said of something else. Hence the saying of Aristotle (*Metaphysics* 8. 10): "To be is to be united and to be one; but not to be is not to be united but to be several." And simple arguments considered through themselves signify some-

quid; non autem esse, aut non esse aliquid, nisi disposita. Solo autem modo indicativo esse aliquid aut non esse indicatur; non reliquis, nisi ad indicativum reductis: ut, *abi.* i.e. jubeo te abire. *Fiat voluntas tua,* i.e. precamur ut fiat. *Utinam dis-* 5 *solverer,* i.e. cupio dissolvi. *Quid est Dialectica,* i.e. quæro quid sit.

Cùm autem in axiomate argumentum cum argumento disponatur, horúmque unum necesse sit antecedere, alterum sequi; hinc partes axiomatis (*Aristot. terminos* vocat) duæ 10 sunt, antecedens & consequens: illa vulgò minor terminus, sive subjectum, hæc terminus major seu prædicatum nominatur; quia id continet, quod de subjecto prædicatur sive dicitur. Verùm hæc nomina angustiora sunt, quàm illa, ut infra patebit.

15 Axiomatis affectio communis est crypsis illa triplex, de qua deque ejus triplici medela capite superiore diximus: defectus, cùm pars aliqua deest; ut, *excessit, erupit, evasit; Catilina* scilicet vel quis alius; pluit, *tonat;* Deus nempe vel cœlum. Redundantia, quæ & amplificatio dicitur, est, cùm argumentum 20 ejúsque synonymum ponitur; aut ad id illustrandum quidvis aliud: prioris exemplum est, *Logica* sive Dialectica *est ars bene ratiocinandi:* posterioris est hoc,

Livor iners vitium mores non exit in altos.

thing, but not that something is or is not, unless they are disposed. By the indicative mode alone is indicated that something is or is not, not by the others, unless they are brought to the indicative, as when we say, *Go away,* we mean, *I order*
5 *you to go away. May thy will be done,* means *We pray that it may be done. Would that I might die,* means *I desire to die. What is dialectic?* means *I ask what it is.*

But when in an axiom one argument is disposed with another, one of these of necessity precedes, the other follows;
10 therefore the parts of the axiom (Aristotle calls them *terms*) are two, the antecedent and the consequent. The first is commonly called the minor term or the subject, the second the major term or the predicate, since it contains what is predicated or said of the subject. The latter names are less inclusive
15 than the former, as will appear below.

The common affect of an axiom is that triple crypsis of which and of the triple remedy of which we spoke in the preceding chapter: a defect appears when some part is absent, as in *he departed, he broke away, he escaped,* that is, Catiline or
20 some one else did; and in *it rains, it thunders,* that is, God or the heavens do. Redundancy, also called amplification, appears when the argument and its synonym are given, or when for making one thing clear another is given. An example of the first of these is the statement: *Logic or dialectic is the art*
25 *of thinking well.* An example of the second is

> Envy, the sluggard's vice, in noble minds
> Cannot find place.

Inversio est, cùm antecedentis loco ponitur consequens: ut, *quæstus magnus est pietas cum animo sua sorte contento,* i.e. pietas cum animo sua sorte contento est magnus quæstus.

Duæ sunt reliquæ axiomatis affectiones; quarum altera ex 5 dispositione oritur, altera ad judicium pertinet. Nam intellectus cùm disponit argumenta, vel componit ea inter se, vel dividit: compositio autem illa & divisio nihil aliud sunt quàm affirmatio & negatio. Cùm verò de dispositione illa judicium fert, judicat eam vel veram esse vel falsam. Quemadmodum 10 autem dispositio est prior judicio, sic esse & non esse prius quiddam est & simplicius quàm affirmare & negare, & utrumque hoc quàm verum aut falsum judicare.

Axioma igitur est affirmatum aut negatum.

Duplex est hic modus enuntiandi, non duæ sunt species 15 enuntiati sive axiomatis: contradictione enim idem axioma affirmatur & negatur: sed affirmatio & negatio enuntiationis, i.e. enuntiandi species sunt, non enuntiati; nam & affirmatio & negatio dici potest enuntiatio, enuntiatum verò nequaquam; axiomatis igitur utraque est affectio, non axioma.

20 *Axioma affirmatum est quando vinculum ejus affirmatur: negatum, quando negatur.* Vinculum n. axiomatis forma est; vinculi vi axiomatis materia disponitur & quasi animatur; vinculo affirmato aut negato, axioma ipsum affirmatur aut

There is inversion when the consequent is put in place of the antecedent, as in the statement: *The great desideratum is piety with a mind contented with its lot,* that is, piety with a mind contented with its lot is the great desideratum.

5 There are two remaining affects of the axiom, one of which is derived from disposition, the other pertains to judgment. For when the intellect disposes arguments it either arranges them among themselves or divides them, but such composition and division are nothing other than affirmation and 10 negation. But when it gives judgment of that disposition, it judges it either true or false. But in whatever way disposition is prior to judgment, similarly being and not-being are prior to and simpler than affirming and denying, and either of the latter is prior to and simpler than judging the true or 15 the false.

An axiom is, therefore, affirmed or denied.

This is a duplex mode of announcing, and there are not two species of the thing announced or the axiom, for by contradiction the same axiom is affirmed and denied, but the 20 affirmation and denial are species of enunciation, that is, of enunciating, not of the enunciate, for both affirmation and negation can be called enunciation but never an enunciate; therefore either is an affect of the axiom, but not the axiom itself.

25 *An axiom is affirmed when its band is affirmed, and is denied when its band is denied.* For the band is the form of the axiom; by the force of the band the matter of the axiom is disposed and as though animated; when the band is affirmed

negatur: affirmatio itaque & negatio sunt vinculi affectiones, adeóque axiomatis ejúsque specierum. Vinculum autem est vel verbum vel Grammatica conjunctio, ut postmodum patebit, cùm axioma in species dividetur.

5 Affirmatio autem hæc & negatio nihil aliud est, ut suprà diximus, quàm compositio & divisio: affirmatur enim axioma, cùm ejus consequens per affirmationem vinculi cum antecedente componitur; negatur, cùm negato vinculo, consequens ab antecedente dividitur. Negatio igitur axiomatica non est, 10 quemadmodum erat topica non ens, sed entis tantummodo ab ente divisio.

Hinc nascitur axiomatum contradictio, quando idem axioma affirmatur & negatur.

CAPUT III.

De Vero & falso.

A*XIOMA deinde est verum aut falsum.*

Hoc scilicet ex affirmatione & negatione fit judicium: cùm enim affirmantur quæ affirmanda sunt, & negantur quæ neganda, axiomata judicantur vera; & contrà. Unde *Arist.* de Interpret. 1. *in compositione & divisione est verum aut falsum.* Falsum autem non docetur hoc modo in 20 arte, sed judicatur: nam enuntiatio falsa non minus axioma

or denied the axiom itself is affirmed or denied; thus affirmation and denial are affects of the band, therefore of the axiom and its species. But the band is either a verb or a grammatical conjunction, as later will appear, when the axiom is divided 5 into species.

As we said above, this affirmation and negation is nothing else than composition and division, for the axiom is affirmed when its consequent is combined with the antecedent through affirmation of the band, and is denied when, by the denial of 10 the band, the consequent is divided from the antecedent. Negation is therefore not axiomatic, just as I showed that non-being is topic, but is only division of being from being.

Thence rises the contradiction of axioms, when the same axiom is affirmed and denied.

CHAPTER III.

Of the true and the false.

AN axiom, then, is true or false.

This judgment is evidently derived from affirmation and negation, for when the things which ought to be affirmed are affirmed and the things which ought to be denied are denied, the axioms are judged true, and con-20 versely. Therefore Aristotle (*De interpretatione* 1) writes that "in composition and division lies the true or the false." But the false is not taught in this way in art but is judged, for a false enunciation is not less an axiom than a true one, for

est, quàm vera, eadem enim utrobique dispositio est: non idem de syllogismo ac methodo dici poterit.

Axioma verum est, quando pronuntiat uti res est: falsum, contrà.

5 Sic enim *Plato,* in Cratylo. Ad judicium itaque faciendum, non modò artis documenta, sed etiam rerum ipsarum cognitio requiritur; quia res ipsa veritatis norma & mensura est.

Axioma verum est contingens aut necessarium. Contingens, quando sic verum est, ut aliquando falsum esse possit. 10 *Ut, audentes fortuna juvat.*

Itaque veritatis hujus contingentis judicium, opinio dicitur. Quæ præteritorum & præsentium homini certa esse potest, futurorum per naturam non admodum potest. Deo autem etsi tempora omnia præsentia non sunt, ut vulgò receptum 15 est, præsentia enim mutare potest, præterita non item, opinio tamen in Deum non cadit, quia per causas æque omnia cognoscit.

De contingentibus autem, præteritis etiam, & præsentibus humanum judicium certa quidem opinio dicitur, non tamen 20 scientia: ea enim ex argumentis, quorum est immutabilis affectio, oritur; cujusmodi in contingenti axiomate non disponuntur. Neque idcirco non est opinio præteritorum & præsentium, quòd manifesta sunt, immo tum maximè opinari contingentia dicimur; nam dubia si sunt, sive contingentia sive 25 necessaria, ne opinamur quidem, sed dubitamus: & necessaria

they have the same disposition. The same cannot be said of the syllogism and of method.

An axiom is true when it speaks as the thing is; false when it does the opposite.

5 Thus Plato pronounces in the *Cratylus.* So to making a judgment not merely the documents of the art but a knowledge of the things themselves is required, since the thing itself is the norm and measure of truth.

A true axiom is contingent or necessary. It is contingent 10 *when it is true in such a way that sometimes it can be false. For example: Fortune friends the bold.*

So the judgment of this contingent truth is called opinion, which in past and present things can be certain to man, but in future things according to nature cannot be certain. But 15 though all times are not present to God, as is popularly supposed, for he is able to change the present but not the past, yet opinion is not to be attributed to God, since he knows all things equally through their causes.

But human judgment about contingent things, both past 20 and present, is indeed called settled opinion, yet not knowledge, for knowledge comes from arguments that have an immutable affect, but they are not so disposed in the contingent axiom. Nor is it not to be called opinion about past and present things because they are plain, but there especially 25 we say that contingent things are matters of opinion, for if they are doubtful, whether contingent or necessary, we do not have opinion, but we doubt, and though necessary things are

tametsi sunt atque certissima, si causam nescimus, etiam ea duntaxat opinamur.

At, inquies, præterita & præsentia non sunt contingentia, sed necessaria, quia sunt immutabilia; nam neque factum in-5 fectum fieri potest; & quicquid est, quandiu est, necesse est esse. Respondendum, necesse quidem esse, ut quod fuit, fuerit, & quod jam est, sit; nec tamen sequi, ut quod fuit vel est, sit propriè necessarium. In axiomate enim contingenti, præterito, vel præsenti quæ videtur esse necessitas, absoluta non est, neque 10 ex rerum dispositarum natura, sed ex conditione duntaxat & lege contradictionis pendet: dum enim aliquid est, non esse non potest; neque dum verum est, esse falsum: & tamen quod nunc verum est, fieri potest ut aliquando falsum fuerit, aut futurum sit. Idem de futuris dicendum; siquid futurum 15 certò est, id necesse est fore quidem verum (omne n. axioma verum est aut falsum) non tamen necessarium. Id nisi teneatur, omne contingens futurum erit necessarium, quod implicat contradictionem. Hoc etiam monendum, futura quidem ipsa neque vera esse neque falsa, neque contingentia, 20 neque necessaria, nondum n. sunt, sed affirmatio solùm de iis aut negatio in futurum; déque præteritis eodem modo sentiendum.

Axioma est necessarium, quando semper verum est, nec falsum potest esse.

25 Nec supervacua posterior hæc clausula est: semper n. esse verum etiam contingens potest; necessarium autem non modò

fully certain, if we are ignorant of their cause, we evidently have opinion about them also.

You may object that past and present things are not contingent, but necessary, since they are immutable, for what is
5 done cannot be made undone, and whatever is, as long as it is, necessarily is. It may be replied that what has been has necessarily been and what now is necessarily is, but it does not follow that what has been or is should be strictly speaking necessary. For in a contingent axiom, whether past or pres-
10 ent, what seems to be necessity is not absolute, and does not depend on the nature of the things disposed, but on the condition and the law of contradiction, for while anything is, it is unable not to be, nor while it is true can it be false; and yet it is possible that what is now true at some time may have been
15 false or may in the future be false. So it can be said of future things; if something is certain to happen, it necessarily is going to be true (for every axiom is either true or false) but it is not necessary. If this is not held, every contingent future thing will be necessary, which implies a contradiction. The
20 caution also must be given that future things themselves are neither true nor false nor contingent nor necessary, for they do not yet exist, but there is merely affirmation or negation of them in the future; and about past things an opinion of the same sort should be held.

25 *An axiom is necessary when it is always true and cannot be false.*

The last little clause is not superfluous, for the contingent can always be true, but the necessary not merely is always

semper est verum, sed falsum esse non potest. Sic etiam *Aristot. Post.* 1. 26.

Contrà, quod semper falsum est, nec verum potest esse, axioma impossibile dicitur. Sic etiam *Aristot.* Phil. *δ*. 12.

5 Hæc autem immutabilitas veritatis in necessario, & falsitatis in impossibili, ab argumentorum quæ in iis disponuntur vel summa consensione, vel infesta semper dissensione pendet. Pari ratione mutabilitas veri aut falsi in contingenti & possibili ex levi argumentorum in iis dispositorum consensione aut 10 dissidio perspicitur.

Ex quo doctrina illa quatuor formularum modalium, *necesse est, impossibile est, possibile est, contingens est,* quàm inutiliter ab *Aristot.* introducta sit, facile apparet: ut, *necesse est hominem esse animal; impossibile est hominem esse* 15 *equum; possibile est Socratem esse divitem; contingens est Socratem esse doctum.* Hæ quatuor modales dispositionem purarum enuntiationum quodammodo afficiunt: pura est, *omnis homo est animal;* modalis, *necesse est omnem hominem esse animal:* hîc *omnem hominem esse animal,* licet in-20 verso ordine, subjectum est enuntiationis modalis; modus *necesse* est prædicatum. Verùm quid attinet quomodo partes axiomatis inter se affectæ sint, signis aut modis exprimere, cùm id ex argumentis ipsis in eo dispositis possit rectius judicari, & ad hos modos alii complures, *facile, difficile, hone-*25 *stum, turpe,* &c. non inutiliùs possint adjungi?

Equidem secundarias, quas vocant, modales primariis hisce

true but cannot be false. Thus says Aristotle in the *Posterior Analytics* 1.26.

On the contrary, what is always false and unable to be true is called an impossible axiom. Thus Aristotle writes in *Metaphysics* 4.12.

But this immutability of truth in the necessary and of falsity in the impossible depends on the full consent or always hostile dissent of the arguments which are disposed in them. From like reason the mutability of true or false in the contingent and the possible is understood through the easy consent or dissent of the arguments disposed in those categories.

From this it is easily apparent how uselessly was introduced by Aristotle that doctrine of the four modal formulas, namely, *it is necessary, it is impossible, it is possible, it is contingent,* as in *It is necessary that man is an animal; it is impossible for a man to be a horse; it is possible for Socrates to be rich; it is contingent that Socrates is learned.* These four modals affect in some way the disposition of the pure enuntiates; the pure is *Every man is an animal;* the modal *It is necessary that every man is an animal;* here *every man is an animal,* though in inverse order, is the subject of a modal enunciate; the mode *it is necessary* is the predicate. Indeed of what value is it to express by signs or modes the way in which the parts of the axiom are affected among themselves, when this can be more rightly judged from the arguments disposed in the axiom, and to these modes many others, *easy, difficult, honest, base,* etc., can with advantage be added?

Indeed I should esteem the secondary modals, as they are

potiores existimem: quibus vulgò dividuntur enuntiationes in *exclusivas,* quarum notæ sunt *solus, tantùm, duntaxat,* &c.; ut, *sola fides justificat: exceptivas,* quarum notæ sunt *præter, præterquam, nisi,* &c. Ut, *nemo præter te sapit:* & *restrictivas,* quarum notæ sunt *qua, quatenus, quoad, secundum quid,* &c. Ut, *homo qua animal, sentit.* Et exclusiva quidem est vel subjecti vel prædicati: subjecti, quæ notâ exclusivâ præpositâ, excludit omnia subjecta alia à prædicato. Sed frustra hanc regulam ratio dictarit, si Logicis quibusdam modernis, & nominatim *Keckermanno* licebit, eam statim, conflato ad id ipsum canone, funditus evertere. *Exclusiva,* inquit, *subjecti non excludit concomitantia:* ut, *solus pater est verus Deus. Hîc* inquit, *non excluditur concomitans, filius, & spiritus sanctus.* At quis non videt subornatum hunc canonem, ad locum illum luculentissimum *Joan.* 17. 3. ludificandum. Haud paulò utilior est canon ille restrictivæ enuntiationis, quem tradit l. 2. c. 4. (restrictiva autem est quæ ostendit quatenus subjectum prædicato convenit) *prædicatum,* inquit, *contradictorium nulla limitatione subjecto conciliatur;* ex *Aristot.* 2. *top.* c. ult. Sect. 4. Quid evidentius dici potuit? & tamen reperti sunt qui interpositis quibusdam distinctiunculis, *accidens posse existere sine subjecto* (quod repugnat) *in cæna Domini* contendant: deinde, qui similib. confictis distincti-

called, more important than the primary ones; by the secondary modals the enuntiations are commonly divided into *exclusives,* of which the signs are *alone, merely, simply,* etc., as when it is said that *Faith alone justifies; exceptives,* the signs
5 of which are *except, besides, unless,* as in *No one knows except you;* and *restrictives,* of which the signs are *as, to what extent, as far as, according as,* as in *Man as animal thinks.* An exclusive is either of the subject or the predicate. An exclusive of the subject, when the sign of the exclusive is prefixed, excludes
10 all other subjects from the predicate. But reason would in vain dictate this rule if certain modern logicians, among whom Keckermann may be named, are permitted at once to overturn it completely by producing a canon for the purpose. "The exclusive," he says, "does not exclude the
15 concomitants of the subject, as in the statement: *The Father alone is true God.* Here," he says, "the concomitant is not excluded, namely the Son and the Holy Spirit." But who does not see that this canon is provided for making sport of that abundantly clear passage John 17. 3? Not in the least more
20 useful is that canon of restrictive enunciation which he gives in book 2, chapter 4 (the restrictive is that which shows how far the subject agrees with the predicate) where he says: "By no limitation is a contradictory predicate conciliated with the subject," from Aristotle, *Topics* 2, the last chapter, section 4.
25 What that is more obvious can be said? And yet they can be found who by interposing some little distinctions contend that *in the Lord's supper an accident can exist without a subject,* which is contrary to reason. Then there are those who by

unculis, *humanam naturam Christi adeoque corpus infinitum esse* disputantes, parem contradictionem committant. Sed omissis Theologorum paradoxis, ad præcepta Logica redeamus.

5 *Axioma necessarium affirmatum appellatur* κατὰ παντὸς *de omni.*

Id est, cum consequens sive prædicatum, ut vocant, axiomatis, de omni & toto antecedente sive subjecto semper verum est. Sic etiam *Aristot.* 1. prior. 1. & post. 1. 4. & hoc etiam 10 nonnunquam καθόλου, i.e. *de toto,* vocat, *Post.* 2. 13.

Axiomata artium sic κατὰ παντὸς *esse debent.*

Nempe de omni & de toto vera, non falsa; necessaria, non fortuita, alioqui non scientiam pariunt, sed opinionem; affirmata denique, non negata: affirmatum enim est firmum, 15 certum, brevissimum; negatum verò est vagum, incertum, infinitum, nihilque docet: ut si quis definiret Logicam, non esse artem bene loquendi, non doceret quid Logica sit, sed quid non sit; eáque definitio omnib. artibus præter Grammaticam æque ac Logicæ conveniret. Nonnulli addunt ex hac 20 lege, axiomata artium debere etiam esse generalia. Verùm hæc regula non tantum de omni est, sed de toto: & multa in artibus præcepta specialibus de rebus occurrunt, ut in *Theologia,* de *Christo;* in *Astronomia* de sole & luna reliquísque planetis: in aliis artibus hujusmodi alia, quæ, cùm sint 25 specialia, etsi κατὰ παντὸς dici non possunt, καθόλου tamen possunt, quod satis est. Quòd si quis objicit, ne in generalibus

making up similar little distinctions commit an equal contradiction in arguing that *Christ can have a human nature and an infinite body.* But abandoning the paradoxes of the theologians, let us return to the precepts of logic.

5 *A necessary affirmative axiom is called* κατὰ παντός, *or of the whole.*

That is, when the consequent or the predicate, as they call it, of the axiom is always true about every antecedent or subject, and the whole of it. Thus also Aristotle puts it in the *Prior*
10 *Analytics* 1.1, and in the *Posterior Analytics* 1.4, and he sometimes calls it καθόλου, that is, of the whole (*Posterior Analytics* 2.13).

The axioms of the arts ought thus to be κατὰ παντός.

That is, they should be true of all and of the whole, not
15 false; necessary, not fortuitous, for otherwise they would beget not knowledge but opinion; lastly, they should be affirmed, not denied, for what is affirmed is firm, certain, very brief, but what is denied is vague, uncertain, infinite, and teaches nothing, for if any one should define logic not
20 to be the art of speaking well, he would not teach what logic is but what it is not, and this definition would fit all the other arts, except grammar, as well as logic. Some add as derived from this law that the axioms of the arts should be general. But this rule is not merely of everything but of the whole, and
25 there are many precepts in the arts that deal with special things, as in theology with Christ, in astronomy with the sun and the moon and the other planets; in the other arts there are other things of this sort, which, since they are special,

quidem præcepta artium κατὰ παντὸς esse posse, propter exceptionum multitudinem, ut in Grammatica videre est; respondendum est, anomaliam analogiæ conjunctam, κατὰ παντὸς instar esse.

5 *Sed præcepta artium homogenea etiam & reciproca esse debent.*

Axioma homogeneum est, quando partes sunt essentiales inter se.

i.e. Vel absolute, ut forma formato, genus speciei, membra 10 integro, definitio definito; vel modo quodam, ut subjectum proprio adjuncto.

Id appellatur καθ' αὑτὸ *per se.*

Idcirco etiam partes axiomatis essentiales inter se esse debent, ut præceptum artis esse scientificum possit: accidentis 15 enim, ut testatur *Aristoteles,* nulla est scientia; nulla nisi per essentiam & causam: idem, τὰ καθ' αὑτὸ, & τὰ συμβεβηκότα, i.e. *accidentia,* opponit, *Post.* I. 4. Itaque non satis est, partes esse inter se consentaneas, sed essentiales: quod cùm ex argumentorum inter se summa consensione oriatur, ex qua necessa- 20 rium quoque axioma esse ortum supradiximus, non video quid per hanc regulam καθ' αὑτὸ ad superiorem illam κατὰ παντὸς quod magni sit momenti, accedat; cùm nullum axioma necessarium esse queat, quin ejus partes inter se sint etiam essentiales. Neque verò putem hîc præcipi, ne quid

although they cannot be called κατὰ παντός yet can be called καθόλου, which is enough. Because if any one should object that in general things the precepts of the arts cannot be κατὰ παντός because of the multitude of exceptions, as may be seen
5 in grammar, it must be answered that anomaly joined to analogy is the same as κατὰ παντός.

But the precepts of the arts ought also to be homogeneous and reciprocal.

An axiom is homogeneous when the parts are essential to
10 *each other.*

That is, either absolutely, as form to the thing formed, genus to species, members to the whole, definition to the thing defined, or in some manner, as the subject to its proper adjunct.

15 *This is called* καθ' αὑτό, *or of itself.*

The parts of an axiom ought to be essential to each other in order that a precept of the art may be scientific, for as Aristotle bears witness, there is no knowledge of an accident; none except through essence and cause. He also opposes
20 τὰ καθ' αὑτό and τὰ συμβεβηκότα, that is, *accidents* (*Posterior Analytics* 1.4). So it is not enough that the parts should be consentany with each other, but essential; and because this relation of the parts springs from the most complete consent of the arguments among themselves, from which we have
25 said above that the necessary axiom is derived, I do not see what of great moment is added by this rule καθ' αὑτό to that earlier one κατὰ παντός, since no axiom can be necessary unless its parts are essential among themselves. Nor do I judge that

heterogeneum sive alienum in arte doceatur; neque enim huc pertinet dispositio præcepti cum præcepto, sed argumenti solùm cum argumento, quæ axiomatis doctrina est, & ex homogenei definitione ipsa ejúsque exemplis perspicitur.

5 *Axioma reciprocum est, quando consequens semper verum est de antecedente, non solùm omni & per se, sed etiam reciprocè.*

Ut homo est animal rationale: numerus est par vel impar. Lupus est natus ad ululandum. Id appellatur καθόλου πρῶτον, 10 de toto primum. Nempe quia de nullo prius dicitur; ideóque proximum est & immediatum, proprium & æquale; unóque verbo, reciprocum; ut risibile de homine: omnis enim homo est risibilis; & reciprocè, omne risibile est homo. Hæc regula nisi observetur, vitari tautologia in artibus non potest. Tum 15 enim non reciprocatur axioma, cùm antecedens consequenti non est æquale, aut contra; sed vel speciale alicui generi, vel generale alicui speciei attribuitur: generale autem de specie non dicitur primò; prius enim dicitur de genere. Cùm autem id quod generis est, speciei attribuitur, idem in reliquis specie-20 bus necessario est repetendum, quod in genere semel dictum oportuit. Ad hanc itaque regulam pertinet præceptum artis illud nobile γενικὰ γενικῶς, *generalia generaliter* & semel docenda sunt. Hæc lex brevitati, brevitas autem intelligentiæ & memoriæ consulit.

it is here laid down that nothing heterogeneous or alien should be taught in an art, for there is not here a question of the disposition of precept with precept, but merely of argument with argument, which is the doctrine of the axiom, and is 5 understood from the homogeneous definition itself and its examples.

An axiom is reciprocal when the consequent is always true of the antecedent not merely of the whole and of itself, but also reciprocally.

10 Examples are *Man is a rational animal; number is equal or inequal; the wolf is born to howl.* This is called καθόλου πρῶτον, first of the whole, for the reason that nothing has been spoken of before. Therefore it is proximate and immediate, proper and equal, and in one word, reciprocal, as to be risible 15 of man, for *every man is risible,* and reciprocally, *every risible being is a man.* Unless this rule is observed, tautology in the arts cannot be avoided. For an axiom is not reciprocated when the antecedent is not equal to the consequent, or the contrary, but either the special is attributed to some genus, or the general 20 is attributed to some species; but the general is not said of the species at first, for it is first said of the genus. But when what pertains to a genus is attributed to a species, the same thing which should be said once for all of the genus must needs be repeated for the remaining species. Thus to this rule per- 25 tains that noble precept of art, γενικὰ γενικῶς, that *generals* are to be taught *generally* and once for all. This is the law of brevity, and brevity is mindful of intelligence and memory.

Atque hæ tres sunt leges documentorum artium propriorum. Prima κατὰ παντὸς, lex veritatis; propterea quòd necessariam affirmati axiomatis veritatem ex consentanea partium affectione postulat. Secunda καθ' αὑτὸ, lex justitiæ; quia jus-
5 titiam requirit in essentiali partium cognatione. Peccant ergo in hanc legem, qui Rhetoricam in inventionem, dispositionem, memoriam, &c. distribuunt, cùm Rhetoricæ partes attribuant, quæ Dialecticæ propriæ sunt. Tertia καθόλου πρῶτον lex sapientiæ, meritò dici possit; cùm quia ejus judicium ve-
10 rissima scientia est, ut postea dicetur, tum quia vitia sapientiæ contraria prohibet, inæqualitatem sive inconvenientiam antecedentis cùm consequente & tautologiam.

Dices, duas illas priores leges comprehendi sub hac tertia: & hoc fatendum quidem est: veruntamen ut trigonum tetra-
15 gonus, & tetragonum pentagonus comprehendit, neque idcirco tamen distinctæ figuræ non sunt; ita hæ leges, etiamsi posterior quæque priorem comprehendit, erant tamen perspicuitatis causa distinguendæ.

Atque hujusmodi axiomatum ita reciprocorum judicium
20 *verissima & prima scientia est.* Prima, quia principiorum est, quæ per se indemonstrabilia, suáque luce manifestissima sunt, neque syllogismi aut ullius argumenti clarioris lucem ad scientiam faciendam desiderant: quæ inde verissima quoque sit necesse est.

And these three are the laws of proper lessons in the arts. First κατὰ παντός, the law of truth, because it demands from the consentany affect of the parts the necessary verity of the axiom affirmed. The second is καθ' αὑτό, the law of justice, 5 since it requires justice in the essential relation of the parts. Therefore they sin against this law who distribute rhetoric into invention, disposition, memory, etc., since they attribute to rhetoric things proper to dialectic. The third is properly called καθόλου πρῶτον,, the law of wisdom, both since 10 its judgment is the truest wisdom, as will be said later, and because it prohibits the vices contrary to wisdom, inequality or lack of agreement of the antecedent with the consequent, and tautology.

You say that the first two of these laws are included in the 15 third, and indeed it should be said that just as the tetragon includes the triangle, and the pentagon the tetragon—yet they do not for that reason cease to be distinct figures—these laws, though the later includes the earlier, should be distinguished for the sake of perspicuity.

20 *So the judgment of axioms of this sort which are thus reciprocal is the truest and first knowledge.* It is first because it is knowledge of principles, which, though indemonstrable through themselves, are completely manifest by their own light, and do not need the light of the syllogism or any plainer 25 argument for producing knowledge; it therefore is of necessity completely true as well.

CAPUT IV.

De Axiomate simplici.

A*TQUE hæc de communib. axiomatis affectionibus; species sequuntur.*

Axioma est simplex aut compositum.

Sic etiam *Aristot.* de interpret. 1. 5. Vulgò propositio dividitur in categoricam & hypotheticam, eodem sensu. Sed categorica affirmatam duntaxat propositionem simplicem comprehendit, quæ scilicet de subjecto κατηγορεῖται, i.e. prædicatur.

Axioma simplex est, quod verbi vinculo continetur.

Cùm enim vinculum, ut supradiximus, axiomatis forma & quasi anima sit, hinc efficitur, quemadmodum duæ sunt species vinculorum, verbum & conjunctio, illud simplicis axiomatis, hoc compositi, ut axioma quoque ex ista distributione vinculi, in oppositas formas sive species dividatur. Vinculum autem simplicis axiomatis, non solum est verbum substantivum, quod dicitur, sed quodvis verbum actionem aut passionem significans, vinculi in se vim inclusam habet; & vel totum consequens vel pars consequentis est; ut, *Socrates* scribit. Nam quod nonnulli putant, verbum omne in substantivum & participium resolvi oportere, ut ea ratione verbum substantivum esse vinculum appareat, scilicet, *Socrates* est scribens; id sæpe ineptissimum esse reperietur. Ut siquis hoc, *Socrates* docetur, sic solvat, *Socrates* est doctus: hoc enim aliud longe

CHAPTER IV.

Of the simple axiom.

THUS *much of the common affects of the axiom; the species follow.*

An axiom is simple or compound.

Aristotle says the same thing in *De interpretatione* 1.5.
5 Commonly the proposition is divided into the categorical and hypothetical, with the same meaning. But the categorical comprehends merely the simple affirmed proposition which κατηγορεῖται, that is, is predicated, of the subject.

An axiom is simple which is held by the band of a verb.

10 For since the band, as we said above, is the form and as it were the soul of the axiom, it thence follows that as there are two species of bands, verb and conjunction, the first of the simple axiom, the second of the composite, so the axiom also from the very distribution of the band is divided into opposite
15 forms or species. But the band of the simple axiom is not merely the substantive verb, as it is called, but any verb signifying action or passion has included in itself the power of a band, and is either the whole consequent or part of the consequent, as in the statement: *Socrates writes.* For as to the
20 opinion of some that every verb ought to be resolved into substantive and participle that in that way the substantive verb might appear as the band—to wit, *Socrates is writing*—this opinion is often found very inept. If anyone should try to solve the statement *Socrates docetur* (Socrates is taught)

est. Quidquod etiam verbum substantivum nonnunquam & vinculum & totum consequens includit; ut, *Socrates* est; Mortui non sunt, i.e. non existunt. Quodsi in uno simplici axiomate plura verba occurrunt, ut, Imparia sunt comparata, quo-
5 rum quantitas non est una, sciendum est illud verbum axiomatis vinculum esse, quod Grammatici vocant principale.

Id si affirmatur, axioma simplex est affirmatum; si negatur negatum.

Negatur autem, si negationis nota verbum illud præcedit:
10 nam si sequitur, negatum non est, sed affirmatum: ut, *Socrates* est leo non necessariò, affirmatum est, quia negationis nota sequitur verbum; nec totum consequens negatur, sed modus.

Negationis autem notæ non solùm sunt adverbia negandi, sed etiam particulæ exclusivæ (cujusmodi sunt *unicus* & *solus*)
15 & verba dissensionem vel differentiam significantia; ut, *differre, opponi,* &c.

Exempla nunc videamus. Ignis urit; ignis est calidus; ignis non est aqua. Hîc *ignis* est antecedens, *urit* consequens.

Atque hîc est prima inventarum rerum dispositio, causæ
20 *cum effecto, ut in primo exemplo; subjecti cum adjuncto, ut in secundo; dissentanei cum dissentaneo, ut in tertio.*

Quo modo argumenta quælibet inter se affecta enuntiari possunt, consentanea quidem affirmando, dissentanea ne-

by putting it in the form *Socrates est doctus* (Socrates is a learned man), he would obtain something far different. Further, any substantive verb sometimes includes both the band and the whole consequent, as *Socrates is, The dead are*
5 *not,* that is, they do not exist. But if in a simple axiom several verbs occur—as in the statement *Unequals are comparatives which do not have one quality*—it should be observed that the verb which the grammarians call the principal one is the band of the axiom.

10 *If this verb is affirmed, the simple axiom is affirmed; if it is denied, the simple axiom is denied.*

But it is denied if the sign of negation precedes that verb, for if it follows it is not negated but affirmed; in the example *Socrates is a lion not necessarily,* it is affirmed, since the sign
15 of negation follows the verb, and the whole consequent is not denied, but the mode.

But the signs of negation are not merely the adverbs of negating, but also exclusive particles (of the sort of *unique* and *sole*) and verbs signifying dissent or difference, as *to*
20 *differ, to be opposed,* etc.

Now let us see some examples: *Fire burns; fire is hot; fire is not water.* Here *fire* is the antecedent, *burns* is the consequent.

And here is the first disposition of invented things, of cause with effect, as in the first example; of the subject with the
25 *adjunct, as in the second; of dissentany with dissentany, as in the third.*

By this mode any arguments whatever that are affected among themselves can be enunciated, the consentany by

gando. Exceptis plenis comparationibus, in quibus duo planè distincta axiomata sunt, propositio, & redditio. Nam distributiones, quas etiam excipit *Ramus,* ut, Argumentum est artificiale aut inartificiale, axiomate simplici enuntiari pos-
5 sunt, ut infra docebitur: possunt & diversa, quæ excipiunt alii, si sic enuntias, Aliquis facundus non est formosus: & contraria; ut, virtus non est vitium, *&c.*

Axioma simplex est generale aut speciale.

Hæc distributio est simplicis axiomatis ex adjuncta quan-
10 titate, quæ modos, non species constituit. In axiomate autem composito, quantitatis nulla ratio habetur, sed tantum vinculi, ut infra dicemus.

Axioma generale est, quando commune consequens attribuitur generaliter communi antecedenti.

15 Vulgò etiam vocatur *universale.* Generaliter autem consequens antecedenti attribuitur, quando omni totique sive universo antecedenti attribuitur, omnibúsque iis, quæ sub ejus significatione continentur. Ad axioma igitur generale, tria hæc requiruntur; consequens, & antecedens generale, & gene-
20 ralis attributio. Neque enim ex nota sive signo universali definiendum fuit axioma generale; cùm & sæpissime non adsit nota, & cùm adest, non causa sed signum tantummodo sit axioma esse generale. Indefinita igitur, quæ vulgò vocant, etsi notam non habent generalem, generalia tamen sunt; ut
25 definitiones & reliqua artium præcepta, quæ nemo generalia

affirming, the dissentany by denying. Exception should be made of full comparisons, in which there are two fully distinct axioms, the proposition and the reddition. For distributions, which also Ramus excepts,—as *An argument is artificial or*
5 *inartificial*—can be enunciated by a simple axiom, as will be explained below. And the same is true of the diverse, which others except, if you enunciate them as follows: *Some eloquent man is not beautiful.* Likewise the contraries, as *Virtue is not vice,* etc.

10 *A simple axiom is general or special.*

This is distribution of the simple axiom from the adjunct quantity, which constitutes modes, not species. But in the compound axiom no account is taken of quantity, but merely of the band, as we will explain below.

15 *An axiom is general when a common consequent is generally attributed to a common antecedent.*

Commonly it is called *universal.* But the consequent is generally attributed to the antecedent when it is attributed to every antecedent and all of it, or to it universally, and to all
20 those which are contained under its signification. For a general axiom, therefore, these three things are required: a general consequent and antecedent, and a general attribution. Nor is a general axiom to be defined from a universal particle or sign, since very frequently the sign is not present, and when it is
25 present, it is not the cause but merely the indication that the axiom is general. Indefinites, therefore, as they commonly are called, though they do not have a general sign, are nevertheless general, such as definitions and the other precepts of

esse inficiabitur; nec notam tamen generalem præfixam habent. Notæ axiomatis generalis tam affirmati quàm negati hæ sunt: *omnis, nullus; semper, nunquam; ubique, nusquam,* &c.

5 *Atque hîc contradictio non semper dividit verum & falsum; sed contingentium utraque pars falsa potest esse:* ut,

Omnis *in urbe locus Bajis prælucet amœnis.* Nullus *in urbe locus Bajis prælucet amœnis.*

Itèm non contingentium.

10 Ut, omne animal est rationale; nullum animal est rationale. Hæc enim non contingentia sunt, sed potius absurda; quia consequens speciale antecedenti generali generaliter attribuitur. Falsa igitur pars utraque generalis contradictionis esse potest, vera esse non potest; falsitas quippe multiplex, veritas 15 una est.

Axioma speciale est, quando consequens non omni antecedenti attribuitur.

Speciale dicitur, quia de specie aliqua enuntiatur. Atque ut in generali axiomate consequens generaliter, sive omni & 20 universo antecedenti; ita in speciali specialiter, sive non omni attribuitur.

In hoc axiomate contradictio semper dividit verum à falso.

Id est specialis contradictionis pars una semper vera, pars altera semper est falsa.

25 *Axioma speciale est particulare aut proprium.*

the arts, which no one will deny to be general, yet they do not have the general sign prefixed. These are the signs of the general axiom, both that which is affirmed and that which is denied: *every, none; ever, never; everywhere, nowhere,* etc.

5 *And here contradiction does not always separate the true and the false; but both parts of contingent axioms can be false.*

For example, *Every spot in the city surpasses charming Baiæ; no place in the city surpasses charming Baiæ.*

10 *The same is true of the non-contingent.*

An example is *Every animal is rational; no animal is rational.* For these are not contingents, but rather absurd, since a special consequent is attributed generally to a general antecedent. Therefore both parts of a general contradiction can be

15 false, but both parts cannot be true, since falsity is manifold, but truth is one.

An axiom is special when a consequent is not attributed to every antecedent.

It is called special since it is pronounced about some species.

20 And as in the general axiom the consequent is attributed generally or to every antecedent and to the whole of every one, so in the special axiom it is attributed specially or not to all.

In this axiom contradiction always divides the true from the false.

25 That is, one part of a special contradiction is always true, the other part always false.

A special axiom is particular or proper.

Particulare, quando consequens commune antecedenti particulariter attribuitur.

Est axioma speciale quia de specie aliqua, licet ea quidem incerta & indefinita, enuntiatur: particulariter autem conse-
5 quens attribuitur, quando non universo antecedenti, sed ejus alicui parti attribuitur. Attributionis autem particularis notæ sive signa sunt, *quidam, aliquis, aliquando, alicubi;* & negationes generalium, *nonnulli, nonnunquam, non semper, non omnis,* &c. quæ particulari æquipollent. Commune autem
10 consequens debet esse; ex illa regula, Consequens nunquam minus est antecedente, sed semper vel majus eo vel saltem æquale. Unde *Aristoteles,* prior. 1. 28, negat *singulare de alio prædicari.*

Sequitur nunc contradictio particularium.

15 *Huic autem axiomati generaliter contradicitur.*

Aliquid ignoscendum est; nihil ignoscendum est: aliqua clementia non est laudanda; omnis clementia est laudanda. Hîc particulari affirmato, generale negatum; & particulari negato, generale affirmatum opponitur. Quodsi utraque pars
20 particularis est, non modo nulla est axiomatum contradictio, sed ne oppositio quidem. *Ut,* Quidam homo est doctus, quidam homo non est doctus. Non enim eidem subjecto attribuuntur, quæ lex est oppositorum. Pars igitur utraque vera esse potest; sicuti etiam cùm utraque affirmata est vel negata: ut,
25 Omnis homo est rationalis, quidam homo est rationalis: nullus

It is particular when the common consequent is attributed particularly to the antecedent.

It is a special axiom since it is pronounced about some species, though this is uncertain and indefinite, but the con-
5 sequent is particularly attributed when it is not attributed to the whole of the antecedent, but to some part of it. The indications or signs of particular attribution are *a certain one, some one, sometimes, somewhere,* and negations of general things, as *not none, not never, not always, not every,* etc., which are
10 equal to the particular. But the consequent ought to be common, according to the rule that affirms that the consequent is never less than the antecedent but always more than it or at least equal. Hence Aristotle (*Prior Analytics* 1.28) denies that "a singular thing can be predicated of another."

15 Now follows the contradiction of particulars.

The contradiction to this axiom is a general.

Examples are *Something is to be pardoned; nothing is to be pardoned. Some clemency is not to be praised; all clemency is to be praised.* In these examples, to the particular which is
20 affirmed is opposed the general that is denied, and to the particular that is denied the general that is affirmed is opposed. Because if either part is particular not merely is there no contradiction of the axioms, but no opposition—as in the example: *A certain man is learned; a certain man is not learned*
25 —for they are not attributed to the same subject, which is the law of opposites. Either part therefore can be true, as also when either is affirmed or denied, as in the statements: *Every man is rational; a certain man is rational. No man is irrational;*

homo est irrationalis, quidam homo non est irrationalis. In his non modo contradictio nulla, sed consensio summa est, generis nempe & speciei.

Axioma proprium (quod alii singulare vocant) *est, quando* 5 *consequens antecedenti proprio attribuitur.* Antecedens autem Logicè proprium dicitur quando rem vel personam singularem designat; sive proprio nomine exprimatur, sive non: qualia sunt etiam demonstrativa; ut, *hic homo.* Secundò, quæ per synecdochen generis dicuntur; ut poëta pro *Homero* aut 10 *Virgilio,* Philosophus pro *Aristotele* aut *Platone* & similia. Ad consequens autem hujus axiomatis quod attinet, id vel commune esse potest vel proprium.

Proprii contradictio est quando utraque pars est propria: in quo discrepat à particulari, cujus pars altera duntaxat particu-15 laris esse debet; consentit cum generali, cujus pars utraque generalis; ut, *Fabulla est bella:* cujus negatio & contradictio est, *Fabulla non est bella.* Atque hæc de axiomate simplici.

APPENDIX.

AD HAS axiomatis simplicis affectiones addunt *Aristotelici* æquipollentiam & conversionem.

Æquipollentia definitur, *enuntiationum verbis discrepantium convenientia re atque sensu:* sic, *aliquis homo est doctus,* &, *non omnis homo est doctus,* idem valent, &

a certain man is not irrational. In these examples not merely is there no contradiction but there is complete consent, to wit, of genus and species.

An axiom is proper (or what others call singular) *when* 5 *the consequent is attributed to its own peculiar antecedent.* But the antecedent is logically called proper when it designates a particular thing or person, whether he is indicated by his proper name or not. Demonstratives may be used, as in *this man.* Secondly, the particular is expressed by synec- 10 doche of the genus, as the Poet for Homer or Vergil, the Philosopher for Aristotle or Plato, and the like. But so far as the consequent of this axiom is concerned, it can be either common or proper.

There is contradiction of the proper axiom when both parts 15 are proper; in this it is different from the particular, of which one part only ought to be particular, but agrees with the general, both parts of which ought to be general, as *Fabulla is beautiful.* The negation and contradiction of this is *Fabulla is not beautiful.* So much for the simple axiom.

APPENDIX.

TO these affects of the simple axiom the Aristotelians add equipollence and conversion.

Equipollence is defined as *agreement in fact and sense of propositions discrepant in word;* thus *Some man is learned* and *Not every man is learned* are of the same value, 25 and so are similar statements, as has been said above in dis-

similia, ut suprà in notis est dictum. Æquipollentia itaque cum in verbis duntaxat, non in rebus, posita sit, ad Grammaticam vel ad Rhetoricam & verborum copiam remittenda est.

Conversio est prædicati unius enuntiationis in locum sub-
5 jecti transpositio ad probandam alteram enuntiationem, quæ ex ea transpositione sive conversione efficitur. Ea triplex affertur; simplex, per accidens, & per contrapositionem. Simplex, quæ fit manente eadem enuntiationis & quantitate & qualitate: fítque etiam tripliciter; in universali negante; ut,
10 *nullus homo est lapis, ergo nullus lapis est homo:* in particulari affirmante; ut, *aliquis homo est albus, ergo aliquod album est homo:* in affirmante denique universali & necessaria; ut, *omnis homo est risibilis, ergo omne risibile est homo.* Et hæc est una omnium conversionum verissima, quæ & *recipro-*
15 *catio* dicitur, proprii scilicet cum suo subjecto, definiti cum sua definitione.

Conversio per accidens mutat enuntiationis quantitatem; universalem scilicet affirmantem in particularem: ut, *omnis homo est animal, ergo quoddam animal est homo.* Per acci-
20 dens hanc dici volunt, quia aliud prius sequitur, nempe, *quidam homo est animal,* ex quo hoc deinde, simplici conversione, *ergo quoddam animal est homo.*

Conversio per contrapositionem mutat enuntiationis qualitatem; universalem scilicet affirmantem in negantem: vel, in
25 qua loco subjecti & prædicati, ponitur utriusque conversi contradictio: ut, *omnis homo est rationalis; ergo quodcunque non*

cussing the signs. So equipollence when it resides in words only, not in things, should be turned over to grammar or rhetoric and copious supply of words.

Conversion is the transposition of one predicated proposition to the place of a subject for the proof of another proposition; the proof is secured through this transposition or conversion. Conversion is of three sorts, simple, by accident, and through contraposition. Simple conversion is that which is carried on when the quantity and quality of the proposition remain the same. It is done in three ways: first, in universal negating, as *No man is a stone, therefore no stone is a man;* second, in particular affirming, as *Some man is white, therefore something white is a man;* thirdly, in universal and necessary affirming, as *Every man is risible, therefore every risible being is a man.* And this one is the truest of all conversions, which is also called *reciprocation,* namely of something proper with its subject, of the thing defined with its definition.

Conversion through accident changes the quantity of the proposition, which affirms the universal in the particular, as *Every man is an animal, therefore a certain animal is a man.* They wish this to be called conversion through accident, since another follows the first, to wit: *A certain man is an animal.* From that is derived, by a simple conversion, *Therefore a certain animal is a man.*

Conversion by contraposition changes the quality of a proposition, namely the universal affirmative into a negative; in this type in the place of the subject and the predicate is placed the contradiction of the converse of either one, as *Every man*

est rationale, non est homo: omne mortale est genitum; ergo quod non est genitum, non est mortale; vel, quod est non genitum, est non mortale: admittendi ad sacramenta, habent pœnitentiam & fidem; ergo qui hæc non habent, non sunt admittendi. Tres hosce modos conversionum ex *Aristot.* petunt: duos priores ex 1. Prior. c. 2. Tertium ex 2. Top. c. 1. syllogisticæ reductionis gratia, cujus inutilitas infra ostendetur, ab ipso inventos.

Conversione autem hac ne decipiamur fortè, neque enim fidissima est, cautiones quædam adhiberi solent: prima, ne termini sint figurati; ut, *panis est corpus Christi.* Secunda, ne quid mutiletur; ut, *quidam cernit cæcum, ergo cæcus cernit quendam:* totum enim prædicatum non est *cæcum,* sed *cernit cæcum;* ut etiam in hac; *omnis senex fuit puer; ergo quidem puer fuit senex;* non enim *puer,* sed *fuit puer* totum prædicatum est; convertendum ergo, *quidam qui fuit puer, est senex.* Tertia, ut casus obliqui à conversione facti, reddantur recti; ut, *aliqua arbor est in agro; ergo aliquod quod est in agro, est arbor,* non sic, *ergo aliquis ager est in arbore.*

Sed, omissis istis cautionibus, expeditior via est, conversionem omnem si dubia sit, tanquam sophisma petitionis principii rejicere; ut quæ sine medio termino probare rem dubiam conetur: de quo sophismate infra monebimus.

is rational, therefore whatever is not rational is not a man; every mortal is begotten, therefore what is not begotten is not mortal; or *what is non-begotten is non-mortal; those to be admitted to the sacraments are they who have penitence and* 5 *faith, therefore those who do not have them are not to be admitted.* They derive these three modes of conversion from Aristotle, the first two from the *Prior Analytics* 1. 2, the third from the *Topics* 2. 1; they were invented by him for the sake of syllogistic reduction, the inutility of which will be shown 10 below.

Lest we should be deceived by this conversion, for it is not very trustworthy, certain cautions are provided. First, lest the terms be figurative, as *Bread is the body of Christ.* Second, lest something is mutilated as *Some one sees the blind man, hence* 15 *the blind man sees some one;* for the whole predicate is not *blind man,* but *sees the blind man,* as also in the following: *Every old man has been a boy, therefore every boy has been an old man;* for the whole predicate is not *boy* but *has been a boy;* therefore it must be converted thus: *A certain one who* 20 *has been a boy is an old man.* Thirdly, that cases which have been made oblique by conversion should be restored to the direct form, as *Some tree is in the field, therefore something that is in the field is a tree;* but not in the form, *therefore some field is in the tree.*

25 But, omitting all cautions, it is a more expeditious way to reject every conversion, if there is any doubt, as a sophism of the *petito principii,* as something that attempts to prove a doubtful thing without a middle term; of this sophism we shall speak below.

CAPUT V.

De Axiomate copulato.

AXIOMA compositum est quod vinculo conjunctionis continetur.

Hoc genus axiomatis *Aristoteles* totum prætermisit. Vulgò *propositio hypothetica* vocatur; i.e. conditiona-
5 lis; angustè nimis; cùm ea vox compositis non omnib. conveniat, ut suo loco patebit. *Compositum* autem dicitur, quia sententia est multiplex, quæ in plures resolvi simplices potest: nec tamen dicendum est, ex simplicib. axiomatis componi, sed ex argumentis, quæ conjunctionis vinculo composita, multi-
10 plicem sententiam efficiunt: idcirco autem axioma componitur, quia argumenta in eo conjuncta consentiunt & compositionem appetunt. Nulla autem hîc ratio habetur quantitatis, generale sit an speciale, sed tantum compositionis. Ut autem verbum fuit vinculum simplicis, ita conjunctio est axiomatis
15 compositi, ejúsque proinde forma & quasi anima est.

Itaque è conjunctione affirmata vel negata, affirmatur vel negatur. Conjunctione non negata, negatum axioma non erit, etiamsi partes omnes erunt negatæ.

Contradictionísque pars vera est, pars falsa. De qua vulgus
20 Logicorum silet.

CHAPTER V.

Of the copulate axiom.

A *COMPOUND axiom is that the band whereof is a conjunction.*

This genus of axiom Aristotle entirely passes over. It is commonly called a *hypothetical proposition,* that 5 is, a conditional one, but too narrowly, for this word would not be suitable to all compounds, as in its place will appear. But it is called *compound* since the statement is multiplex, for it can be resolved into several simple statements. But it should not be said that it is composed of simple axioms but of 10 arguments which, being held together by the band of the conjunction, bring about a multiplex statement. And the axiom is compound for the reason that the arguments joined in it consent and desire composition. But no account is here taken of quantity, whether general or special, but merely of 15 composition. But as the verb was the band of the simple axiom, so the conjunction is the band of the composite axiom, therefore it is the form and as it were soul of it.

So from the affirmation or denial of the conjunction, the axiom is affirmed or denied. If the conjunction is not denied, 20 the axiom will not be denied, even though all its parts are denied.

Part of the contradiction is true, part false. This is something of which the mass of logicians is silent.

Enuntiatum compositum est pro sua conjunctione congregativum aut segregativum.

Congregativum est cujus partes tanquam simul veræ, conjunctione sua congregantur. Conjunctione videlicet non solùm illa Grammatica verùm etiam sententiarum quavis relatione. Cùm autem relatio ista, sive Grammatica sive Logica, multiplex sit, essentiæ, consequentiæ sive causæ, quantitatis, qualitatis, temporis, loci, relatio quidem essentiæ (cujus notæ sunt *is qui, id quod)* & loci (cujus notæ sunt *ubi, ibi)* ad simplicia axiomata referenda est; de reliquis suo loco.

Congregativum enuntiat omnia consentanea affirmando, omnia dissentanea negando. Hoc est, si unum consentaneorum subjecto attribuatur, alterum quoque attribuitur; & contrà, uno negato, alterum negatur: si unum dissentaneorum de subjecto affirmatur, alterum negatur; & contrà. Ita semper consentanea simul hîc affirmanda vel neganda sunt, dissentanea non simul.

Congregativum verò est copulatum aut connexum. Copulatum, cujus conjunctio est copulativa, ut Æneid. 1.

> *Unà Eurúsque Notúsque ruunt, crebérque procellis*
> *Africus.*

Hîc igitur negatio erit & contradictio, negata conjunctione; *non unà Eurúsque Notúsque ruunt* &c. *Socrates & doctus*

A compound enunciate is according to its conjunction congregative or segregative.

That is congregative of which the parts as though simultaneously true are held together by its conjunction. That is,
5 it is held together not merely by the grammatical conjunction but by some relation of the statements. But though this relation, whether grammatical or logical, is multiplex, being of essence, consequence or cause, quantity, quality, time, and place, yet the relation of essence (the signs of which are *he*
10 *who, that which*) and of place (the signs of which are *where, there*) is to be referred to the simple axiom; the rest will be treated in their place.

The congregative enunciate expresses all the consentanies by affirming, all the dissentanies by denying. That is, if one
15 of the consentanies is attributed to the subject, the other is attributed also, and on the contrary, if one is denied, the other is denied; if one of the dissentanies is affirmed of the subject, the other is negated, and contrariwise. So the consentanies here must always be affirmed or denied at the same time, but
20 the dissentanies not at the same time.

The congregative enunciate is either copulative or connex. The copulative is that whereof the conjunction is copulative as in *Æneid* 1:

The east and south winds as though one do blow,
25 The Afric oft with these his blasts conjoins.

Hence in this statement there will be denial and contradiction when the conjunction is denied:

The east and south winds not as one do blow, etc.

erat & formosus: Socrates non & doctus erat & formosus. Quòd si hoc modo negaretur, *Socrates nec doctus erat nec formosus* (qui modus contradictionis est adhibendus cùm omnes partes sunt falsæ) contradictio non esset axiomatica; 5 non enim vinculum negaretur, sed partes: copulatio enim significat utrumque simul verum esse, ejus negatio non utrumque; at hæc negatio neutrum: acsi dictum esset, *Socrates & non doctus & non formosus erat:* deinde, in axiomate composito contradictionis pars una vera, altera est falsa; hîc autem 10 utraque: hoc ergo axioma, *Socrates nec doctus erat nec formosus,* est potius axioma copulatum affirmatum, cujus partes negantur. Copulati autem negatio per axioma etiam discretum fieri potest, cùm partes non omnes falsæ sunt; ut infra intelligitur. Conjunctio denique hîc sæpe non adest, sed intel- 15 ligitur.

Verum autem enuntiati copulati judicium pendet ex omnium partium veritate; falsum, ex una saltem parte falsa. Hoc est axioma copulatum judicatur esse verum, si omnes partes simul veræ sunt; falsum, si vel una pars erit falsa. Idem tradit 20 *Gellius, l.* 16. *c.* 8. In copulato enim axiomate, veritas omnium partium spectatur, quia partes omnes absolute enuntiantur tanquam simul veræ.

Huic generi affine est enuntiatum relatæ qualitatis, cujus conjunctio Logica potius est quàm Grammatica, nempe *ipsa* 25 *relatio.*

Socrates was both learned and handsome; Socrates was not both learned and handsome. The negation may have the form: *Socrates was neither learned nor handsome* (a mode of contradiction employed when all the parts are false), but if this
5 form should be used the contradiction would not be axiomatic, for the band is not denied, but the parts, for the copulation signifies that both are true at the same time, the denial of it that both are not true; but this negation that neither of them is true, as though it were said: *Socrates was not learned and*
10 *was not handsome.* Then in a compound axiom one part of the contradiction is true, the other is false, but here both are false. Hence the axiom *Socrates was neither learned nor handsome* is rather a copulative affirmed axiom, of which the parts are denied. But the negation of the copulate
15 through the axiom can also be discrete, when the parts are not all false, as will be seen below. Moreover, the conjunction in this case often is not present but is understood.

A true judgment of a copulative enunciate depends on the truth of all the parts; a false judgment on at least one false
20 *part.* That is, a copulative axiom is judged to be true if all the parts are true at the same time; false if even one part is false. Gellius (16. 8) is of the same opinion. For in a copulative axiom the truth of all the parts is seen, since all the parts are absolutely enunciated as true at the same time.

25 *Akin to this genus is the enunciate of related quality, the conjunction of which* is logical rather than grammatical, to wit, *the relation itself.*

Related quality, however, is full similitude, as the signs

Relata autem qualitas est plena similitudo: ut notæ ipsæ testantur; *qualis, talis, quemadmodum, sic.* Eclog. 3.

Tale tuum carmen nobis, divine poëta,
quale sopor fessis in gramine.——

5 Hîc copulatum judicium est tanquam diceretur, Sopor est fessis gratus, & sic tuum carmen nobis gratum est: cujus negatio, Non tale tuum carmen, quale sopor, *&c.*

Ad hunc etiam locum pertinet relatio quantitatis in plenis comparationibus: quarum notæ sunt, cùm à pari, *idem quod,* 10 *tam quàm, tanto quanto, tot quot, eò quò;* tum à majori, *non solùm, sed etiam;* tum à minori, *non modò non, sed ne* (quæ nota est copulati axiomatis affirmati, cujus partes negantur) *cùm tum.* Relatio autem hæc & qualitatis & quantitatis si hypotheticè non absolutè enuntiatur ad connexum potius refe-15 renda est.

Relationes autem loci ad axioma simplex rectius referuntur, ut supra est dictum. Neque enim in hujusmodi exemplo, *ubi amici ibi opes,* est copulatum judicium, sed simplex & quidem generale; scilicet, omnem divitem amicos habere.

themselves testify: *of such a sort . . . such, just as . . . so.* This is illustrated in the third *Eclogue:*

> So me thy song as sleep on grass doth queme
> The traveler his weary limbs to drench.

5 Here the copulative judgment is as though it should be said: *Sleep doth queme the traveler, and likewise thy song doth queme me.* The negation of this is *Thy song doth not, as sleep* etc.

To this place also pertains the relation of quantity in full 10 comparisons, of which the signs are, in comparison by an equal, *the same as, so . . . as, by as much . . . by so much, as many . . . so many, by what . . . by that.* The sign when a greater is used is *not merely . . . but also;* when a lesser *not merely not . . . but not* (which is the sign of the 15 affirmed copulative axiom, of which the parts are denied), *as . . . so especially.* But this relation of both quality and quantity if hypothetically it is not absolutely enunciated must be referred rather to the connex.

Relations of place, however, are more properly referred to 20 the simple axiom, as is said above. For not even in an example of this sort—*Where are friends, there is wealth*—is there a copulative judgment, but a simple and indeed general one, to wit: *Every rich man has friends.*

CAPUT VI.

De Axiomate connexo.

AXIOMA connexum est congregativum, cujus conjunctio est connexiva.

Ut *si, nisi* affirmativè. Idem enim valet *nisi,* quod *si non:* quo non totum axioma, sed antecedens tantum
5 negatur: ut *Æneid.* 2.

——si miserum fortuna Sinonem
finxit, vanum etiam mendacémque improba finget.

Cujus negatio est, negata conjunctione, *Non si miserum fortuna Sinonem finxit, vanum etiam mendacémque improba*
10 *finget.*

Conjunctio etiam hæc interdum negatur apertiùs, negando consequentiam. Ut, non continuò, non illicò, non idcirco, non ideo: his enim formulis non consequens axiomatis, id n. contradictionem non efficeret, sed ipsa partium consequentia
15 quæ Logica conjunctio est apertius negatur: ut pro *Amer. Non continuò, si me in sicariorum gregem contuli, sicarius sum. De Fato: Nec si omne enuntiatum verum est aut falsum, sequitur illicò causas esse immutabiles.*

Affirmatio enim significat, si sit antecedens, etiam conse-

CHAPTER VI.

Of the connex axiom.

T*HE congregative axiom whose conjunction is connexive is called connex.*

Its conjunctions when affirmative are such as *if, unless*. *Unless* is of the same value as *if not*, by which is denied
5 not the whole axiom, but the antecedent merely. Illustration is found in *Æneid* 2:

> If Fortune wrought for Sinon misery,
> In malice she'll make him a liar vain.

The denial of this, with denial of the conjunction, is

10 > Nor, if Chance wrought for Sinon misery,
> Shall she in hate make him a liar vain.

This conjunction is also sometimes more plainly denied by denying the consequence, as by *not necessarily, not directly, not therefore, not on that account.* By these formulas the con-
15 sequent of the axiom is not openly denied, for that would not bring about contradiction, but rather the very consequence of the parts which constitutes logical conjunction. This is illustrated in *Pro Amerino:* "I am not of necessity a murderer, though in the company of murderers." And in *De Fato:*
20 "Neither if every enunciation is true or false doth it follow therefore that the causes are immutable."

For affirmation signifies that if there is an antecedent there

quens esse. Negatio itaque & contradictio statuit, si sit antecedens, non ideo consequens esse.

Potest & connexo per axioma discretum contradici: ut, *quamvis omne enuntiatum sit verum aut falsum, non tamen*
5 *causæ sunt immutabiles;* quod sequente capite liquebit.

Sed cùm judicabis connexum absolute, i.e. per se suáque natura *verum esse, necessarium quoque judicabis: & intelliges hanc necessitatem ex necessaria partium connexione oriri, quæ ipsa potest esse vel in falsis partibus.*

10 *Ut, si homo est leo, est etiam quadrupes,* necessarium connexum est; quia argumentorum, quæ hîc connectuntur, leonis scilicet & quadrupedis, connexio est necessaria, speciei scilicet cum genere. Unde efficitur axioma generaliter verum ac proinde necessarium; *omnis leo est quadrupes:* quod in
15 connexo indicium est absolutæ veritatis. Sic, si *Socrates est homo, est etiam animal,* absolutè verum est & necessarium, quia omnis homo est animal: hujúsque connexi consequens falsum esse non potest, nisi antecedens quoque falsum sit, quod aliud signum est absolutæ veritatis.

20 Quòd si consequens falsum fuerit, falsum item est antecedens. *Si illud, hoc: si non hoc, ne illud quidem.* Atque ita, ut jam demonstravimus, si connexio absolute vera est, erit quoque necessaria: sin ex conditione & pacto, sine quo con-

is also a consequent. So negation and contradiction assert that although there is an antecedent, there is not for that reason a consequent.

It is possible also for a connex axiom to be contradicted by
5 means of a discrete axiom, as *Any proposition whatever may be true or false, but its causes are not immutable.* This will appear in the following chapter.

But when you will judge that a connex is absolutely, that is, through itself and its nature, *true, you will also judge that it*
10 *is necessary, and you will observe that this necessity springs from the necessary connection of the parts, which can appear even in false parts.*

To illustrate, in the statement *If a man is a lion he is also a quadruped,* the connex is necessary, because the connection of
15 the arguments which are here connected, to wit, lion and quadruped, is necessary, that is, of species with genus. Whence is obtained an axiom generally true and accordingly necessary: *Every lion is a quadruped;* this is an indication of absolute truth in the connex. Thus, since every man is an animal, it is
20 absolutely true and necessary to say: *If Socrates is a man he is also an animal.* But the consequent of this connex cannot be false, unless the antecedent is also false, which is another sign of absolute truth.

For if the consequent is false, the antecedent is also false.
25 The signs are *if that . . . this, if not this . . . neither that as well.* And so, as we have now demonstrated, if the connection is absolutely true, it will also be necessary; if however it is true merely according to the conditions and agreement

nexum per se suáque natura verum non esset, erit tantummodo contingens.

Quod si connexio sit contingens & pro sua tantum probabilitate ponatur, judicium ejus tantum opinio fuerit.

5 Ut, *Terent. Andr.*

Pamphile, si id facis, hodie postremum me vides.

Hoc est, si *Philumenam* uxorem ducis, ego hodie moriar: quod nemo sequi existimaverit, nisi hoc posito, *Charinum,* qui hoc dicit, *Philumenam* perditissimè amare. Per se enim 10 nulla est connexionis necessitas inter nuptias *Pamphili* & interitum *Charini.* Qui autem ex amoris vehementia sic existimabit, ejus judicium non erit scientia, sed opinio.

Ut autem judicare possimus, quæ connexio sit absolutè vera, quæ non, spectanda argumenta sunt, quæ in axiomate 15 connectuntur, consentiant inter se nec ne, & quo modo. Ut *si dies est, lux est,* connexum est necessarium, quia dies sive sol ortus est causa lucis. *Si dies est, Dio ambulat,* connexum est falsum aut contingens; quia nulla est affectio absolutè consentanea inter diem & *Dionem.*

20 *Connexo axiomati affinis est ista consequentiæ relatio:* quæ à nonnullis, *relatio causæ* dicitur; & axioma efficit, quod *Stoici causale* nominant; *Laërt.* in *Zenone:* quia nempe antecedens

without which the connex through itself and its nature cannot be true, it will be merely contingent.

For if the connection is contingent and is laid down as true merely because of its probability, the judgment of it will be 5 *opinion only.*

This is illustrated by Terence in the *Andria:*

> If thou do that, Pamphilus, this is the last day that ever thou shalt see me.

That is if you take Philumena as your wife, I shall die 10 today, something that no one will think possible unless it is first taken for granted that Charinus, who says this, loves Philumena desperately, for in itself there is no necessity for connection between the marriage of Pamphilus and the death of Charinus. But any one who because of the violence of love 15 thinks there is such a connection will have a judgment that will be not knowledge but opinion.

But that we may be able to judge which connection is absolutely true, which not, the arguments which are connected in the axiom should be inspected to see whether they are con- 20 sentany with each other or not, and in what way. The connex is necessary in the example *If it is day, it is light;* for day or the sunrise is the cause of light. In the example *If it is day, Dion is walking,* the connex is false or contingent, since there is no absolutely consentany affect between day and Dion.

25 *Akin to the connex axiom is that relation of consequence* which by some is called *the relation of cause,* and produces an axiom which the Stoics, according to Laërtes (*In Zenone*)

est causa consequentis, adeóque vinculum ejus conjunctio causalis *cùm, quia, quoniam;* quibus respondet *ideo* vel *etiam:* ut, *cùm Tullius sit orator, est etiam peritus benè dicendi.* Quanquam autem relata ista connexis affinia sunt, non nihil 5 tamen discrepant: in antecedente enim connexi quædam conditio est, in hoc relato nulla: connexum potest ex falsis partibus verum esse, relatum hoc sive causale non potest esse verum, nisi antecedens verum fuerit: ut, *quia dies est, sol est supra horizontem.*

10 Affinis est & relatio temporis axiomati connexo, ut ait ipse *Ramus* infra *c.* 13.

Relatio autem temporis has habet notas, *tum cùm, donec dum, quandiu tandiu:* ut apud *Ovid.* in epist.

Cùm Paris Oenone poterit spirare relicta,
15 *ad fontem Xanthi versa recurret aqua.*

Sic, *Donec eris felix, multos numerabis amicos.*

Potest etiam connexum enuntiari sine ulla non modò relationis verùm etiam connexionis nota: ut, *posita causa, ponitur effectum. Fac hoc, & vives. Ovid in epist: sume fidem &* 20 *pharetram, fies manifestus Apollo.* Nonnunquam etiam duob. negativis: *Cic.* pro *Milone: non hoc fragile corpus humanum mente regitur, & non regitur mente universum mundi corpus.*

call *causal,* since the antecedent is the cause of the consequent, and moreover its band is a causal conjunction, as *because, since, whereas;* to these corresponds *therefore,* or *certainly,* as *Since Tully is an orator, he is certainly skillful in speaking*
5 *well.* But though these relatives are akin to connexes, yet they are somewhat discrepant, for in the antecedent of the connex there is a condition, but none in the relative; the connex can be true with false parts, but this relative or causal cannot be true unless its antecedent is true, as *Since it is day, the sun is*
10 *above the horizon.*

The relation of time is also akin to the connex axiom, as Ramus himself says in chapter thirteen below.

The relation of time has as its signs *then . . . when, at the time when, while, as long as . . . so long,* as in the
15 *Epistles* of Ovid:

> When Paris apart from Oenone can breathe,
> To their well shall the waters of Xanthus recur.

Another example is *During the time when you are fortunate, you will number many friends.*

20 A connex can be expressed not merely without any sign of relation but even of connection, as *The cause being laid down as true, the effect is laid down;* and *Do this and you live.* Ovid gives an example in his *Epistles:*

> Now take the lyre and quiver—Apollo plain thou art.

25 Sometimes also two negatives are used, as by Cicero in *Pro Milone:* "This fragile human body is not ruled by the mind, and the universal frame of the world is not ruled by a mind."

CAPUT VII.

De Axiomate discreto.

AXIOMA segregativum est, cujus conjunctio est segregativa.

Ideóque argumenta dissentanea enuntiat.

Enuntiatum segregativum est discretum aut disjunctum.

5 *Discretum, cujus conjunctio est discretiva.* Discretum dicitur, quòd conjunctione illa segregativa discernuntur & segregantur ea potissimum quæ leviter & ratione tantum dissentiunt.

Itaque è dissentaneis præcipuè diversa enuntiat.

10 *Præcipuè,* quia diversorum notæ, *non hoc, sed illud,* ut superiore libro dictum est, in diversis nonnunquam solent oppositis inservire. Ut autem diversorum ita etiam discreti axiomatis doctrina distinctionib. duntaxat, non conclusionibus, idonea est; & à reliquis propterea Dialecticis, qui 15 omnia ad syllogismum referunt, omissa. Sed rationis usus quicunque in Logica prætermittendus non erat. Exempli gratia: *Tuscul.* 5. *Quanquam sensu corporis judicentur, ad animum referri tamen.* Cujus negatio & contradictio est, *non quamquam corporis sensu judicentur, tamen ad animum re-* 20 *ferri:* vel, *quanquam sensu corporis judicentur, non tamen ad animum referri.* Nam *tamen* est hîc conjunctio præcipua.

CHAPTER VII.

Of the discrete axiom.

A SEGREGATIVE axiom is one whose conjunction is segregative.

Therefore it expresses dissentany arguments.

The segregative axiom is discrete or disjunct.

5 *That is discrete of which the conjunction is discretive.* It is called discrete because by that conjunction segregatives are discerned and those especially are segregated which dissent easily and by reason only.

So among the dissentanies it especially enunciates diverse 10 *arguments.*

Especially, because the signs of the diverse arguments, *not this . . . but that,* as was said in the book above, sometimes are used for diverse opposites. But the doctrine of the discrete axiom as of diverse arguments is suitable for distinctions 15 merely, not for conclusions, and therefore is omitted by the other dialecticians, who refer everything to the syllogism. But any use of reason is not to be passed over in logic. For the sake of example, consider *Tusculan Disputations* 5: "Although they be judged by the sense of the body, yet they are 20 to be referred to the spirit." The negation and contradiction of this is *Nor though they be judged by the sense of the body are they therefore to be referred to the spirit;* or *Though they be judged by the sense of the body, yet they are not to be referred to the spirit.* For *yet* is here a special conjunction.

Quemadmodum autem copulati & connexi axiomatis negatio & contradictio discretum esse potest, ita vicissim copulatum vel connexum discreti: ut, *quanquam culpa vacat, non tamen suspicione caret:* cujus per copulatum contradictio est, *& culpa vacat, & suspicione caret;* vel per connexum, *si culpa vacat, etiam suspicione caret.*

Discretum enuntiatum judicatur esse verum & legitimum, si partes non solum veræ, sed etiam discretæ sint; falsum vel ridiculum contra.

Ut, *quanquam* Ulysses *formosus erat, tamen non erat infacundus,* falsum est, quia antecedens est falsum. Sed si consequens modò verum est, axioma verum erit, etiamsi antecedens verum esse tantummodo concedatur. Hoc autem, *Quanquam Menelaus formosus erat, tamen erat facundus,* non est discretum, sed ne segregativum quidem: omnis enim segregativi axiomatis partes tanquam non simul veræ segregantur, hic verò tanquam simul veræ congregantur. *Quanquam* Ulysses *facundus erat, non tamen erat indisertus,* est ridiculum, quia partes non sunt discretæ sed oppositæ.

Just as the negation and contradiction of the copulate and the connex axiom can be discrete, so in turn the copulate or the connex can be the negation and contradiction of the discrete, as *Though he is without fault, yet he does not escape suspicion.* This is contradicted through the copulate: *He is without fault and he escapes suspicion.* It is also contradicted through the connex: *If he is without fault he also escapes suspicion.*

A discrete enunciate is judged to be true and legitimate if the parts are not merely true but also discrete; otherwise it is false or ridiculous.

The example *Although Ulysses was handsome, yet he was not without eloquence* is false because the antecedent is false. But if the consequent is true, the axiom will be true, even though the antecedent is merely conceded to be true. But this—*Though Menelaus was handsome, yet he was eloquent*—is not discrete, not even segregative, for all the parts of a segregative axiom are segregated as not true at the same time, but here they are congregated as true at the same time. It is ridiculous to say that *Although Ulysses was eloquent, yet he was not ineloquent,* since the parts are not discrete but opposite.

CAPUT VIII.

De Axiomate disjuncto.

A*XIOMA disjunctum est axioma segregativum, cujus conjunctio est disjunctiva.*

Ut, *aut dies est, aut nox est. Aut vera est hæc enunciatio aut falsa.* Nam ut ex *Cicerone* citatur hoc exem-
5 plum, *omnis enuntiatio vera est aut falsa,* videtur esse distributio potius quàm disjunctio. Distributio autem quatenus de toto diviso partes enuntiantur, axioma simplex & generale est, adeóque non compositum nedum disjunctum. Neque enim distributionis partes, quamvis inter se oppositæ, oppositionem
10 vel disjunctionem ullam faciunt, sed eidem toti subjiciuntur, & in ejusdem simplicis axiomatis consequente verbi vinculo cum toto, quod antecedens est, consentiunt; at extra distributionem, ubi non de toto, sed de aliqua ejus parte vel specie enuntiantur, tum demum axioma disjunctum efficiunt; ut,
15 quod supra posuimus, *hæc enuntiatio aut vera est aut falsa.*

Hîc significatur è disjunctis unicum verum esse.

Nempe quia opposita hic sola disponi debent. Atque id semper à disserente significatur, tametsi aliquando accidit, ut disjunctorum vel plura uno, vel nullum omninò verum sit.
20 Negatio igitur & contradictio erit, *non aut dies aut nox est.*

Et contradictione significatur, non necessariò alterutrum verum esse.

CHAPTER VIII.

Of the disjunct axiom.

A *DISJUNCT axiom is a segregative axiom the conjunction of which is disjunctive.*

Examples are *Either it is day or it is night;* and *This enunciation is either true or false.* From Cicero is cited
5 the example: *Every enunciation is true or it is false,* but this seems to be distribution rather than disjunction. But a distribution, so far as the parts of a divided whole are enunciated, is a simple and general axiom, therefore neither compound nor disjunct. Neither do the parts of a distribution,
10 though opposite among themselves, produce any opposition or disjunction, but are subjected to the same whole, and in the consequent of the same simple axiom agree by means of the band of the verb with the whole which is the antecedent. But aside from distribution, in instances where they are af-
15 firmed not of the whole but of some part or species of it, they indeed produce a disjunct axiom, as in the one we gave above: *This enunciation is either true or false.*

Here it is indicated that one only of the disjuncts is true.

The reason is that here only opposites should be set forth.
20 And this is always signified by one who argues, though sometimes it happens that more than one of the disjuncts or none at all of them is true. Hence there will be negation and contradiction, as *It is not either night or day.*

And by contradiction is signified that neither one is neces-
25 *sarily true.*

Nam si disjunctio absolutè vera est, est etiam necessaria; partésque disjunctæ sunt opposita sine ullo medio. De quibus vide superioris libri caput de contradicentibus.

Veruntamen quamvis absolutè vera disjunctio, necessaria 5 *quoque sit; tamen nihil necesse est partes separatim necessarias esse.*

Ut, *cras aut pluet aut non pluet,* disjunctio est necessaria, quia ex contradicentibus constat, quæ sunt contraria sine medio: & tamen, *cras pluet* & *cras non pluet,* utrumque con- 10 tingens axioma est. Sic, *homo aut bonus est aut non bonus,* &c.

Nam disjunctionis necessitas pendet è necessaria partium oppositione & disjunctione non ex earum necessaria veritate.

Hinc argumentum illud dissolvitur *Chrysippi Stoici* aliorúmque veterum, apud *Ciceronem* de Fato; quo probare sunt 15 conati, futura omnia esse necessaria & quasi fatalia, eò quòd necesse sit ea aut vera esse aut falsa. Disjunctio quidem, ut diximus, necessaria est; pars tamen disjunctionis alterutra talis erit, qualis causa ejus est; sive necessaria, sive contingens, i.e. vel libera, vel fortuita.

20 Atque hæc de necessaria disjunctione, cujus judicium scientia est.

Disjunctio autem sæpe est ex conditione.

Ut si quæratur utrum Cleon venerit an Socrates, quia ita pactum sit alterutrum tantum venturum esse.

For if the disjunction is absolutely true, it is also necessary, and the parts are disjunct opposites without any mean. On this see the chapter on contradictories in the first book.

Nevertheless, though any disjunction absolutely true is also 5 *necessary, yet there is no necessity for the parts separately to be necessary.*

For example, *Tomorrow it will rain or it will not rain* is a necessary disjunction since it is made up of contradictories which are contrary without any mean, and yet of the two 10 statements—*Tomorrow it will rain* and *Tomorrow it will not rain*—either is a contingent axiom. The same is true of *A man is either good or he is not good,* etc.

For the necessity of disjunction depends on the necessary opposition and disjunction of the parts, not on their necessary 15 *truth.*

Thence is annulled that argument of Chrysippus the Stoic and other ancients, according to Cicero's *De fato;* they attempted by it to prove that all future things are necessary and as it were fated, because these necessarily are either true or 20 false. A disjunction, indeed, as we have said, is necessary, but one part or other of the disjunction will be such as is its cause, whether necessary or contingent, that is, either free or fortuitous.

So much for necessary disjunction, the judgment of which 25 is knowledge.

A disjunction is often conditional.

For example, it may be asked whether Cleon or Socrates was coming, since it has been agreed that one or the other only should come.

Itaque si disjunctio sit contingens (contingens autem est, si partes medium habent) *non est absolute vera, sed tantum opinabilis.*

Qualis est frequenter in hominum usu. Ut *Cæsar* ad ma-
5 trem: *hodie me aut pontificem videbis, aut exulem. Ovid.* in epistola *Leandri.*

Aut mihi continget felix audacia salvo,
aut mors solliciti finis amoris erit.

CAPUT IX.

De Syllogismo & ejus partibus.

ATQUE ejusmodi dispositio est axiomatica sive noëtica axiomatis per se manifesti: sequitur dianoëtica. *Dianoëtica est cùm aliud axioma ex alio deducitur.*

Vox *Græca* διάνοια, mentis & rationis discursum significat; qui tum fit maximè cùm sententia alia ex alia ratiocinando deducitur.

15 *Dispositio dianoetica est syllogismus aut methodus.*

Syllogismus est dispositio dianoetica qua quæstio cum argumento ita disponitur, ut posito antecedente, necessariò concludatur.

Est dianoia: est ergo discursus mentis ac rationis quo aliud
20 ex alio ratiocinando colligitur: eam ratiocinantis quasi collectionem vox ipsa syllogismi significat: quæ quidem collectio

So if a disjunction is contingent (and it is contingent if the parts have a mean) *it is not absolutely true but merely a matter of opinion.*

This is frequently exemplified in the practice of men, as 5 when Cæsar said to his mother: "Today you will see me pontifex or an exile." Ovid writes in the *Epistle of Leander:*

> Either good hap shall now unto me fall,
> Or else fierce death, the end of loving thrall.

CHAPTER IX.

Of the syllogism and its parts.

THE axiomatic or noëtic disposition of the axiom manifest through itself is as I have presented it; there follows the dianoëtic.

A dianoëtic disposition is found when one axiom is deduced from another.

The Greek word διάνοια signifies discourse of mind and 15 reason, which most appears when one opinion is by reasoning deduced from another.

A dianoëtic disposition is a syllogism or method.

A syllogism is a dianoëtic disposition by which a question is so disposed with its argument that if the antecedent is given, 20 of necessity a conclusion is drawn.

It is dianoia; therefore it is a discursive process of the mind and reason by which one thing is gathered from another by reasoning; the word syllogism itself signifies this gathering

sive deductio ab intellectûs humani imbecillitate profecta est: quæ cùm rerum veritatem & falsitatem primo intuitu perspicere in axiomate non potest, ad syllogismum se confert, in quo de consequentia & inconsequentia earum judicare possit.

5 *Cùm itaque axioma dubium est, quæstio efficitur, & ad ejus fidem tertio argumento est opus cum quæstione collocato.*

Quæstionis partes vulgò termini appellantur; & antecedens quidem minor terminus, consequens major terminus dicitur; quia antecedente latius ferè est consequens. Tertium autem 10 argumentum ab *Aristot. medium* & *medius terminus* dicitur. Non quo semper medius inter duos quæstionis terminos in syllogismo collocetur, sed eò quòd quasi arbiter de consensu eorum inter se aut dissensu, disceptat & judicat. Atque hæc sunt tria illa argumenta, ex quibus solis omnis syllogismus con- 15 ficitur; duo scilicet quæstionis, & tertium argumentum; quæ vulgò *tres termini* dicuntur. Termini autem isti non semper simplices sunt voces, sed orationes nonnunquam longiusculæ; nec semper casibus rectis, sed obliquis interdum efferuntur.

Partes syllogismi duæ sunt; antecedens & consequens. 20 *Antecedens syllogismi pars est, in qua quæstio cum argumento disponitur.*

Syllogismi antecedens partes duas habet, propositionem & assumptionem: quæ vulgò *præmissæ* nominatur.

together as it were by the reasoning man. Such gathering up or deduction has arisen from the weakness of the human intellect, which because it is not able by the first intuition to see the truth and falsity of things in the axiom, turns to the
5 syllogism in order to judge of their consequence and lack of consequence by its means.

When an axiom is thus doubtful, it becomes a question, and to produce confidence in it there is need for a third argument properly disposed with the question.

10 The parts of the question are commonly called terms; the antecedent is called the minor term, the consequent the major term, since the consequent is usually more extensive than the antecedent. The third argument, then, is called by Aristotle *the mean* and *the middle term*. This does not mean that the
15 middle term will always be placed between the two terms of the question in the syllogism, but that it determines and judges like a judge of the consent or dissent between them. And these are the three arguments from which only every syllogism is made up, namely two of the question and one as
20 the third argument; they commonly are called *the three terms*. But these terms are not always simple words, but speeches somewhat long, nor are they always brought forward in direct cases, but sometimes in the oblique.

The parts of the syllogism are two: the antecedent and the
25 *consequent. The antecedent is the part of the syllogism in which the question is placed with the argument.*

The antecedent of the syllogism has two parts, the proposition and the assumption; it is commonly referred to as the *premises.*

Propositio est prior pars antecedentis, qua quæstionis saltem consequens cum argumento disponitur.

Saltem; quia nonnunquam *tota* quæstio cum argumento in propositione disponitur, ut infra patebit.

5 Propositio vulgò *major* dicitur; vel quia majorem vim habet (est enim argumentationis quasi basis & fundamentum) vel quia major terminus, i.e. consequens quæstionis in propositione collocatur.

Assumptio est secunda pars antecedentis, quæ assumitur è 10 *propositione.*

Assumitur enim inde vel tertium argumentum vel tota assumptio, ut infra perspicietur. Hinc itaque argumentum tertium, sive medius terminus, dignoscitur, quòd bis ponitur ante conclusionem. Assumptio vulgò *minor propositio* dici- 15 tur, vel quia minorem vim obtinet, ex propositione videlicet deductam; vel quia minor terminus, i.e. antecedens quæstionis, in ea sæpe disponi soleat, non semper, ut infra intelligemus.

Syllogismi autem pars consequens est, quæ complectitur 20 *partes quæstionis, eámque concludit. Unde complexio* & *conclusio* dicitur.

Hinc sequitur, conclusionem & verbis & terminorum ordine, eandem planè esse cum proposita quæstione oportere; alioqui syllogismi fidem claudicare, & quasi depositum non 25 reddere. Secundo hinc intelligitur illa regula, *tertium argumentum sive medius terminus nunquam ingreditur conclusionem.* Ratio est, quia medium non est id quòd concluditur,

The proposition is the first part of the antecedent, in which the consequent at least of the question is placed with the argument.

At least; since sometimes the *whole* question is disposed
5 with the argument in the proposition, as will appear below.
The proposition is commonly called the *major,* either because it has greater force (for it is as it were the basis and foundation of the argument) or because the major term, that is, the consequent of the question, is put in the proposition.
10 *The assumption is the second part of the antecedent, which is taken out of the proposition.*

For from the proposition is taken either the third argument or the whole assumption, as will be made plain below. Hence the third argument or middle term is distinguished, because
15 it is expressed twice before the conclusion. The assumption is commonly called *the minor proposition,* either since it has less force, deduced, of course, from the proposition, or since the minor term, that is the antecedent of the question, is often given in it, but not always, as we shall explain below.
20 *But the consequent is the part of the syllogism which comprehends the parts of the question and concludes it. For that reason it is called the complexion and conclusion.*

Thence it follows that the conclusion both in words and in order of terms ought to be clearly the same as the question
25 proposed; otherwise confidence in the syllogism is weak, and it does not, as it were, return its deposit. Secondly there follows the rule that *the third argument or middle term never enters the conclusion.* The reason is that the mean is not that

neque de quo quicquam; sed id, quo adhibito, quæstio concluditur, vel duo ejus termini inter se consentire aut dissentire judicantur. Medius itaque terminus aut ulla pars ejus in conclusione si sit, syllogismum vitiosum facit; id facillime deprehenditur, si non solum quæstio proposita, sed præterea aliquid quod bis erat in præmissis repetitum, conclusionem intrat.

Cùm autem in omni syllogismo, ut ex ejus definitione constat, quæstio cum argumento ita disponatur, ut posito antecedente, i.e. concessis præmissis, necessariò concludatur: quæ necessitas non consequentis, sed consequentiæ, non materiæ, sed formæ est, hinc intelligitur, nullam in syllogismi forma differentiam esse contingentis & necessarii, sed syllogismum omnem necessariò concludere, teste etiam *Aristot.* Prior. I. 33; eámque necessitatem ex legitima dispositione quæstionis cum tertio argumento, non ex necessaria partium in antecedente dispositarum veritate pendere. Unde & illi redarguuntur, qui vulgò dividunt syllogismum in dialecticum & apodicticum, probabilem scilicet & demonstrativum, sive necessarium cùm & illa distinctio axiomatum sit, & syllogismi consequentia tam in contingenti, immo in falso necessaria sit, quàm in vero & necessario; immo ex falsis præmissis conclusio nunc vera nunc falsa necessariò sequatur: ut, *omnis leo est quadrupes: Socrates est leo; ergo Socrates est quadrupes.* In

which is concluded, nor that of which anything is concluded, but is that which by its presence permits the conclusion of the question, or the judgment that its two terms consent or dissent each with the other. But if the middle term or any part of it
5 is in the conclusion, it makes the syllogism vicious. This is most easily discerned if not merely the question proposed but in addition something which was twice repeated in the premises enters the conclusion.

But since in every syllogism, as is established from its
1 definition, a question is so disposed with its argument that when an antecedent is laid down, that is when premises are granted, it is necessarily concluded—this necessity being not of the consequent but of the consequence, not of matter but of form—, it is to be understood thence that there is no dif-
15 ference between the form of the contingent and that of the necessary syllogism, but that every syllogism necessarily concludes, as Aristotle witnesses in the *Prior Analytics* 1.33; this necessity depends on the legitimate disposition of the question with the third argument, not on the necessary
20 truth of the parts disposed in the antecedent. Wherefore are refuted those who commonly divide the syllogism into the dialectic and apodictic, the probable, to wit, and the demonstrative or necessary, since that is a distinction of the axioms, and the consequences of the syllogism are as necessary in
25 the contingent, yes, in the false, as in the true and necessary. Indeed from false premises a conclusion, sometimes true, sometimes false, follows necessarily, as *Every lion is a quadruped, Socrates is a lion, therefore Socrates is a quadruped.*

quo simile quiddam habet syllogismus axiomati connexo, & fortasse originem ab eo ducit: nam ut connexum necessarium esse potest ex falsis partibus, modò ipsa connexio sit vera; ut, *si leo est quadrupes, & Socrates leo, Socrates necessariò est* 5 *quadrupes;* sic syllogismus necessariò concludit ex veris quidem partibus nil nisi verum, ex falsis & falsum & verum, modò ipsa dispositio sit legitima.

Quòd autem *Aristotelici* syllogismum dividunt in verum & falsum sive apparentem; verum, cujus materia vera est, 10 in dialecticum sive probabilem, cujus materia contingens est, & apodicticum sive demonstrativum ac necessarium, eúmque vel perfectum, quæ vocatur διότι sive à priori, quo accidens de subjecto per causam vel efficientem vel finalem positam quidem affirmatur, remotam verò negatur; & in imperfectum 15 quæ vocatur τοῦ ὅτι sive à posteriori, quo accidens de subjecto per effectum probatur, hæc quidem divisio, qualiscunque est, cùm axiomatis propria sit, & vel ad formam syllogismi ut in dialectico & apodictico, vel omninò ad artem, ut in falso sive sophistico nihil pertineat, melius rejicitur.

Appendix de paralogismis qui hac generali doctrina syllogismi redarguuntur.

ATQUE hæc syllogismi doctrina generalis fuit. Ut rectum quidem index est sui & obliqui, & veritatis doctrina rectè tradita, errorem omnem ipsa per se indicat atque etiam redarguit. Verùm cùm non sit ea cujusque

In this the syllogism has a sort of likeness with the connex axiom, and perhaps derives its origin from it, for as the connex can be necessary when the parts are false, provided the connection itself be true—as *If a lion is a quadruped, and* 5 *Socrates is a lion, Socrates is necessarily a quadruped*—thus the syllogism from true parts necessarily concludes nothing except what is true, and from false parts concludes both the false and the true, provided the disposition itself is legitimate.

The Aristotelians divide the syllogism into true and false 10 or apparent; and the true, of which the matter is true, they divide into dialectic or probable—of which the matter is contingent—, and apodictic or demonstrative and necessary. The last may be perfect, and called διότι or *à priori;* in this kind the accident is affirmed of the subject through a cause, 15 either efficient or final, that is posited, or the accident is denied through a cause that is removed. Or it may be imperfect and called τοῦ ὅτι or *à posteriori;* in this type the accident is proved from the subject through the effect. But this division, of whatever kind it is, since it is proper to the axiom, 20 and in no way pertains either to the form of the syllogism, as in the dialectic and apodictic types, or to the art of logic in any way, as in the false or sophistic type, is better rejected.

An appendix of the paralogisms which are refuted by this general doctrine of the syllogism.

25 So much for the general doctrine of the syllogism. As the right is the touchstone of itself and of the wrong, the doctrine of truth itself when rightly presented indicates

hominis perspicacia aut ingenii felicitas, ut vel omnes technas adversarii animadvertere ex ipsis regulis, vel omnes artis regulas memoria tenere semper queat, alienum non erit de præcipuis captionibus quæ committere in hanc generalem 5 syllogismi doctrinam solent, seorsim hîc aliquid monere.

Cùm itaque syllogismi doctrina generali doceamur, tria duntaxat argumenta sive tres terminos in syllogismo disponi oportere, hinc facilè perspicuum est, peccare omnem syllogismum in hanc doctrinam generalem, in quo termini vel 10 plures ternis disponantur, vel pauciores: termini autem non tam sunt verba, quàm verborum sensus & significationes.

Peccatur autem terminis pluribus, vel apertius vel tectius. Apertius, (ut puerilia de accentu, figurâ dictionis, plurium, quæ dicitur, interrogationum, & similia omittam) cùm tres 15 termini distinctè numerantur in propositione: ut, *qui est bonus & dialecticus, is est bonus dialecticus; Cleanthes est bonus & dialecticus; ergo, est bonus dialecticus.* Hæc fallacia *compositionis* dicitur; quia divisa male componit. Contra; *qui est bonus dialecticus, is est bonus & dialecticus; Cleanthes* 20 &c. Hæc fallacia est *divisionis;* quia composita male dividit; vel quia composita proponit, divisa concludit. Idem committitur etiam sine conjunctione: ut, *bonus citharœdus est bonus; Nero est bonus citharœdus; ergo, bonus. bonus* duplici signi-

through itself and also refutes every error. But since every man has not such perspicacity or happy native endowment that he can recognize all the devices of an adversary by means of the rules themselves, or is able always to remember all
5 the rules of the art, it will not be out of place separately here to give some advice on the special captions which are normally considered in this general presentation of the syllogism.

So since we are taught by the general doctrine of the syllogism that three arguments or terms merely ought to be dis-
10 posed in the syllogism, it is thence easily to be seen that according to this general doctrine every syllogism is faulty in which are disposed more or fewer than three terms. And the terms are not so much words as the meanings and significations of words.

15 The error of too many terms can be either open or hidden. It is open (for I omit puerilities of accent, of the figure of diction, of several interrogations, as it is called, and the like) when three terms are distinctly numbered in the proposition, as *He who is good and a dialectician, he is a good dialectician;*
20 *Cleanthes is good and a dialectician, therefore he is a good dialectician.* This is called the fallacy of composition, since it brings together badly things which are separate. The contrary is *He who is a good dialectician, he is good and a dialectician; Cleanthes,* etc. Here the fallacy is one of division,
25 since it divides badly things that are composed, or since it sets forth composed things and concludes divided things. The same is done without a conjunction, as *A good flute-player is good, Nero is a good flute-player, therefore he is*

ficatione cum *citharœdo* disponitur, in propositione; quatuor ergo termini. Sic etiam cùm non iisdem verbis aliud planè proponitur, aliud assumitur: ut, *dextera Dei est ubique; humanitas Christi sedet ad dextram Dei; ergo, humanitas Christi* 5 *est ubique.*

Tectius verò peccatur, vel *homonymia,* vel *amphibolia.*

Homonymia sive æquivocatio est, primò, cùm simplicis vocis seu termini unius, significatio duplex ponitur: ut, *leo est bestia; leo est Papa; ergo, Papa est bestia.* Secundò, cùm 10 argumentum in una parte propriè, in altera tropicè ponitur; vel in una parte pro reipsa, in altera pro artificiali aliqua notione rei. Hujusmodi sunt artium vocabula: ut, *potens est participium; rex est potens; ergo, rex est participium. Animal est genus; homo est animal; ergo, homo est genus.*

15 Amphibolia sive ambiguitas vel in syntaxi est, vel in ipsa re. In syntaxi; ut, *pecunia quæ est Cæsaris, possidetur à Cæsare; hæc pecunia est Cæsaris; ergo, possidetur à Cæsare.* Ambiguitas in ipsa re, quæ & *prava expositio* vocatur, fit, cùm affectio rei non eadem assumitur quæ proponitur; mutata au-20 tem affectione, mutatur argumentum; ut, *quas carnes emisti, comedisti; crudas emisti; ergo, crudas comedisti.* Hîc propositio & de carnibus & de substantia carnium loquitur; assump-

good. In the proposition *good* is disposed with *flute-player* in a double meaning; therefore there are four terms. Thus it is also when with different verbs one thing is plainly laid down, and another assumed, as *The right hand of God is* 5 *everywhere, the humanity of Christ sits at the right hand of God, therefore the humanity of Christ is everywhere.*

The covert error of too many terms occurs in *the use of homonyms* or in *ambiguity.*

Homonymy or equivocation is, first, when a double sig- 10 nification is given for a simple word or one term as *Leo* (the lion) *is a beast, Leo is pope, therefore the pope is a beast.* Secondly, when an argument is used literally in one part, figuratively in the other, or in one part for the thing itself, in the other for some artificial notion of the thing. 15 Of this sort are the vocables of the arts, as *Potent is an adjective, the king is potent, therefore the king is an adjective. Animal is a genus, man is an animal, therefore man is a genus.*

Amphiboly or ambiguity is either in syntax or in the thing 20 itself. To illustrate it in syntax, *Cæsar's money should be possessed of Cæsar, this is Cæsar's money, therefore it should be possessed by Cæsar.* Ambiguity in the thing itself, which is called also perverse exposition, is produced when the affect of the thing as assumed is not its affect as proposed, but 25 by a change of affect the argument is changed, as *You have eaten the meat you bought, you bought raw meat, therefore you have eaten raw meat.* Here the proposition speaks of meat and of the substance of meat, but the assumption speaks

tio, de qualitate earum: dicendum ergo erat, *quales carnes emisti*, &c. Eadem est fallacia cum id quod in *abstracto*, quod aiunt, proponitur, in *concreto* assumitur: ut, *candidum est disgregativum visus; paries est candidus; ergo, paries est dis-* 5 *gregativum visus.* Etiam cùm in ipsa copula quartus terminus latet: ut, *fortitudo non est clementia; principis est fortitudo; ergo, principis non est clementia.* Hîc verbum *est* in majore *esse*, in minore *habere* significat; casuúmque mutationem rectorum in obliquos inducit; qui quatuor esse terminos decla- 10 rant. *Nullus puer diu vixit; Nestor fuit puer; ergo, Nestor non diu vixit.* Hîc major de eo qui est, minor de eo qui fuit puer loquitur; qui duo termini sunt. Quatuor denique sunt termini cùm plus est in conclusione quàm in præmissis.

Pauciores autem termini sunt ternis, cùm tertium argu- 15 mentum deest. Hoc fit quoties vel idem sensu vel æque obscurum pro argumento sumitur; (idem enim non est tertium; æque obscurum non est argumentum) quæ *petitio principii*, vel, ejus quod erat in principio nominatur; quia postulatur ipsa quæstio ut gratis, i.e. sine argumento concedatur: ut, 20 *ensis est acutus; gladius est ensis; ergo, gladius est acutus.* Vel, *quod omnis homo est, id singuli homines sunt; omnis homo est justus; ergo, singuli homines sunt justi.* Huc refer jactatum illud, Quæ non amisisti habes, cornua non amisisti, ergo

of the quality of it; the statement, therefore, should be *What sort of meat,* etc. The fallacy is the same when that which is proposed in the abstract, as they say, is assumed in the concrete, as *Whiteness tends to disintegrate the sight, a wall is*
5 *white, therefore a wall tends to disintegrate the sight.* Also when the fourth term is latent in the copula itself, as *Fortitude is not clemency, fortitude is of the prince, therefore clemency is not of the prince.* Here the verb *is* has in the major the sense *to be,* in the minor the sense of *have,* and
10 it brings on the mutation of direct cases to oblique; these things show that there are four terms. Another example is *No boy has lived long, Nestor was a boy, therefore Nestor did not live long.* Here the major speaks of one who is a boy, the minor of one who was a boy; this makes two terms.
15 There are, then, four terms when there is more in the conclusion than in the premises.

But the terms are fewer than three when the third argument is lacking. This is produced when either a thing the same in sense or a thing equally obscure is taken for an argu-
20 ment (for the same thing is not a third, and a thing equally obscure is not an argument); this is called begging of the question or of what was in the question, since the question itself is postulated in order that it may be conceded gratis, that is, without an argument, as *A brand is sharp, a sword is*
25 *a brand, therefore a sword is sharp.* Or *What every man is, that individual men are; every man is just, therefore individual men are just.* Here also I classify the debated syllogism *What you have not lost you have, you have not lost your*

cornua habes. Habere & amittere privantia sunt & quidem sine medio quatenus talia, ergo non amittere & habere sunt idem, nullus itaque hic est medius terminus, sed perinde ac si diceres; Quæ habes, habes, cornua habes, ergo habes. Hujus generis est, cùm tertium argumentum non integrum è propositione assumitur: ut, *omnes apostoli sunt duodecim; Petrus & Joannes sunt apostoli; ergo, Petrus & Joannes sunt duodecim*. Hîc *omnes* collectivè sumptum, pars est tertii argumenti, quod totum erat in assumptione assumendum. Ad hoc sophisma referendæ sunt denique omnes conversiones enuntiationum; quoties rem dubiam non argumento sive medio termino, sed conversione sola probare contendunt: de qua suprà monuimus. Atque his ferè modis in formam syllogismi generalem peccatur.

Materia syllogismi vitiosa est, quoties antecedentis pars vel altera vel utraque est falsa: id fit tot modis, quot sunt argumentorum genera. Quorum cùm veritas tum falsitas quanquam in axiomate judicatur, propterea tamen quòd argumenta ipsa in syllogismo disponuntur, qui modi præcipuè nominantur à Dialecticis vel materia sola, vel partim materia, partim forma vitiosi, eos hîc breviter attingemus.

Primus est materiæ solius: dicitúrque *non causæ ut causæ*. Causæ autem nomen hîc usurpatur pro quovis argumento, etiam non effecti ut effecti, non subjecti ut subjecti, & sic de-

horns, therefore you have horns. To have and *to lose* are privatives and such as have no mean at all; therefore *not to lose* and *to have* are the same; so there is no middle term here, but it is as though you said: *What you have you have,*
5 *you have horns, therefore you have them.* It is of this type when a third argument not entire is assumed from the proposition, as *All the apostles are twelve, Peter and John are apostles, therefore Peter and John are twelve.* Here *all* taken collectively is part of the third argument, and this whole was
10 to be assumed in the assumption. To this sophism, then, are to be referred all those conversions of axioms which attempt to prove a doubtful thing not by argument or a middle term but by conversion alone, of which we gave warning above. For the most part errors in the general form of the syllogism
15 are of these kinds.

The matter of the syllogism is faulty as often as part of the antecedent, either one or the other, is false; this can happen in as many modes as there are kinds of argument. Albeit the truth and falsity of these modes is judged in the
20 axiom, yet because the arguments themselves are disposed in the syllogism we shall touch briefly here on those modes especially that are called faulty by the dialecticians either because of their matter alone or partly because of their matter, partly because of their form.

25 The first fallacy is of the matter alone and is called *of non-cause as cause,* for the name of cause is usurped here by any sort of argument, even that of non-effect as effect, non-

inceps. Hanc captionem singulorum argumentorum definitiones facile refellunt.

Secundus est quæ vocatur fallacia *accidentis,* sive, quod idem est, à dicto secundum quid ad dictum simpliciter: vel
5 contrà, à dicto simpliciter ad dictum secundum quid; quoties id quod adjuncti est, subjecto attribuitur; aut contrà quod subjecti, adjuncto: ut, *quæ non restituenda sunt domino furioso, non restituenda sunt domino; arma non restituenda sunt domino furioso; ergo, non domino:* vel contra: *quæ restitu-*
10 *enda sunt domino, etiam domino furioso; arma domino; ergo, domino furioso.* In his propositio semper falsa est.

Tertius est *ignoratio elenchi; (elenchus* autem est redargutio quælibet sive vera sive falsa) cùm leges oppositionis non observantur eidem numero, secundum idem, ad idem, & eodem
15 tempore: ut, *cæci vident; qui carent visu, sunt cæci; ergo, qui carent visu, vident.* Propositio distinguenda est; nempe, qui fuerunt cæci, nunc vident. Sic; *is qui non videt, cæcus est; dormiens non videt; est ergo cæcus.* Ad idem non est: propositio enim de potentia, assumptio de actu videndi loquitur; vel
20 quatuor sunt termini, & prava expositio dici potest. Aliis ignoratio elenchi est, cùm vel planè mutatur & torquetur status

subject as subject, and so on. The definitions of single arguments easily disprove this caption.

The second is what is called the fallacy of the *accident*, or, what is the same thing, from a qualified saying to an un-
5 qualified saying, or on the contrary from an unqualified to a qualified one; this occurs as often as what belongs to the adjunct is attributed to the subject, and on the contrary what belongs to the subject is attributed to the adjunct, as *What are not to be restored to an insane master are not to be re-*
10 *stored to a master, arms are not to be restored to an insane master, therefore not to a master;* or on the contrary *What are to be restored to a master are to be restored even to an insane master, arms are to be restored to a master, therefore to an insane master.* In these the proposition is always false.

15 The third is ignorance of the elench (an elench is any sort of refutation whether true or false), when the laws of opposition are not observed for the same number, according to the same thing, in relation to the same thing, and at the same time, as *The blind see, those who lack sight are blind,*
20 *therefore those who lack sight see.* The proposition should be distinguished, to wit, *Those who were blind now see.* Another example is *He who does not see is blind, the sleeping man does not see, he is therefore blind.* But it is not in relation to the same thing, for the proposition speaks of
25 power, the assumption of the act of seeing; or there are four terms and it can be called a perverse exposition. In other cases there is an ignorance of the elench when either the state of the controversy is evidently changed and twisted, or

controversiæ, vel conclusio adversarii non directè opponitur nostræ thesi secundum canones legitimæ oppositionis.

Quartus est fallacia *consequentis*, sive comparatorum, quæ è contrariis quidem sunt orta, sed parium collatione tractata, 5 cùm disputatur, contraria esse contrariorum consequentia: quam regulam esse fallacem, l. 1. c. 18. copiosè ostenditur: ut, *quæ eidem æqualia, inter se æqualia; ergo, quæ eidem sunt inæqualia, inter se sunt inæqualia*. Ut, 2. et 2. sunt inæquales ad 5; ergo sunt inter se inæquales. Duo latera quadrati sym-10 metra non sunt diagonio; ergo non sunt inter se.

CAPUT X.

De Syllogismo simplici contracto.

SYLLOGISMUS *est simplex aut compositus.*

Simplex, ubi pars consequens quæstionis disponitur in propositione, pars antecedens in assumptione.

Ut syllogismi forma generalis erat dispositio quæstionis 15 cum argumento, ita specialis quæque dispositio quæstionis cum argumento cujusque speciei forma est. Ex. gr. *homo est animal: Socrates est homo; ergo Socrates est animal.* Hinc facile perspicitur, si quæstionis terminus major non disponatur in propositione majore, minor in minore, syllogismum

a conclusion of the opponent is not directly opposed to our thesis according to the canons of legitimate opposition.

The fourth is the fallacy of the *consequent* or of comparatives—which are indeed sprung from contraries, but treated
5 by the collation of equals—when it is argued that contraries are the consequents of contraries. In book 1, chapter 18, it is fully shown that the rule is fallacious, as *Things equal to the same thing are equal to each other, therefore things unequal to the same thing are unequal to each other,*
10 as *Two and two are unequals with respect to five, therefore they are unequal to each other. Two symmetrical sides of a quadrate are not equal to the diagonal, therefore they are not equal to each other.*

CHAPTER X.

Of the simple abridged syllogism.

THE syllogism is simple or compound.

It is simple when the consequent part of the question is placed in the proposition, the antecedent part in the assumption.

As the general form of the syllogism was the placing of the question with the argument, thus the special form is the
20 placing of the question with an argument of whatever species it may be. For example, *Man is an animal, Socrates is a man, therefore Socrates is an animal.* Thence it is easily seen that if the major term of the question is not placed in the major proposition, the minor in the minor, the syllogism is not

non esse legitimum. Quòd si aliquando usu venit, ut antecedens quæstionis in propositione & consequens in assumptione disponi videatur, intelligere debemus syllogismi partes inverti: ut, *Socrates est homo: homo est animal; ergo Socrates est animal.*

Sequitur jam syllogismi simplicis distinctio in adjunctos modos, qui ex partium, i.e. axiomatum affectione oriuntur.

Syllogismus simplex est affirmatus è partib. omnib. affirmatis. Negatus ex negata antecedentis parte altera cum complexione. Non ex omnib. negatis, ut affirmatus ex omnibus affirmatis; nisi enim argumentum tertium cum altera parte quæstionis consentiat, nihil probat.

Ut autem syllogismorum tota ratio intelligatur (quod hoc loco fieri commodissimè posse arbitror) sciendum est eam duab. præcipuè legibus fundari; altera parium, altera generis ex loco petita. Ex parium loco; *quæ conveniunt in uno aliquo tertio, conveniunt inter se; & contrà, quæ non in uno tertio, non inter se.* Ex loco generis; *quod generi generaliter attribuitur, id omnib. etiam attribuitur speciebus quæ sub eo genere continentur.* Hæc regula vocatur in scholis, *dictum de omni & nullo.* Illa à Geometris primùm sensu præeunte facilius inventa est; & præcipitur *Aristot.* 1. Prior. c. 1. Ut

legitimate, because if at any time it happens in practice that the antecedent of the question seems to be placed in the proposition and the consequent in the assumption, we ought to understand that the parts of the syllogism are inverted, 5 as *Socrates is a man, a man is an animal, therefore Socrates is an animal.*

Now follows the distinction of the simple syllogism into its adjunct modes which spring from the affect of the parts, that is, the axioms.

10 *The simple syllogism is affirmed by all the affirmative parts. It is denied when either part of the antecedent, with the conclusion, is denied.* It is not negated by all the negatives as it is affirmed by all the affirmatives, for unless a third argument consents with one of the two parts of the question, 15 it proves nothing.

But that the whole reason of syllogisms may be understood (which I judge can be most conveniently done in this place) it must be known that it is founded on two laws especially, one from the place of equals, the other from that of 20 genus. From the place of equals: *Things which agree in some third thing agree among themselves;* and on the contrary: *Things which do not agree in a third thing do not agree among themselves.* From the place of genus: *What is generally attributed to a genus is also attributed to all the* 25 *species contained under the genus.* In the schools this rule is called *the dictum of all and none.* It was first easily found out by the geometers, since sense led the way, and it is taught by Aristotle in the *Prior Analytics* 1. 1: *If the norm*

enim illic norma, *si duab. lineis æque conveniat, eas lineas demonstrat convenire inter se, sive esse æquales;* eodem planè modo medius terminus si duob. conclusionis terminis conveniat, velut norma demonstrat, convenire duos illos inter se; & 5 contrà. Itaque si quæstio affirmanda est, quærendum est per omnes inventionis locos argumentum quod utrique parti quæstionis conveniat: si neganda est, quærendum quod uni parti conveniat, ab altera dissentiat; nam si ab utraque parte dissentit, tertium argumentum esse non poterit, nihil n. probabit. 10 Ex. gr. quæritur *an Socrates sit animal?* Si affirmanda est hæc quæstio, ad illa duo argumenta quæ in quæstione sunt, *Socrates* & *animal,* quærendum aliquod tertium argumentum est, quod cum utraque parte quæstionis consentiat. Ejusmodi autem est *homo:* nam *homo* convenit cum *animali,* ut species cum suo 15 genere; cum *Socrate,* ut genus cum sua specie; ergo *Socrates* & *animal* conveniunt inter se; adeóque *Socrates est animal.* Sin neganda est quæstio, ut, *Socrates non est bestia,* quærendum est argumentum tertium, quod ab altera tantùm parte dissentiat. Hujusmodi autem est *homo: homo* n. non est 20 *bestia,* at *Socrates* est *homo; ergo Socrates non est bestia.* Sin medius cum neutro quæstionis termino conveniat, neutrius norma esse potest; neque ostendit, inter se conveniant, nécne; neque *de omni* dicit neque *de nullo;* adeóque nec probat quicquam nec refellit. Unde illa regula; *ex utraque præmissa* 25 *negata nihil concluditur; Aristot.* 1. prior. c. 24. ut, *nullus*

agrees with two lines equally, it demonstrates that they agree between themselves or are equal; by the same method, it is plain, the middle term, if it agrees with the two terms of the conclusion, as a norm shows that the two agree among
5 themselves, and the reverse. So if a question is to be affirmed there must be sought through all the places of invention an argument that agrees with both sides of the question; if it is to be denied, an argument must be sought that agrees with one side and dissents from the other, for if it dissents from
10 both sides it cannot be a third argument, for it will prove nothing. For example, it is asked *whether Socrates is an animal.* If this question is to be affirmed, in addition to the two arguments in the question, namely *Socrates* and *animal,* some third argument must be sought, which will agree with
15 either side of the question. Of this sort is *man,* for *man* agrees with *animal* as a species with its genus, with *Socrates* as a genus with its species; hence *Socrates* and *animal* agree among themselves; and it is clear that *Socrates is an animal.* If the question should be denied, as *Socrates is not a beast,*
20 a third argument must be sought which dissents from one part merely. But of this sort is *man;* for *a man is not a beast,* but *Socrates is a man, therefore Socrates is not a beast.* But if the middle may agree with neither term of the question, it can be the norm of neither, nor does it show whether they
25 agree among themselves or not, it does not speak of *all* and does not speak of *none,* and indeed it does not either prove or refute anything. Thence comes the rule of Aristotle (*Prior Analytics* 1.24): "From the denial of both premises

lapis est animal: nullus homo est lapis; nullus igitur homo est animal. Excipitur tamen ab hac regula, si medius terminus sit negatus, vel duplex negatio sit in majore: ut, *quod non sentit, non est animal: planta non sentit; ergo*
5 *planta non est animal.* Hîc enim major, quæ videtur esse negata, æquipollet affirmatæ; eadémque est acsi diceret, *omne quod sentit, est animal:* negationésque istæ topicæ potius & infinitæ, quàm axiomaticæ sunt, partiúmque negationes non totius axiomatis, hoc potius modo enuntiandi, *quod est non*
10 *sentiens, est non animal:* & hoc affirmatum planè axioma est. Sed hac de re plura dicemus infra cap. 12. ad secundam speciem explicati. Cur autem complexio, negata antecedentis parte altera, negata quoque esse debet, ratio est, trita illa regula, *conclusio sequitur partem debiliorem:* negatúmque de-
15 bilius est affirmato, particulare generali, contingens necessario. Regulæ autem ratio est, quia conclusio est præmissarum quasi effectum: nullum autem effectum est toto genere dignius aut fortius sua causa. Fallit ergo hic paralogismus: *qui non differt à bruto, differt à Sophronisci filio: Socrates non*
20 *differt à Sophronisci filio; ergo non à bruto.* Hæc conclusio non sequitur, uti debuit, assumptionem negatum, sed propositionem affirmatam: & enim *non differt à bruto* non propo-

nothing is concluded," as *No stone is an animal, no man is a stone, therefore no man is an animal.* But there is exception to this rule if the middle term is denied, or there is a double denial in the major, as *What does not perceive is*
5 *not an animal, a plant does not perceive, therefore a plant is not an animal.* For here the major, which seems to be negated, is equivalent to an affirmative, and is the same as if one said *Everything which perceives is an animal.* These denials are rather topical and infinite than axiomatic, and
10 negations of the parts, not of the whole axiom, especially in the following mode of statement: *What is not sentient is not an animal;* and this when affirmed is plainly an axiom. But of this we shall speak further in chapter twelve below, on the second species of the fully developed syllogism. But
15 the reason why, when either part of the antecedent is denied, the complexion also ought to be denied, is given by that trite rule: *The conclusion follows the weaker part,* for what is denied is weaker than what is affirmed, the particular is weaker than the general, and the contingent than the
20 necessary. The reason, however, of the rule is that the conclusion is as it were an effect of the premises, but no effect is in its whole genus worthier or stronger than its cause. Therefore the following paralogism is fallacious: *He who does not differ from a brute differs from the son of Soph-*
25 *roniscus, Socrates does not differ from the son of Sophroniscus, therefore he does not differ from a brute.* This conclusion does not follow, as it ought, the denied assumption, but the affirmed proposition, for *does not differ from a brute* is

sitionis totius, sed antecedentis duntaxat ejus est negatio: idémque valet, acsi affirmatum sic esset; *qui idem est cum bruto*. Sequitur autem conclusio sive consequens partem antecedentis negatam non affirmatam, quia si partes conclusionis 5 non consentiunt in argumento tertio, non consentiunt inter se: sequitur partem specialem, non generalem, quia genus concludit speciem, non species genus; juxta illud superius dictum *de omni & nullo*.

Syllogismus simplex (nimirum qui ex simplicibus axio- 10 *matis constat) est vel generalis, vel specialis, vel proprius.*

Generalis è propositione & assumptione generalibus.

Non ex generali etiam conclusione, ut patebit infra.

Specialis est ex altera tantum generali.

Hæc enim regula firmissima quoque est, *ex utraque præ-* 15 *missa particulari nihil concluditur*. Exigit enim dictum *de omni & nullo* partem antecedentis unam saltem generalem: nec non in duabus particularibus quatuor sunt termini: cùm enim individua, quæ vocant, *vaga*, particulares propositiones faciunt, fit ut de alio subjecto major, de alio minor ferè loqua- 20 tur: ut, *quoddam animal est homo: quoddam animal est brutum; ergo quoddam brutum est homo. Quidam sunt divites: quidam sunt docti; ergo quidam docti sunt divites.*

the denial not of the whole proposition but merely of its antecedent, and is of the same force as though it were affirmed in the form: *who is the same as a brute.* The conclusion or consequent also follows the denied and not the affirmed part of the antecedent, since if the parts of the conclusion do not agree in the third argument they do not agree among themselves; it follows the special part, not the general, since genus includes species, but species does not include genus, according to that dictum given above *of all and none.*

The simple syllogism (that is, the one consisting of simple axioms) *is either general, or special, or proper.*

It is general when made up of a proposition and an assumption that are both general.

But it is not general because of a general conclusion, as will appear below.

It is special when proposition alone or assumption alone is general.

For this rule is also perfectly firm: *From premises both of which are particular nothing is concluded.* For the dictum *of all and none* requires at least one general part in the antecedent, and besides in two particular premises there are four terms, for since individual *vague* things, as they are called, make particular propositions, it comes about that the major is affirmed of one subject and the minor commonly of another, as *Some animal is a man, some animal is a brute, therefore some brute is a man. Some men are rich, some men are learned, therefore some learned men are rich.*

Proprius est ex utraque propria.

Cur autem ex utraque propria cùm non ex utraque particulari, quia nempe hæc certa sunt & de eodem dicta, illa vaga, *ut suprà.*

5 Hinc liquet, cur ut axioma, ita syllogismus specialis in particularem & proprium dividi non potuerit, cùm syllogismus proprius non sit species syllogismi specialis. Quare autem partes omnes non sint propriæ, i.e. axiomata propria, infra etiam apparebit. Et syllogismus quidem proprius, etsi ab 10 *Aristotele* neglectus, ab aliis rejectus sit, usum tamen frequentissimum habet.

Simplex syllogismus est contractus partibus, vel explicatus.

Aristoteles in tres figuras dividit syllogismum; primam, secundam, & tertiam. Verùm hanc *Rami* dichotomiam esse 15 commodiorem & naturæ ordini aptius respondere, res ipsa demonstrabit.

Contractus syllogismus est, cùm exemplum pro argumento ita subjicitur particulari quæstioni, ut utramque ejus partem antecedere & assumptione affirmatum esse intelligatur.

20 Exempli gratia: *quædam confidentia est virtus, ut constantia. Quædam confidentia non est virtus, ut audacia.*

In his, ut cernimus, primò, quæstio particularis duntaxat proponitur; generale enim, ut inquit *Aristot.* pr. 1. 6. & 2. 7. in hac specie, quæ tertia nimirum *Arist.* figura est, conclu-

The proper syllogism has both the proposition and the assumption proper.

The reason why the proper syllogism requires that both be proper and the particular does not require that both be
5 particular is that the proper are certain and said of the same thing, while the particular are vague, *as was said above.*

Thence it is clear why like the axiom the special syllogism cannot be divided into particular and proper, since the proper syllogism is not a species of the special syllogism. But why
10 all the parts are not proper, that is, proper axioms, will appear below. And the proper syllogism, though neglected by Aristotle and rejected by others, yet is very frequently used.

A simple syllogism is either contracted in its parts or ex-
15 *plicated.*

Aristotle divides the syllogism into three figures, first, second, and third. But the fact itself will demonstrate that the dichotomy of Ramus is more convenient and more in harmony with the order of nature.

20 *A syllogism is contracted when an example, brought in instead of an argument, is so subjected to the particular question that it is seen to precede both parts of it and to be affirmed by the assumption.*

For example: *A certain confidence is a virtue, as con-*
25 *stancy. A certain confidence is not a virtue, as audacity.*

As we see, in these there is first proposed a question merely particular, for, as Aristotle (*Prior Analytics* 1.6 and 2.7) says, nothing general can be concluded in this species,

dere non licet: addo etiam, neque proprium; quæ ratio est, cur syllogismus generalis non ex omnibus generalibus & proprium non ex omnibus propriis definitur, cùm in hac specie consequens sive conclusio debeat semper esse particularis, etiamsi 5 utraque pars antecedentis generalis aut propria fuerit: unde sequitur, particulares duntaxat quæstiones in hac specie concludi. Deinde exemplum speciale pro argumento subjicitur sive subjungitur, ut *constantia.*

Hujus autem syllogismi dispositio specialis hæc esse intel- 10 ligitur, si contractum explicamus (tametsi nunquam ferè nisi contractus in usu occurrit) ut exemplum sive argumentum tertium, primò utramque partem quæstionis in præmissis, quod aiunt, antecedat, sive præmissæ utriusque subjectum sit.

Hîc autem argumentum sive exemplum utramque partem 15 *quæstionis antecedere intelligitur,* quia quæstionis pars utraque argumento sive exemplo attribuitur, i.e. de eo vel affirmatur vel negatur; perinde quasi explicatè diceretur, *constantiam esse virtutem, & esse confidentiam; ergo quandam confidentiam esse virtutem.* Item, *audaciam non esse virtutem,* 20 *& tamen esse confidentiam; ideóque quandam confidentiam non esse virtutem.* Exemplum ergo sive argumentum tertium in contracto, etsi quæstioni subjicitur, tamen si contractum explicas, & propositionis & assumptionis antecedens sive subjectum esse reperitur. Est autem contractus enthymematis

which is the third Aristotelian figure. Neither, I add, can the proper be concluded; this is the reason why the general syllogism is not defined by having all its arguments general, and the proper syllogism by having all its arguments proper, 5 since in this species the consequent or the conclusion ought always to be particular, though both parts of the antecedent were general or proper. Thence it follows that particular questions only are concluded in this species. Then a special example is subjected or subjoined in the place of an argu- 10 ment, as *constancy*.

This special disposition is understood to belong to this syllogism if we expand what is contracted (though in practice it almost never occurs except in the contracted form), in order that, in the first place, an example or third argument 15 may antecede, as they say, both parts of the question in the premises, or may be the subject of both premises.

Here, moreover, the argument or example is understood to antecede both parts of the question, since both parts of the question are attributed to an argument or example; that 20 is, are either affirmed or denied of it. It is as though it were explicitly said: *Constancy is a virtue and is confidence, therefore a certain confidence is a virtue.* And also: *Audacity is not a virtue, and yet is confidence, hence a certain confidence is not a virtue.* Therefore the example or third argument in 25 the shorter form, even though subjected to the question, when the contraction is expanded is found to be antecedent or subject of both proposition and assumption. And there is a certain short species of enthymeme, which, when it is

quædam species, quæ, cùm explicatur, in peculiarem quandam syllogismi formam resolvitur, ideóque erat specialiter docenda. Secundò, postulat hujus syllogismi dispositio, ut assumptio semper affirmetur. Cùm enim tertium argumentum speciale exemplum sit, adeóque species antecedentis sive minoris termini quæstionis qui in assumptione semper disponitur, atque ita antecedens sit tertii argumenti genus; necesse est, genus de specie semper affirmari.

Atque ista expositio quæstionis per exemplum quod subjicitur, principium syllogismi partibus explicati ab Aristot. 1. pr. 6, &c. *efficitur, tanquam per se pleno syllogismi judicio clarior & illustrior.*

Prior ergo est ordine syllogismus contractus explicato, cùm quia clarior, tum quia simplicior: est autem ita clarus, ut mens eum, sicuti est contractus, antè percipiat, quàm partibus explicari possit; ideóque usus disserendi contracta hac forma contentus, formam explicatam rarissime solet adhibere. Claritas autem ejus eximia vel hinc perspicitur; quòd cùm duo duntaxat hujus speciei sint sophismata, eorum inanitatem contracta hujus syllogismi forma facilius detegit quàm explicata, *ut infra ostendetur.*

Ad tollendum itaque dubitationem, non hîc supplendæ syllogismi partes, ut in enthymemate, sed contrahendæ; contractum quippe explicato hîc est explicatius, & ab judicio syllo-

expanded, is resolved into a sort of peculiar form of the syllogism, and therefore was especially to be taught. Second, the disposition of this syllogism demands that the assumption should always be affirmed. For when the third argu-
5 ment is a special example and even a species of the antecedent or minor term of the question which is always placed in the assumption, and the antecedent is thus the genus of the third argument, it is necessary that as the genus it should always be affirmed of the species.

10 *And this exposition of the question through an example which is subjected is made by Aristotle* (*Prior Analytics* 1.6, etc.) *the simplest form of the syllogism explicated in its parts, as though in itself clearer and plainer than the full judgment of the syllogism.*

15 The contracted syllogism is therefore prior in order to the explicated form, since it is both clearer and simpler; indeed it is so clear that even contracted as it is the mind grasps it before it can be explicated in its parts. Therefore the practice of thinking, content with this contracted form, is accustomed
20 very seldom to employ the explicated form. The great clarity of this form is also seen in another way, for when there are at least two sophisms of this form, their emptiness is more easily revealed by the contracted form of this syllogism than by the fully developed form, *as will be shown below.*

25 Hence for taking away uncertainty the parts of a syllogism of this sort are not to be given in full, as for the enthymeme, but contracted, since the contracted form is more explicate than the explicated form, and by it one is as it were sum-

gismi ad axiomatis clarius judicium hîc est quasi provocandum & regrediendum.

Quod ad modos attinet hujus speciei, si contractam tantummodo formam spectamus, pluribus non est opus quàm duo-
5 bus; uno affirmato, altero negato: quia non refert, utrum exemplum subalterna sit species an specialissima. Sin explicatam hanc speciem spectamus, plures habet modos quàm species reliquæ: quatuor autem sunt affirmati, totidem negati; quorum duo sunt generales, quatuor speciales, duo proprii:
10 quatuor autem sunt in hac specie speciales modi, cùm in reliquis bini tantum sint; quia in hac specie propositio potest esse vel generalis vel particularis, in reliquis verò nunquam particularis est. Exempla hæc sunt.

Primus modus est affirmatus generalis: ut, *constantia est*
15 *virtus: constantia est confidentia; ergo quædam confidentia est virtus.*

Secundus est negatus generalis: ut, *audacia non est virtus: audacia est confidentia; ergo quædam confidentia non est virtus.*

20 Affirmatus specialis duplex est; tertius & quartus. Tertius, cujus propositio est particularis: ut, *quidam sapiens est dives: omnis sapiens est laudabilis; ergo quidam laudabilis est dives.*

Quartus, cujus propositio est generalis: ut, *omnis sapiens est laudabilis, quidam sapiens est pauper; ergo quidam pauper*
25 *est laudabilis.*

Negatus item specialis est duplex; quintus & sextus. Quintus, cujus propositio est particularis: ut, *quidam stultus non*

moned and turned back from the judgment of the syllogism to the clearer judgment of the axiom.

As to the modes of this species, if we look merely at the contracted form, there is no need for more than two, one af-
5 firmed, the other negated, since it does not matter whether an example is a subaltern species or a very special one. If we look at this explicated species, it has more modes than the other species have; four are affirmed, and as many denied, two of which are general, four special, two proper. There
10 are four special modes in this species, while in the others there are merely two, since in this species the proposition can be either general or particular, but in the others it is never particular. Examples follow.

The first mode is a general affirmative, as *Constancy is a*
15 *virtue, constancy is confidence, therefore some confidence is a virtue.*

The second is a general negative, as *Audacity is not a virtue, audacity is confidence, therefore some confidence is not a virtue.*

20 The special affirmative is duplex, making the third and the fourth. The third has a particular proposition, as *Some wise man is rich, every wise man is praiseworthy, therefore some praiseworthy man is rich.*

The fourth, with a general proposition, as *Every wise man*
25 *is praiseworthy, some wise man is poor, therefore some poor man is praiseworthy.*

Similarly the special negative is duplex, making the fifth and the sixth. The fifth has a particular proposition, as *Some*

est fortunatus: omnis stultus est contemptus; ergo quidam contemptus non est fortunatus.

Sextus, cujus propositio est generalis: ut, *stultus non est beatus: quidam stultus est fortunatus; ergo quidam fortu-* 5 *natus non est beatus.*

Reliqui duo proprii sunt, cùm exemplum est species specialissima sive individuum. Affirmatus est, *Socrates est Philosophus: Socrates est homo; ergo quidam homo est Philosophus.* Negatus est, *Thersites non est Philosophus: Thersites* 10 *est homo; ergo quidam homo non est Philosophus.*

Contracti syllogismi duo vitia sive sophismata sunt, quæ definitione præcaventur. Unum, si quæstio sive conclusio particularis non sit: ut, *omnis homo est rationalis: omnis homo est animal; ergo omne animal est rationale,* ratio est, quia id 15 quod non generaliter attribuitur in assumptione (non enim omne animal est homo) non potest esse generale subjectum conclusionis. Alterum est, cùm assumptio est negata: ut, *homo est animal: homo non est bestia; ergo bestia non est animal.* Quæ duo sophismata in contracta hujus syllogismi 20 forma, facilius, ut suprà dixi, deteguntur, & primo statim intuitu ridentur: ut, *omne animal est rationale, ut homo: quædam bestia non est animal, ut homo.*

fool is not fortunate, every fool is despised, therefore some despised man is not fortunate.

The sixth has a general proposition, as *A fool is not happy, some fool is fortunate, therefore some fortunate man is not* 5 *happy.*

The other two are proper, since the example is a very narrow species or indivisible. The affirmative is *Socrates is a philosopher, Socrates is a man, therefore some man is a philosopher.* The negative is *Thersites is not a philosopher,* 10 *Thersites is a man, therefore some man is not a philosopher.*

There are two vices or sophisms of the contracted syllogism which are guarded against by the definition. First, if the question or conclusion is not particular, as *Every man is rational, every man is an animal, therefore every animal is* 15 *rational.* This is vicious because what is not generally attributed in the assumption (for not every animal is a man) is not able to be a general subject of the conclusion. The second is when the assumption is negated, as *A man is an animal, a man is not a beast, therefore a beast is not an animal.* As I 20 said above, these two sophisms are easily detected in the short form of this syllogism, and frequently are laughed at by first intuition, as *Every animal is rational, as man; some beast is not an animal, as man.*

CAPUT XI.

De Prima specie syllogismi simplicis explicati.

SYLLOGISMUS explicatus præter ipsum nomen aliam definitionem non desiderat. Dicitur *explicatus,* non quod semper omnibus occurrat partibus explicatus, sic enim vix millesimus quisque syllogismus occurrit, sed quod
5 partes non modo in forma integra, verùm etiam in enthymemate semper distinctas habet.

In syllogismo explicato propositio est generalis aut propria; & conclusio similis antecedenti aut parti debiliori.

Similis, nempe & qualitate & quantitate: *antecedenti,* utri-
10 que scilicet ejus parti, propositioni & assumptioni, si ipsi inter se similes sunt, sive affirmatæ sive generales sive propriæ; sin dissimiles, parti debiliori, ut suprà.

Syllogismi explicati species duæ sunt. Prima, ubi argumentum semper sequitur, negatum in altera parte.

15 Hæc prima species explicati, *figura secunda* ab *Aristotele* dicitur. Prior autem hæc species efficitur, quia dispositio ejus est simplicior, ut ex altera specie collata comperiemus. Sequitur autem semper argumentum partem utramque quæstionis, consequentem in propositione, antecedentem in assumpti-
20 one: unde ab *Aristot.* pr. 1. 5. *prædicatum de ambobus* dici-

CHAPTER XI.

Of the first species of the simple explicated syllogism.

THE explicated syllogism does not need other definition than its name. It is called *explicated* not because it always occurs explicated in all its parts, for hardly one syllogism in a thousand is found in that form, but be-
5 cause not merely in the integral form but even in the enthymeme the parts are always distinct.

In the explicated syllogism the proposition is general or proper, and the conclusion similar to the antecedent or the weaker part.

10 *Similar,* namely in quality and quantity. *To the antecedent,* that is, to either part of it, proposition and assumption, if they are similar to each other, whether affirmed or general or proper; if they are dissimilar, to the weaker part, as above.

15 *There are two species* of the explicated syllogism. *The first is where the argument always follows, being denied in one of the parts.*

This first species of the explicated syllogism is called by Aristotle the second figure. But this species is formed first,
20 since its disposition is simpler, as we may learn by comparing it with the other species. But the argument always follows both parts of the question, in the proposition the consequent, in the assumption the antecedent, whence by Aristotle (*Prior Analytics* 1.5) it is said to be predicated of both. But the

tur. Negatum autem dicitur argumentum in altera parte, quia pars altera, vel propositio nempe vel assumptio semper est negata. Unde cùm negata etiam conclusio semper necessariò sit, sequitur, hujus speciei modos omnes negatos esse, & negatas duntaxat quæstiones hac specie concludi, quæ omnis in refutationibus est posita.

Modi hujus syllogismi sex sunt; & omnes quidem, ut diximus, negati; duo generales, duo speciales, duo proprii.

Generalis primus, cujus propositio negatur: *Turbatus non benè utitur ratione: sapiens bene utitur ratione; sapiens igitur non est turbatus.* Hoc exemplum in sua crypsi sic apud *Ciceronem* est 3 *Tuscul. Quemadmodum oculus conturbatus non est probè affectus ad suum munus fungendum, & reliquæ partes totúmque corpus à statu cùm est motum, deest officio suo ac muneri; sic conturbatus animus non est probè affectus ad exequendum munus suum. Munus autem animi est ratione uti: & sapientis animus ita semper affectus est, ut ratione optimè utatur; nunquam igitur est perturbatus.* Crypsis hîc unica redundantia est: nam ordo partium rectus est, nec ulla pars deest: prosyllogismus unus est propositionis; illustratur enim propositio similitudine plena, cujus redditio est ipsius propositionis sententia.

Generalis secundus, cujus assumptio negatur *res mortalis est composita: animus non est compositus; animus igitur non est mortalis.* Hic syllogismus crypsi involutus est apud *Cic.* 1. *Tuscul.* quo is judicat animum immortalem esse. *In animi*

argument is said to be negated in one of the parts, since one of them, whether proposition or assumption, is always denied. Thence, since the conclusion is always of necessity denied, it follows that all the modes of this species are denied,
5 and that denied questions alone are included in this species, which is concerned entirely with refutations.

There are six modes of this syllogism, all, as we have said, denied, two of them general, two special, two proper.

The first is general with the proposition denied: *The be-*
10 *wildered man does not use reason well, the wise man uses reason well, therefore the wise man is not bewildered.* This example in its crypsis is to be found in Cicero (*Tusculan Disputations* 3): "And when the eye is troubled, it is not honestly affected to the fulfilling of its duty, and the rest of
15 the parts, and also the whole body when it is moved from its state, wanteth its office and function; so a troubled mind is not honestly affected to fulfil his duty. But the duty of the mind is to use reason, and a wise man is always so affected that he useth reason most excellently; he is therefore never
20 troubled." Here the single crypsis is redundance, for the order of the parts is right, nor is any part lacking; there is one prosyllogism of the proposition, for the proposition is illustrated by a full similitude, the reddition of which is the meaning of proposition.

25 In the second general mode the assumption is denied, as *A mortal thing is composite, the spirit is not composite, therefore the spirit is not mortal.* This syllogism involved with crypsis is found in Cicero (*Tusculan Disputations* 1) when

autem cognitione, inquit, *dubitare non possumus, nisi fortè in physicis plumbei sumus, quin nihil sit animis admixtum, nihil concretum, nihil coagmentatum, nihil duplex. Quod cùm ita sit, certè nec secerni, nec dividi, nec discerpi, nec*
5 *distrahi potest; nec interire igitur: est enim interitus quasi discessus & secretio ac diremptus earum partium quæ ante interitum junctione aliqua tenebantur.* In hoc exemplo partium ordo invertitur: nam postremo in loco propositionis sententia ponitur, interitum esse scilicet rerum compositarum:
10 assumptio occurrit prima, *in animi autem cognitione* &c. Et ornatur synonymis: conclusio media est atque à causa illustratur, *ergo nec secerni &c., nec interire igitur.*

Specialis primus est, cujus propositio negatur: *lividus non est magnanimus: Maximus est magnanimus; Maximus igitur*
15 *non est lividus.* Hoc judicio *Ovidius* 3. de *pont. eleg.* 3. concludit.

> *Livor, iners vitium, mores non exit in altos:*
> *Utque latens ima vipera serpit humo.*
> *Mens tua sublimis supra genus eminet ipsum.*
> 20 *Grandius ingenio nec tibi nomen inest.*
> *Ergo, alii noceant, miseris, optentque timeri,*
> *tinctáque mordaci spicula felle gerant.*
> *At tua supplicibus domus est assueta juvandis;*
> *in quorum numero me precor esse velis.*

he judges that the spirit is immortal, saying: "For we cannot doubt in our minds, unless we be perchance ignorant in physical things, but that there is nothing knit to souls, nothing connexed, nothing copulate, nothing joined, nothing
5 double, which, when it is so, can never be parted, nor divided, nor severed, nor drawn asunder, neither perish therefore, for perishing is as it were a departure and separation or breach of those parts which before the perishing were joined together." In this example the order of the parts is inverted,
10 for the assertion, namely that compound things are subject to ruin, is put in the last place of the proposition; the assumption occurs first: "We cannot doubt in our minds" etc. It is also adorned with synonyms; the conclusion is medial and is illustrated by the cause, "can never be parted" etc. "neither
15 perish therefore."

In the first special mode the proposition is denied, as *The envious man is not magnanimous, Maximus is magnanimous, therefore Maximus is not envious.* With this judgment Ovid (*Epistles from Pontus* 3.3) concludes:

20 Envy and sloth are not in the high mind,
Rather with vipers them on ground we find.
In highest things thy mind excels we see,
Nor can thy name express the soul in thee.
Let others joy in raising cruel fear
25 And armed with poisoned arrows domineer;
But thou art wont to help complaining men,
Amongst which number pray let me be then.

Hujus etiam exempli crypsis redundantia sola est: propositio suos habet prosyllogismos, & livor pro livido ponitur, adjunctum pro subjecto; & illustratur à contrario abjecto; isque à simili, *vipera:* assumptio, i.e. *Maximi* magnanimitas, illustratur partim à minori totius generis magnanimitate, partim à notatione nominis ejus, i.e. *Maximi;* cujus parem esse animi magnitudinem demonstrat: conclusio negat *Maximum* esse lividum, partim quia dissimilis sit lividorum, quos describit ab effectis, *ergo alii noceant* &c.; partim, quia ipse faciat quæ magnanimus consuevit, qui disparatus à livido est; *at tua supplicibus* &c.

Specialis secundus est, cujus assumptio negatur: *Saltator est luxuriosus: Muræna non est luxuriosus; Muræna igitur non est saltator. Cic.* pro *Muræn. Nemo enim ferè saltat sobrius, nisi fortè insanet: neque in solitudine neque in convivio moderato atque honesto. Intempestivi convivii, amœni loci, multarum deliciarum comes est extrema saltatio. Tu mihi arripis id quod necesse est omnium vitiorum esse postremum: relinquis illa quibus remotis, hoc vitium omnino esse non potest: nullum turpe convivium, non amor, non comessatio, non libido, non sumptus ostenditur: & cùm ea non reperiantur quæ voluptatis nomen habent quæque vitiosa sunt, in quo ipsam luxuriam reperire non potes, in eo te umbram luxuriæ reperturum putas?* Hujus etiam syllogismi partes

The crypsis of this example is redundance alone; the proposition has its prosyllogisms, and envy is put for the envious man, the adjunct for the subject, and it is illustrated by the contrary of magnanimous, that is abject, and this
5 contrary by a similar thing, a *viper;* the assumption, that is the magnanimity of Maximus, is illustrated partly by the lesser magnanimity of the whole race, partly by the meaning of his name, that is *Maximus,* to which he shows that the magnitude of his mind is equal. The conclusion denies that
10 Maximus is envious, partly because he is unlike the envious, whom he describes from the effects of envy—"Let others joy in raising" etc.—partly because he does what the magnanimous man who is different from the envious is accustomed to do: "But thou art wont to help" etc.

15 In the second special mode the assumption is denied: *A dancer is lustful, Muræna is not lustful, therefore Muræna is not a dancer.* Cicero says in *Pro Muræna:* "For no man almost being sober danceth, unless perchance he be mad, neither alone, nor at a moderate and honest banquet, for
20 excess in dancing is the companion of untimely banquets, pleasant places, and many delights. But thou accusest him of that which of necessity is the hindmost of all vices; thou leavest those whereby when they are removed this vice ought not to be at all; no filthy banquet, no love, no gluttony, no
25 lust, no prodigality is shewed; and since we find not these things which have the name of pleasure and are vices, dost thou think to find the shadow of lechery in that man in whom thou canst not find lechery itself?" The parts of this

prosyllogismis exornantur. Propositionis sententia his verbis continetur, *intempestivi convivii* &c. quam prosyllogismus præcedens illustrat à contrariis, *nemo ferè saltat sobrius* &c. Assumptio per partes explicatur, *nullum turpe convivium,* 5 &c. & à minoribus quibusdam illustratur: cujus etiam prosyllogismus præcedit, reprehensio nempe *Catonis,* quòd postularet consequens, non probato antecedente. Postremo loco ponitur conclusio, quæ negat *Murænam* esse saltatorem, repetendo quædam quæ in assumptione præcesserant; & inter-10 rogatione fortius negando.

Hoc judicii modo *Ovidius* 1. Trist. *eleg.* 1. tripliciter concludit, dum carminum suorum excusationem exponit:

Carmina proveniunt animo deducta sereno;
nubila sunt subitis tempora nostra malis.
15 *Carmina secessum scribentis & otia quærunt.*
Me mare, me venti, me fera jactat hyems.
Carminibus metus omnis abest; ego perditus ensem
hæsurum jugulo jam puto jamque meo.
Hæc quoque quæ facio, judex mirabitur æquus;
20 *scriptáque cum venia qualiacunque leget.*

Tres hîc syllogismi sunt qui in unum sic reduci possunt: *Ut quis possit carmina bona scribere, oportet is lætus sit, otiosus, securus: ego nec lætus sum, nec otiosus, nec securus; ergo*

syllogism also are ornamented by prosyllogisms. The assertion of the proposition is contained in the words "untimely banquets" etc.; the preceding prosyllogism illustrates this by contraries, "no man almost being sober danceth" etc.; 5 the assumption is explained through its parts, "no filthy banquet" etc.; and it is illustrated by certain minors; its prosyllogism, to wit, the rebuke of Cato precedes, because, though the antecedent was not proved, he was demanding the consequent. In the last place is put the conclusion, which 10 denies that Muræna is a dancer by repeating certain things which preceded in the assumption, and by more strongly denying by interrogation.

By this mode of judgment Ovid (*Tristia* I. I) concludes in a three-fold manner, when he sets forth the apology for 15 his poems:

> They that make verses should not troubled be;
> Our time is clouded with adversity.
> They that write verses should enjoy their ease,
> The seas, the winds, the fierce winter me press.
> 20 Good poets should not fear, but I fear death,
> I dread lest swords shall take away my breath.
> Then what is here a right judge will admire,
> If reading them they satisfy desire.

There are here three syllogisms which can thus be re- 25 duced into one: *In order that anyone may be able to write good poems, it is necessary that he should be happy, at leisure, and secure; I am neither happy, nor at leisure, nor*

bona carmina non scribo. Pro assumptionibus prosyllogismi à dissentaneis & impedientibus causis ponuntur. Deinde conclusio sequitur, non ipsa quidem sed ejus consectarium; mirum esse si bona sunt; sed potius cum venia esse legenda, quia
5 non sunt bona.

Proprius primus est, cujus propositio negatur: ut, *Agesilaus non est pictus ab Apelle: Alexander est pictus ab Apelle; Alexander igitur non est Agesilaus.*

Proprius secundus est, cujus assumptio negatur: ut, *Cæsar*
10 *oppressit patriam: Tullius non oppressit patriam; ergo Tullius non est Cæsar.*

Sophismata hîc duo sunt; quorum unum utrique explicati speciei commune est, alterum primæ speciei proprium. Commune est, cùm propositio est particularis; quæ ex communi
15 explicatorum regula generalis aut propria esse debuit.

Sophisma primæ speciei proprium est, cùm argumentum tertium in altera parte antecedentis non negatur, ut definitio primæ speciei præcipit: unde illud vulgò dictum, Ex duabus affirmatis in secunda figura, nihil concluditur. Excipiendum
20 tamen est, si propositio fortè axioma reciprocum sit: ut, *homo est animal rationale: Socrates est animal rationale; ergo Socrates est homo.* Verùm hîc potius inversio partium propositionis intelligenda est; *animal rationale est homo:* atque ita ad sequentem speciem syllogismi referetur.

secure; therefore I do not write good poems. For the assumptions are given prosyllogisms from dissentany and impeding causes. Then follows the conclusion, not the conclusion itself, indeed, but its consectary that it would be mar-
5 velous if they were good, or rather that they are to be read with indulgence since they are not good.

In the first proper mode the proposition is denied, as *Agesilaus was not painted by Apelles, Alexander was painted by Apelles, therefore Alexander is not Agesilaus.*

10 In the second proper mode the assumption is denied, as *Cæsar oppressed his native land, Tully did not oppress his native land, therefore Tully is not Cæsar.*

Two sophisms are to be considered here, one of which is common to both species of explicated syllogism, the other
15 proper to the first species. In the common form the proposition, which from the common rule of fully developed syllogisms should be general or proper, is particular.

A sophism is proper to the first species, when the third argument is not negated in the second part of the antecedent,
20 as the definition of the first species teaches; thence comes that popular dictum: *From two things affirmed in the second figure, nothing is concluded.* But an exception must be made if the proposition happens to be a reciprocal axiom, as *Man is a rational animal, Socrates is a rational animal, there-*
25 *fore Socrates is a man.* But here one should understand rather an inversion of the parts of the proposition: *A rational animal is a man;* then it can be referred to the following species of syllogism.

CAPUT XII.

De Secunda specie Syllogismi simplicis explicati.

S*ECUNDA species explicati syllogismi est, quando argumentum antecedit in propositione, sequitur affirmatum in assumptione.*

Hæc species ab *Aristotele, prima figura* dicitur; sed naturæ
5 ordine est postrema. Cùm enim in reliquis speciebus dispositio quæstionis cum argumento tertio simplex & uniusmodi sit, in hac specie duplex est; in propositione enim argumentum antecedit quæstionis consequentem, utpote specialius; in assumptione sequitur quæstionis antecedentem, utpote generalius; unde
10 fortè medius terminus in hac solùm figura propriè dicitur. Quòd autem propositio nunquam particularis, conclusio semper antecedenti similis aut parti debiliori est, id habet commune cum explicata specie priore; hoc etiam cum contracta, affirmatum esse in assumptione; nisi in contracta, quæstionis
15 antecedens ut generalius de argumento; in hac, argumentum de antecedente quæstionis affirmatur.

Hæc maxime figura fundatur dicto illo *de omni* & *nullo:* antecedens enim sive subjectum propositionis continet genus, adeoque est semper generalis, subjectum assumptionis conti-
20 net speciem quæ de illo genere affirmatur. Assumptio itaque semper esse debet affirmata. Ex quo sequitur, quicquid de

CHAPTER XII.

Of the second species of simple explicated syllogism.

IN THE second species of explicated syllogism the argument is antecedent in the proposition and follows affirmatively in the assumption.

This species is called by Aristotle the *first figure,* but in
5 the order of nature it is the last. For while in the remaining species the disposition of the question with the third argument is simple and of one kind, in this species it is double, for in the proposition the argument precedes the consequent of the question, as though more special; in the assumption
10 it follows the antecedent of the question, as more general. Hence perhaps in this figure only is it properly called the middle term. But because the proposition is never particular, the conclusion is always like the antecedent or the weaker part; this it has in common with the first explicated
15 species. And it has in common with the contracted form that it is affirmed in the assumption, except that in the contracted form the antecedent of the question as more general is affirmed of the argument, and in this the argument is affirmed of the antecedent of the question.

20 This figure is made firm above all by that dictum *of all and none,* for the antecedent or subject of the proposition contains the genus, therefore is always general; the subject of the assumption contains the species which is affirmed of that genus. So the assumption ought always to be affirmed.

genere in propositione dicitur, id de eo quod in assumptione species esse illius generis affirmatur, in conclusione rectissimè concludi. Quòd si genus illud subjectum scil. propositionis termino infinito negante, seu topicè contradictorio exprimitur, 5 non negata continuò censenda erit assumptio, quamvis esse videatur; assumit n. tantummodo genus ex propositione termino illo topicè duntaxat contradictorio expressum, ipsa nihil axiomaticè negat: ut, *quisquis non credit, damnatur: aliquis Judæus non credit; ergo aliquis Judæus damnatur.* Hîc pro- 10 positionis subjectum est genus *quisquis non credit, i.e.* omnis non credens sive infidelis: *Judæus* est ex numero sive specie non credentium, id quod assumptio non negat, sed affirmat æquè acsi sic diceret, *aliquis Judæus est non credens.*

Ex hac autem affirmatione sequitur, nullum argumentum 15 ab antecedente quæstionis dissentaneum, in hac secunda specie locum habere. De cætero, hæc species neque ad particulares quæstiones, ut contracta, neque ad negatas, ut prior species explicati, restringitur; sed ad omnia quæstionum genera concludenda rectè adhibetur.

20 Restant hujus speciei modi; qui quanquam partim affirmati sunt partim negati, plures tamen non sunt quàm in altera specie, ubi omnes erant solùm negati. Æqualitatis ratio est

From this it follows that whatever is said of the genus in the proposition is in the conclusion rightly concluded of that which in the assumption is affirmed to be a species of that genus. Because if that genus as subject, namely of 5 the proposition, is expressed by an infinite negating term, or topically by a contradictory, the assumption will be judged as not continuously negated, however it seems to be, for it merely assumes from the proposition the genus expressed by that term which is but topically contradictory, and itself 10 axiomatically denies nothing, as *Whoever does not believe is damned, a certain Jew does not believe, therefore a certain Jew is damned.* Here the subject of the proposition is the genus *whoever does not believe,* that is, all not believing or infidel. A Jew is one of the number or species of the non- 15 believing, something the assumption does not deny, but affirms as much as though it should say *A certain Jew is non-believing.*

From this affirmation it follows that no argument dissentany from the antecedent of the question has a place in 20 this second species. Besides, this species never is restrained to particular questions, as is the contracted species, nor to negatives, as is the first species of the explicated syllogism, but is rightly employed in demonstrating all genera of questions.

25 There remain the modes of this species, which though they are partly affirmed, partly denied, yet are not more in number than in the other species where all were merely denied. The reason of the equality is that by the affirmation

quòd assumptionis affirmatio, & solius inde propositionis negatio negatorum numerum minuit. Modi igitur hujus speciei sex itidem sunt; tres affirmati, tres item negati; utrique rursum sunt generales, speciales & proprii.

5 Primus est affirmatus generalis: ut, *omne justum est utile: omne honestum est justum; omne igitur honestum est utile.* Quod *Cic.* 2. *Off.* ita concludit: *quicquid justum sit, id etiam utile esse censent: item quod honestum, idem justum: ex quo efficitur, ut quicquid honestum sit, idem sit utile.* Proposi-
10 tionis prosyllogismus a testimonio Stoicorum primo in loco ponitur, deinde omnes partes syllogismi ordine sequuntur. Partes hujus syllogismi sunt axiomata relatæ essentiæ quæ simplicium axiomatum vim habent.

Secundus modus est negatus generalis: *Timidus non est*
15 *liber: avarus est timidus; avarus itaque non est liber.* Hoc ita concluditur & judicatur ab *Horatio,* epist. *l.* 1. 16.

Quò melior servo quò liberior sit avarus,
in triviis fixum, cùm se demittit ob assem,
non video. Nam qui cupiet, metuet quoque: porro
20 *qui metuens vivit, liber mihi non erit unquam.*

In hoc exemplo duplex est crypsis, inversio partium & prosyllogismus. Primo in loco ponitur conclusio, eáque duabus prosyllogismis illustratur; primò à pari, quod *avarus* non *sit liberior servo:* secundò ab effectis, quod *se demittit ob assem.*

of the assumption and then the denial of the proposition alone the number of negatives is diminished. Therefore the modes of this species are also six, three affirmed, three denied; and both again are general, special, and proper.

5 First is the general affirmative mode, as *Every just thing is useful, every honest thing is just, therefore every honest thing is useful.* Cicero (*De officiis* 2) puts it thus: "Whatsoever is just that also they think to be profitable; also whatsoever is honest, that is just; from whence ariseth that whatsoever 10 is honest, that is also profitable." The prosyllogism of the proposition is in the first place laid down from the testimony of the Stoics, then all the parts of the syllogism follow in order. The parts of this syllogism are axioms of related essence which have the force of simple axioms.

15 Second is the general negative mode: *A fearful man is not free, a miser is fearful, therefore a miser is not free.* In this way it is argued and judged by Horace (*Epistles* I. 16):

> The miser for a groat kneels in the street;
> That he is freer than a slave complete
> 20 I do not see; he that desires doth fear,
> And he that fears his freedom doth not bear.

In this example there is a double crypsis, inversion of the parts and a prosyllogism. The conclusion is put in the first place and is illustrated with two prosyllogisms, first by an 25 equal, because the miser is not "freer than a slave"; secondly by its effects, because he "for a groat kneels in the street."

Tum ponitur assumptio, *qui cupiet, metuet quoque.* Propositio postremo in loco ponitur,

qui metuens vivit, liber mihi non erit unquam.

Sic *Terent.* in *Eunuch.* concludit & judicat: *consilii expers,* 5 *consilio regi non potest: amor est consilii expers; consilio itaque regi non potest.* Syllogismus his verbis sequitur:

Here, quæ res in se neque consilium neque modum
habet ullum, eam consilio regere non potes.
In amore hæc omnia insunt vitia; injuriæ,
10 *suspiciones, inimicitiæ, induciæ,*
bellum, pax rursum: incerta hæc si tu postules
ratione certâ facere, nihilo plus agas,
quàm si des operam, ut cum ratione insanias.

In hoc exemplo propositio suo loco est, *quæ res in se* &c. 15 Pro assumptione ponitur ejus prosyllogismus variorum amoris adjunctorum, quæ consilium impediunt; amor consilii expers est, *quia in amore hæc insunt vitia,* &c. Conclusio sequitur, *incerta hæc,* &c. Cujus sententia comparatione parium comprehenditur, ergo si amorem consilio regere vis, *nihilo plus,* 20 &c.

Tertius modus est affirmatus specialis: *Consules propter virtutem facti, studiosè remp. tueri debent: Cicero est propter virtutem factus consul; Cicero igitur studiosè remp. tueri*

Then the assumption is laid down, "he that desires doth fear." The proposition is laid down in the last place:

And he that fears his freedom doth not bear.

Thus Terence in the *Eunuchus* argues and judges: *That*
5 *which is void of counsel cannot be ruled by counsel, love is void of counsel, therefore it cannot be ruled by counsel.* The syllogism follows in these words:

> Master, that thing which hath in it neither counsel nor moderation, that thou canst not govern by
> 10 counsel. In love are all these vices, injuries, suspicions, enmities, flatteries, war, peace again; these uncertain things if thou wouldst guide by certain reason, thou dost no more than if thou shouldst labor to be mad with reason.

15 In this example the proposition is in its place, "that thing which hath in it" etc. Instead of the assumption is given its prosyllogism of the various adjuncts of love which impede counsel; love is neglectful of counsel since "in love are all these vices" etc. The conclusion follows, "these uncertain
20 things" etc. Its meaning is expressed by the comparison of equals; therefore if you wish to rule love by counsel "thou dost no more" etc.

The third is the special affirmative mode: *Consuls chosen because of their virtue ought carefully to guard the state,*
25 *Cicero has been made consul because of his virtue, therefore Cicero ought carefully to guard the state.* Thus the orator

debet. Sic orator diligentiam suam, Agr. 2. concludit & judicat: *Nam cùm omnium consulum,* ait, *gravis in repub. custodienda, cura ac diligentia debet esse, tum eorum maximè, qui non in incunabulis, sed in campo sunt consules facti. Nulli populo Rom. pro me majores nostri sposponderunt mihi creditum est: à me petere quod debeo, me ipsum appellare debetis. Quemadmodum cùm petebam, nulli me auctores generis mei vobis commendarunt: sic siquid deliquero, nullæ sunt imagines, quæ me à vobis deprecentur. Quare modò ut vita suppetat (quanquam ego sum is qui eam possim ab istorum scelere insidiísque defendere) polliceor hoc vobis, Quirites, bona fide, remp. vigilanti homini, non timido, diligenti, non ignavo, commisistis.* Partes hujus syllogismi prosyllogismis ornantur. Propositio à minori illustratur: cujus sententia est comparationis redditio, diversis illustrata; *nam cùm omnium consulum gravis,* &c. *tum eorum maximè:* diversa sunt, *non in incunabulis, sed in campo.* Assumptio sequitur, *nulli populo Rom.* &c. quæ iisdem rursus diversis illustratur, & à simili; meis, non majorum meritis; in campo, non in incunabulis: similitudo his verbis continetur; *quemadmodum cùm petebam,* &c. Tandem conclusionis sententia sequitur illustrata, primùm testimonio promissi, obligationis vim habentis,

argues and gives judgment for his diligence, saying (*On the Agrarian Law* 2): "For as the great care and diligence as well of all the consuls ought to be placed in defending the commonwealth, so above all of those who not in the cradle
5 but in the camp were made consuls. None of our ancients promised to the people of Rome for me that I ought to be trusted; to ask of me that I ought, you should make your demand upon myself. Likewise when I did ask the consulship, none of our ancestors commended me to you; therefore
10 if I neglect anything there are no renowned ancestors who shall intercede with you on my behalf. Yet while my life lasts (I being he who am able to defend it from their wickedness) I promise this to you, O Quirites, that you have committed the commonwealth to the providence of a good trust,
15 to a watchful man, not a coward, to a diligent man, not a sluggard." The parts of this syllogism are adorned with prosyllogisms. The proposition is made clearer by the lesser, whose meaning is the reddition of the comparison, illustrated by various things: "For as the great care and diligence as well
20 of all the consuls" etc. "so above all of those"; the various things are "not in the cradle but in the camp." The assumption follows: "None of our ancients promised to the people of Rome" etc., which again is illustrated by the same various things and by a comparison, for he mentions his own merits,
25 not those of his ancestors, and in the field, not in the cradle. A similitude is contained in the words: "Likewise when I did ask" etc. Then the idea of the conclusion follows, illustrated first by the testimony of promise, having the force of obliga-

polliceor, &c. Deinde diverso & disparato; *quare modò,* &c. Ergo *Cicero* erit vigilans, non timidus; diligens, non ignavus.

Aliud exemplum: *quod optatum redierit, gratum est: Lesbia Catullo optata rediit; grata igitur est.*

5 *Si quicquam cupidóque optantíque obtigit unquam &*
insperanti, hoc gratum est animo propriè.
Quare hoc est gratum, nobis quoque charius auro,
quod te restituis, Lesbia, mi cupido.
Restituis cupido atque insperanti ipsa refers te
10 *nobis; ô lucem candidiore nota!*
Quis me uno vivit felicior, aut magis hac quid
optandum vita dicere quis poterit?

In hoc exemplo propositio videtur esse composita, simplex tamen est, & syllogismus simplex; quia simplex est dispositio
15 argumenti cum partibus quæstionis. Duplex hîc crypsis est, inversio & redundantia. Primo loco est propositio *si quicquam cupido,* &c. i.e. quicquid cupido; *si* enim non semper connexi nota est. Assumptio est in quarto & quinto versu, *Lesbia Catullo* optata rediit. Conclusio est versu tertio illu-
20 strata à minori, *quare hoc est gratum & auro charius.* Tribus postremis versibus iteratur sententia conclusionis, primùm ab

tion—"I promise" etc.; then by the diverse and disparate: "while my life lasts" etc. Therefore Cicero was vigilant, not timid, diligent, not slothful.

As another example: *A longed-for thing that has come back is pleasing, Lesbia who was longed for has come back to Catullus, therefore she is pleasing.*

> That which we long for with desires great
> Is acceptable to us when we ha't.
> Wherefore this grateful is, more dear than gold,
> That Lesbia is come, our friend of old.
> Thou dost our wishes grant, our hope restore;
> O light most clear! who is there that is more
> Happy than I, who have what I desire?
> For any wish there's nought I can require.

In this example the proposition seems to be composite, but it nevertheless is simple, and the syllogism is simple since the disposition of the argument with the parts of the question is simple. The crypsis is double here, inversion and redundance. In the first place is the proposition "if we long for anything" etc., that is "that which we long for," for *if* is not always the sign of a connex. The assumption is in the fourth and fifth verses, that Lesbia who was longed-for has returned to Catullus. The conclusion in the third verse is illustrated by the lesser, "wherefore this grateful is" and "more dear than gold." In the last three verses the idea of the conclusion is repeated first with the adjunct time, "O light," then with an

adjuncto tempore, *ô lucem:* deinde à pari, *nemo me felicior, aut magis hac quid,* &c.

Quartus modus est negatus specialis: *deceptor amantis puellæ non est laudandus: Demophoon est deceptor amantis* 5 *puellæ; Demophoon igitur non est laudandus. Phyllis* apud *Ovidium* ita judicat *Demophoontem* laudandum non esse.

Fallere credentem non est operosa puellam
gloria: simplicitas digna favore fuit.
Sum decepta tuis & amans & fœmina verbis;
10 *dii faciant laudis summa sit ista tuæ.*

Propositio suum obtinet locum cum prosyllogismo adjunctæ simplicitatis, ut causæ cur deceptor non sit laudandus. Assumptio sequitur, sum *decepta tuis,* &c. Conclusionis sententia imprecatione continetur, *dii faciant,* &c.

15 Quintus modus est affirmatus proprius: ut, *Octavius est hæres Cæsaris: ego sum Octavius; sum igitur hæres Cæsaris.*

Sextus modus est negatus proprius: ut, *Antonius non est filius Cæsaris: tu es Antonius; non es igitur filius Cæsaris.*

Hujus itaque speciei laus est præ cæteris, quòd omnia 20 quæstionum genera concludat; nempe generales, speciales vel proprias, eásque vel affirmatas vel negatas; & præsertim ge-

equal, no one is "more happy than I, or what more than this" is to be desired?

The fourth mode is the negative special: *The deceiver of a loving maid is not to be praised, Demophoon is the deceiver* 5 *of a loving maid, therefore Demophoon is not to be praised.* According to Ovid, Phyllis thus judges that Demophoon is not to be praised:

> It is no glory virgins to deceive,
> Who love a man and wish him for to have;
> 10 Simplicity should rather favor gain.
> But I that love and eke a woman am
> Deceived am by these with flattering style.
> The gods thy praises make it all the while!

The proposition obtains its place with the prosyllogism of 15 added simplicity, as the cause why the deceiver is not to be praised. The assumption follows, "Deceived am" etc. The idea of the conclusion is contained in the imprecation, "The gods thy praises make it" etc.

The fifth mode is the affirmative proper, as *Octavius is* 20 *the heir of Cæsar, I am Octavius, therefore I am heir of Cæsar.*

The sixth mode is the negative proper, as *Antonius is not the son of Cæsar, you are Antonius, therefore you are not the son of Cæsar.*

So the reputation of this species is greater than that of the 25 others because it concludes all genera of questions, to wit, general, special, or proper, and all these either affirmative or negative, and especially the general affirmative; that is the

nerales affirmatas: ob quam potissimum causam *Aristoteles* speciem hanc & reliquis anteposuit, quod primus ejus modus nempe *affirmatus generalis* sit maximè scientificus, Post. 1. 11. cùm præcepta artium solus demonstret, & reductionem 5 reliquarum ad hanc figuram sive speciem laboriosè & subtiliter excogitavit verum non sic præstat hæc species cæteris duabus, ut earum idcirco ad hanc reductio cum tanta ut fit, alphabeti vexatione elaboranda fuerit, quandoquidem & reliquæ species non imperfectæ sunt, nec minus necessariò conclu- 10 dunt, id enim syllogismi speciebus commune cunctis est, quæstiones denique illas, quæ ad ipsarum judicium rectè referuntur, interdum aptius concludunt, quàm in hac specie, concludi queunt. Meritò itaque *Galenus,* l. 2. de placit. Hippoc. & *Plat.* reductionem hanc omnémque ejus supellectilem abe- 15 cedariam tanquam vanissimæ subtilitatis doctrinam inanem ac futilem post *Antipatrum* & *Chrysippum* explodit. *Et Keckermannus* ipse, in *P. Ramum* ferè iniquior, reductionem tamen illam quam vocant *per impossibile,* ad eos duntaxat refutandos inventam, homines sanè absurdos & raròadmodum reper- 20 tos, qui utraque præmissa concessa, conclusionem negent, fatetur se potius propter consuetudinem scholarum, quàm propter magnum ejus usum retinuisse. At consuetudo certè gnaviter nugandi ejicienda è scholis potius, quàm retinenda erat.

25 Tres hîc paralogismi refellendi sunt; quorum duo sunt utrique speciei explicatæ communes, propositio nimirum particularis, & conclusio partis non debilioris: utriusque exem-

cause above all why Aristotle (*Posterior Analytics* 1.11) puts this species before all the others, because its first mode, to wit, the *affirmed general* syllogism, is especially scientific, since it alone can demonstrate the precepts of the arts, and he
5 laboriously and subtly excogitates the reduction of the others to this figure or species; but this species does not so much surpass the other two that the reduction of them to this figure should be carried out with so much vexation of the alphabet as usually appears; and since the remaining species are not
10 imperfect, and not less necessarily bring a conclusion, for that is common to all species of syllogism, sometimes they better conclude those questions which are properly referred to their judgment than they can be concluded in this species. So properly Galen (*De placitis Hippocratis et Platonis* 2) fol-
15 lowing Antipater and Chrysippus, explodes this reduction and all its added alphabetical work as an empty and futile doctrine of the vainest subtlety. And Keckermann himself, who is usually rather unfair to Peter Ramus, says of the reduction which they call *by impossibility*—invented merely
20 for refuting those absurd and very rare men who when both premises are conceded deny the conclusion—that he retains it rather on account of the custom of the schools than on account of its great use. But certainly the habit of learned vaporing should rather be ejected from the schools than re-
25 tained.

Here three paralogisms are to be disproved, two of which are common to both the explicated species, to wit the proposition of the particular and the conclusion of the part not

plum hoc esse potest: *quoddam animal est rationale: bestia est animal: ergo bestia est rationalis.* Et prӕterea totum medium, nempe *quoddam animal,* non assumitur.

Proprius in hac specie paralogismus est argumenti negatio 5 in assumptione: ut, *omnis homo est animal: equus non est homo; ergo equus non est animal.*

Hîc etiam *solus* & *unicus* pro negandi particulis habendi sunt; paritérque reddunt assumptionem captiosam: ut, *quicquid est in mea domo, est in oppido: unicus fons est in mea* 10 *domo; ergo unicus fons est in oppido.* Sic, *quicquid est risibile, est animal: solus homo est risibilis; ergo solus homo est animal.* Tam enim hӕ particulӕ quàm negatio in minore, ostendunt non reciprocum esse majorem; adeóque conclusionem ex majore per minorem, vel generale ex proprio non 15 sequi.

Expendenda porrò hîc definitionis verba sunt; quӕ non tam assumptionem ipsam quàm argumentum in assumptione affirmatum significant. Cùm enim propositionis antecedens (quod tertium argumentum est) negatione infinita to- 20 pica duntaxat exprimatur, assumptionis consequens (quod etiam tertium argumentum est) eandem negationem retinere debet; alioqui non sequeretur argumentum affirmatum in assumptione, sed contradictione sublatum. Negatio autem hӕc non dicenda est vel assumptionis vel argumenti negatio, sed 25 argumenti infiniti affirmatio: tum enim demum negatur in assumptione argumentum, cùm illius negatio propositionis

weaker; this can serve as an example of both: *Some animal is rational, a beast is an animal, therefore a beast is rational.* And besides the whole middle, to wit, *some animal,* is not assumed.

The paralogism peculiar to this species is the negation of the argument in the assumption, as *Every man is an animal, a horse is not a man, therefore a horse is not an animal.*

Here also *single* and *unique* are to be taken for particles of negating; they equally render the assumption captious, as *Whatever is in my house is in the town, there is a single fountain in my house, therefore there is a single fountain in the town.* Also *Whatever is risible is an animal, man alone is risible, therefore man alone is an animal.* For these particles, like negation in the lesser, show that the greater is not reciprocal; and therefore the conclusion from the greater through the lesser, or the general from the proper, does not follow.

Therefore words of definition are here to be considered, which do not signify so much the assumption itself as the argument affirmed in the assumption. For when the antecedent of the proposition (which is the third argument) is expressed by an infinite negation merely topical, the consequent of the assumption (which is also the third argument) should retain the same negation; otherwise the argument would not follow, being affirmed in the assumption but taken away by contradiction. But this negation is not to be called negation either of the assumption or of the argument, but the affirmation of an infinite argument; for the argument is denied in the assumption only when the negation of that

affirmationi opponitur. Exempli gratia: *qui non est dives, contemnitur: Posthumus non est dives; ergo Posthumus contemnitur.* Assumptionem hîc non negari probat affirmatio conclusionis: sed perinde est acsi hoc modo argumentaretur:
5 *omnis homo qui non est dives, contemnitur: Posthumus est homo qui non est dives; ergo Posthumus contemnitur.* Vel hoc modo: *omnis non dives contemnitur: Posthumus est non dives; ergo contemnitur.* Sed hæc ex iis etiam quæ suprà ad definitionem ipsam hujus speciei diximus, puto non esse
10 obscura.

Præterea in quibusdam exemplis, quorum propositio est reciproca, videtur interdum syllogismus iste habere assumptionem negatam; cùm dicendum sit potius, partes propositionis inverti quæ si in ordinem revocentur, syllogismus erit
15 in prima specie explicati: ut *Joan.* 8. 47. *Qui ex Deo est, verba Dei audit: vos ex Deo non estis; ergo verba Dei non auditis.* Propositio invertenda est: *qui verba Dei audit, is ex Deo est: vos non estis ex Deo; ergo verba Dei non auditis.*

proposition is opposed to its affirmation. For the sake of example, *Since he is not rich he is despised, Posthumus is not rich, therefore Posthumus is despised*. The affirmation of the conclusion here proves that the assumption is not to be denied, but it is just as though it were argued in the following mode: *Every man who is not rich is despised, Posthumus is a man who is not rich, therefore Posthumus is despised;* or as though it were argued in this mode: *Every one not rich is despised, Posthumus is not rich, therefore he is despised*. But I judge that these things are not obscure after what I have said above on the definition of this species.

Besides in these examples of which the proposition is reciprocal, the syllogism seems sometimes to have a denied assumption; though it rather should be said that the parts of the proposition are inverted, since if they are put back in order, the syllogism will be of the first species of the explicated type, as John 8.47: *He that is of God hears the words of God, you are not of God, therefore you do not hear the words of God*. The proposition is to be inverted: *He that hears the words of God is of God, you are not of God, therefore you do not hear the words of God*.

CAPUT XIII.

De Syllogismo connexo primo.

ADHUC simplex syllogismus fuit.

Syllogismus compositus est syllogismus ubi tota quæstio est pars altera propositionis affirmatæ & compositæ; argumentum est pars reliqua.

5 Negat *Aristoteles* ullam esse syllogismi speciem præter tres figuras: & tamen ipse sæpe utitur composito, qui ad nullam ex tribus figuris referri potest. Verùm usus, optimus magister, docet, sæpius in communi hominum sermone ac disputationibus, compositos adhiberi syllogismos, quàm simplices: ut qui 10 multas quæstiones, multa argumenta commodè satis disponant, quæ syllogismi simplices respuunt. *Theophrastus* etiam & *Eudemus, Aristotelis* discipuli, quin etiam *Stoici,* & post eos *Cicero* & *Boëthius,* usum præceptorem secuti, compositos non omiserunt. Syllogismus autem compositus dicitur non tam 15 quod ex compositis axiomatis, nam & simplex potest ex compositis, nimirum relatis constare, sed à composita dispositione quæstionis totius cum tertio argumento in propositione; unde assumptio tota etiam assumitur; & conclusio non partim ex propositione partim ex assumptione, sed tota ex propositione 20 deducitur: propositio enim cùm sit composita, duas reliquas syllogismi partes (quæ axiomata simplicia sunt) conjuncti-

CHAPTER XIII.

Of the first connex syllogism.

HITHERTO the simple syllogism has been treated. A composite syllogism is a syllogism in which the whole question is one part of an affirmed and compound proposition; the argument is the other part.

5 Aristotle denies that there is any species of the syllogism besides the three figures; and yet he often uses the compound syllogism, which can be referred to none of the three figures. But experience, the best school master, teaches that in the common speech of men and in disputations compound sylло-
10 gisms are more often brought forward than simple ones, and that they sufficiently well dispose of many arguments which simple syllogisms reject. Even Theophrastus and Eudemus, disciples of Aristotle, and also the Stoics, and after them Cicero and Boethius, following experience as their teacher,
15 do not omit compound syllogisms. But the compound syllo-gism is not so called because made up of compound axioms, for the simple syllogism can also be made up of compound and even relate axioms, but because of the compound disposition of the whole question with the third argument in the proposi-
20 tion, whence the whole assumption is assumed; and the con-clusion is deduced not partly from the proposition, partly from the assumption, but entirely from the proposition; for when the proposition is compound, the two remaining parts of the syllogism (which are simple axioms) are held as conjuncts

onis vinculo conjunctas complectitur: pars illa efficit assumptionem quæ argumentum continet, altera conclusionem. Propositio autem debet esse affirmata, quia negata si esset, composita esse desineret, ipsa enim compositio negatione dissolve-
5 retur. Propositionem autem negatam efficit, ut de axiomate composito suprà dictum est, non partium sed conjunctionis negatio: ut, *si non est animal, non est homo;* hæc propositio ex omnibus etiam partibus negatis affirmata est: rectè igitur inde assumitur atque concluditur, *at non est animal, ergo*
10 *neque homo.* Sin hoc modo dicerem, *non si non est animal, idcirco non est homo,* ex hac negata propositione nihil omnino deduci aut concludi posset. In syllogismis itaque compositis ex ipsa conjunctionis vi deducuntur assumptio & conclusio. Ex duobus enim quæ in propositione conjunguntur, aut unum
15 assumitur ut alterum concludatur, aut unum tollitur ut alterum tollatur.

Tollere autem in syllogismo composito, non est negare, sed specialem contradictionem ponere.

Specialis autem contradictio, ut in axiomate simplici jam
20 diximus, particularis est aut propria. Tollere igitur propositionis partem aliquam in assumptione aut conclusione, est ejus contradictionem particularem aut propriam ponere. Particulari autem generaliter contradici, generali particulariter, ibidem etiam docemur. Exemplis rem planam suo quamque loco
25 faciemus.

by the band of the conjunction; the part which contains the argument effects the assumption, the other effects the conclusion. But the proposition ought to be affirmative, since if it is negative it ceases to be compound, for the compounding
5 itself would be dissolved by negation. But as was said above of the compound axiom, it is the denial not of the parts but of the conjunction that makes the proposition negative, as *If he is not an animal, he is not a man*. This proposition is affirmative with all its parts denied; rightly therefore it is thence
10 assumed and concluded *But he is not an animal, therefore he is not a man*. But if I should speak in this mode, *It is not true that if he is not an animal therefore he is not a man,* from this denied proposition nothing at all could be deduced or concluded. So in compound syllogisms from the very force of
15 the conjunction an assumption and conclusion are deduced. For of two things which are joined in the proposition, either one is assumed that the other may be concluded, or one is taken away that the other may be taken away.

But to take away in a compound syllogism is not to deny,
20 *but is to lay down a special contradiction.*

But a special contradiction, as we just now said in discussing the simple axiom, is either particular or proper. Therefore to take away some part of the proposition in the assumption or the conclusion is to make a particular or proper con-
25 tradiction of it. And we are also taught about that that the particular is generally contradicted and the general is particularly contradicted. We shall in its place make the matter plain with examples.

Sequitur nunc compositi syllogismi distributio: cujus genera ex propositionum compositione oriuntur: propositiones axiomata composita semper sunt: ex quatuor autem axiomatum compositorum generibus copulatum si affirmatum sit, 5 non habet locum in composito syllogismo; si negatum, æquipollet interdum disjuncto: discretum syllogismi expers est quia diversa ex quibus constat, nec planè consentiunt, & tamen ita leviter dissentiunt, ut uno posito vel remoto, non tamen sequatur alterum poni vel removeri; aut vim habet connexi.

10 *Syllogismus itaque compositus est connexus aut disjunctus.*

Syllogismus connexus est syllogismus compositus propositionis connexæ. Vel, cujus propositio est axioma connexum.

Cùm autem axiomati connexo affine sit relatum temporis, ut ibidem ostendimus, etiam syllogismi connexi propositio po-15 terit relata esse temporis: nam quantitatis, qualitatis, loci propositiones relatæ in simplicibus syllogismis locum habent; quia in iis propositionibus quæstionis duntaxat consequens cum argumento disponitur. Relatum denique consequentiæ, de quo supra cap. 6. syllogismis idoneus non est.

20 *Syllogismus connexus est duorum modorum.*

Primus modus syllogismi connexi est, qui assumit antecedens & consequens concludit.

Quo modo *Cicero* judicat & concludit l. 2. de divinatione: *si dji sunt, divinatio est: sunt autem dii; divinatio est igitur.*

There now follows the distribution of the compound syllogism, the kinds of which spring from the compounding of propositions. Propositions are always composite axioms; but of the four genera of composite axioms the copulate, if it is
5 affirmed, does not have a place in the compound syllogism; if it is denied, it is sometimes equivalent to the disjunct. The discrete is without part in the syllogism, since the diverse things of which it consists do not plainly agree, and yet so lightly disagree that if one is laid down or removed, it does
10 not therefore follow that the other is laid down or removed; or it has the force of a connex.

Hence a compound syllogism is connex or disjunct.

A connex syllogism is a compound syllogism with a connex proposition, or one of which the proposition is a connex
15 axiom.

But since the relative of time is akin to the connex axiom, as we have showed in its place, the proposition of the connex syllogism also may be a relative of time, for related propositions of quantity, quality, or position have a place among the
20 simple syllogisms, since in these propositions the consequent of the question alone is placed with the argument. The relative of consequence, then, with which I dealt above in chapter six, is not suitable for syllogisms.

The connex syllogism is of two sorts.

25 *The first sort of the connex syllogism is that which assumes an antecedent and concludes a consequent.*

In this sort Cicero judges and concludes in *De divinatione* 2: "If there are gods there is divination, but there are gods, therefore there is divination."

Aliud ex 3. *Offic. Atque si etiam hoc natura præscribit, ut homo homini, quicunque sit, ob eam ipsam causam, quòd is homo sit, consultum velit, necesse est secundum eandem naturam; omnium utilitatem esse communem. Quod si ita est,*
5 *una continemur omnes & eadem lege naturæ. Idque ipsum si ita est, certè violare alterum lege naturæ prohibemur. Verum autem primum; verum igitur & extremum.*

Propositio hujus syllogismi est sorites (de quo infrà) trium gradium, *si hoc natura præscribit, ut,* &c.

10 *Frequenter hîc non assumitur idem sed majus.*

Ut 1 *Catil. Si te parentes odissent, discederes: nunc patria te odit (quæ communis est omnium nostrum parens) multo magis ergo discedes.* Sed *majus illud* facile contineri in propositione poterit hoc modo; si propter odium parentum disce-
15 deres, multo magis propter odium patriæ. *At illud; ergo hoc multo magis.*

Simili ratione concluditur etiam majus vel minus: ut *Cic.* pro *Quint. Etsi vadimonium deseruisset, non debuisses tamen ad extrema jura descendere:* at non deseruit; multò minus
20 ergo debuisti, vel multo magis non debuisti.

Concludendi modus, ut supradiximus, *hîc idem est quando propositio est relata temporis.*

Another is to be found in *De officiis* 3: "And if also nature prescribeth this, that a man to a man, whatsoever he be, for that same cause that he is a man will use consultation, it is necessary according to the same nature that the profit of all
5 should be common. Which if it be so, all of us are contained in one and the same law of nature, and if this be so indeed we are certainly forbidden by the law of nature to violate one another. But the first is true, the last therefore is also true."

10 The proposition of this syllogism is a sorites (to be treated below) of three grades: "If also nature prescribeth this, that" etc.

Frequently here not the same but a greater is assumed.

This is illustrated in the first *Against Catiline: If your*
15 *parents hated you, you would depart; now your native land (which is the common parent of all of us) hates you; so much the more, therefore, you should depart.* But the formula *that the more* is easily contained in a proposition of this mode: *If on account of the hatred of your parents you should depart,*
20 *you should much more on account of the hatred of your fatherland.* The form is *but that . . . therefore this much more.*

By a similar method either more or less is concluded, as by Cicero in *Pro Quinto: Even though he had forfeited his recognizances, you still should not have invoked the severest*
25 *penalties of the law.* But he has not deserted; therefore much less you ought, or much more you ought not.

The mode of concluding, as we said above, *is here the same when the proposition is a relative of time.*

Ut, *cùm Paris Oenonem deseret, Xanthus recurret: Paris Oenonem deseruit; Xanthus ergo recurret.*

Sed tamen relata temporis ut & reliqua axiomata composita, id quod supra monuimus, ad syllogismum simplicem perti-
5 nebunt quoties non tota quæstio in propositione disponitur: quod quidem semper fit, cùm de certo & definito tempore quæstio est: ut si quæratur an hoc tempore sit æstas, hujusmodi erit syllogismus: *cùm sol est in cancro, æstas est: at hoc tempore sol est in cancro; ergo hoc tempore æstas est.*

CAPUT XIV.

De Syllogismo Connexo secundo.

SECUNDUS *modus connexi tollit consequens, ut tollat antecedens.*

Hæc enim vis connexi axiomatis est, si consequens non sit, nec esse antecedens. Sic *Cicero* 4 de fin. *docent nos,* inquit, *Dialectici,* &c. *Si illud, hoc: non autem hoc; igitur ne*
15 *illud quidem.*

Sequuntur exempla: *si ulli rei sapiens assentietur unquam, aliquando etiam opinabitur: nunquam autem opinabitur; nulli igitur rei assentietur.* Hîc consequens contradictione speciali in assumptione tollitur, *aliquando, nunquam;* conclu-
20 sio etiam antecedenti specialiter contradicit; *ulli rei, nulli rei.*

For example, *When Paris deserts Oenone let Xanthus turn back, Paris has deserted Oenone, therefore let Xanthus turn back.*

But nevertheless the relatives of time, like the other com-
5 pound axioms, as we have indicated above, pertain to the simple syllogism as often as not the whole question is placed in the proposition, as is always done when there is a question of a certain and definite time; if it should be asked whether at this time it is summer, the syllogism will be of
10 this mode: *When the sun is in cancer it is summer, but at this time the sun is in cancer, therefore at this time it is summer.*

CHAPTER XIV.

Of the second connex syllogism.

THE second sort of the connex takes away the consequent that it may take away the antecedent.

For this is the force of the connex axiom, that if
15 the consequent is not, the antecedent is not. Thus Cicero (*De finibus* 4) says that "the dialecticians teach us, etc.: If that is true this is true, but this is not true, therefore that is not true."

Examples follow: *If a wise man ever assents to anything he will sometimes conjecture, but he will never conjecture, there-*
20 *fore he will assent to nothing.* Here by a special contradiction the consequence is taken away in the assumption, *sometimes . . . never;* also the conclusion specially contradicts the antecedent, *anything . . . nothing.*

Eodem syllogismo *Ovid.* 2. de *Trist.* stultitiam suam judicat:

Si saperem doctas odissem jure sorores,
numina cultori perniciosa suo.
5 *At nunc (tanta meo comes est insania morbo)*
saxa memor refero rursus ad icta pedem.

Propositio est, *si saperem, Musas odissem:* cujus prosyllogismus est ab adjuncta pernicie. Assumptio, at non odi; quæ à simili exprimitur, *at nunc saxa memor,* &c. Ergo non sapio:
10 cujus conclusionis sententia in parenthesi est; *tanta meo,* &c. Atque in hoc exemplo est contradictio propria.

Hæ duæ syllogismi species sunt omnium usitatissimæ.

Non enim ea solùm argumenta quæ in simplicibus & disjunctis syllogismis disponi non possunt, in connexis facile dis-
15 ponuntur, sed etiam ex iis quæ possunt aliis formis concludi, multa in his speciebus facilius & promptius concluduntur: immo nullum omnino argumentum, quod in syllogismo usum habet, has connexi species respuit.

Præter hos duos connexi syllogismi modos nonnulli duos
20 alios adjiciunt; quorum prior tollit antecedens ut tollat consequens, posterior assumit consequens ut concludat antecedens. In quos modos etsi communis fortè sermo, boni etiam authores nonnunquam incidunt, tamen cùm in syllogismo non veritas partium sed necessitas consequentiæ spectetur, tenen-
25 dum est, vitiosos esse eos modos qui ex veris verum juxta & falsum possunt concludere. Prior ergo hîc modus qui tollit

With the same syllogism Ovid (*Tristia* 2) judges his folly:

> If I were wise those sisters I should hate,
> Deities hurtful to whom on them waits;
> But now (so great my foolishness is seen),
> 5 I build them altars whom my hurt have been.

The proposition is *If I were wise, I should hate the Muses;* its prosyllogism is from the adjunct harm. The assumption is *but I have not hated,* which is expressed by a comparison: "I build them altars" etc. *Therefore I am not wise* is the con-
10 clusion, with its meaning given in the parenthesis: "so great" etc. There is also a proper contradiction in this example.

These two species of syllogism are the most frequently used of all.

For not those arguments alone which cannot be placed in
15 simple and disjunct syllogisms are easily placed in connex syllogisms, but also many of those that can be concluded by other forms can be in these species more easily and promptly concluded; indeed no argument at all, which is employed in the syllogism, rejects these species of connex.

20 In addition to these two sorts of the connex syllogism, some add two others, the first of which takes away the antecedent that it may take away the consequent, and the second assumes the consequent that it may conclude the antecedent. Though common speech perchance falls into these sorts of syllogism,
25 good authors never do, and since in the syllogism not the truth of the parts but the necessity of the consequence is considered, it must be held that those sorts are vicious which from

antecedens est prioris legitimi modi paralogismus, affinis negatæ assumptioni in secunda specie explicati: ut, *si homo est leo, sentit: non est leo; ergo non sentit.* Et hoc: *si Dio est equus, est animal: at non est equus; ergo non est animal. Si*
5 *orator est, homo est: non est orator; ergo nec homo.* Hoc si sic resolvas in secundam speciem explicati, *omnis orator est homo,* fallacia patebit. Immo sine ista reductione per se etiam patet: tollit enim antecedens, quod minus est, ut tollat consequens, quod majus est: à minore autem ad majus nulla est
10 hujusmodi consequentia.

Modus posterior, qui assumit consequens ut concludat antecedens, est captio posterioris legitimi modi, affinis paralogismo ex omnibus affirmatis in prima specie explicati: ut, *si homo est leo, sentit: at sentit; ergo est leo.* Utrumque hunc
15 paralogismum *Aristoteles* appellat fallaciam consequentis; quæ toties fit quoties propositio non est reciproca.

Sed est etiam aliud sophisma secundi modi, cùm assumptio non tollit contradictione speciali; id est, quando consequenti vel generali generaliter, vel particulari particulariter contra-
20 dicit. Generalis contradictionis exemplum est, *si omne animal est irrationale, omnis etiam homo est irrationalis: at nullus*

true arguments are able to conclude true and false together. Therefore here the prior sort which takes away the antecedent is the paralogism of the prior legitimate sort akin to the negated assumption in the second explicated species, as *If a man is a lion he perceives, he is not a lion, therefore he does not perceive.* And this: *If Dio is a horse he is an animal, but he is not a horse, therefore he is not an animal. If he is an orator he is a man, he is not an orator, therefore he is not a man.* The fallacy will appear if you resolve this into the second species of the explicate syllogism as follows: *Every orator is a man.* Indeed without this reduction it is plain through itself, for it takes away the antecedent, which is less, that it may take away the consequent, which is greater; but from the minor to the major there is no succession of this kind.

The last sort, which assumes the consequent that it may conclude the antecedent, is a fallacious argument of the last legitimate mode, akin to the paralogism from affirmative arguments only in the first species of the explicate syllogism, as *If a man is a lion he perceives, but he perceives, therefore he is a lion.* Both of these paralogisms Aristotle calls fallacies of the consequent, which appear as often as a proposition is not reciprocal.

There is also another sophism of the second sort, when the assumption does not take away by a special contradiction, that is, when it contradicts the consequent, either a general one generally or a particular one particularly. An example of a general contradiction is *If every animal is irrational every man is irrational, but no man is irrational, therefore no animal*

homo est irrationalis: nullum ergo animal est irrationale. Particularis hoc: *si homo est rationalis, aliquod animal est rationale: sed aliquod animal non est rationale; ergo nec homo.*

CAPUT XV.

De Syllogismo disjuncto primo.

SYLLOGISMUS *disjunctus est syllogismus compositus propositionis disjunctæ.*

Modi duo sunt. Sic etiam *Cic.* in *Top. & Stoici apud Laërtium.*

Primus tollit unum, & reliquum concludit.

Ut, *aut dies est, aut nox: at dies non est; ergo nox est.* Vel,
10 *nox non est; dies ergo est.*

Ciceronis pro *Cluentio* judicium tale est: *sed cùm esset hæc illi proposita conditio, ut aut justè piéque accusaret, aut acerbè indignéque moreretur; accusare quoquo modo posset, quàm illo modo mori maluit.* Disjunctio clarior sic erit: *aut*
15 *accusandum aut moriendum: non moriendum; accusandum igitur.* In hoc exemplo, ut est apud Cic. est partium inversio, totusque Syllogismus in axiomate relato consequentiæ involvitur. Propositio non est absolutè vera, sed ex conditione. Assumptio & conclusio per comparationem minoris ponuntur;
20 ita, ut conclusio præcedat.

Sic idem 2 *Philip.* ratiocinatur: *nunquamne intelliges tibi statuendum esse, utrum illi qui istam rem gesserunt, homici-*

is irrational. The particular is this: *If a man is rational, some animal is rational, but some animal is not rational, therefore a man is not rational.*

CHAPTER XV.

Of the first disjunct syllogism.

A *DISJUNCT syllogism is a compound syllogism with a disjunct proposition.*

There are two sorts. So says Cicero in the *Topics,* and the Stoics according to Laërtius.

The first takes away one and concludes the other.

For example, *It is either day or night, but it is not day,* 10 *therefore it is night.* Or *It is not night, therefore it is day.*

There is such a judgment by Cicero in *Pro Cluentio:* "But when as this condition was proposed to him, that either he should accuse justly and piously or die sharply or unworthily, he would rather accuse after that manner than die after this." 15 The disjunction would be clearer in this form: *There must be either accusation or death, there is not to be death, therefore there must be accusation.* In this example, as it is in Cicero, there is an inversion of the parts, and the whole syllogism is involved in the related axiom of succession. The proposition 20 is not absolutely true, but conditional. The assumption and the conclusion are established through comparison of the lesser, in such a way that the conclusion may precede.

Thus in the same way it is argued in the second *Philippic:* "Dost thou not understand it must be determined that either

dæ sint an vindices libertatis? Attende, &c. *Nego quicquam esse medium. Confiteor illos nisi liberatores populi Rom. conservatorésque reip. sint, plus quàm sicarios, plus quàm homicidas, plus quàm parricidas esse: siquidem est atrocius*
5 *patriæ parentem,* &c. *Si parricidæ, cur honoris causa à te sunt & in hoc ordine & apud populum Rom. semper appellati? Cur* &c? *Atque hæc acta per te. Non igitur homicidæ. Sequitur ut liberatores tuo judicio sint; quandoquidem tertium nihil potest esse.* Quæstio hîc proponitur initio de
10 *Cæsaris* interfectoribus, *utrum,* &c. Propositio proponitur axiomate connexo, *confiteor illos nisi,* &c. quod æquipollet disjuncto, *aut vindices sunt libertatis aut plus quàm homicidæ:* illustratur enim ea pars disjunctionis à majori: & præcedit prosyllogismus, quo ostenditur disjunctionem hanc esse sine me-
15 dio, & proinde necessariam. Assumptio sequitur, *non sunt homicidæ;* idque confirmatur prosyllogismo à testimonio & factis ipsius *Antonii.* Prosyllogismus concluditur in secundo connexo, si parricidæ, cur, &c? *at hæc acta per te; non igitur homicidæ.* Conclusio denique sequitur, *ut liberatores fuerint;*
20 idque repetito propositionis prosyllogismo confirmatur, *quandoquidem tertium sive medium nihil potest esse.*

Si partes disjunctæ propositionis sint duabus plures, judicandi concludendique ars erit eadem.

those who have done this thing are homicides or revengers of liberty? But attend, etc. I deny that there is any mean; I grant that they are, except they be deliverers and conservers of the Roman commonwealth, more than villains, more than 5 homicides, more than parricides; if truly it be cruelty rather to be a father to the country, etc. If they be parricides, why were they honored of thee, and called to this order by the Roman people? Why, etc. And these things were done by thee. They are not, therefore, homicides. It followeth, then, 10 that by thine own judgment they are deliverers, whenas truly there can be no third admitted." Here the question about the murderers of Cæsar is propounded at the beginning: "either" etc. The proposition is laid down in a connex axiom: "I grant that they are, except" etc., which is of equal weight with the 15 disjunct: *Either they are avengers of liberty or more than homicides,* for this part of the disjunction is made plain by the greater. The prosyllogism precedes, by which it is shown that this disjunction is without a middle and therefore necessary. The assumption follows: "They are not homicides," 20 and this is confirmed by the prosyllogism with the testimony and deeds of Antony himself. The prosyllogism is concluded in the second connex: "If they be parricides, why etc.? And these things were done by thee. They are not, therefore, homicides." Then follows the conclusion: "They are deliverers," 25 and this repetition of the proposition is confirmed by the prosyllogism: "Truly there can be no third" or mean.

If the parts of a disjunct proposition are more than two, the art of judging and concluding will be the same.

Quamvis autem disjunctionis partes esse possint sæpenumerò plures quàm duæ, id quod in disparatis accidit, ipsius tamen propositionis duæ tantummodo partes sunt; quarum una est quæstio, altera est argumentum. In hoc modo ubi quæ- 5 stio semper concluditur, tertium argumentum plura opposita comprehendit, quæ omnia in assumptione tollenda sunt, ut quæstio concludatur: nam oppositorum plura simul affirmari nequeunt, negari plura simul queunt.

Sic *Cic.* judicat *Rabirium cum consulibus esse oportuisse.* 10 *Aut enim cum consulibus, aut cum seditiosis, aut latuisse: at nec cum seditiosis fuisse, nec latuisse; fuisse ergo cum consulibus.* Pro *Rabir. Atqui videmus ait hæc in rerum natura tria fuisse, ut aut cum Saturnino esset, aut cum bonis, aut lateret. Latere autem, mortis erat instar turpissimæ: cum Saturnino* 15 *esse, furoris & sceleris; virtus & honestas & pudor cum coss. esse cogebat.* Propositio per se clara est. Assumptionis partes prosyllogismis illustrantur, primo à simili, deinde ab adjunctis. Conclusio prosyllogismo ab efficiente illustratur.

Notandum est in hoc modo non ita exigi specialem con- 20 tradictionem, ut in reliquis; neque enim ad consequentiæ necessitatem pertinet in hoc modo, ut in reliquis, sed ad assumptionis solius veritatem. Si ergo assumptio generalem contradictionem ferre potest, per consequentiam licebit uti: ad consequentiæ enim rationem sufficit, alterum quovis modo

Though the parts of the disjunction can frequently be more than two, as happens in disparates, the parts of the proposition itself are two only, one of which is the question, the other the argument. In this sort where the question is always concluded, the third argument comprehends several opposites, which are all to be taken away in the assumption, that the question may be concluded, for several opposites cannot at the same time be affirmed, but several can at the same time be negated.

Thus Cicero judges that Rabirius should have been with the consuls: *Either he was with the consuls or with the seditious or he was hidden, but he was not with the seditious nor was he hidden, therefore he was with the consuls,* as we read in *Pro Rabirio:* "And we see these three to be in the nature of things, to wit that either he should be with Saturninus, or with the good, or that he should lie hid. But to lie hid is proper to the dead and rotten; to be with Saturninus of fury and wickedness; virtue and honesty and shamefastness constrained him to be with the consuls." The proposition is clear through itself. The parts of the assumption are made clear by prosyllogisms, first from the similar, then from the adjuncts. The conclusion is illustrated by a prosyllogism with an efficient.

It should be observed that in this mode the special contradiction is not so much sought for as in the rest, for in this mode it does not pertain to the necessity of the sequence, as in the rest, but to the truth of the assumption alone. If therefore the assumption can bear a general contradiction, it will

tolli, ut reliquum concludatur, eademque conclusio erit, sive specialis sive generalis in assumptione contradictio fuerit, in altero verò modo secus erit, ubi contradictio in ipsam conclusionem cadit.

CAPUT XVI.

De Syllogismo disjuncto secundo.

D*ISJUNCTUS secundus è propositione partibus omnibus affirmata assumit unum & reliquum tollit.*

Secundus efficitur, quia minus generalis est primo, utpote proprietatibus quibusdam astrictus, quibus prior immunis erat. Proprietates autem hæ sunt, 1. partium omnium propositionis affirmatio, non totius modò propositionis, id enim syllogismis omnibus compositis commune est; & affirmari quidem propositio vel omnibus negatis partibus potest. 2. assumptio affirmatur, quoniam in propositione affirmata fuerat. 3. in conclusione semper est negatio, eáque specialis contradictio: in primo quidem conclusio nonnunquam negatur; sed hoc tum fit cùm pars propositionis quæ concluditur negata fuit. Exempli gratia: *aut dies est, aut nox: dies est; ergo nox non est.*

Ejusmodi syllogismus efficitur è propositione copulata ne-

consequently be allowable to use one, for it suffices to the explanation of the sequence that one should be taken away in any manner, that what remains may be concluded, and the conclusion will be the same whether there was a special or a 5 general contradiction in the assumption, but in the other sort, where the contradiction falls in the conclusion itself, it will be otherwise.

CHAPTER XVI.

Of the second disjunct syllogism.

THE second disjunct syllogism from a proposition affirmed in all its parts assumes one and takes away the rest.

It is constituted the *second,* since it is less general than the first, being restricted by certain properties from which the first was immune. These properties are as follows: 1, The affirmation of all the parts of the proposition, not merely of 15 the whole proposition, for this is common to all composite syllogisms, and a proposition can indeed be affirmed even though all the parts are denied. 2, The assumption is affirmed, since it has been affirmed in the proposition. 3, In the conclusion there is always a denial, and it is a special con-20 tradiction; in the first conclusion it is sometimes denied, but this is done when part of the proposition which is concluded has been denied. For the sake of example: *Either it is day or night, it is day, therefore it is not night.*

A syllogism of this sort is made from a denied copulative

gata, quæ negata complexio, vel, quod Græcis idem est, negata copulatio dicitur, *& disjunctionis affirmatæ vim obtinet.*

Non & dies, & nox est: at dies est; non igitur nox est. De hac negata copulatione sic *Cic.* in *top. non & hoc, & illud:* 5 *hoc autem; non igitur illud.*

Pertinet autem ad hunc secundum duntaxat modum negata copulatio; quod cum in hujusmodi propositione quævis opposita disponi possint, ex uno eorum negato, nisi in iis qui medio carent, non necessariò alterum affirmatur & concludi- 10 tur, quod fit in primo modo, sed ex altero affirmato alterum negatur, quæ communis est regula omnium oppositorum, & fit duntaxat in hoc secundo.

Ad sophismata quod attinet horum modorum, primi quidem nullum occurrit. Secundi quæ sunt, ex definitione re- 15 darguuntur. Primum est, si aliqua pars propositionis negata erit: ut, *leo aut animal est, aut non est homo; at non est homo; ergo nec animal.* Secundum est, si assumptio sit negata; ut in exemplo superiore. Tertium est, si specialis contradictio non erit in conclusione: ut hoc; *aut homo est animal, aut omne* 20 *animal est irrationale; sed homo est animal; ergo nullum animal est irrationale.*

proposition, which is called a denied complex, or, what is the same in Greek, a denied copulation, and *gains the force of an affirmative disjunction.*

It is not both day and night, but it is day, therefore it is not
5 *night.* Of this denied copulation Cicero writes as follows in the *Topics:* "Not both this and that, but this, therefore not that."

To this second sort merely the denied copulation pertains, because when in a proposition of this sort any opposites can
10 be laid down, when one is denied, except in those that lack a middle term, the other is not of necessity affirmed and concluded, as is done in the first sort, but from the affirmation of the one comes the denial of the other, which is the common rule of all opposites and is done merely in this second type.
15 As to the sophisms of these modes, there is in fact none connected with the first. Those connected with the second are refuted by the definition. In the first some part of the proposition is denied, as *A lion is either an animal or it is not a man, but it is not a man, therefore it is not an animal.* The second
20 is if the assumption is denied, as in the example above. The third is if there will not be a special contradiction in the conclusion, as *Either a man is an animal or every animal is irrational, but a man is an animal, therefore no animal is irrational.*

Appendix de enthymemate, dilemmate, & sorite.

EXPOSITIS omnibus cùm simplicis tum compositi syllogismi speciebus, sequitur axiomatis & syllogismi communis affectio, vel potius anomalia, de qua antediximus, crypsis. Quæ in omni cùm loquendi usu tum scri-
5 bendi genere tam frequens est, idque brevitatis plerumque causa, ut nemo ferè syllogismos integros sine crypsi aliqua vel loquatur vel scribat.

Sed quoniam crypsis ejúsque triplex modus syllogismorum omnes species afficiunt, ea re dicendi locus de syllogismi cryp-
10 sibus antè non erat, quàm de syllogismi speciebus cunctis dictum esset.

Si qua pars syllogismi defuerit, enthymema dicitur.

Ut ab exemplo: *Themistocli licuit urbem relinquere; ergo mihi.* addatur propositio; *quod Themistocli licuit, licet &*
15 *mihi.* Ab inductione: *inventio & dispositio in argumentis versantur; ergo Logica tota.* addatur assumptio; *Logica tota est eorum inventio & dispositio.*

Hoc etiam perpetuò observandum est, si conclusionis prædicatum deest, deesse majorem; si subjectum, minorem: si
20 utrumque; syllogismi compositi majorem vel potius majoris

An appendix of the enthymeme, dilemma, and sorites.

AFTER the exposition of all the species of the simple as well as the compound syllogism, there follows the common affect of the axiom and syllogisms, or rather the anomaly of which we spoke before, the crypsis.
5 In every exercise of speech and genus of writing this is so frequent, and the more because of its brevity, that generally no one speaks or writes integral syllogisms without some crypsis.

But since the crypsis and its triple mode affect all species
10 of the syllogism, there was therefore no place for speaking of the crypses of the syllogism before all the species of the syllogism had been discussed.

If some part of a syllogism is lacking, it is called an enthymeme.

15 This appears in the following argument by example: *It was proper for Themistocles to abandon the city, therefore it is proper for me to do so.* The proposition may be added: *What was proper for Themistocles is proper for me.* An example in arguing by induction is *Invention and disposition*
20 *are found in arguments, therefore the whole of logic.* The assumption may be added: *The whole of logic is the invention and disposition of them.*

It should be perpetually observed that if the predicate of a conclusion is lacking, the major is lacking; if the subject, the
25 minor; if both, the major of a compound syllogism or rather

antecedentem, quæ cum tota quæstione ut cum consequente disponitur; quod indicat plenum syllogismum fore compositum, & antecedens pars enthymematis erit antecedens majoris; totúmque enthymema convertetur in majorem propo-
5 sitionem syllogismi connexi: ut, *virtus reddit beatos; vitium ergo miseros.* In antecedente hujus enthymematis nec antecedens nec consequens quæstionis apparet: totum igitur converte in axioma connexum aut disjunctum, plenum syllogismum compositum esse intelliges; ut, *si virtus reddit beatos,*
10 *vitium reddit miseros; at illud; hoc igitur. non est nox; ergo est dies.* Totum converte in axioma disjunctum, majorem supplebis, & syllogismum plenum disjunctum conficies: *aut dies est, aut nox; non nox, ergo dies.*

Si quid ad tres illas syllogismi partes accesserit, prosyllo-
15 *gismus dicitur.* Est enim ad partem aliquam syllogismi addita probatio.

Partium etiam ordo sæpe confunditur. Quod utrumque accidit in dilemmate & sorite.

Dilemma est specialis quædam crypsis non syllogismi, sed
20 syllogismorum; à duplici propositione dictum, quam *lemma Stoici* vocant, vulgò *disjunctivus, biformis, & syllogismus cornutus,* quasi cornibus feriens: cujus vis in duobus axiomatis connexis citra syllogismi formam satis manifesta est: ut illud *Martialis;*

the antecedent of the major, which is disposed with the whole question as with the consequent. This indicates that the full syllogism will be compound, and the antecedent part of the enthymeme will be the antecedent of the major, and the
5 whole enthymeme will be converted into the major proposition of a connex syllogism, as *Virtue makes men blessed, vice therefore makes them miserable.* In the antecedent of this enthymeme neither the antecedent nor the consequent of the question appears; convert the whole therefore into a connex
10 or disjunct axiom and you know that the full syllogism is compound, as *If virtue makes them happy, vice makes them miserable; but that . . . therefore this; It is not night, therefore it is day.* Convert the whole into a disjunct axiom, you will supply the major and will produce a full disjunct syllo-
15 gism, as *Either it is day or night, it is not night, therefore it is day.*

If anything is added to those three parts of the syllogism, it is called a prosyllogism, for it is an added proof for some part of the syllogism.

20 *The order of the parts is often confounded.* Both of these happen also in the dilemma and the sorites.

The dilemma is a special kind of crypsis, not of a syllogism, but of syllogisms, so called from a double proposition, which the Stoics call a *lemma,* and which generally is called the *dis-*
25 *junctive, biformed,* and *cornute syllogism,* as though striking with horns. The force of this in two connex axioms beyond the form of the syllogism is sufficiently manifest, as in that saying of Martial:

hæc, si displicui, fuerint solatia nobis;
hæc fuerint nobis præmia, si placui.

Et illud in evangelio: *si bene locutus sum, cur me cædis; si male, testare de malo.* Et reciprocum illud insigne *Protagoræ magistri* ad *Euathlum* discipulum, apud *Gellium, l.* 5. *c.* 10. & 11: *si contra te lis data erit, merces mihi ex sententia illa debebitur, quia ego vicero; sin verò secundum te judicatum erit, merces mihi ex pacto debebitur, quia tu viceris.* Cui contrà *Euathlus; & ego bone magister, utrovis modo vicero,* &c. Hujusmodi est etiam illud apud *Aristot.* Rhet. 2. 23. *non agendum esse cum populo; quia, si justa dixeris, hominibus invisus eris, si injusta, Deo.* Immo agendum esse cum populo: *nam, si injusta dixeris, hominibus gratus eris; si justa, Deo.*

Explicatur autem hæc crypsis axiomate disjuncto; tot deinde syllogismis connexis vel etiam categoricis, quot erant disjuncti axiomatis membra: ut illud *Biantis* consilium de uxore non ducenda: *aut formosam duces, aut deformem; si formosam, communem; si deformem, pœnam: neutrum autem bonum; non est igitur ducenda uxor.* Vel categoricè sic; *communis non est ducenda; formosa erit communis; ergo,* &c. *pœna non est ducenda; deformis erit pœna; ergo,* &c. Sed axioma illud disjunctum partes omnes disjunctas non enumerat:

When my verse takes not, this will be an ease;
A high reward in case it thee do please.

And there is that passage in the Gospel: "If I have spoken evil, bear witness of the evil; but if well, why smitest thou
5 me?" And as reciprocal that striking saying of Protagoras the teacher to Euathlus the pupil, according to Gellius 5. 10 and 11: "If judgment is given against you the money will be due me for that reason, since I win; but if the decision is favorable to you the money will be due me according to our agreement,
10 since you win." To whom Euathlus answered: "Good teacher, I win whichever way it goes" etc. Of the same sort is the saying in Aristotle (*Rhetoric* 2. 23): "You should not speak in the assembly, for if you speak justly you will be hateful to men, if unjustly to God. Indeed you should speak in the as-
15 sembly, for if you speak unjustly you will be pleasing to men, if justly to God."

This crypsis is explained by a disjunct axiom, and then by as many connex syllogisms or even categories as there were members of the disjunct axiom, as in that advice of Bias on
20 not marrying: *You will marry either a beautiful or an ugly woman; if she is beautiful, she will be a harlot, if ugly, an affliction; neither is good; therefore one should not marry.* Or categorically thus: *A harlot is not to be married, a beautiful woman will be a harlot, therefore* etc. Or it may be put
25 *An affliction is not to be married, an ugly wife will be an affliction, therefore* etc. But that disjunct axiom does not enumerate all the disjunct parts, for there is a wife who occupies

est enim media quæ nec formosa nec deformis est; & neutrius connexi consequens est vera; fieri enim potest, ut nec formosa communis, nec deformis pœna sit futura.

Sorites & syllogismus crypticus multarum propositionum 5 continua serie ita progredientium, ut prædicatum præcedentis propositionis perpetuò sit subjectum sequentis, donec tandem consequens propositionis ultimæ concludatur de antecedente primæ: ut, *homo est animal; animal est corpus sentiens; corpus sentiens est vivens; vivens est substantia; ergo homo est* 10 *substantia. Græcè* autem sorites, *acervalis Latinè à Cicerone* dicitur; quia minutatim addit, & quasi acervum efficit.

Adhibetur ferè vel ad summum genus de infima specie, vel ad causam primariam, licet remotam, effecto attribuendam; & illud quidem per genera subalterna, ut in exemplo superi- 15 ore; hoc per causas medias, ut in exemplo sequente: *quos Deus prænovit, eos prædestinavit; quos prædestinavit, eos vocavit; quos vocavit, eos justificavit; quos justificavit, eos glorificavit; ergo, quos prænovit, eos glorificavit.*

Utitur autem sorites & subalternis generibus & subordinatis 20 causis quasi tot mediis terminis ad probandum conclusionem; tot nempe quot sunt termini inter subjectum primæ propositionis & prædicatum conclusionis: quot autem termini medii, tot sunt syllogismi.

Est itaque progressio enthymematica syllogismos uno pau-

the middle between beautiful and ugly; and the consequent is true of neither connex, for it can happen that a beautiful wife will not be a harlot nor an ugly one an affliction.

The sorites is a cryptic syllogism of many propositions so 5 progressing in a continued series that the predicate of the preceding proposition is constantly the subject of the following, until the consequent of the last proposition is concluded of the antecedent of the first, as *A man is an animal, an animal is a sentient body, a sentient body is living, anything living is* 10 *substance, therefore man is substance*. It is called in Greek a sorites and by Cicero in Latin *acervalis,* since it adds bit by bit and makes as it were a heap of things.

It is generally used either in moving to the highest genus from the lowest species or in attaining to a primary cause, 15 though remote, to be assigned to an effect; the first is done through subaltern genera, as in the example given above, the second through mean causes, as in the example following: "Whom he did foreknow, he also did predestinate. . . . Whom he did predestinate, them he also called; and whom 20 he called, them he also justified; and whom he justified, them he also glorified." *Therefore whom he did foreknow, them he glorified.*

The sorites uses both subaltern genera and subordinate causes as so many middle terms for proving a conclusion, so 25 many indeed as there are terms between the subject of the first proposition and the predicate of the conclusion; there are, then, as many syllogisms as there are middle terms.

So it is an enthymematic progression containing syllogisms

ciores continens quàm propositiones. Syllogismus principalis habet pro majore propositionem conclusioni proximam; pro minoris termino minore, subjectum conclusionis; pro termino majore, subjectum propositionis majoris: ex. gr. *quos justificavit, glorificavit; quos prænovit, justificavit; quos ergo prænovit, glorificavit.* Reliqui sunt minorum prosyllogismi, & præcedens quisque probatio sequentis.

Unde intelligitur soritæ crypsis triplex, & defectus, & redundantia, & inversio. Si igitur partium, sive species sive causæ sint, non erit recta subordinatio firmáque connexio, sorites probus non erit: ut, *ex malis moribus existunt bonæ leges; ex bonis legibus salus reip.; ex reip. salute bona omnia; ergo ex moribus malis bona omnia.* Hîc causæ per se male subordinantur causæ per accidens.

Fallit hic etiam: *si nullum tempus esset, nox non esset; si nox non esset, dies esset; si dies esset, aliquod tempus esset; ergo, si nullum tempus esset, aliquod tempus esset.* Nam si nullum tempus esset, certè nec dies esset: fallit ergo in propositione secunda; quæ non verè continuatur; sed ponit effectum, sublata causa. Cætera sorites vitia habet cum aliis syllogismi speciebus communia.

one less in number than its propositions. The principal syllogism has for its major the proposition nearest the conclusion; for the minor term of the minor, the subject of the conclusion; for the major term the subject of the major proposition, for 5 example, *Whom he justified, he glorified; whom he foreknew, he justified; whom, therefore, he foreknew, he glorified.* The rest are prosyllogisms of the minors, and each one that precedes is a proof of what follows.

Thence is understood the triple crypsis of the sorites: de-10 fect, redundance, and inversion. If therefore there is not a proper subordination and firm connection of the parts, whether they are species or causes, the sorites will not be sound, as *From evil customs arise good laws, from good laws the health of the state, from the health of the state all good 15 things, therefore from evil customs arise all good things.* Here the causes through themselves are badly subordinated to the cause through an accident.

There is a fallacy here also: *If there were no time, there would be no night; if there were no night, it would be day; 20 if there were day, there would be some time; therefore, if there were no time, there would be some time.* For if there were no time, certainly there would be no day; it is fallacious therefore in the second proposition, which is not truly continued but lays down an effect when the cause has been re-25 moved. The sorites has all the other vices in common with the other species of syllogism.

CAPUT XVII.

De Methodo.

METHODUS *est dispositio dianoëtica variorum axiomatum homogeneorum pro naturæ suæ claritate præpositorum, unde omnium inter se convententia judicatur memoriáque comprehenditur.*

5 Methodi permagnus est in omni vita usus, magna proinde laus. Hanc *Plato,* in *Philebo* esse ait *donum hominibus divinitus datum. Aristoteles* etiam *ordinem in maximis bonis* numeravit. *Fabius, nec mihi,* inquit, *errare videntur, qui ipsam rerum naturam stare ordine putant; quo confuso, peritura* 10 *sunt omnia.*

Est autem methodus dispositio variorum axiomatum homogeneorum, i.e. eorum quæ ad eandem rem pertinent, eandémque ad finem referuntur. Homogenea nisi fuerint, subordinata sibi invicem esse non poterunt, adeóque ne ordinata 15 quidem. Itaque Arithmeticum in Geometria, Geometricum in Arithmetica veluti heterogeneum & alienum methodus excludit. Pro naturæ autem suæ claritate axiomata quæque præponenda sunt, prout argumenta priora, notiora, illustriora complectuntur. Prima autem præcedant an orta à primis pa-20 rum refert, cùm utrorumque eadem affectio sit.

Atque ut spectatur in axiomate veritas aut falsitas, in syl-

CHAPTER XVII.

Of method.

METHOD is a dianoëtic disposition of various homogeneous axioms arranged one before another according to the clarity of their nature, whence the agreement of all with relation to each other is judged and
5 *retained by the memory.*

There is very great use of method in all life, therefore great glory is given to it. Plato in the *Philebus* says that it is "a gift divinely given to men." Aristotle also numbers "order among the greatest goods." Fabius writes: "They do not seem to me
10 to err who think that the very nature of things stands in order, and that if order is lost everything will perish."

Method, then, is a disposition of various homogeneous axioms, that is, of those which pertain to the same thing, and are referred to the same end. If they were not homogeneous,
15 they could not be mutually subordinate to each other, therefore could not be at all ordered. So method excludes arithmetic in geometry, and geometry in arithmetic as heterogeneous and alien. Axioms are to be arranged one before another according to the clarity of their nature, as they ex-
20 press arguments that are prior, better known, and clearer. It makes little difference whether prime arguments or arguments derived from primes precede, since both have the same affect.

So as truth or falsity is seen in the axiom, in the syllogism

logismo consequentia & inconsequentia; sic in methodo consideratur, ut per se clarius præcedat, obscurius sequatur; omninóque ordo & confusio judicatur. Sic disponetur ex homogeneis axiomatis primo loco absoluta notione primum,
5 *secundo secundum, tertio tertium, & ita deinceps.*

Prius autem sicut & posterius quinque modis dicimus: tempore, ut senem juvene; natura, ut causam effecto, genus specie; quicquid denique existendi consecutione est prius; i.e. quod alio posito, ponitur; & quo posito, aliud non ponitur, ut
10 unitas binario: nonnunquam etiam ubi consecutio reciproca est, quod simul est tempore, natura tamen est prius, ut sol suo lumine. Bifariam etiam dicitur prius natura; generante scilicet, ut partes toto, simplex composito, media fine; vel intendente, ut totum partibus, compositum simplici, finis mediis.
15 Prius dispositione sive loco dicitur, quod initio est propius; ut in dicendo, narratio confirmatione. Prius dignitate; ut magistratus cive, aurum argento, virtus auro. Prius denique cognitione, quod cognitu facilius est: idque vel in se, vel nobis: in

consequence and inconsequence, so in method care is taken that what is clearer in itself should precede, what is more obscure should follow; and in every way order and confusion are judged. Thus the first in absolute idea of the homogene-
5 *ous axioms is disposed in the first place, the second in the second, the third in the third, and so on.*

The prior as well as the posterior we speak of in five modes. First is that of time, as an old man is before a youth. Next is that of nature, as a cause is before an effect, a genus before a
10 species. Then comes whatever is before in consecutiveness of existing, that is, what is given when something else is given, and which when it is given does not require that another be given, as unity in relation to something consisting of two; for sometimes where there is reciprocal consecutiveness a thing
15 is before by nature which is simultaneous in time, as the sun in relation to its light. That which is before by nature is also spoken of in two ways; a thing may be before in production, as the parts are before the whole, the simple before the composite, the means before the end; or it may be before in in-
20 tention, as the whole is before the parts, the compound before the simple, the end before the means. Fourth, anything is prior in disposition or place which is nearer the beginning, as in speaking narration is before confirmation, or something may be before in dignity, as the magistrate to the citizen, gold
25 to silver, virtue to gold. Finally, a thing is prior in cognition which is easier to grasp, either in itself or in us—in itself because it is before by nature, in us because it is later and pre-

se quod naturâ est prius; nobis, quod posterius est, & sensibus objectum: illa perfectior est cognitio, hæc imperfectior.

Ideóque methodus ab universalibus, ut quæ causas contineant, ad singularia perpetuò progreditur. Adeóque ab ante-
5 cedentibus omninò & absolutè notioribus ad consequentia ignota declarandum.

Unde intelligitur agi hîc de methodo tradendi sive docendi, quæ analytica rectè dicitur, non inveniendi. Methodus n. inveniendi quæ à *Platone* dicitur *synthetica,* procedit à singu-
10 laribus quæ tempore sunt priora, sensibúsque se prius offerunt; quorum inductione generales notiones colliguntur: methodus autem docendi sive inventa & judicata disponendi, de qua hic agitur, contraria via ut etiam docet *Arist.* 1. Metaph. c. 1. & 2 procedit ab universalibus, quæ natura sunt priora &
15 notiora; non quo prius aut facilius cognoscantur, sed quòd posteaquam sunt cognita, præcedunt notionis natura & claritate quanto sunt à sensibus remotiora. Sic generales rerum species (ut Optici etiam docent) citius in sensus incurrunt: ut advenientem aliquem, judico prius animal esse quàm homi-
20 nem, & hominem quàm *Socratem.* Atque hanc solam methodum *Aristot.* passim docuit.

Sed methodi unitatem exempla doctrinarum & artium præcipuè demonstrant, præcipuéque vendicant.

Quibus quamvis omnes regulæ generales sint & univer-

sented to the senses; the first is more perfect cognition, the second less perfect.

So method continually progresses from universals, as those which contain causes, to particulars. Indeed from antecedents
5 in every way and absolutely more known one must proceed to unknown consequents.

Thence it is to be understood that here is treated the method of presenting or teaching, which is properly called analytic, not the method of inventing. For the method of inventing
10 which by Plato is called *synthetic* proceeds from single things which are before in time and first offer themselves to the senses; by induction from these general notions are collected; but the method of teaching or of disposing what have been invented and judged is the subject of this section. A contrary
15 way, as Aristotle (*Metaphysics* I. I and 2) teaches, proceeds from universals, which by nature are before and better known; not since they are known first or more easily, but because after they are known they have precedence by the nature and clarity of the notion in proportion as they are more remote from
20 the senses. Thus the general species of things (as the opticians also teach) strike the senses more quickly than particulars, as when something is coming I judge it is an animal before I judge it is a man, and a man before Socrates. Aristotle in many passages teaches this as the only method.

25 *But the examples of sciences and arts especially demonstrate and especially defend unity of method.*

In these all rules should be general and universal, yet their

sales, tamen earum gradus distinguuntur: quantóque unaquæque generalior erit, tanto magis præcedet.

Generalissima loco & ordine prima erit, quia lumine & notitia prima est.

5 *Subalternæ consequentur, quia claritate sunt proximæ: utque ex his natura notiores præponentur, minus notæ substituentur.*

Tandémque specialissimæ constituentur.

Definitio itaque generalissima prima erit; causas n. conti-
10 net. Definitioni consectaria subjungentur, sive proprietatum si quæ sunt & ex definitione per se non patent, explicationes. Distributio sequetur.

Quæ si multiplex fuerit, præcedet in partes integras partitio, sequetur divisio in species. Partésque ipsæ & species eodem
15 *ordine sunt rursus tractandæ ac definiendæ, quo distributæ fuerint.*

Et transitionum vinculis si longior inter eas intersit explicatio, colligandæ sunt: id n. auditorem reficit ac recreat.

Transitio autem vel perfecta est vel imperfecta. Perfecta,
20 quæ breviter & quid dictum sit & quid sequatur, ostendit: qualis illa hujus libri secundi initio; *adhuc prima Artis Logicæ pars fuit,* &c. Imperfecta est quæ alterutrum duntaxat ostendit vel quid dictum sit, vel quid sequatur: qualis illa l. 1. c. 18. *argumenta simplicia ita fuerunt,* &c.

grades are distinguished, and in proportion as any one is more general it will the more take precedence.

The most general will be first in place and order, since it is first in light and knowledge.

5 *The subaltern follow, since they are next in clarity; and of these the ones better known by nature are put first and the less known are ranged beneath.*

Last are put the most restricted.

So definition as the most general will be the first, because 10 it contains the causes; the consectaries will be subjoined to the definition; or distribution will follow the explications of the proprieties, if there are some and they are not clear of themselves from the definition.

If this is multiplex, partition into integral parts will pre- 15 *cede, and division into species will follow. On the other hand, the parts themselves and the species are to be treated and defined in the same order in which they have been distributed.*

And if a rather long explication intervenes between these, 20 *they are to be joined together by bands of transition, for this restores and refreshes the hearer.*

A transition is either perfect or imperfect. One is perfect which briefly shows both what has been said and what follows, as does the beginning of this second book: "Up to this 25 point has been treated the first part of the art of logic" etc. An imperfect transition is that which shows in some other way merely what has been said or what follows, such as that at the beginning of book 1, chapter 18: "Simple arguments are as I have said" etc.

Exemplo sit Grammatica. Hujus definitio, ut quæ generalissima sit, ex lege methodi primo loco statuatur; ars scilicet bene loquendi: secundo loco erit Grammaticæ partitio, in etymologiam & syntaxin; tum etymologia, quæ de vocibus agit, 5 definiatur; dein vocis partes in literis & syllabis, speciésque in vocibus numeri & sine numero subsequantur, exituúmque transitiones suis locis collocentur: atque ita omnium etymologiæ partium definitiones, distributiones, colligationes, exempla denique specialissima in singulis disponentur: idémque 10 in syntaxi fiet. Hanc viam omnes artes sibi proposuerunt.

Moderni quidam duplicem methodum instituunt, *syntheticam* & *analyticam:* illam scientiis theoreticis tradendis, Physicæ putà vel Mathematicæ magis accommodatam; qua partes scientiæ ita disponuntur, ut à subjecto contemplationis uni- 15 versali ad particularia, à simplicibus ad composita progressus fiat: sic Physica exorditur à corporis naturalis definitione; ad ejus deinde causas vel partes effectionésque generales ad species denique progreditur. Methodum analyticam definiunt, qua ita disponuntur partes scientiæ practicæ ut à notione finis 20 fiat progressus ad notitiam principiorum vel mediorum, ad illum finem assequendum: sic in Ethicis à fine, scilicet beatitudine, ad media, nempe virtutes proceditur: Verùm cùm hac

Grammar may be taken as an example. Its definition, since that is the most general rule of an art, according to the law of method should be determined in the first place; to wit, it is the art of using words correctly; in the second place will
5 be the partition of grammar into etymology and syntax; then etymology, which deals with words, should be defined; then should follow the parts of a word in letters and syllables, and species in words with number and without number, and the transitions of the terminations should be collected in their
10 places; and thus also the definitions of all the parts of etymology, the distributions, the connections, and finally the most special examples in single instances will be arranged; and in syntax the same thing will be done. All the arts have set for themselves this course.

15 The moderns indeed set up a double method, the *synthetic* and *analytic*, as more fit for teaching the theoretical sciences, for example physics or mathematics; by this method parts of the science are so disposed that there is progress from the universal subject of contemplation to particulars, from the simple
20 to the composite. Thus physics sets out from the definition of a natural body; then there is progress toward its causes or parts and general doings and then to the species. They define the analytic method as that by which the parts of a practical science are so disposed that from the notion of the end prog-
25 ress is made toward the notion of beginnings or means, for the sake of understanding that end; thus in ethics progress is from the end, to wit, beatitude, to the means, namely, the virtues. But since both of these methods proceed in one and the same

utraque methodus una eadémque via, à definitione scilicet generalissima, sive illa subjectum sive finem generalem contineat, ad minus generalia, à notioribus ad minus nota, à simplicibus ad composita æque utrobique dividendo progre-
5 diatur, non videtur ob diversam in definitione generali, illic subjecti, hîc finis mentionem, duplicem esse methodum constituendam; sed unam potius, artium quidem tradendarum, eámque analyticam esse dicendam.

Atqui methodus non solùm in materia artium & doctri-
10 *narum adhibetur, sed in omnibus rebus quas facilè & perspicuè docere volumus.*

Ideóque poëtæ, oratores, omnésque omninò scriptores, quoties docendum sibi auditorem proponunt, hanc viam sequi volunt, quamvis non usquequaque ingrediantur atque in-
15 *sistant.*

Sic Virgilius, in Georgicis, distribuit propositam materiam in quatuor partes, ut antedictum est: primóque libro res communes persequitur, ut astrologiam, meteorologiam, déque segetibus & earum cultu disserit, quæ pars operis prima erat;
20 túmque transitio adhibetur initio secundi libri,

hactenus arvorum cultus, &c.

Dein scribit generaliter de arboribus, tum specialiter de vitibus. Sic toto opere, generalissimum, primo; subalterna, medio; specialissima, extremo loco ponere studuit
25 Eandem *Ovidius,* in Fastis, dispositionis hujus gratiam sequitur. Proponit initio summam operis:

tempora cum causis Latium digesta per annum, &c.

way, that is, from a very general definition—whether that contains a subject or a general end—to a less general, from the more known to the less known, from the simple to the composite by dividing equally on both sides, it does not seem 5 that on account of a diverse mention in the general definition, there of the subject, here of the end, a double method is constituted, but rather that the method of teaching the arts is to be called one and that analytic.

Method is also applied not merely to the material of the arts 10 *and doctrines, but to all things which we wish to teach easily and perspicuously.*

Therefore the poets, orators, and all writers of every sort, as often as they set out to teach an auditor, wish to follow this course, though they do not always move in it and insist on it.

15 Thus in the *Georgics* Vergil distributes the matter before him into four parts, as was said above; in the first book he deals with general matters, as astrology, and meteorology, and discusses cornfields and the cultivation of them, which was the first part of the work; then at the beginning of the 20 second book a transition is used:

Thus far of tillage, etc.

Then he writes generally on trees, next specially on vines. So in the entire work he endeavors to put first the most general, in the middle the subaltern, and the most special in the 25 last place.

In the *Fasti* Ovid also uses the advantages of this disposition. At the beginning he sets forth the sum of his work:

I'll sing of times that pass throughout the year, etc.

Mox imploratione facta, partitionem anni statuit. Tum communes differentias interpretatus diei fasti, nefasti, *&c.* tandem unumquemque mensem suo loco persequitur, & ordinis hujus à generalibus ad specialia studium suum præfa-5 tione indicat.

hæc mihi dicta semel, totis hærentia fastis,
ne seriem rerum scindere cogar, erunt.

Oratores in procemio, narratione, confirmatione, peroratione hunc ordinem affectant, eumque artis & naturæ & rei 10 *ordinem appellant, & interdum studiosius assectantur.*

Ut in *Verrem, Cicero* primùm proponendo tum partiendo. *Quæstor* inquit *Cn. Papyrio cos. fuisti ab hinc annos quatuordecim, & ex illa die ad hanc diem quæ fecisti, in judicium voco,* &c. Propositio hîc & definitio summæ rei est, tanquam 15 in hoc judicio generalissima. Partitio sequitur: *hi sunt anni,* &c. *quare hæc eadem erit quadripartita distributio totius accusationis meæ.* Quas partes quatuor earúmque partium particulas deinceps suo quamque ordine & loco tractat, & transitionibus copulat; tres primas tertio libro; & sic deinceps.

20 *Hæc igitur in variis axiomatis homogeneis suo vel syllogismi judicio notis methodus erit, quoties perspicuè res docenda erit.*

*At cùm delectatione motúve aliquo majore ab oratore quovis aut poeta, ut quibuscum vulgo potissimum res est, ducen-*25 *dus erit auditor, crypsis methodi ferè adhibebitur; homogenea*

Having made his invocation, he next lays down the division of the year. Then having interpreted the common differences between holiday and working day, etc., he goes through each month in its place, and in his preface indicates his liking
5 for this order from general to special:

I say these things for the whole calendar
But once, not to break off my further course.

Orators in the introduction, narration, confirmation, and peroration affect this order, and call it the order of art and
10 *nature and fact, and commonly follow it closely.*

In his *In Verrem* Cicero does this, first in laying down, then in distributing; he writes: "Thou hast been quæstor this fourteen years since Cnæus Papyrius was consul, and I accuse thee of all things which thou hast done from that day to this"
15 etc. Here is the proposition with the definition of the chief matter, as the most general thing in this judgment. The partition follows: "All these years, etc. And therefore into these four parts my whole accusation shall be parted." These four parts and the small parts of these parts he then treats, each in
20 its order and place, and binds together with transitions, the first three in the third book, and so on.

This then will be the method in diverse homogeneous axioms known either by their own judgment or by that of the syllogism, as often as a thing is to be clearly taught.

25 *But when the auditor is to be allured with pleasure or some stronger impulse by an orator or a poet—for they commonly make that their chief concern—a crypsis of method will usu-*

quædam rejicientur, ut definitionum, partitionum, transitionúmque lumina. Quædam assumentur heterogenea, velut digressiones à re, & in re commorationes. Et præcipuè rerum ordo invertetur.

5 Sed oratoribus & poetis sua methodi ratio relinquenda est; vel saltem iis, qui oratoriam & poeticam docent.

ally be employed; some homogeneous axioms will be rejected, as the lights of definitions, partitions, and transitions. Certain heterogeneous axioms will be taken up, as digressions from the fact and lingerings on the fact. And especially the order
5 *of things will be inverted.*

But their own doctrine of method is to be turned over to the orators and poets, or at least to those who teach oratory and poetics.

PRAXIS LOGICÆ

Analytica ex Dounamo.

Ad Cap. Tertium Ramiæ Dialecticæ.

EXEMPLUM *primum est causæ procreantis & conservantis ex Ovidii primo de Remed.*

Ergo ubi visus eris nostra medicabilis arte,
ſac monitis ſugias otia prima meis.
5 *Hæc, ut ames, faciunt: hæc quæ ſecere tuentur;*
hæc sunt jucundi causa, cibusque mali.
Otia si tollas, periere Cupidinis arcus,
contemptæque jacent & sine luce ſaces.

In singulis, quæ ad efficientis doctrinam illustrandam afferuntur, exemplis, tria consideranda sunt, efficiens, effectum, efficiendi modus. In hoc exemplo effectum est amor, efficiens est otium, quod amorem efficit duplici modo, tum procreando, tum conservando, ut in secundo disticho Poeta docet. Dispositio autem hujus exempli (ut pleniorem ejus analysin instituam) syllogistica est. Quæstio, quam Poeta concludendam proponit, hæc est; fugiendum esse otium ei, qui ab amore immunis esse velit: eáque duobus syllogismis concluditur: in

An Analytic

PRAXIS OF LOGIC

from Downham.

On the Third Chapter of the Dialectic of Ramus.

THE first example is of the procreant and conserving cause, from Ovid (*De remediis* 1):

> Therefore when thou shalt look in this our medicinal art,
> 5 My admonition do, set idleness apart.
> This causeth thee to love, this doth defend it still,
> This is the cause of joy, as meat sometimes breeds ill.
> Take, lastly, sloth away, god Cupid's bow is lost,
> His torches lose their light, contemned away they're tost.

10 In single examples which are brought forward to illustrate the doctrine of the efficient, three things are to be considered, the efficient, the effect, the mode of effecting. In this example, love is the effect, idleness is the efficient, which brings about love in a double manner, both by procreating and by con-15 serving, as the poet shows in the second distich. But the disposition of this example (that I may begin a fuller analysis of it) is syllogistic. The question which the poet proposes to be concluded is this: *Idleness should be avoided by him who wishes to be immune from love.* This is concluded in two

priori argumentum tertium ducitur ab effectis quidem otii, amoris verò causa procreante & conservante, hoc modo: amoris procreans & conservans causa vitanda est ei, qui ab amore ipso liber esse velit; otium verò amoris procreans & conservans
5 causa est. Otium igitur fugiendum est ei, qui ab amore liber esse velit. Propositio deest. Assumptio in secundo disticho primò simpliciter proponitur, deinde altera ejus pars de conservante per similitudinem cibi illustratur. Conclusio præcedit in primo disticho. Secunda ratio est consectarium ex as-
10 sumptione prioris syllogismi deductum. Otium est causa procreans & conservans amoris; ergo sublato otio, amor tollitur. Cujus propositio & fundamentum est Logicum illud axioma; sublata causa, tollitur effectum, quæ propositio si addatur, plenus erit syllogismus.

15 Exemplum secundum ibid. ex *Æneid.* 4.

Non tibi diva parens generis nec Dardanus auctor
perfide: sed duris genuit te cautibus horrens
Caucasus. Hyrcanæque admorunt ubera Tigres.

Hic effectum est Æneas. Causæ efficientes, pater, mater,
20 nutrix, modus autem efficiendi non unus: parentes enim liberos efficiunt procreando, nutrix verò conservando. Disponitur autem hoc exemplum axiomate discreto. Anchises & Venus

syllogisms; in the first the third argument is obtained from the effect of leisure, which is the procreating and conserving cause of love, in this manner: *The procreating and conserving cause of love should be shunned by him who himself wishes to be free from love itself, but idleness is the procreating and conserving cause of love, therefore idleness should be shunned by him who wishes to be free from love.* The proposition is lacking. The assumption is in the second distich first proposed simply, then the second part of it on the conserving cause is illustrated through the similitude of food. The conclusion precedes in the first distich. The second reason is a consectary deduced from the assumption of the first syllogism: *Idleness is the procreant and conserving cause of love, therefore if idleness is taken away love will be taken away.* The proposition and foundation of this is that logical axiom: *If the cause is taken away, the effect is taken away;* if this proposition is added, the syllogism will be full.

The second example of the same thing is from *Æneid* 4:

> Th' art no god's child, ne Dardanus's son;
> Thou rather from the steep, hard rocks didst come
> Of Caucasus; it seemeth of that breed
> Hyrcanian tigers thee with breasts did feed.

Here the effect is Æneas. The efficient causes are father, mother and nurse, but the mode of effecting is not one, for the parents are the efficients in procreating a child, but the nurse in conserving. This example moreover is disposed with a discrete axiom. As it seems to Dido, Venus and Anchises are

non sunt Æneæ parentes, ut Didoni placet, sed horrens Caucasus & duræ cautes: Hyrcanæ autem tigres ut nutrices ubera admoverunt.

Exemplum tertium est solitariæ causæ *cap.* 4. ex *Æneid.* 9.

5 *Me, me: adsum, qui feci, in me convertite ferrum*
O Rutuli, mea fraus omnis: nihil iste nec ausus,
nec potuit.——

In hoc exemplo effectum est cædes Rutulorum. Efficiens hujus cædis Nysus. Quod autem ad modum attinet efficiendi, 10 effecit, ut ipse de se ait, solus. Dispositio autem hujus exempli syllogistica est. Qui solus auctor est cædis, is solus est occidendus. Ego verò, inquit, solus auctor cædis sum; ergo, &c. Propositio deest: assumptio continetur versu 2. Mea fraus, *i.e.* culpa omnis, quam probat remotione sociæ causæ, nihil 15 iste nec ausus est, *&c.* Conclusio versu 1. Me, me scilicet occidite, in me convertite ferrum, &c.

Ejusdem causæ exemplum aliud, in oratione *Ciceronis* Pro *Marcello. Nam bellicas laudes solent quidam extenuare verbis, eásque detrahere ducibus & communicare cum multis, ne* 20 *propriæ sint imperatorum: & certè in armis militum virtus, locorum opportunitas, sociorum auxilia, classes, commeatus multum juvant: maximam verò partem, quasi suo jure, for-*

not the parents of Æneas, but the horrid Caucasus and its hard crags; moreover, the Hyrcanian tigers presented their breasts as nurses.

A third example, illustrating the single cause discussed in 5 chapter 4, is taken from *Æneid* 9:

> Lo, here I am who only did this deed;
> Latians, against me turn your swords with speed.
> 'Twas my deceit; he could it never do
> Ne would his courage serve him thereunto.

10 In this example the effect is the slaughter of the Rutili. The efficient of this slaughter is Nysus. But as to the mode of effecting, as he says of himself, he effected alone. But the disposition of this example is syllogistic; he who is alone the author of the slaughter should alone be killed; he says: *I alone* 15 *am the author of this slaughter; therefore* etc. The proposition is lacking; the assumption is contained in verse three: "my deceit," that is, all the blame, which he proves by the removal of an associated cause: "Ne would his courage" etc. The conclusion is in verse two, to wit, *Kill me:* "against me turn your 20 swords" etc.

There is another example of this cause in the oration of Cicero *Pro Marcello:* "For warlike praises they are wont to extenuate truly by words, and to detract them from their leaders, to communicate them with many, lest they should 25 be proper to their commanders. And certainly in war the strength of the soldiers, opportunity of places, help of fellows, ranks, and provision do much avail. But Fortune as it

tuna sibi vendicat, & quicquid est prosperè gestum, id penè omne ducit suum. At verò hujus gloriæ, Cæsar, *quam es paulò antè adeptus, socium habes neminem: totum hoc quantum-cunque est quod certè maximum est, totum, inquam, est*
5 *tuum. Nihil tibi ex ista laude centurio, nihil præfectus, nihil cohors, nihil turma decerpit: quin etiam illa ipsa rerum humanarum domina fortuna in istius se societatem gloriæ non offert: tibi cedit, tuam esse totam ac propriam fatetur.* Hoc exemplum continet plenam comparationem à minore ad majus,
10 ad amplificandam Cæsaris laudem clementiæ. In protasi exemplum est causarum, quæ cum aliis efficiunt. Effectum est victoria; efficiens imperator, non quidem solus, sed cum aliis, quarum alia principalis est, & imperatori quasi socia fortuna: aliæ adjuvantes & ministræ, cujusmodi quinque recensentur,
15 militum fortitudo, locorum opportunitas, sociorum auxilia, classes, commeatus. In apodosi exemplum habemus solitariæ causæ: effectum est clementia in Marcellum, præstita. Cujus causa & quidem sola est ipse *Cæsar;* eáque illustratur remotione causarum adjuvantium. Scopus *Ciceronis* est, ut ostendat
20 *Cæsarem* plus laudis ob clementiam mereri, quàm propter res gestas: ídque ostendit ex collatis inter se efficiendi modis, quod nimirum rerum gestarum *Cæsar* non solus auctor fuerit, clementiæ verò præstitæ solus. Jam verò efficiens plus laudis

were by her own right challangeth the chiefest part to herself, and whatsoever is prosperously carried, that altogether she leadeth. But yet of this glory, O Cæsar, which a little before thou didst obtain thou hast no companion; all that, how much
5 soever it is, which truly is the chiefest, all that, I say, is thine. The centurian, president, ranks, and companies have taken from thee none of this praise. Yea, even the lady of human affairs, Fortune, offereth not herself into the society of this glory; to thee she giveth place and confesseth it all and wholly
10 to be thine." This example contains a full comparison from the lesser to the greater, for amplifying the fame of the clemency of Cæsar. In the protasis there is an example of the causes which work with others. The effect is victory; the efficient is the emperor, not indeed alone but with others, the chief of
15 which and as it were the companion of the emperor is Fortune; the others are aiding and ministering causes, of which five are listed in this way: "the strength of the soldiers, opportunity of places, help of fellows, ranks, and provisions." In the apodosis we have an example of the solitary cause; the
20 effect is unusual clemency towards Marcellus, of which the cause and the only cause is Cæsar himself; and this is made more striking by the removal of the aiding causes. The purpose of Cicero is to show that Cæsar merits more praise because of his clemency than on account of his deeds; and he
25 shows this from the methods of working compared with each other, because Cæsar was not the sole author of the things accomplished, but was the sole author of the unusual clemency. The efficient which acts alone surely merits more of

vel vituperationis meretur, quæ sola quid facit; quæ verò cum aliis, minus. Sic igitur hæc ratio potest concludi. Cujus *Cæsar* solus auctor est, id plus meretur laudis, quàm cujus solus non est auctor. Rerum in bello gestarum solus auctor non est; clementiæ verò in Marcellum præstitæ solus; proinde clementia *Cæsaris* plus meretur laudis, quàm res in bello gestæ. Hujus syllogismi assumptio tantum in hoc exemplo proponitur; ejúsque prior pars enumeratione causarum adjuvantium, posterior remotione earundem illustratur.

Ibidem exemplum causæ instrumentalis primo de *Nat. deor. Quibus oculis animi intueri potuit vester Plato fabricam illam tanti operis, qua construi à Deo atque ædificari mundum facit? Quæ molitio? quæ ferramenta? qui vectes? quæ machinæ? qui ministri tanti operis fuerunt?* Syllogismus sic sese habet. Qui instrumenta non habuit, is mundum non creavit. Deus instrumenta non habuit; ergo, *&c.* Hujus syllogismi propositio falsissima deest; conclusio præcedit; assumptio sequitur: eaque per inductionem quandam specierum illustratur. Utraque autem tum assumptio tum conclusio per interrogationem ἐμφατικώτερον negatur.

praise or vituperation, but an efficient which acts with others deserves less. So this reasoning can be concluded as follows: *That of which Cæsar is the sole author merits more praise than that of which he is not the sole author; he was not the* 5 *sole author of the deeds accomplished in war; but he was the sole author of the unusual clemency toward Marcellus; hence the clemency of Cæsar merits more praise than the things accomplished in war.* Only the assumption of this syllogism is given in this example; the first part of it is made plainer by 10 the enumeration of the assisting causes, the posterior part by the removal of them.

There is also an example of the instrumental cause in *De natura deorum 1:* "For by what eyes of the mind could your Plato behold the frame of so great a work, whereby he maketh 15 it constructed and builded of God? what labor? what iron engines? what levers? what devises? what ministers were there of so great a work?" Thus the syllogism goes: *He who did not have instruments did not create the world, God did not have instruments, therefore* etc. The wholly false proposi- 20 tion of this syllogism is lacking; the conclusion precedes; the assumption follows; and this is made plainer through a certain induction of species. Both assumption and conclusion are negated ἐμφατικώτερον through interrogation.

PETRI RAMI VITA
Ex
JOANNE THOMA FREIGIO,
Recisis digressionibus, descripta.

PETRUS RAMUS natus est anno millesimo quingentesimo decimo quinto. Ejus avus, ut ipse in præfatione suæ Regiæ Professionis memorat, in *Eburonum* gente, familia imprimis illustri fuit: sed patria à *Carolo,*
5 *Burgundionum* duce, capta & incensa, in *Veromanduorum* agrum profugus, ac spoliatus, carbonariam facere coactus est: hinc *Ramo carbonarius pater* probri loco objectus: sed pater Agricola fuit. Puer vix è cunis egressus, ut ipse in *Scheckiano* epilogo de se narrat, duplici peste laboravit. Juvenis invita
10 modísque omnibus repugnante fortuna, *Lutetiam* ad capessendas artes ingenuas venit. Erat statura corporis grandi ac generosa, vultu mitissimo, moribus integerrimis, valetudine firma ac robusta, quam perpetua abstinentia continentiáque & continuo labore etiam firmiorem reddidit. *Lutetiæ* Magisterii
15 titulum suscepturus, problema hoc sumpsit; *quæcunque ab Aristotele dicta essent, commentitia esse.* Attoniti novitate atque insolentia problematis examinatores ac magistri, per diem integrum, sed irrito conatu, Magistrandum, ut vocant,

THE LIFE OF PETER RAMUS

taken from

JOHN THOMAS FREIGIUS,

With the digressions omitted.

PETER RAMUS was born in the year 1515. His grandfather, as he himself tells in the preface of his *Professio regia,* was originally of a good family of the district of Liége, but when his native place was captured and laid waste
5 by Charles, duke of Burgundy, he was exiled to Vermandois, where his poverty forced him to make charcoal. For that reason it was charged against Ramus as a ground for reproach that his father was a charcoal burner, but his father was a farmer. As a child he was hardly out of the cradle, as he him-
10 self tells in the epilogue to his *Defensio adversus Jacobum Schecium,* before he was twice attacked by pestilence. As a youth with fortune unfavorable and in every way opposed to him, he came to Paris to learn the liberal arts. He was tall and well-built, with a very pleasant face, thoroughly virtuous
15 in his habits, and of excellent and well-established health, which by continuous abstinence and continency and steady labor he rendered still firmer. When about to take the degree of Master of Arts at Paris, he undertook this problem: *Whatever has been said by Aristotle is false.* Astonished by the
20 novelty and haughtiness of the problem, the examiners and masters for an entire day, but in vain, fought against his re-

oppugnarunt. Ex hoc fortuito successu, ansam deinceps seriò & liberè in *Aristotelem* animadvertendi & inquirendi arripuit. Logicámque imprimis, utpote instrumentum reliquarum artium expolire instituit (ut ipse pluribus persequitur in *epilogo*
5 *l.* 5. Scholarum Dialecticarum) sed annum agens ætatis primum & vigesimum hæc moliri incœperat. Septimo pòst, primam, ut putatur, Dialecticam & *Aristotelicas* Animadversiones ad Academiam *Parisiensem* edidit: sequente anno *Euclidem,* Latinè, quam & præfatione commendavit. Ex eo tem-
10 pore multos adversarios contra se irritavit, & præsertim duos homines, quos *Talæus* in Academia sua dum contentionem totam enarrat, non nominat tamen. Vix, inquit, *Aristotelicæ* Animadversiones lectæ erant, cùm *P. Ramus* repentè ad prætorii tribunalis capitalem contentionem per certos homines
15 falso Academiæ nomine rapitur, novíque criminis accusatur, quòd scilicet, *Aristotelem* oppugnando, artes enervaret: hac enim oratione *Aristotelea* actio instituta est. Hinc *Aristoteleorum* clamoribus agitatus, ad summum *Parisiensis* curiæ consilium traducitur. Id cum ex adversariorum sententia non
20 procederet, novis artibus à senatu *Parisiensi* ad regiam cognitionem res defertur: constituuntur judices quinque, bini ab utraque parte, quintus à rege nominatur; causam de singulis animadversionum capitibus dicere jubetur *Ramus:* qui tametsi de quinque judicibus tres infensissimos habebat, tamen
25 ut mandato regio obtemperaret, ad diem constitutam adfuit;

ceiving the degree of Master, as it is called. From this fortuitous success he then took occasion of animadverting and inquiring seriously and freely into Aristotle. He decided to perfect logic first as the instrument of the other arts (as he
5 himself explains in detail in the epilogue to book five of the *Scholæ Dialecticæ*), and he had begun to carry out his plans in his twenty-first year. Seven years later, he presented to the university of Paris what is called his first *Dialectica* and the *Aristotelicæ Animadversiones*. In the following year he
10 presented Euclid, in Latin, graced with a preface. From this time he irritated many adversaries against him, and especially two men whom Talon does not name in his *Academia,* though he narrates the whole contention. Hardly, he says, were the *Aristotelicæ Animadversiones* read than Peter Ramus was
15 hurriedly dragged away to a capital trial at the tribunal of the *prévôt* by certain men falsely using the name of the University and was charged with a new crime, to wit that by opposing Aristotle he weakened the arts; for by this speech the Aristotelian trial was begun. Being driven thence by
20 the clamors of the Aristotelians, he was taken to the highest council of the court of Paris. When this would not proceed according to the opinion of his adversaries, by new arts the affair was taken from the parliament of Paris to the jurisdiction of the king; five judges were appointed, two by either
25 side, and the fifth named by the king. Ramus was ordered to state the case concerning single heads of the animadversions. Though of five judges three were thoroughly hostile, Ramus, that he might obey the royal mandate, was present on the ap-

scriba unus aderat, qui rationes *Rami* & judicum sententias
exciperet. Biduo magna contentione de Dialecticæ artis definitione & partitione, quæ in Logici Organi libris nullæ essent,
concertatum est. Tres *Aristotelei* judices primo die, contra
5 omnes bene descriptæ artis leges, judicarunt ad Dialecticæ
artis perfectionem definitione nihil opus esse. Qui duo judices
à *Ramo* lecti erant, contrà censuerunt. Postridie tres judices
Aristotelei vehementer conturbati, de Partitione assentiuntur,
causámque in aliam diem rejiciunt. Verùm ne non damnare-
10 tur *Ramus,* novum consilium initur, ut ab initio tota dispu-
tatio retexatur, judicata pridie, pro nihilo habeatur. Ab ista
judicum inconstantia provocat *Ramus;* sed frustrà; judicium
n. sine provocatione tribus illis judicibus datur; condemnan-
tur triumvirali illa sententia non solùm Animadversiones *Ari-*
15 *stotelicæ,* sed Institutiones etiam Dialecticæ: auctori interdici-
tur, ne in posterum vel docendo vel scribendo, ullam Philosophiæ partem attingeret: ludi etiam magno apparatu celebran-
tur, in quibus *Ramus* & *Ramea* Dialectica ludibrio habetur.
Ab his difficultatibus unus omnium *Carolus Lotharingus*
20 *Ramum* liberavit: *Henrico* enim regi persuaserat, Philosophiam semper liberam esse oportere. Hinc *Ramus* pristinæ
docendi ac scribendi libertati restitutus, per annos quatuor
summa in pace studiis operam dedit. Anno ætatis trigesimo
primo Orationem de studiis Philosophiæ & Eloquentiæ con-

pointed day; a single secretary was present to write down the reasons of Ramus and the opinions of the judges. For two days there was a debate with much disputing on the definition and partition of the art of dialectic, which are not in the books
5 of the *Organon of Logic.* On the first day the three Aristotelian judges, contrary to all the laws of a well-described art, judged that for the perfection of the art of dialectic there was no need of definition. The two judges chosen by Ramus held the contrary opinion. Finally the three Aristotelian judges, violently
10 agitated, gave their assent on the subject of partition and adjourned the case to the second day. But lest Ramus should not be convicted a new plan was brought forward, namely, that the whole debate should be gone over again and what had been decided the day before annulled. Ramus appealed from
15 this inconstancy of the judges, but in vain, for sentence without appeal was given by the three hostile judges. By that sentence of the three were condemned not merely the *Aristotelicæ Animadversiones* but also the *Institutiones Dialecticæ;* the author was interdicted from touching on any part of phil-
20 osophy in his future teaching or writing. Even plays were given with a great to-do in which Ramus and the Ramistic dialectic were made sport of. From these difficulties one man alone, Charles of Lorraine, freed Ramus, for he persuaded King Henry that philosophy ought always to be free. Being
25 in this way reinvested with his previous liberty of teaching and writing, for four years Ramus applied himself to his studies in complete peace. In the thirty-first year of his age he delivered an oration recommending the union of the studies

jungendis habuit: cum *Talæo* fratre (sic eum perpetuo vocat) professionis partes ita divisit, ut *Talæus* matutinis horis philosophiam, ipse pomeridianis Eloquentiam doceret: in poetis, oratoribus, philosophis omnísque generis authoribus explicandis, usum dialecticæ demonstravit: id *Ramo* postea crimini datum est, quòd in philosophico studio non Philosophos, sed, contra leges Academiæ, pro philosophis Poetas explicaret: purgat se *Ramus;* petítque ut gymnasium suum *Præleum* per probos & doctos homines invisatur. Sed judex quidam, nobilis adolescens, datus, discipulos *Rami* indicta causa, condemnat; publicis & scholis & sigillis & tabulis prohibet; omnibus denique Academiæ muneribus & præmiis excludit. Ab hac sententia tam nova discipuli *Rami* ad *Julianense* philosophorum comitium provocant, & absolvuntur, modò præceptor eorum jurejurando confirmet, libros, Academiæ legibus definitos, à se esse prælectos. Confirmat *Ramus:* paulò tamen pòst ab eodem judice adolescente, non discipuli, ut antea, sed magistri eorum oppugnantur: *Ramo* injungitur, ut in publicis scholis disciplinam suam ipse detestaretur & ejuraret. Is ad superiores Academiæ ordines secundò provocat: sed cùm vitandi tumultus causa, scripto se absens, defenderet, adolescens

of philosophy and eloquence; with his brother Talon (for this he always called him) he so divided the parts of the profession that Talon in the morning could teach philosophy, and he himself in the afternoon could teach eloquence. He
5 demonstrated the service of dialectic in explaining the poets, orators, philosophers and authors of all sorts. It was later charged against him as a crime that in the school of philosophy he did not explain the philosophers, but, contrary to the laws of the university, the poets instead. Ramus cleared himself
10 and sought to have his Collége de Presles inspected by upright and learned men. But a certain judge who was appointed, a youth of noble family, condemned the disciples of Ramus without trying the case, prohibited them from attending the public schools and from receiving official documents or
15 having their names in the records, and then excluded them from all the benefits and honors of the university. From a sentence so new as this the pupils of Ramus appealed to the assembly of philosophers at the church of Saint Julien, and were acquitted with the condition that their teacher should
20 confirm with an oath that he lectured on the books prescribed by the laws of the university. Ramus gave assurance that he would do so. But a little later not the pupils as before but their masters were attacked by the same youthful judge. It was enjoined upon Ramus that in the public schools he should
25 solemnly renounce and abjure his method. A second time he appealed to the higher orders of the university; but when he wished to defend himself in writing without a personal appearance in order to avoid a tumult, that youthful judge,

ille judex, etsi duabus appellationibus rejectus, tertiò judicat ac damnat. Quartò provocat *Ramus:* cùm provocationis diem accusator antevertisset, coactus est *Ramus* subito in senatum venire: hîc iterum *Carolus Lotharingus* unico præsidio
5 fuit: accusationem cujusdam audiit gavissimam *Ramum* Academicum nominantis, qui de humanis divinisque legibus dubitaret, qui lubricos *D. Augustini* locos ad effrænatam atque impiam libertatem suis auditoribus proponeret, & quo facilius incautis animis abuteretur, omnes Logicas disputationes tol-
10 leret. Contra has caluminas facile se defendit *Ramus*. Decretum est itaque in senatu, uti *Ramus* discipulíque ejus in pristinum atque integrum statum restituerentur. Ipse anno ætatis trigesimo sexto cùm *Blessiis Carolus Lotharingus* ad *Henricum* regem de disciplina *Ramea* retulisset, in numerum
15 atque ordinem Regiorum Professorum per literas regias honorificè ad se scriptas, est cooptatus. Gratias itaque & regi *Henrico* & *Carolo Lotharingo* publicè egit; sibíque persuasit, se à rege in præstantissima reip. parte esse collocatum; sibíque adeo dies ac noctes esse summo studio enitendum, ne tanto
20 muneri ac professioni eloquentiæ simul & philosophiæ deesset: unde animos adolescentium tanta audiendi & proficiendi cupiditate inflammavit, ut schola regia, licet ad audiendum amplissima, plerumque tamen auditorum concursum frequentiámque capere minime potuerit. Adversariorum petulantiam

though his judgment had been overthrown by two appeals, a third time judged and condemned him. Ramus appealed a fourth time; when the accuser set ahead the day of appeal, Ramus was forced to come unexpectedly into the senate; here
5 again Charles of Lorraine was his only defense. He heard a very severe accusation by a certain one calling Ramus an academician who was uncertain about human and divine laws, who set forth to his hearers obscene passages of Saint Augustine tending toward unrestrained and impious liberty,
10 and who, that he might more easily take advantage of unguarded minds, dispensed with all logical disputations. Ramus easily defended himself against these calumnies. So is was decreed in the senate that Ramus and his pupils should be restored in every respect to their former condition. In his
15 thirty-sixth year, since Charles of Lorraine had spoken to King Henry at Blois of the learning of Ramus, he was received into the number and rank of the regius professors by means of royal letters honorably written to him. Hence he publicly gave thanks to King Henry and to Charles of Lorraine, and
20 persuaded himself that he had been placed by the king in the most important part of the state, and that he would therefore work day and night with the greatest zeal, lest he should be inadequate to so great an office and to the professorship of both eloquence and philosophy. As regius professor he in-
25 flamed the spirits of the young men with such a desire of hearing and profiting that the regal school, though it had capacity for many hearers, often was quite unable to hold all who assembled to hear him. He bore and wholly defeated

summa constantia tulit atque pervicit; symbolúmque ejus hoc fuit, *labor omnia vincit.* Anno 1552 cùm in *Cameracensi* schola frequentissimis auditoribus Dialecticam suam auspicaretur, inter strepitus, clamores, sibilos nihil commotus, per intervalla clamorum, incredibili constantia perexit & peroravit: qua ejus virtute consternati inimici, in posterum minus ei molestiæ exhibuerunt. In *Heidelbergensi* etiam Academia, principis autoritate ad profitendum adductus, consimiles æmulorum clamores invicto animo pertulit. Adversus doctos aliquot homines *Goveanum, Gallandium, Perionium, Turnebum, Melancthonem,* pari silentio est usus. Viginti annis abstemius fuit, donec sanitatis causa medici vino uti suaserunt: vini enim fastidium ceperat ex quo infans in cellam vinariam clam parentibus irrepens, se tam immodicè ingurgitavit, ut mortuo similis humi reperiretur. Pro lectulo stramentis ad senectutem usque usus est. Coelebs tota vita permansit. *Prælei* gymnasii labore (qui ipsi sine ullo publico stipendio erat mandatus) contentus fuit. A discipulis suis oblata munera, quamvis debita, tamen non accepit. Anno 1556. *Ciceronianum* edidit de Optima juventutis instituendæ ratione. Pronuntiationem Latinæ linguæ in Academia *Parisiensi* tunc temporis inquinatissimam, corrigendi author cumprimis fuit, reclamantibus licet *Sorbonistis,* pravarum omnium consuetudinum propug-

the impudence of his adversaries with the greatest constancy; and this was his motto: *Labor omnia vincit.* When in the year 1552 he began his lecture on dialectic to a large audience in the college of Cambrai, in the midst of noises, shouts and
5 whistles, he was wholly unmoved, and with marvelous firmness in the intervals of uproar went through and concluded; his enemies, struck with consternation by such a display of virtue, thereafter gave him less annoyance. Also in the university of Heidelburg, where he was brought to give instruc-
10 tion by the authority of the prince, with inconquerable spirit he went through a similar uproar by the envious. Against certain learned men, Govéa, Galland, Périon, Turnèbe, and Melancthon, he used equal silence. For twenty years he drank no wine, until the doctors persuaded him to use it for the sake
15 of his health, for he began to have a distaste for wine at the time when in childhood, slipping into the wine cellar without the knowledge of his parents, he guzzled so immoderately that he was found lying on the ground as though dead. Instead of a good bed he used straw to his old age. He remained
20 celibate his entire life. He was content in the labor of the college of Presles (which was given to him without any public stipend). The money offered to him by his pupils, though due, he did not accept. In the year 1556 he published the *Ciceronianus* on the best method of instructing youth. He was
25 one of those most responsible for correcting the pronunciation of the Latin language in the University of Paris where in the course of time it had become very corrupt. The Sorbonists objected, for they were such obstinate supporters of all bad

natoribus tam obstinatis, ut sacerdotem quendam novatæ pronuntiationis coram senatu *Parisiensi* insimulatum, quasi ob hæresin, ut aiebant, Grammaticam, amplissimis proventibus ecclesiasticis privandum contenderent: & lite quidem
5 superiores videbantur discessuri, nisi *P. Ramus* cæteríque professores regii ad curiam convolantes, judicii tam alieni insolentiam dissuasissent. Verùm illius temporis tam crassa ignorantia fuit, ut libris editis proditum sit, in ea Academia doctores extitisse, qui mordicus defenderent, *ego amat* tam com-
10 modam syntaxin esse, quàm *ego amo;* ad eámque pertinaciam comprimendam, authoritate publica opus fuisse. In Mathematicis quid effecerit *Ramus,* Scholæ Mathematicæ aliáque ejus opera testantur. Ea meditantem, belli civilis calamitas interpellavit; acceptis igitur à rege literis, ad regiam *Fontisbelaquei*
15 bibliothecam profectus, Mathematicas prælectiones ab initio plenius & uberius retractavit. Tum in *Italiam* cogitabat, quo ipsum *Bononia* honorificè invitarat; vel saltem in *Germaniam:* sed viis omnibus terror mortis intentatus, rumor etiam *Prælei* sui indignis modis direpti ac bibliothecæ spoliatæ, ad regiam
20 *Vincennarum* propius urbem revocarunt. Sed & alia vis etiam gravius urgebat, ut è *Vincennis* per invia itinera profugiendum esset, & subinde variis in locis delitescendum: in fuga tamen & latebris otium hospitésque sui cupidissimos reperit; in eóque otio Scholas Physicas conscripsit, vel potius inchoavit.

customs that when a certain priest was charged before the parliament of Paris with using the new pronunciation they declared he should be deprived of his very large ecclesiastical revenues for this grammatical heresy, as they called it. The 5 superiors seemed at the point of giving up the struggle, but Peter Ramus and other regius professors hastening to the court persuaded it against the presumption of a judgment so alien from its powers. Indeed so crass was the ignorance of that time that it is revealed in printed books that doctors 10 existed in that university who with tooth and nail maintained that *ego amat* was quite as good syntax as *ego amo;* there was need for the public authority to repress their zeal. What Ramus accomplished in mathematics the *Scholæ Mathematicæ* and other of his works bear witness. While he was engaged on 15 these, the calamity of civil war interrupted him; as a result of letters from the king, he went at once to the royal library of Fontainebleau, and completely rewrote his mathematical lectures in a fuller and richer form. Then he was thinking of going to Italy where the university of Bologna had honorably 20 invited him, or at least to Germany, but the danger of death which menaced all the roads and the rumor that his college of Presles had been broken up by unworthy means and his library ruined called him nearer the royal city of Vincennes. But another force urged him yet more strongly to flee from 25 Vincennes by lonely paths and then to lie hidden in various places, but in flight and in concealment he found leisure and hosts eager to receive him; in this leisure he wrote his *Scholæ Physicæ,* or rather began them. When the civil war broke out

Erumpente rursus bello civili, in Optimatum castra profugit: eo tumultu post sex menses sedato, reversus, nihil in bibliotheca præter inania reperit scrinia; mathematicas tantùm commentationes *Resnerus* (qui *Parisiis* permansit) direptoribus
5 commodùm eripuit. Impendente jam tertium civili bello, impetravit à rege *Carolo* ad invisendas exteras Academias annuam dimissionem, quasi legationem liberam. In extremis regni finibus, vix militum quorundam manus, nisi prolato in medium diplomate regio, effugisset. Ter dimissus, ter repe-
10 titus, tandem velocitate summa eo pervenit, ubi sicariis licentia nequaquam pareat. Adventus ejus in *Germaniam* bonorum ac doctorum omnium singulari humanitate & gratulatione exceptus est. *Argentorati Joannes Sturmius,* ejus Academiæ author simul & rector, peramanter eum accepit. Deinde
15 Academia tota adjunctis etiam quibusdam ad ampliorem gratulationem comitibus & baronibus, liberalissimè tractavit: quo die, denique, nobilissimæ nuptiæ in eo loco celebrabantur, in prytaneum summus urbis magistratus, publicæ gratulationis gratia cum *Sturmio* eum adduxit. *Bernam* præteriens, tantùm
20 vidit, nec tamen sine Consulis *Stegeri* honorifica liberalitate, atque *Halleri, Aretii* aliorúmque doctissimorum hominum amica gratulatione discessit. *Tiguri, Henricus Bullingerus* simulatque in urbem ingressus est *Ramus,* gratulator primus affuit, cœnámque ei apparavit, eruditissimis convivarum,

again he fled to the camp of the nobles. When after six months these tumults were calmed, he returned to find nothing in his library except empty shelves and drawers. His mathematical commentaries alone were opportunely snatched away from the plunderers by Resner (who remained in Paris). Since civil war was then impending for the third time, he asked from King Charles leave for a year to visit foreign academies as a free ambassador. On the borders of the kingdom he would hardly have escaped the hands of some soldiers if he had not showed them the royal warrant. Three times dismissed, three times taken again, yet with the greatest speed he came to a country where there was no license for assassins. On arriving in Germany he was welcomed with singular kindness and joy by all good and learned men. At Strassburg, John Sturm, both founder and rector of the University of Strassburg, most lovingly received him. Afterwards the whole university, with which, in order to show him greater honor, certain counts and barons joined, treated him most graciously; and then, on a day when a splendid marriage was celebrated there, the highest magistrate of the city led him with Sturm into the city hall for the sake of public manifestation of respect. Passing by Bern he merely saw it, yet not without the honorable liberality of the *avoyer* Steger, and he departed amid manifestations of friendliness by Haller, Arétius, and other learned men. At Zurich, Henry Bullinger appeared to welcome him before anyone else, as soon as Ramus entered the city, and prepared him a banquet that was made very agreeable by the learned words of the other

Josiæ Simleri, Rodolphi Gualteri, Lodovici Lavateri sermonibus longè gratissimam. Postridie cùm ab eodem *Bullingero* in aulam publicam deduceretur, miratus quid sibi vellet in eum locum frequentissimus civium cujusque ordinis conven-
5 tus, quæsivit ex eo, ecquæ illic etiam, ut *Argentinæ,* nobiles nuptiæ celebrarentur. Cui *Bullingerus,* Tibi, inquit, nostra civitas nuptias istas celebrat. Præbuit ei *Heidelberga* amicum *Ursinum, Olivianum,* hospitem etiam *Immanuelem Tremellium,* fautorem denique, ipsum *Electorem Palatinum,* qui
10 discedentem *Ramum,* aurea imagine sua donavit. Inde *Francofurtum* pergens, à primariis aliquot civibus honorificè est acceptus: deinde *Noribergam* ad præstantissimos opifices & mechanicos aliósque viros doctos & præsertim *Joachimum Camerrarium* profectus, est: hîc jurisconsultorum collegio
15 mandatum à senatu est, ut *P. Ramo* convivium publico urbis nomine instruerent. Inde *Augustam* perexit ubi urbis consul primarius eum liberalissimè tractavit, adhibitis in convivium eruditis variæ doctrinæ convivis, sed imprimis *Hieronymo Wolfio,* & *Tichone Bracheo,* cum quo post prandium in sub-
20 urbanum consulis deductus, varios sermones de studiis mathematicis habuit. Rumore tandem restitutæ pacis revocatus, *Lausannam* contendit: hîc à viris doctis exoratus, Logicam ἀκρόασιν dies aliquot maximo concursu exhibuit. *Geneva* cum doctissimis hominibus tum de cæteris liberalibus studiis, tum
25 de Logicis collocutio illi assidua fuit, maximè cum *Francisco de Cretensi* & *Andrea Melvino, Scoto.* Cum aliis multis eru-

guests, Josias Simler, Rudolph Gualter, and Lodovic Lavater. When on the next day he was taken into the public hall by Bullinger, he wondered what the great crowd of citizens and people of every rank was doing there, and asked his host if there as at Strassburg a splendid wedding was being celebrated. Bullinger replied: "Our state celebrates this wedding for you." Heidelburg presented to him as friends Ursinus and Olivianus, and as his host Immanuel Tremellius, and then as a patron the Elector Palatine himself, who bestowed his image in gold on Ramus at his departure. Thence going to Frankfort he was honorably received by several of the best citizens. Then he visited at Nürnberg the chief artists and mechanics and other learned men, especially Joachim Camerarius; here it was asked from the senate by the society of jurisconsults that a banquet should be officially prepared for Peter Ramus in the name of the city. Next he passed through Augsburg where the burgomaster of the city treated him most courteously, asking as guests with him at a banquet men erudite in various subjects, but especially Jerome Wolf and Tycho Brahe; after the meal he was taken with the latter to the villa of the burgomaster and they had various discussions on mathematical studies. Called back by the rumor that peace had been restored, he hastened to Lausanne; here on the request of the scholars of the place, for some days he presented to a great crowd a logical ἀκρόασιν. At Geneva he was fully occupied in converse with the most learned men on other liberal studies as well as on logic, especially with Franciscus Portus, the Cretan, and Andrew Melville, a Scotchman. With

ditissimis viris, in *Italia Commandino* & *Papio,* in *Anglia Dio* & *Acontio,* in *Germania Chytræo,* aliisque permultis amicitiam per literas jam antè coluerat. Nobiles & inclytæ civitates eum magnis & honorificis muneribus, & sexcentorum corona-
5 torum oblato stipendio appetiverunt. *Joannes* electus rex *Pannoni* amplissimo stipendio *Albæ Juliæ* regendam Academiam illi obtulit. *Cracoviam* liberalissimè, immo in *Italiam* mille ducatorum stipendio *Bononiam* invitatus, patriam tamen deserere noluit: itaque *Carolus* ix. petitum undique calumniis
10 domi, invidorúmque morsibus, non solùm præsenti ope sublevavit, sed honore auxit & amplificavit, eíque vacationem à laboribus concessit. Tandem, anno 1572 in illa *Parisiensi Christianorum* ac civium internecione, indignissime periit. Necis causam sunt qui in æmulos ejus conferant: plerique
15 eandem quæ cæteris ea nocte trucidatis fuisse existimant. Legatum annuum Mathematico Professori in *Parisiensi* Academia luculentum testamento reliquit.

FINIS.

many other men of great erudition, in Italy with Commandino and Papio, in England with Dee and Acontius, in Germany with Chytræus and a large number of others he had previously cultivated friendships through letters. Noble and famous
5 states endeavored to secure him by offering great and honorable rewards; he was even promised a stipend of six hundred crowns. Having been elected king of Hungary, John offered him the headship of the university at Stuhlweissenburg, with a large salary. He had a most generous offer from Cracow,
10 and was even invited into Italy to Bologna at a stipend of a thousand ducats, but was unwilling to desert his native land. So Charles IX not merely made a gift as a temporary assistance to Ramus, who was assailed on all sides at home by calumnies and by the teeth of the envious, but improved and strengthened
15 his position by showing him honor, and granted him leave from his labors. Yet in the year 1572 in that slaughter of Christians and citizens at Paris, he most undeservedly perished. There are some who hold that his death was caused by those who were envious of him, and many think the cause was
20 the same as that for which others were killed that night. In his will he left a splendid annual legacy for a professor of mathematics in the university of Paris.

The End.

NOTES

The Translation

MILTON'S *Artis Logicæ Plenior Institutio* has never before been translated. Since the Ramistic logic it presents is now obsolete, the words of Milton cannot always easily be rendered into the English of the present, though equivalents can be found in the translations of Ramus made in the sixteenth and seventeenth centuries; to them, therefore, I have often resorted. Their language will be intelligible to any one acquainted with Ramistic terminology, and Milton's treatise can hardly be easy reading for one who is not. From the translators of Ramus come also, sometimes with modification, many of the renderings of illustrative quotations from the classics; others are from well known writers of Milton's time; a few have been made for the occasion.

The Text

The text is that of the edition of 1672. There is no proof of the issue of an earlier edition and a copy dated 1673 is identical with those of 1672 except for the title page (see *Notes and Queries,* CLXV (1933), 56).

The present text was set up from a copy in the library of Columbia University. The proof was compared also with three other copies, one in the library of Duke University and two in that of the editor. There is but one variation between these copies which suggests a change in type during printing (see the note on page 36, line 10). Reference has also been made to the text given in the editor's copy of the first collected edition of Milton's prose, with the imprint Amsterdam, 1698,

to that in Symmons' edition (London, 1806), and to that in the Pickering edition (London and Boston, 1851), which was "printed from the original editions."

The abbreviation CAP. in headings, and other abbreviations such as q; have been expanded, the long s modernized, and the page of *Typographi Errata* incorporated in the text without remark. In a few instances the arrangement on the page has been normalized without any change in the wording. All other modifications, no matter how slight, are mentioned in the textual notes. The mock accents of the original have been preserved, and any used contrary to the habits of Milton and his contemporaries have been corrected, but none of those lacking have been supplied. No table of contents is given in the first edition; I have put one together from the chapter headings.

In spite of the *Typographi Errata,* errors in the text of 1672 are numerous; most of them can doubtless be imputed to the printer, though probably some to Milton or his amanuensis. Those which occur in quotations from his acknowledged sources can, when obvious blunders, be corrected with certainty. There are, however, passages in which the wording of the sources is deliberately modified. In some instances I have supported an emendation of what seems a printer's error by giving in the notes a passage which Milton apparently had in mind as he wrote, but which he does not quote. The punctuation has been modified only when it seemed thoroughly misleading, and never without mention in the notes.

Milton's chief sources are the *Dialectica* of Peter Ramus, the

Commentarii on it by George Downham, and the *Petri Rami Vita* by Freigius, all more fully described in the table of abbreviations. Though I have made no systematic collation of the six editions of the *Dialectica* available to me, I have observed no important differences between them and believe that readings attributed to Ramus in the textual notes give the text generally printed. Assignment of a reading to Downham means that it occurs in the editor's copy of the edition of 1669 and in many instances in the copy of the edition of 1605 in the library of Columbia University.

In a number of copies the stubs of two leaves cut or torn from the volume appear between pages four and five; copies which lack the stubs appear to have been rebound. Sig. B2, which should appear on page three, is lacking. Page three and the upper part of page four have wide spaces between the paragraphs, as though the amount of matter on the pages had been reduced. The stubs in one of the editor's copies show that the beginning of three words now occurring in the text on page three were in the earlier form lower on the page than at present. Page one and the lower half of page four seem, however, to have been unmodified. Additional matter, if any, would therefore have been on pages two and three or on three alone. The stubs, though apparently of sufficient size to show the ends of words near the bottom of page three, are quite blank there. The lower part of page two is now occupied by the beginning of chapter two; in addition to the title there are but four lines of text. It seems possible that the lower part of that page was originally blank and that the new

chapter began at the head of page three. The printer then perhaps decided not to begin the chapter on a fresh page and moved enough matter from page three to fill out page two; he also borrowed a little from four for three. No blank space is left at the bottom of a page after the end of a chapter nor does any chapter begin at the top of a new page until chapter fifteen is reached. Thereafter the majority of the chapters begin on fresh pages without respect to the space left at the bottom of the preceding page, though a considerable number still do not. One of the editor's copies, apparently in its original binding, permits examination. It indicates that the cancellation was made early in the history of the volume, for the portrait is on one half of the sheet of which pages one and two, sig. B, make up the other half. The blank sheet before the portrait is attached to that of pages three and four. Between the portrait and page one intervene the title-page, preface, and errata, in all sixteen pages, sigg. [A3]—A5. The portrait is that later given in the second edition of *Paradise Lost* and reproduced in Volume II of the present edition.

Abbreviations

Abbreviations immediately following words from the present text indicate the source of the reading adopted. Words directly following the square bracket are from the edition of 1672; words from other sources are preceded by abbreviations.

A Artis Logicæ Institutio *in* Joannis Miltoni Opera Omnia Latina, Amstelodami, 1698

B Fr. Burgersdicii Institutionum Logicarum Libri Duo, Cantabrigiæ, 1668

C	The editor's conjecture
D	Commentarii in P. Rami . . . Dialecticam, auctore Georgio Dounamo
D1605	*Ibid.*, Francofurti, 1605
D1669	*Ibid.*, Londini & Cantabrigiae, 1669
F	Petri Rami Vita, per Ioann. Thomam Freigium *in* Petri Rami Praelectiones in Ciceronis Orationes Octo Consulares, Basileæ, 1575
M	Joannis Miltoni Angli, Artis Logicæ Plenior Institutio, ad Petri Rami Methodum Concinnata, Londini, 1672
Mc	*Ibid.*, in the library of Columbia University
Md	*Ibid.*, in the library of Duke University
Med1	*Ibid.*, in the library of the editor, first copy
Med2	*Ibid.*, in the library of the editor, second copy
P	*Ibid.*, in The Works of John Milton (Pickering edition), London & Boston, 1851
R	P. Rami Veromandui Regii Professoris, Dialecticæ Libri Duo
R1595	*Ibid.*, Spiræ, 1595
R1640	*Ibid.*, Cantabrigiæ, 1640
R1669	*Ibid.*, Londini & Cantabrigiæ, 1669
Rtal	*Ibid.*, Audomari Talaei Praelectionibus Illustrati, Francofurti, 1583
Rich	The Logicians School-Master: or, A Comment upon Ramus Logick. By Alexander Richardson. London, 1657

NOTES ON THE LATIN TEXT

TITLE-PAGE

concinnata. AP] concinnata, Analytica AP] Annalytica

PREFACE

PAGE 2

—HEADING PRÆFATIO] PRÆFATIO

PAGE 4

—2 se fuse] sefuse —4 longiore] Longiore —19 *Aristotile*] *Aristtotile*

PAGE 16

—12 inornata] in ornata —15 accuratior] acuratior

FIRST BOOK, CHAPTER 1

PAGE 18

—CHAPTER HEADING CAPUT] CAPUT. —1 Eodémque] Eodèmque —3 à] ὰ λόγῳ] λόγω —6 facultate.] facultate —11 διαλέγεσθαι D] διαλέγεθαι

PAGE 20

—4 διαλέγεσθαι D] διαλέγεθαι

FIRST BOOK, CHAPTER 2

PAGE 20

—CHAPTER HEADING *déque* RD] *Déque*

PAGE 22

—5 Phædro] phædro —12 continet] , continet —14 genesin,] genesin —15 inventorúmque] inventorùmque —17 *aliquid*] *aliqnid* *est.*] *est,* —19 id est, ut D] id —20 *Boethius*, D] *Boethius*

PAGE 24

—13 ex] Ex —23 loquendi] loqendi

PAGE 26

—4 Rhet. 1.2. D] Rhet. 1.12. —9 affectionem D] affectíonem

FIRST BOOK, CHAPTER 3

PAGE 28

—20 dici,] dici.

PAGE 30

—5 deor.] deor;

FIRST BOOK, CHAPTER 4

PAGE 36

—9 ubi Mc ed] Md ONLY U LEGIBLE —10 causæ Md Med1] Mc Med2 causa —17 Nat. D] nat —18 Hoc] hoc

PAGE 38

—9 déque] dèque

FIRST BOOK, CHAPTER 5

PAGE 40

—4 proximè C] proximæ —5 consilium] concilium sciénsque] scíensque —9 itaque] itáque

PAGE 42

—2 testantur] Testantur —3 literæ.] literæ: —16 Rhet. 1.10 D] Rhet. 2.20

PAGE 44

—18 Et] *Et* —19 de Fato D] de, Fato

PAGE 46

—5 *solet*. RD] *solet* —6 Sic D] *Sic* *videntur* D] *videnter* —11 *minus* D] *nimus* —14 *cæteroqui*] *cœteroqui* —17 Et] *Et*

PAGE 48

—18 earum] éarum —22 ex hypothesi] exhypothesi

FIRST BOOK, CHAPTER 6

PAGE 50

—13 definitio] difinitio —14 effectum D] affectum

PAGE 52

—4 propriam. D] propriam:

FIRST BOOK, CHAPTER 7

PAGE 54

—5 sub] sub, —6 effectúmque] effectùmque —8 materiæ C] materia Rich the efficient and matter were combined together —15 *Aristotelis*] *Aristotilis*

PAGE 56

—20 nempe] neme

PAGE 58

—4 definitio D] definitis —21 Quòd si] Quòdsi

PAGE 60

—21 suprà dictum] supràdictum

PAGE 62

—4 *hac* RD] *hæc*

FIRST BOOK, CHAPTER 8

PAGE 62

—18 *optimum*. D] *optimum:*

PAGE 66

—4 *Phil*. δ D] *Phil*.8 —21 *Phil*. δ D] Phil.8 Et] *Et*

FIRST BOOK, CHAPTER 9

PAGE 70

—18 notiores;] notiores

PAGE 72

—8 Ut] *Ut* —12 specialia] speciala

PAGE 74

—3 *recludit* RD] *recluàit*

FIRST BOOK, CHAPTER 10

PAGE 80
—12 insunt D] in sunt —17 differentias D] differantias Geometricis D] Geometrecis
PAGE 82
—15 *concomitantia*] *concomitentia* —17 effectorum] effectoram argumentum C] argumentorum
PAGE 84
—7 *gloriæ* RD] *gloria* —*postest:* RD] *potest.*

FIRST BOOK, CHAPTER 11

PAGE 84
—8 *subjicitur,*] *subjicitur.* —12 *Aristotele,*] *Aristotele.* —13 extrinsecus D] extrinsicus
PAGE 86
—7 Phil. ϛ D] Phil.S —9 excipias.] excipias, —13 subjecto. Sublato] subjecto sublato —19 *consequentia*] *consequantia*
PAGE 88
—2 *multa* MD some eds. of R] other eds. of R *juncta* —7 lac D] làc certior] certlor
PAGE 90
—8 qualitatibus] qualitatibus, —12 dicuntur] dicunter —18 dictum] dicium —20 positóque] positóq
PAGE 92
—13 Secundus] Secudus —19 recipiuntur] receipiuntur
PAGE 94
—1 αἰὼν D] ἄιον —1 ἀἐι ὂν D] ἀεὶ ὢν —9 Cic.] Cic —19 *Pœnorum* D] *pœnorum*
PAGE 96
—2 *Sidonia* D] *Sidonio* —4 adjuncti] adjunctti *Est* R] *Et*

FIRST BOOK, CHAPTER 12

PAGE 98
—17 ideóque] idéoque
PAGE 102
—7 levissimam D] levissiman —11 nec ei] necei
PAGE 106
—15 *Paulò*] *Pauló*
PAGE 108
—1 *judicentur* D] *judicantur* —11 opposita] opposia

FIRST BOOK, CHAPTER 13

PAGE 108

—18 *sunt*] sunt —20 'αντικείμενα D] 'αντεκείμενα

PAGE 110

—3 nunquam] nunqam —15 *Ad idem*, i] Ad idem, î

PAGE 112

—20 *Multis:*] *Multis.*

PAGE 114

—5 i.e.] i.e,

FIRST BOOK, CHAPTER 14

PAGE 116

—9 'αντικείμενα D] ἀντικεμένα —13 distributionem] distribu-tiònem —21 negationis M] D abnegationis

PAGE 118

—1 *Phil.* γ D] *Phil.V* —2 negationis M] D abnegationis —3 præceptorem D] ptaeceptorem

PAGE 122

—6 discipulis] discipul is —10 non D] Non —14 *non*] *Non* —15 *nulla.*] *nulla:*

PAGE 124

—2 dicatur. Id] dicatur, id —3 reponas] IN THE TEXT reponat; IN THE *Typographi Errata* teponas —3–4 *Philos.* ς D] *Philos.*5 —5 id C] idne —6 *affirmantia,*] *affirmantia.* —15 mutuæ D] mutua

PAGE 126

—2 *reliquum* RD] *roliquum* —9 *Top.* 6.4 D] *Top.* 3 —11 definitionem D] difinitionem

PAGE 128

—3 *Tum* RD] IN THE TEXT *Tu;* IN THE *Typographi Errata Cum* —9 *ne quis* RD] *nequis* —11 ferreæ RD] ferrea —12 varia] Varia

FIRST BOOK, CHAPTER 15

PAGE 132

—7 verum etiam] verumetiam

PAGE 134

—7 *Phil.* κ D] *Phil. x*

FIRST BOOK, CHAPTER 16

PAGE 136

—18 1 Post.] D 2 Post.

PAGE 138
—2 Expressè] Expressé —15 *resistito* RD] *risistito* —20 nonnihil] nonnîhil

FIRST BOOK, CHAPTER 17

PAGE 144
—2 *Phys.* 1 D] Phys. 2 —5 *ademptio* D] *ademtio* —9 justum;] justum —12 inest D] in est potest, D] potest? —16 dicitur.] dicitur,

PAGE 146
—2 item. D] item: —11–12 attribuuntur,] attribuuntur.

PAGE 148
—4 peccatum] pecatum —25 forma] IN THE TEXT (MISPLACED) forma; IN THE *Typographi Errata* formæ

FIRST BOOK, CHAPTER 18

PAGE 150
—19 *Inter*] Inter

PAGE 152
—16 insignis D] in signis —21 *redditióque*] *redditíoque*

PAGE 154
—3 redditio] reddîtio —22 *Phil.* δ D] *Phil.* 8

PAGE 156
—16 *perinde ac si* D] *perinde, acsi* —20 concipitur.] concipitur:

PAGE 158
—15 *Philippic* D] *Philipic*

PAGE 160
—4 si] si, —10 *Philip.*] *Philip:* —15 verò D] veró

PAGE 164
—12 *dici* D] *diei*

FIRST BOOK, CHAPTER 19

PAGE 170
—12 *non tam, quam*] non, tam, quam

PAGE 172
—6 Ingentes] Ingentis —8 *verò*] *veró* —18 inhonestum] in honestum —20 Sic] *Sic*

PAGE 174
—2 *Thersites* RD] *Thersies* —17 verùm] Verùm

PAGE 176
—12 *si siet* RD] *sisi ét* —21 *Sufficimus*] *sufficimus*

FIRST BOOK, CHAPTER 20

PAGE 178

—1 adeóque] adéoque —2 definitionem] definitionen —19 3 R] 2 D 2 *Sævior* RD] *Sevior*

PAGE 180

—9 *sævior es* RD] *sæviores* —13 quoniam] quòniam

PAGE 182

—15 *protulerunt* D] *portulerunt* —18 majus,] majus

PAGE 186

—4 *accipere*] *accipcre* —9 2 Agr. *Quæ* RD] 1 Agr. *quæ* —14 Sic] *Sic* —23 si] Si

FIRST BOOK, CHAPTER 21

PAGE 192

—12 Phil. *δ* D] Phil. 8

PAGE 196

—2 *Cn.* RD] *En.* —20 *sic* D] *Sic*

PAGE 198

—1 *poëta* D] *poïta* —20 *Aliquando* RD] *Aliquanào*

PAGE 200

—16 *imponunt.* Quod] *imponunt,* quod —19 Top. 2.10] Top. 24 D Top. 24 —23 idcirco] Idcirco

PAGE 202

—23 *porticibus* RD] *poriùcibus* *sic* RD] *Sic*

PAGE 204

—8 *.] *

FIRST BOOK, CHAPTER 22

—CHAPTER HEADING *Dissimilibus* RD] *Similibus*

PAGE 206

—7 *linguâ* R] *linguá*

FIRST BOOK, CHAPTER 23

PAGE 210

—7 vim] vîm

PAGE 212

—2 notatio D] noatio —22 conjugata] Conjugata

PAGE 214

—6–7 definiunt] definitiunt —17 est.] est:

PAGE 216

—15 effecta] affecta

FIRST BOOK, CHAPTER 24

PAGE 218
—9 veriloquium D] veroloquium
PAGE 220
—3 proculdubio] procludubio —16 *focus* RD] *locus*
PAGE 222
—1 *appellentur* RD] *appellantur*

FIRST BOOK, CHAPTER 25

PAGE 228
—8 *Thebas.* D] *Thebas* —12 procemio AP] proæmio
PAGE 230
—6 ratione] ratíone —7 duo genera] duogenera —8 *finem.*] *finem.* Eff. R finis. Efficiens APPARENTLY THE Eff. OF Efficiens, WHICH M DID NOT WISH TO QUOTE, WAS COPIED IN ERROR.

FIRST BOOK, CHAPTER 26

—CHAPTER HEADING *De* RD] *Dc*

PAGE 232
—1 *Phil.* δ. 25 D] *Phil.* 8.15 —8 *dispositionem*] *dispositionēm* —17 facultas D] facultate —22 ideóque] idéoque
PAGE 234
—3 regulas] Regulas
PAGE 236
—3–4 efficientes D] efficientis

FIRST BOOK, CHAPTER 27

PAGE 238
—7 significat. D] significet, —9 et idea] Et idæa —11 μ. 5. sed D] *v*.5. Sed —13 Ideas] Idæas —16 *Phil.* δ. D] *Phil.* 8 Invent. 1. D] Invent. 1
PAGE 240
—4 *Porphyrius*] *Porphirius* —11 *subalternum* RD] *subalternnm* —16 *subalterna* RD] *subalterua*
PAGE 244
—1 species] spicies
PAGE 246
—12 virtutem D] Virtutem —16 *perspicientia* RD] *perspicentia*

PAGE 248

—2 ipsas C] ipsa RD *Distributio generis in species . . . Distributio generis in formas specierum eadem est* *formæ* RD] *forma* —22 Phœbe RD] Phæbe

PAGE 250

—7 capitibus] captibus —17 *mœnia* RD] *mænia*

PAGE 252

—1 accommodantur D] accomodantur —7 *exhauriunt* D] *exhauriun* —13 distributio] distributîo

FIRST BOOK, CHAPTER 28

PAGE 254

—6 dividitur D] diuiditur

FIRST BOOK, CHAPTER 29

PAGE 256

—CHAPTER HEADING *Adjunctis* D] *Adjnnctis* —13 divites, D] divites

PAGE 258

—19 idem vel solus] C eadem vel sola; CF. THE TITLE OF 1.4, ABOVE, AND D 1.3, P. 57: eadem vel sola id efficit —20 accidens.] accidens:

FIRST BOOK, CHAPTER 30

PAGE 260

—6 accipit.] accipit, —19 definitionis] difinitionis

PAGE 262

—17 Itaque] Itaq

FIRST BOOK, CHAPTER 31

PAGE 266

—16 primariò] Primariò —19 definiuntur. B (2.2.14)] definiuntur,

PAGE 268

—15 subjecto,] subjecto

PAGE 270

—1 eclipsis] ecclipsis —20 descriptionémque] descriptîonémque

PAGE 274

—6 à] á —7 quòd,] quòd.

PAGE 276

—1 *Enceladóque* RD] *Enceladóq*

FIRST BOOK, CHAPTER 32

PAGE 280

—14 quæritur] queritur

FIRST BOOK, CHAPTER 33

PAGE 284

—4 accurata D] acurata

PAGE 286

—15 *cœpissent* RD] *cæpissent* —19 versibus, R] versibus. —20 Σαλαμῖνος RD] Σαλαμίνος νῆας,] νηᾶς. —21 Ἀθηναίων] Αθηναίων —22 naves,] naves.

PAGE 288

—1 victi RD] Victi —4 Atque] Atq —13 ut RD] Ut —15 *vitulam* RD] *vitilam*

PAGE 290

—5 *Fecit. certa crux. Nullas fecit. sperata libertas* MRt (WITH QUOTES, NOT ITALICS)] R1640 R1669 *Fecit: certa crux. Nullas fecit: sperata libertas* R1595 Fecit. Certa crux. Nullas fecit. Sperata libertas.

SECOND BOOK, CHAPTER 1

PAGE 296

—2 finis,] finis —19 clariùs] clarîus

SECOND BOOK, CHAPTER 2

PAGE 298

—15 *Galeno, & Gellio* D] *Gellio, Galeno* —16 8.] 8. & —18 , *effatum*, & D] ; *effatum*

PAGE 300

—2 ideóque] idéoque —6–7 orationis] Orationis —18 autem est] autem cum argumento est D autem hîc, ut Aristoteli etiam κατηγόρημα non modo . . . significat

PAGE 302

—13 angustiora] angustoria —22 posterioris] posterioris

PAGE 304

—21 Vinculum] Vinculum. D vincula axiomatum formæ sunt

SECOND BOOK, CHAPTER 3

PAGE 312

—25 non] Non

Page 314

—2 *duntaxat*, & c.] *duntaxat*. & c —19 *contradictorium* Med] Mc Md *contradi orium* —23 distinctiunculis] dístinctiunculis

Page 316

—11 *debent*.] *debent*, —24 quæ C] in quibus D de rebus specialibus multa multis in artibus præcipi solent . . . præcepta de hujusmodi rebus singularibus concepta, quæ

Page 318

—3 anomaliam D] anomalium —16 *αὐτὸ* D] *αὐτὸ* —21 *αὐτὸ* D] *ἀυτὸ*

Page 322

—24 necesse] ncesse

SECOND BOOK, CHAPTER 4

Page 324

—CHAPTER HEADING Axiomate] Axoimate —5 in] în

Page 328

—1 comparationibus RD] comprationibus —17 omnibúsque] omnibúsq

Page 330

—7 *Bajis* RD] *bajis* —8 *Bajis* RD] *bajis* —14 multiplex D] mutiplex —25 *proprium* RD] *propium*

Page 334

—3 speciei] specici

Page 336

—7 accidens] acccidens

SECOND BOOK, CHAPTER 5

Page 342

—10 simplicia D] simpliciæ APPARENTLY, BUT NOT CLEARLY PRINTED —19 *copulativa*, R] *copulativa*. —20 *procellis* RD] *procellis*.

Page 344

—2 Quòd si] Quòdsi —6 utrumque] ut*r*umque

SECOND BOOK, CHAPTER 6

Page 348

—3 Ut *si*] *Ut*, *si* D quales sunt *si* —13 axiomatis, id] axiomatis id. —15 pro] pro. D1605 Pro D1669 Pro. —17 *Fato*] Fato

Page 350

—2 *antecedens*] *antecèdens* —21 *quidem*.] *quidem*,

PAGE 354
—14 *relicta,* D] *relicta.*

SECOND BOOK, CHAPTER 7

PAGE 358
—13 autem,] autem.

SECOND BOOK, CHAPTER 8

PAGE 360
—19 omninò] ominnò
PAGE 362
—2 *disjunctæ* RDM (IN THE *Typographi Errata,* WHERE THE PAGE-NUMBER IS OMITTED)] *disjuncta*
PAGE 364
—4 Ut] *Ut*

SECOND BOOK, CHAPTER 9

PAGE 370
—11 est,] est. —19 distinctio] distinctîo
PAGE 372
—15 τοῦ B 2.24] τοὺ —APPENDIX-HEADING *paralogismis*] *parologismis* —20 Ut D] Et —21 index] D judex
PAGE 374
—14 dicitur,] dicitur —15 *qui* C] *quia*
PAGE 376
—7 æquivocatio] aquivocatio —17 *Cæsare* AP] *Casare*
PAGE 380
—22 dicitúrque] dicitùrque
PAGE 382
—17 Sic] *Sic*

SECOND BOOK, CHAPTER 10

PAGE 384
—CHAPTER HEADING *De*] *Dc*
PAGE 386
—12 quæstionis] quæstonis
PAGE 388
—6 inventionis C] inventiones B (2.16) *Ad inventionem argumentorum dialecticorum spectat locus* —9 nihil] nihil. —15 genus] e INVERTED —23 adeóque] adéoque
PAGE 390
—14 *debiliorem*] *dibiliorem*

PAGE 392
—2 idémque] îdémque —22 *docti sunt*] *dicti sum*
PAGE 394
—18 *quæstioni* RD] *quastioni*
PAGE 396
—6 quæstiones] quæstionis D particulares enim quæstiones solæ in hac specie concluduntur
PAGE 398
—16 ideóque] idéoque
PAGE 402
—12 præcaventur] precaventur —20 suprà dixi] supràdixi

SECOND BOOK, CHAPTER 11

PAGE 404
—20 *ambobus* D] *ambabus*
PAGE 406
—25 Hic] Hîc
PAGE 408
—3 *concretum, nihil* M] RD *concretum, nihil copulatum, nihil* —11 à] á —12 *&c.,*] *&c,* —14 *Maximus est magnanimus* RD] *Maximus est*
PAGE 410
—9 &c.] &c —21–22 *reperiantur* RD] *reperiannur*
PAGE 412
—2 &c. D] &c: —4 Assumptio D] assumptio —5 &c. D] &c; —7 Postremo D] postremo —18 *hæsurum* RD] *hæsûrum*
PAGE 414
—16 primæ D] prima

SECOND BOOK, CHAPTER 12

PAGE 424
—11 *polliceor hoc vobis* RD] *polliceor vobis* —18 &c. D] &c,
PAGE 426
—6 *gratum est* M] RD *est gratum* —9 *te* RD] *te.*
PAGE 430
—3 Post. 1 D] post. l —27 debilioris] dibilioris
PAGE 432
—13 adeóque] adéoque
PAGE 434
—1 *qui* D] *quia* —14 inverti D] inverti?

SECOND BOOK, CHAPTER 13

PAGE 436
—19 propositione (1)] propositîone
PAGE 438
—10–11 *si non est animal, idcirco non est* M] D si est animal, idcirco est THE CHANGE FROM THE READING OF D IS MADE IN THE *Typographi Errata.*
PAGE 444
—1 *Paris* DR] *paris* —2 *deseruit* D] *deseret* —9 *æstas*] *estas*

SECOND BOOK, CHAPTER 14

PAGE 444
—10 *tollat* RD] *iollat*
PAGE 448
—16 propositio] proposirio

SECOND BOOK, CHAPTER 15

PAGE 450
—12 *piéque*] *pièque* —18 absolutè] absoluté —19 minoris D] mînoris —21 *Philip.* R] *Philip*
PAGE 452
—12 *plus quàm* D] *plusquam*

SECOND BOOK, CHAPTER 16

PAGE 460
—4 cùm] cùm,
PAGE 462
—13 *nox,*] *nox* —21 *disjunctivus, biformis,*] *disjunctivus biformis*
PAGE 464
—3 *cædis* D] *cœdis* —10 Rhet. 2 D] Rhet. 3
PAGE 466
—7 ultimæ] ultima B (2.13.6) *prædicatum ultimum concludatur de subjecto primo*
PAGE 468
—12 *reip.;*] *reip.*

SECOND BOOK, CHAPTER 17

PAGE 470
—14 adeóque] adéoque —16 heterogeneum] heterogenium

PAGE 474

—3 *Ideóque*] *Idéoque* —12 judicata D] judcata —13 agitur, contraria] agitur. Contraria —22 *exempla* RD] *exempli*

PAGE 476

—8 *specialissimæ* RD] *specialissima* —9–10 continet.] continet —11 explicationes.] explicationes

PAGE 478

—5 speciésque] specièsque

PAGE 480

—12 *omninò*] *omninó*

PAGE 482

—11 *Verrem*] *verrem*

PAGE 484

—1–2 *transitionúmque* R] *transitionùmque*

THE PRAXIS

PAGE 486

—HEADING *Analytica* AP] *Analitica*

PAGE 488

—7 simpliciter D] simplicitur —15 ibid.] ibid

PAGE 490

—13 deest D] de est

PAGE 492

—10 protasi D] proto —17 præstita. D] præstita,

THE LIFE OF PETER RAMUS

PAGE 496

—13 robusta F] rebusta —14 *Lutetiæ*] *Lutitiæ*

PAGE 498

—1 oppugnarunt F] opugnarunt —10 contra se] contrase —17 *Aristotelea* F] *Aristotelêa* —21 quinque,] quinque

PAGE 500

—10 ut F] Ut

PAGE 502

—5 usum F] Usum

PAGE 506

—19 Anno] Anno.

PAGE 508

—20 propius F] proprius —21 è F] é —23 hospitésque] hospitèsque —24 eóque] eòque

PAGE 510
—8 quorundam] quorundum —14 accepit. Deinde F] accepit deinde —24 cœnámque F] coenámq

PAGE 512
—1 *Lavateri* F] *Lavalteri* —8 *Olivianum* F] *Olevianum*

PAGE 514
—3 jam antè C] jaxantè —8 *Bononiam*] *Bononian*

COLUMBIA UNIVERSITY PRESS
Columbia University
New York

FOREIGN AGENT
OXFORD UNIVERSITY PRESS
Humphrey Milford
Amen House, London, E.C. 4